INSIDER

JOSÉ LUIS LLOVIO-MENÉNDEZ

INSIDER

MY HIDDEN LIFE AS A REVOLUTIONARY IN CUBA

TRANSLATED BY EDITH GROSSMAN

BANTAM BOOKS
TORONTO · NEW YORK · LONDON · SYDNEY · AUCKLAND

INSIDER
A Bantam Book/July 1988

LIBRARY OF CONGRESS

Library of Congress Cataloging-in-Publication Data
Llovio-Menéndez, José Luis.
    Insider: my hidden life as a revolutionary in Cuba/José Luis Llovio
-Menéndez; [translated by Edith Grossman].
        p.   cm.
    Includes index.
    ISBN 0-553-05114-8
    1. Llovio-Menéndez, José Luis.   2. Cuba—Politics and
government—1959–   3. Revolutionists—Cuba—Biography.   I Title.
F1788.22.L58A3   1988
972.91'064—dc19
                                                        87-33479
                                                           CIP

Published simultaneously in the United States and Canada

Bantam Books are published by Bantam Books, a division of Bantam
Doubleday Dell Publishing Group, Inc. Its trademark, consisting of the
words "Bantam Books" and the portrayal of a rooster, is Registered
in U.S. Patent and Trademark Office and in other countries. Marca
Registrada. Bantam Books, 666 Fifth Avenue, New York, New York 10103.

PRINTED IN THE UNITED STATES OF AMERICA

DH   0 9 8 7 6 5 4 3 2 1

*To my father and uncle,
who did not live to know the truth.*

To judge revolutions and those who make them, it is necessary to observe them at close range and judge them from a distance.

—SIMÓN BOLÍVAR
FEBRUARY 9, 1815

ACKNOWLEDGMENTS

I begin this book with a request: that the reader view my narrative through a lens different from the one to which he or she is accustomed. For those who have lived in socialist countries no such approach will be necessary; many of my observations may seem even too obvious for the telling. But these memoirs have been written for the general reader, who in all likelihood has never glimpsed life under socialism first-hand, let alone lived it.

During the years since I left Cuba, and particularly during the writing of this book, I have had to resort to that lens more than once in order to understand certain actions I took and the decisions that prompted them. The course of my life sometimes seems astonishing, even to me. If I have succeeded here, what happened to me will be understood against this backdrop of repression, paranoia, and deceit.

These memoirs are based on four different sources of information. First, there are the notes that I meticulously wrote day after day in my years inside the revolution. For a high-ranking official to keep such notes is not unusual behavior in Cuba. Information is the most important tool for survival. I had to remember everything I did or said or heard, in order not to fail. The more information I got, the safer I was.

Second, there are my transcriptions of Fidel Castro's and Ché Guevara's conversations. Our talks were not recorded, but I wrote them up immediately after they occurred, trying to preserve the accuracy of these men's words while they were fresh in my mind. I kept my transcriptions of talks with Ché before and after I went to live in Cuba, because of the curiosity I developed about him from the first time we met. I was fascinated by this unusual Communist revolutionary whose views about the revolution were so uniquely his. In Fidel's case, it was very different. I needed to know how this man thought; my life depended on it. Only a small part of these conversations has been used here.

Third, almost all the excerpts of Fidel's speeches are taken from the official translations of the Revolutionary Government. The speeches I could not get in English were rendered by the book's translator.

Fourth are the anecdotes of my childhood and early youth which I have tried to re-create to the best of my recollection. The Library of Congress has been an invaluable resource for verifying the dates and events in my records.

Only one person's identity has been changed. Because he is still living in Cuba, he has been completely disguised to ensure his safety.

It is impossible to name all the people who in one way or another helped me as I wrote this book. I am very grateful for the moral support I had from my family and so many friends in the past four years.

My first thought is of Maggie, without whom it would have been impossible to accomplish this complex task. Her close collaboration has been invaluable, and I could never have succeeded without her. Then, my thanks to Bella Linden, lawyer and friend.

I would also like to express my gratitude to my very capable translator, Edith Grossman, and to the staff of Bantam Books, for their deep professionalism and the respect with which they treated my work—my life. Individually, I want to thank Steve Rubin, Vice President and Editor-in-Chief, who saw the potential and had faith; Nessa Rapoport, my editor, who with intelligence, grace and unusual devotion asked all the right questions; and Linda Loewenthal, for many hours of expert labor and brainpower.

CONTENTS

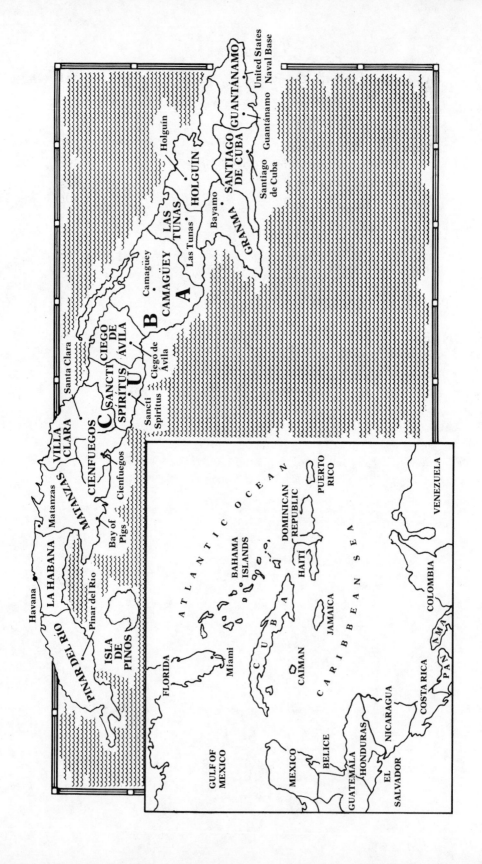

PROLOGUE:
THE KOALA

As far as anyone knew, I was one of them. I applauded Fidel in the Plaza; I dutifully lived the part of a faithful member of his bureaucracy. Trapped since 1965, I had made my decision from the minute of my arrival: To escape Fidel's Cuba, I would mask every feeling, hide from the world and even from myself every human instinct, create a facade of pure Communist revolutionary devotion in order to put my plan into action.

On a spring weekend in 1972, I was at home, alone. It was very unusual for me to have time to myself, not working overtime in my office, or summoned to a mobilization in the fields, or by the military committee. Finally I would be able to tackle the pile of old papers and junk that had accumulated for years in the spare room of our apartment.

For several dreary hours I was an archeologist of the recent past. With each layer of envelopes and discarded artifacts the years peeled away. It was tedious work. Should I keep the back issues of *Granma*, the party paper? Perhaps I would need them to decipher a change in policy that might jeopardize my precarious safety. Here were piles of old public documents that I'd read and rarely consulted again. Here were my notes of official meetings and unofficial conversations related to any aspect of the country that would help me in my work or might prevent unforeseeable problems in the future.

As I worked I dug back in time, through the notes that had allowed me to survive these years. Toward the bottom of the pile I discovered a rusty trunk I barely recalled owning. The lid groaned as I pried it open with a screwdriver.

Inside I found more documents I no longer needed. I was about to toss the trunk and its contents aside when my groping fingers touched a tattered carton. As I pulled it up indifferently for inspection, my hand brushed against a hard woolly object beneath it.

To my astonishment I found that I was holding the plush koala bear, worn and shabby from use and age, that had been my daughter's favorite toy, the one she had taken to bed with her every night.

The discovery shattered me. Instinctively I began to caress the little bear as it evoked a torrent of sweet memory. In an instant, the child I had not seen for five years was in the room with me, a living presence. I watched her blond hair shake with her laughter; I felt her hand. I had not cried since 1957, when my grandmother died. Now I squeezed the koala in the stuffy spare room, tears streaming down my face.

Suddenly I was no longer invisible, no more a stranger to myself. The capacity to feel love and sorrow, and the anguished uncertainty about whether or not I would see my daughter again, flooded me, dissolving the life-preserving anesthetic I had so carefully absorbed.

I could afford none of this. Knowing that I could be so unexpectedly vulnerable was terrifying. A child's toy had proved I was not master of myself. At any cost I had to stop my own weakness or I was finished. Abruptly, koala in hand, I walked out the door. A few steps down the hallway I stopped at the hinged slot in the wall and stuffed the bear down the chute into the building's incinerator.

Nothing mattered anymore. In the battle for my life I had destroyed the one thing left to remind me of the time I had been a feeling man. It was only then that I knew: However long my struggle, I would succeed. I would get out.

ENCOUNTERS

ABROAD

The first time I had left Cuba in self-imposed exile, I never could have imagined that one day I would find myself trapped in the country of my birth. It was 1958, and after fighting six years as a revolutionary against the dictator Fulgencio Batista, I was studying medicine at the Sorbonne, in Paris. Although in my years underground I had learned many brutal truths, politically I was still a child. I would pay dearly for my naïveté.

Home then was never far from my thoughts. I was still haunted by my memories of many friends who died in bloodshed. My youth had been spent fighting, and now I had to adapt to a very different way of life. There were many of us from the island in Paris in that fall of 1958, generally students who had left Cuba for a variety of personal and political reasons. As a group, we wanted the world to understand the necessity for revolution in our country, and so we organized demonstrations and sometimes we collected money. Once, a group of us even climbed the steps of the Eiffel Tower and hung from its top an enormous July 26th Movement banner.

My doubts about Fidel Castro notwithstanding—my concern about where his hunger for power might take him—I considered myself a revolutionary, and I cared passionately about Cuba's future. Although I was far away in Europe, I could never abandon the cause—Batista's overthrow—or my solidarity with my *compañeros*.

We Cubans in Paris followed the course of the struggle in *Le Monde* and in letters from home. Although the news was often sketchy, we did know of the general strike Fidel had called on April 9, 1958. In the government action against the strikers, ninety people had been killed in Havana and some thirty others were shot dead in Santiago de Cuba.

Two factors had doomed the strike. One was lack of organization; Fidel's July 26th Movement had not yet recovered from the loss of Frank País, second-in-command to Fidel. Secondly, Fidel did not have the support of the established Communist party [the PSP], which was, in turn, influential in Cuba's trade unions.

As a result of the strike's failure, Fidel made a pair of pragmatic decisions. He resolved to establish closer clandestine relations with the Communists, even as he emphasized for public consumption the ideological independence of the Movement. For those who might fear a creeping Red tinge to the rebellion, Fidel was reassuring. The revolution is green, he said repeatedly, like the palm tree. On at least one occasion, Fidel explicitly asserted his politics.

"Not Communism or Marxism," he had said clearly, in English, in a 1958 television interview in the Sierra Maestra. "Our philosophy is representative democracy."

Secondly, he reversed himself on the issue of unity among the revolutionary factions. In December of 1957, after rejecting the Pact of Miami, which sought to unify the various revolutionary factions, Fidel in the summer of 1958 had promoted a second similar Pact of Caracas, thereby bringing the revolutionary groups under his now unquestioned overall leadership.

After his first few months in the Sierra Maestra, Fidel saw very little direct combat as the revolution moved toward triumph. Indeed, there were few large-scale military operations on either side during the Cuban revolution and no widespread devastation. At its peak, the summer of 1958, the rebel army numbered no more than three thousand *compañeros*.

In May 1958, Batista had launched his single major offensive, "Operation Summer." But internecine conflicts in the government, low morale in the army, and constant harassment by the guerrillas had defeated Operation Summer at the outset. By August, Fidel was in absolute control of the Sierra Maestra. His brother, Raúl Castro, had formed a new guerrilla base, the Frank País Second Front, to the north of the Sierra in the Mayarí region. And Batista's army was in full retreat.

Fidel's new second-in-command, Camilo Cienfuegos, and the Argentine doctor-revolutionary, Ernesto "Ché" Guevara, had by then pushed their twin offensives from Oriente into Las Villas Province, while guerrillas of the students' Revolutionary Directorate and Segundo Frente, or Second Front, led by Gutiérrez Menoyo rose up in the Escambray district of Las Villas. With defeat certain, Batista's senior officers opened secret peace negotiations with Fidel. This process was mooted on January 1, 1959, when the dictator fled to the Dominican Republic. Five and a half years after his famous suicidal raid on the Moncada Barracks, Fidel marched again into Santiago de Cuba, this time as the undisputed leader of the Cuban revolution.

In Paris, I experienced a complex personal estrangement from the triumph. On the one hand, as a revolutionary I rejoiced at Batista's final removal and was heartened by the generally positive international response to his downfall. I joined enthusiastically in a symbolic takeover of the Cuban Embassy.

At the same time, the euphoria of victory and its clear popularity in the world community outside the United States provoked in me an anguished guilt. I was mortified at the thought that I might have been mistaken to leave the struggle. Despite my misgivings about Fidel, it seemed as if he would never dare turn away from democracy in the face of such universal expectations that Cuba would at last be free and independent, a model new country.

I knew many of the revolutionary leaders from our struggle against Batista. They often came through Paris or sent their friends to see me. I could always go back and be fully accepted into revolutionary society. But my doubts wouldn't leave me and intuition said: Wait, let us see how Fidel behaves now that power is his. Many of my Cuban friends in Paris were heading home. From Cuba, I received constant messages from old friends such as Camilo Cienfuegos that I, too, should return at once. There were many government jobs open. Then came the tide of bearded *compañeros* from the clandestine days urging me to come home.

I thought they talked too much of Fidel, but I was impressed by their news of his early reforms. Land was to be given to the *campesinos*, property belonging to Batista officials was confiscated, and social reforms such as free health care and education were being considered. Undoubtedly, Fidel was making good on his political platform. But I decided to wait until summer and my school vacation before seeing for myself what the revolution had wrought.

I flew home in July 1959 with a planeful of other Cubans. I was overjoyed to be going back, excited to see my family and friends and very anxious to see revolutionary Cuba myself. As we descended toward Havana along the northern coast of Matanzas Province we could see the distinctive green of sugar cane and palm trees. An infectious, unrestrained jubilation spread through the passenger cabin, and we all started shouting, applauding, and singing.

The spirit in the airport was equally raucous. You could feel the heat—the tropical heat of Cuba's brilliant, burning summer sun and the emotional heat of a new revolution. A trio of Cuban *guaracheros*, or popular musicians, greeted us at the gate performing old Cuban songs with guitar and maraca accompaniment. Several bearded men in uniform wandered around the airport, to no apparent purpose. Outside and inside the terminal, I saw men everywhere carrying machine guns, rifles, and revolvers; not menacingly but casually, part of the disordered, effervescent atmosphere. In all this noise and excitement, none of us minded that our luggage had been temporarily lost.

On the way into the city the roadways were lined with Cuban flags flying the standard of the July 26th Movement. It was pandemonium. Cars and trucks and motorcycles went tearing past and around us. Heedless of the speed limit, they honked their horns indiscriminately and ignored the most basic safety rules. Everyone was smiling and laughing.

The Havana Hilton, where I spent my first night, was a new hotel, an artifact of Batista's final days that now brimmed with revolutionaries. They, too, were wildly ecstatic, happy to welcome another *compañero* home to the new Cuba, to down a few *mojitos*, the national rum drink, and to spin for hours happy and sad stories of the struggle. Some were now revolutionary government ministers, others *comandantes*, and still others were again attending the reopened university. But no one paid attention to rank. Powerful or obscure, black or white, Catholic or Protestant, everyone was first a Cuban—equal, united, and free.

Outwardly, all of Cuba seemed to be of a single, confident mind and heart. I saw this unity in everyone I met as I traveled east through Matanzas, Las Villas, and then to Camagüey Province and Ciego de Avila, where my family had gathered to meet me. With them, I shared a different joy, a cheerful, hearty reunion after fourteen months of separation.

My father had begun a new life in Venezuela for over a year, and my mother and brother, who had been living in a rented house in Ciego de Avila, were at last ready to join him. But beneath the excitement of the family reunion and their eager anticipation of being with my father soon, I perceived a deep unease.

The revolution, said my uncle Sergio, "is green, but green like a watermelon. On the inside it is red. Fidel is deceiving us. This is Communism."

My aunts and my mother felt the same way. "What we have to do is get out before it's too late," they all said. They wouldn't hear my arguments that they were being influenced by deliberate counterrevolutionary rumors. Every one of them was convinced that Communism in Cuba would deprive them of their liberty and would spell the end of free enterprise. And they were very frightened.

Still the revolutionary idealist, I rejected these fears as groundless. Whatever Fidel intended for Cuba, I believed, it was not Communism. Likewise, it was inconceivable to me that the Cuban people would allow a Communist takeover of their revolution.

This analysis, however, ignored certain portents. By and large, Cubans were friendly toward the people of the United States, despite the U.S. government's long record of interference in Cuban affairs. Cubans drove American cars, used American goods, could travel to Miami in forty-five minutes and were very influenced by U.S. culture. But their charismatic new leader most assuredly was not of the same disposition. The normal nationalism of Fidel's early speeches was threaded throughout with an insistent, anti-imperialist, anti-Yanqui tone. This attitude affected the revolutionaries around Fidel, and it served to deepen their bitter memory of the aid the United States had given to Batista. Cuban-U.S. amity was further strained by Washington's objections to the terms of Fidel's land expropriations— the distribution of the property of the wealthy landowners, many of whom were American companies and individuals, to the *campesinos*. Along with other slights, there was President Dwight Eisenhower's refusal to meet with Fidel during his visit to the United States in the spring of 1959. Eisenhower explained he was "playing golf" that day and offended Fidel by sending Vice President Nixon in his stead.

These mutual irritations, from a Cuban point of view, were seen in an historical context of flagrant disregard by the United States of the island's sovereignty and independence. They had begun in 1898 with the close of the Spanish-American War, when U.S. troops occupied the island for four years.

When independence for Cuba was granted in 1901, her new constitution included the hated Platt Amendment, a provision that allowed the United States to intervene at will in Cuban domestic affairs, forbade Cuba to make any treaties or alliances without the United States' approval, and barred any foreign military bases on the island except, of course, for North American installations such as the naval base at Guantánamo, which was established with a ninety-nine-year lease in 1902.

The United States exercised the powers of the amendment directly with marine occupation from 1906 to 1909, then again in 1912, and once more from 1917 to 1923. Whether or not U.S. troops were stationed in Havana, from 1902 until 1959 the most powerful man on the island was always the United States ambassador.

Another source of irritation among the majority of the revolution's fighters was the early appointment by Fidel of PSP members to some key governmental posts. Most of us saw these party members as hack opportunists, men who'd openly opposed the revolutionary struggle until victory was assured. I didn't for a moment believe they could influence Fidel or that he shared any of their philosophy; after all, Batista, too, had had two Communist ministers in his regime.

But what I most seriously misjudged was the power of Fidel's personality. Perhaps because I had not been exposed to his magnetism, I started noticing the exaggerated devotion to Fidel without fully comprehending how strong it truly was. In my mind, revolutionary ideals could never be replaced by a revolutionary idol.

Yet I recall one of the many conversations I had that summer of 1959 with Camilo Cienfuegos. Camilo, second only to Fidel in the guerrilla command, was good-natured, very honest, and intelligent. He disliked Communism and had been particularly angered at the 1956 Soviet invasion of Hungary. In 1959, Camilo told me, he was equally opposed to the many extralegal trials and executions of former Batista officials in Cuba, a view that brought him into direct conflict with Raúl Castro, the strongest advocate of this violent, summary justice.

But this principled independence of mind deserted Camilo when it came to Fidel. He professed to me an almost mystical admiration for the man. One afternoon on the beach at Bacuranao, east of Havana, I asked Cienfuegos what he thought of the foreign press allegations that the revolution was Communist.

He replied using my old nickname, *Flaco* ("Slim").

"Look, Slim, you know that I'm one hundred percent *Fidelista*. Do you remember that day when we were in the clinic together and I said you looked like Frankenstein? I also told you that what we needed in Cuba was a brave, upright, just revolutionary leader, someone who would bring together the young people who wanted a better life with no more lies and injustice. Well, I found that leader in Fidel."

Camilo's certainty was startling. "I've had," he said, "I have now, and I always will have absolute confidence in him. If he says we have to be Communists, then I'll be one. But more than anything else, I'll be a *Fidelista.*"

Fidelismo, a term that began to be used even before the Sierra Maestra struggle, was an epithet of pride and blind allegiance to Fidel, the ultimate acknowledgment of his charisma.

"I've always thought that the Popular Socialist Party's leaders are a gang of cowards and opportunists," Camilo went on. "If Fidel decides one day that all of us should be Communist, I'll ask only one thing—that he takes all those cowards out of the government.

"But forget it! He's not an asshole. Fidel knows that if Communism is established here, the Soviet Union will do the same thing to us that she's done in the other Socialist countries."

A CONVERSATION WITH CHÉ

I debated with myself through the summer of 1959 whether I should stay in Cuba, as so many of my friends pressed me to do, or return to my studies in France. By September, I was no surer of Fidel's intentions than I had been in July; I had come looking for answers in Cuba and found only more questions. But my intuitive distrust of Fidel and the way the revolution was centered around him intensified, as I heard, more and more often, the blind loyalty to Fidel in so many people's words. With these misgivings, I finally decided to leave once again for Paris.

I did allow time in my schedule for a several-day visit to Havana, and once again took a room at the Hilton, soon to be renamed the Havana Libre. Among the scores of bearded *compañeros* who were still thronging about its lobby, I was delighted to encounter Jesús Suárez Gayol, a boyhood friend from Camagüey who had also gone on to the university and then fought in the Sierra Maestra. Jesús, now a captain, invited me to come that night to the house of one of his relatives.

At eleven o'clock I found the residence in a pleasant middle-class Havana neighborhood. Soon Jesús and I were deep into a discussion of the only topic in Cuba: the revolution. We must

have been speaking for the better part of an hour when there
came a knock on the door. Since it was then common social
practice in Cuba to appear informally at a friend's house at
almost any hour of the evening, I paid no attention to the fact
that it was close to midnight. Nor, since Jesús had been a guerrilla, did I wonder that his visitor was a weary-eyed revolutionary carrying his sidearm and clad in disheveled olive-drab fatigues.
The surprise was the guest's identity: Comandante Ernesto "Ché"
Guevara.

At the time, this future legend of twentieth-century revolution was already, with Fidel, the popular embodiment of the
romantic guerrilla in Cuba and all over the world. In Europe the
newspapers had been filled with stories of his exploits. He was
above all a symbol of the heroic struggle for freedom—the common man as warrior for liberation.

Ché spoke briefly in an adjoining room with a woman of the
house before joining us in the family's modest living room. My
first impression of him, beyond noting his obvious haggardness
and the exhausted way he slumped into a chair, was that Ché
was much shorter and slighter than he appeared on television
and in the hundreds of photographs I'd seen of him.

When we were introduced, Ché mentioned he'd heard from
mutual friends, perhaps Pepín Naranjo, that I was living in
Paris.

"Are you back home for good or are you just on vacation?"
he asked.

"On vacation," I answered. "I'm going back to France to
finish medical school."

"Yes," he said from his chair, regarding me with his intense
gaze. "But I suppose you'll come back when you finish. We need
a lot of doctors here, and we'll be needing more every day." Then
he added, without expression, "I'm a physician too. So we'll be
colleagues."

I smiled at the sardonic "so we'll be colleagues." Ché and I
were hardly apt to be practicing medicine together one day. I
recognized also in the remark the well-known black wit of this
man—a committed revolutionary who nevertheless appreciated
the irony of his dual avocations for healing and for revolution.
His mordancy mitigated his didacticism—a side of his nature
with which I was about to become acquainted.

"You know?" he said, starting to pace and wheezing from
his chronic asthma. "I don't think our profession will stand up

under the force of this revolution. Like good members of the petite bourgeoisie, they're bound to lick the Americans' boots the first chance they get. Don't you think so?"

No answer was expected.

"Tell me, do you like France?" he went on. "How are things going over there? I admire General de Gaulle, you know. I think he's been very manly in his dealings with the Yanquis. But now he's making a serious mistake by refusing to give Algeria her independence. He's the only Frenchman with enough prestige to pull France out of the chaos she's in now. If he were smarter, he'd nationalize the large private companies and get rid of the bureaucracy and the fascistic army officers. I mean, he could make France symbolize for the world what she once symbolized during the French Revolution, and that would make him the greatest man in contemporary French history. He's already the tallest."

I pointed out that it would be rather difficult for De Gaulle to proceed in this way, even if he was of a mind to.

"Yes! Of course!" Ché agreed at once. "Because there's no revolution! Because they change the head of state but all the machinery of oppression stays the same. Things would be very different if De Gaulle had come to power in a revolution like ours, where an entire nation is behind an indisputably popular leader who represents what is best and purest in José Martí's thought, who has no obligations except those that grow out of his commitment to History.

"De Gaulle's in the situation of so many leaders who represent a class—their own class—and who act on behalf of that class's interests. They couldn't act another way if they wanted to, because their hands would be tied by laws, by the invisible but unbreakable rules that the capitalist system has established. That is why you can't expect the oppressed masses to gain any advantages at all from any movement within the so-called Western democracies—which, incidentally, have very little to do with democracy."

Ché was a very controversial figure of the Cuban revolution. He was attacked by Cuban exiles, the U.S. government, and the international press as a Communist. But because I had heard the same accusation leveled against Fidel and thought it to be untrue, I had assumed that Ché was being similarly maligned. And yet after listening to him talk it was clear to me that he had communistic beliefs.

"Look at our example," he went on. "Who liberated Cuba? The guerrilla, under Fidel's exceptional leadership. And with whose help? First of all, the *campesino*, who saw in the policy of agrarian reform the realization of a hope that until then had been kept dormant by oppression, poverty, and false promises. That *campesino* firmly believed in the revolution and in the guerrillas as its vanguard, which is why a formidable symbiosis was created between the *campesinos* and the leaders of the Rebel Army. The Rebel Army's thinking changed day by day and underwent a real transformation as a result of contact with the *campesino* masses. The Rebel Army learned about the needs and suffering of that class; it experienced the hard reality of those lives."

Although I had few preconceptions about Ché, the evident emotion of his convictions was startling. He soon captivated me, provoking in me the strongest urge to probe him as deeply as possible. His personality was so riveting and his intensity so compelling that I automatically engaged my Marist-taught capacity for memorization, intending to write out his sentences at the earliest opportunity. Ché's magnetism was overwhelming; his intellect was rapier-sharp. I knew myself to be at a wellspring of revolution, and I wanted to preserve what I was hearing.

Ché was totally utopian about the potential for people to remake themselves. "You must have complete faith in man," he lectured us as the night wore on. "You must free him and allow his potential to develop fully, and for that you need the revolution. It is the only key to unlock the doors that will allow man to find himself, to rid himself of alienation, to become truly free and master of his own destiny.

"The Cuban revolution is essentially humanistic. I don't mean in the pseudo-philanthropic, charitable sense that the bourgeoisie or the Church attributes to the word. No, when I use the term, I'm thinking of a new concept: total commitment to the oppressed classes, not superiority to them."

His tiredness and the chronic labor of his breathing, together with the fervor with which he spoke, made the conversation physically taxing for Ché. At one point he forgot my name; Jesús reminded him.

"Comandante?" I asked.

"Call me Ché!" he interrupted. "Don't be so formal, uh ..." He'd forgotten it again.

"José Luis."

"Yes, José Luis."

"Ché," I started again. "You've just come back from a long trip through several underdeveloped countries, I hear. Did you find any similarity between those countries and ours?"

"Yes," he answered in a reflective tone. "I visited a few underdeveloped countries, but I also visited Japan, a developed country, where I observed two very curious things. First, their agrarian reform, favored and imposed by the United States, is the most radical in the world! They permit only one hectare per person. [One hectare equals 2.471 acres.] Yet the United States criticizes our agrarian reform, which allows private ownership of four hundred hectares! What do you think about that?

"Second, I was surprised to see that a country like Japan, without iron or oil, is becoming one of the most powerful nations in the world. And I ask myself why Cuba can't do the same. Why can't we start an aggressive program of industrialization, especially heavy industry?

"As for the Socialist countries, I was really only in one, Yugoslavia—if you can call Yugoslavia Socialist. The system of financial autonomy in business there, with its distribution of profits to the workers, is almost identical to entrepreneurial capitalism. And its market is no different from capitalism. It is ruled by the laws of supply and demand and the price wars they generate."

The conversation was becoming more and more exciting for me. I had known nothing about Japanese or Yugoslavian politics, and I wanted to learn all I could from him.

"I'd like to ask you another question," I said.

He smiled at me quizzically. Ché, stern and unapproachable by reputation, seemed somewhat amused by my directness. He asked Jesús for more coffee and then erupted into another violent asthma attack that sent him searching for his pocket inhaler. As his color returned, he wheezed, "Look what you've done to me! I'll tell you, it's not that I like talking so much, but sharp questions stimulate me. If they didn't, I would have gone to bed a long time ago, which is exactly what I'm going to do in a few minutes. But go on, what's your question?"

I was trying, by indirection, to discover from Ché how open the revolution was, or would be, to the Soviet bloc. "Can we Cubans," I offered, "chart our own course?"

His answer required not a moment's consideration.

"Well, why not? I think we can. It's a nice variant that would allow us to continue making our original revolution on neutral territory. Nonaligned. Right in the middle. And everybody would help us. Our 'Yanqui friends,'" he said with a smile, "as well as the Soviets. Don't the Yanquis send aid to Poland and Yugoslavia? And Nasser? Doesn't he receive aid from both sides? Well, why not Cuba?"

We had been talking now for more than five hours. First light was breaking over Havana as Ché rose to leave. "I don't have much time to sleep," he said with a yawn. "José Luis, we'll see each other soon in Paris. We'll continue our conversation there."

But as Ché reached the door, he turned and added, "Are you sure you don't have any more fucking questions, as you say here?"

I certainly did have one more. Ché had been accused over and over in the press of being a Communist. Assured of his confidence, I ventured a final question that, among Cubans in 1959, would have been considered an impertinence.

"Are you a Communist?" I asked simply.

Ché was at that moment lazily bracing himself against the doorframe. "You've got a lot of balls, José Luis," he said as he walked slowly back into the room. "It's just as well you're not a reporter."

He motioned for Jesús and me to sit. Then he took up a rigid, professorial pace around the room as he instructed us in a synthesized survey of world history, from primitive cultures to the present. It took Ché a good while even to get to the French Revolution, which he examined minutely for us; and he dwelt at great length upon the Bolshevik uprising. With each era he covered he grew more impassioned, pacing, wheezing, and gesturing. At last he concluded:

"If being opposed to injustice, to oppression, to poverty, and to social inequalities means being a Communist, you can be sure I am one! But you could just as well describe me with other words. I've read Marx, Engels, Lenin—and I think any man who doesn't is a fool. I've also read Socrates, Machiavelli, Rousseau, Hegel, and many other philosophers. Although I don't agree with their ideas, I understand that they made a great contribution to the progress of mankind. That's the most important thing. The progress of mankind."

With that, the clock turned past 6:00 A.M. and Ché stood before us, utterly spent. "José Luis," he said, "you want to know too much. It is too late now for going to bed, but not for going to work. Today, you know, is Sunday, the voluntary workday."

Showing me the wryest of small smiles, he added: "Wouldn't you like to come with me?"

I said nothing but only smiled back. Ché nodded and left.

On my way back to the hotel, thinking about all I had heard that evening, I hoped I could meet this enigmatic man again. Although his political beliefs were ones I did not share, there was no mistaking his integrity. Also, if anyone could give me more insight into the revolution I was eager to understand, it was Ché.

In the last week of my trip I decided I would go to the university campus one last time, to the site of the revolutionary struggle that had resulted in the Cuba I was now visiting. Inside the Rectory at the university, I was chatting with a professor when three cars pulled up in front of the building. Fidel, looking sweaty and uncombed, got out of one of the vehicles, holding a big cigar.

Within minutes he was surrounded by hundreds of students, whom he began to question eagerly. What were they studying? What did they think of the new revolutionary laws? Of his proposals for agrarian reform? The meeting was completely spontaneous, a rewarding moment of open discussion, dominated of course by the energetic Fidel.

Commander René Vallejo, Fidel's physician and personal aide (and at that time something of a controversial figure among the revolution's leadership for his deeply held belief in *santería*— Afro-Cuban spiritualism), came up to me during the impromptu gathering and greeted me affectionately. We agreed to meet later for a conversation at the Hilton.

I waited in the lobby for Vallejo about twenty minutes until I saw him come in with Fidel. Vallejo invited me up to the headquarters' living suite on the twenty-fourth floor. When we came in, Fidel had already taken off his belt, pistol, and shoes. He was sweating profusely and his face shone with moisture and grease. Vallejo introduced me, and Fidel offered sodas from the refrigerator. He emptied his in a swallow and disappeared into the adjoining room. Five minutes later he came out half-dressed, barefoot, with his hair wet and uncombed. A more informal head of state was hard to imagine.

Fidel sat down and put on his socks and boots. Then he went again into the next room and came back with his hair combed, tucking his shirt into his fatigue pants. He looked like a water-spout. In all this unselfconscious, hurried attention to his appearance, he did not stop moving or bombarding Vallejo with questions. Still in motion, he then left for an appointment.

Before going back to France, I would have liked to talk to Fidel as directly as I had with Ché. My brief visit home had resolved none of my doubts about the man; all I could say for certain was that he and his revolution were then wildly popular in Cuba. Since I did not have the chance to pose questions of the sort I had asked Ché, I, like everyone else, would have to wait and see where Fidel intended to take the country.

A MEETING IN THE ALPS

In Paris I was living with Count Jocelyn de Noblet d'Anglure and his wife, Marie France, in their large apartment on Square Villaret de Joyeuse, near the Arc de Triomphe. I had met them through the first friend I'd made in France, Hubert de Grandcourt, and now they were part of my new life.

In the year since I'd arrived, I had made many friends through Hubert, Jocelyn, and Marie France. There were several weekend hunting expeditions outside Paris, as well as trips to the Norman coast, where we picked strawberries and swam in the frigid Channel. Sometimes we got together just to talk or to listen to music.

Among these friends were Serge and Patrick Budin, whose parents, Maître Jean Budin and Alla, I also had gotten to know. Maître Budin was an erudite international lawyer, deeply reflective with a refined wit. Alla, his wife, was of Russian descent. She was kindly and spirited, with an explosive Slavic temperament and great *joie de vivre*. We had liked one another immediately, and the Budins had become, in a sense, my surrogate parents.

With two of my other new acquaintances, Christian de Jonquières and Bernard de Castet, I had travelled through Europe in an old, two-cylinder Citroën—and on an exceedingly modest budget. The camaraderie forged among us had continued to grow, helping to fill the emotional void of separation from my family and friends and Cuba.

After my return from Cuba for the fall of 1958, I once again resumed what was beginning to seem like a life sentence of medical school. It had been six years since I'd begun my studies in Havana, and only my unquestioned sense of family duty kept me at them.

Still, there was plenty of time for my social life with Jocelyn and Marie France, the Budins, Bernard, Christian, and all the rest. That winter, too, I learned how to ski.

Then in March of 1960, I contracted a severe case of bronchitis, and a physician recommended that I convalesce in the cold, dry air of the French Alps. If my coughing wasn't too heavy, he said, it would be all right for me to practice my new sport.

The weather was frigid, and the cable car to the top of the mountain, while offering a magnificent view of the valley, also had a crack in its window. The first morning I climbed aboard with my equipment I was nearly numb from the wind before the car reached the top of the trail.

I skied gently down the long slope, taking care at its many dangerous turns and finally stopping to rest from my exertions. Sticking my poles in the snow, I took off my gloves and contemplated the Alpine tranquillity.

My serenity soon was broken by the appearance of another skier above me on the trail, moving very fast. I imagined he knew what he was doing, and that he would reduce his speed before he reached the tricky, flat area where I was resting. Instead, he tried to stop all at once and fell into a tumble, his skis flying into the air.

Although the skier appeared unhurt, I put on my gear quickly and hurried to him while he struggled to rise and gather his own equipment. Only as I reached him did I realize that this "he" was a she. From under the hood of her parka, she looked up at me with deep-blue eyes, intense and shining with fear.

"What's your name?" I asked as I helped her stand.

"Marie Christine," she replied shyly. "And you?"

I gave her my name and then boldly proposed a date. "Suppose we meet at six in the club at the lodge to celebrate your renaissance?"

"I don't know," Marie Christine answered cautiously. "Maybe. I don't . . . I have to go now. Thanks. 'Bye." She made a ninety-degree turn and zigzagged down the hill at a prudent speed. I didn't move until her small silhouette had disappeared into the pine forest below.

It was a long wait that evening at the Whiskey-á-Go-Go; for two hours just me and my hot grog and the roaring fireplace. *It's a shame*, I thought to myself as I gave up my vigil. There had been such sparkle in those beautiful eyes.

Several days later in a café on the Champs Élysées, I happened to look up from my espresso and newspaper when, by incredible luck, there she was again! Shy as before, she smiled when I walked over to her. We drank our coffee together and then I asked for her telephone number. "You can't refuse my next invitation," I said as we rose to leave. "You already stood me up once."

Marie Christine and I dined together the next night in a small restaurant on the Left Bank and then we took a long walk along the Seine to the Île de la Cité. There we sat under the *Vert Galant*, famous according to Parisian legend as spring's harbinger, the first tree in the city to leaf as winter dies.

My first impression of Marie Christine was confirmed. She was very beautiful. She had fine, delicate features, framed by thick ash-blond hair that fell to her shoulders. She was also, at first, given to melancholy, quiet moods that gave her beauty an enigmatic quality.

As we spoke, I was struck by her fineness, a quality that infused every comment she made. Even in her sad moments she radiated a lively inner purity of spirit that evoked in me an idealized love for her. We shared a passion for Mozart and Bach and we admired the same old masters as well as Impressionist painters. Marie Christine was always exquisitely sensitive to nuance in both her thinking and her emotions. Although we spoke to each other in French, she had full command of Spanish and perfect English, which she pronounced with a British accent.

I told her much about myself, my family, and my role in the revolution. But she talked little about herself. I knew she was one of five children in a Catholic family and that she lived on Avenue Montespant close to where it intersects with Avenue Kléber. It was on that corner that she always said farewell. Not until late May, more than two months after our chance encounter in the Alps, did I discover Marie Christine's true circumstances, when she invited me to tea.

Turning onto Avenue Montespant, I found her family's house was almost completely hidden from the street by an iron fence, painted black and reinforced by steel plates. In its center was a large metal gate. I rang the bell and then waited for two or three minutes. A butler, very stern-looking and gray-haired, finally came to answer my ring. "I've been invited to have tea with," I stammered, "with Mademoiselle Marie Christine."

He quietly led me through the entrance hall, to the left, into an opulent room hung with famous paintings under a sparkling chandelier. The room's furniture was very fine, and there were beautiful antique French rugs on the highly polished floor. Awed by such luxury, I asked myself who this girl I'd fallen in love with could be.

Marie Christine came softly to my side, kissed me, and then led me by the arm into another, even grander room. All the rooms of the house were named for their color. In this one, great windows gave a wide view of the garden. We sat on Louis XIV chairs and took our tea from Limoges china that the butler brought to us on a silver tray.

I didn't know what to say. Dozens of questions that never before had occurred to me were beating in my brain. I stared at Marie Christine's hands, delicately pouring our tea. I took a sip, and then blurted out: "You have a very beautiful house."

"Yes, do you like it?" she answered with complete naturalness.

"Very much."

I didn't know how to continue. I was afraid of committing some gaucherie. But when I looked at Marie Christine's face, I understood that it was better to be spontaneous than to mask my surprise.

"And your father, what does he do?" I asked. "I mean, what business is he in?"

"I thought you weren't interested in knowing anything about my family," she said. "I really don't know myself all the businesses he's involved in. It's a little complicated, and I haven't lived with my parents—"

"It doesn't matter," I interrupted her. "It's obvious that your family is very wealthy. I thought you were so, so *normal*."

At this she broke into a giggle. "I always thought I was, too," she said. "Until now."

"I mean average," I added quickly. "Not so rich."

"I'm not rich," she corrected me. "But my father is." She explained that he owned a factory for making essential oils for perfumes in Grasse, in the South of France. It was a family business, inherited from her grandfather. The same was true, she went on, for his property in Boufarik in Algeria and a farm in Seville. He also owned businesses in New York, Brazil, and elsewhere.

"It doesn't matter—that's enough," I interjected. "I would have preferred you broke." I smiled when I added, "Don't tell me that you're a marquise, too."

"I'm not, I don't think. But my father is a count."

"That's the final touch!" I declared. "A little Cuban in love with the daughter of a French millionaire, and a marquise to boot!"

"Not a marquise," she answered. "My father is a count, that is all. And little Cuban? You're not that, either. A giant Cuban, more likely. You're so tall."

I still had not fully absorbed the shock of Marie Christine's position by the time tea was finished and we were saying good-bye in the vestibule. The butler approached circumspectly with my raincoat and helped me into it with a dignified effortlessness. As he made his graceful retreat, Marie Christine took my hand. "I forgot something," she said. "Next week, on the twenty-eighth, my parents are giving me a coming-out party. You're invited, okay?"

"Okay," I replied, and then kissed her.

In a rented tuxedo, I presented myself at the appointed hour on the 28th of May. A servant, dressed as a page, accepted the invitation from me, rapped the floor three times with a long stick, and announced in a loud voice: "MONSIEUR LLOVIO Y MENÉNDEZ." From the receiving line ahead of me I caught a look at Marie Christine, more stunning than ever with her blond hair falling down on her bare shoulders. She smiled sweetly at me, a welcome bit of warmth next to the gelid, appraising glances I received from her parents next to her, the Count and Countess de Chiris.

I affected my most formal air at our introduction, shaking the aloof count's hand firmly and kissing the countess's proffered hand as I uttered the obligatory *"Mes hommages, Madame."*

Marie Christine was the perfect debutante, both demure and lively. I wasn't sure of my own role in her introduction to society until she came to me with a conspiratorial grin and said, "I've been looking for you. You're my official escort at this party."

For the rest of the night we mingled idly with the elegant guests at the sumptuous affair. The furniture had been rear-

ranged for the occasion, and each room was devoted to a theme.
One room featured flamenco songs and guitar players. In the
center were two large tables laden with a variety of Spanish
foods. The next room was done in a Russian theme with gypsy
music and caviar. French *delicatesses* were being served in yet
another room, where violinists played. Despite the countess's
inquisitorial stare, which I felt on me throughout the night, Marie
Christine and I were happily adrift in the glow of our affection.
In all, I enjoyed the splendid party enormously.

The Monday after Marie Christine's coming-out party, still
basking in the magical evening's afterglow, I sat with Jocelyn
and Marie France in their library drinking excellent coffee and
listening to Jocelyn recount his recent trip to Israel. His descriptions were so vivid and entertaining that I felt as if I'd gone to
Israel myself.

Suddenly the doorbell interrupted his narrative. I answered
the ring and found myself face to face with an obviously frightened young woman. She was Marie Christine's maid, and she
had a letter for me from her mistress.

Darling:
I am writing to tell you that my parents are utterly
opposed to us. Now they want to marry me to someone I
hardly know, but I stood up to them as I never have
before. I've confessed to them how deep my love is for
you. I leave tomorrow for Algeria and will not return
until, as my parents say, "I get over this mad, childish
infatuation." They watch me all the time. I can't do
anything without your help. Please, my love, save me!
                                    Marie Christine

In the face of this unexpected crisis, I realized how
much in love with Marie Christine I was. I did not want to
lose her. It didn't seem right that her parents could stand in
the way of our happiness. How could I help her, and help
us? My mind fixed on the only possible solution, drastic as it
seemed. I had to kidnap her.

Back in the library, I showed Jocelyn the letter and
enlisted him in my plan. His lively eyes shone at the prospect of an adventure, and without letting me finish he exclaimed, "You can rely on me!"

A while later, the telephone rang. It was Marie Christine.

"I don't have much time," she told me in a trembling voice. "I leave tomorrow on the six P.M. plane. My mother and a bodyguard will be with me. My father was called suddenly to New York."

"Okay, listen," I said. "I'm determined to keep you from going. Keep your eyes open when you leave the house. I have a plan for when you come out. If it doesn't work, we'll try again at the airport—"

Marie Christine hung up abruptly.

Our first move was to recruit a third confederate, Philippe d'Argencé, a mutual friend, former parachutist, and professional photographer. We called him right away, and within the hour he was with us in the apartment, helping to plan the abduction.

Through the night we refined my original idea into a primary and a backup strategy. First, we would wait for the De Chiris family car at the corner of Avenues Montespant and Kléber. There we expected the heavy afternoon traffic to stop or slow the car long enough for us to rush it. If this failed, Plan B, an airport kidnap, would be attempted.

At four that afternoon we were in place. Jocelyn stayed behind the wheel of his Aronde on Avenue Kléber near the intersection. Philippe took his post at the intersection itself, and I was positioned between the two of them.

It was a cool day and the wind blew cold on our faces and hands. I glanced at Jocelyn, who smiled back at me nervously, then gave a wink and a tilt to his head. Philippe crossed and recrossed the intersection like an honor guard. He kept taking his hands out of his pockets and blowing on them.

Suddenly, the family's elegant English automobile turned the corner behind him and quickly motored away. They had taken us by surprise. Philippe and I ran to the Aronde, where Jocelyn, in his hurry to start it, managed to flood the motor.

"There's nothing to do but let it rest," he said, disgusted with himself. When we finally got it started, Marie Christine was far away. But Jocelyn atoned for his blunder by expertly wheeling the Aronde through the rush-hour traffic and on to Orly Airport ahead of our quarry. We had one more chance to rescue Marie Christine.

At the Air France terminal, Jocelyn again remained in the car at the curb while Philippe and I went inside. He assumed a nonchalant pose near the counter itself while I took a chair opposite him and pretended to read France-Soir. I cut a small hole in the middle of the paper so that I could surreptitiously monitor the area.

Minutes later Marie Christine walked through the door, followed by her mother and a burly older man, the driver-bodyguard. At the counter she stood tense and watchful, chain-smoking while the countess and the bodyguard exchanged whispers next to her. When Marie Christine looked in my direction, I shook the newspaper and caught her attention. The action was on.

"Come on! Hurry!" I shouted to her. As she darted toward me, Philippe closed in on the bodyguard and pinned his arms. The countess screamed, "Help! Help! They're kidnapping a minor!" as we fled out the door to the car.

At this moment the police appeared out of nowhere to block our escape. Then they took us all to the airport prefecture, where Jocelyn, Philippe, and I were put under guard in a corner. Across the room, I watched Marie Christine argue with her mother in a low but very determined voice. Her attitude astonished me: This was not the timid, fearful girl I knew.

The subprefect, once he learned who the countess was, began toadying to her. Then the press and curiosity seekers started crowding into the room. I had to do something fast.

The solution came to me just as the prefect of the airport himself walked into the office. "Quiet!" I yelled. "Everybody listen to me!" The startled crowd fell silent.

"Listen to me, please," I went on in an indignant voice. "It's unheard of for such a thing to happen in France, the country of lovers *par excellence*! They wanted to coerce me, and I have to take advantage of my right to speak to ask only one question. May I?"

The prefect nodded his assent. Marie Christine looked at me with unquestioning love. The countess scowled.

"They've mentioned mademoiselle's minority as the basis for charging that a crime has taken place," I said. "Well then, why don't you ask her for her passport and check her age?"

The subprefect looked crestfallen; he was about to be made foolish, and he knew it. Marie Christine confidently strode forward with her passport and opened it before him.

"Excuse me, Mademoiselle," he croaked. "There's been a mistake. You are free to go wherever you like. Please accept my apologies, and I ask the same of these gentlemen," he concluded, looking at the three of us in the corner.

Madame the Countess was stunned. She rained promises, pleas, and threats on her daughter, but Marie Christine was unmovable. As the prefect's office erupted into cheers and applause from the onlookers, Marie Christine's mother walked silently away, her bodyguard following. Her final gesture was a venomous glare at me.

HAPPY TIMES

We celebrated our success that night at the apartment on Square Villaret. Marie Christine's rescue, everyone agreed, was wondrous confirmation that love conquers all. By the next morning, however, it was time to address practical matters.

Marie Christine and I decided we would marry. Until the ceremony and a place for us to live could be arranged, she needed somewhere safe to stay. The answer to this initial problem, we hoped, would be found with Father Rossi, an old friend of the de Chiris family who had known Marie Christine since her early girlhood.

I rose early to go see him in Pigalle. Downstairs, Jocelyn and Marie France's concierge accosted me harshly. "This is unbearable, Monsieur," she said furiously as she directed my attention outside to a crowd of reporters with their cameras, pads, pencils, and microphones. "They've been disturbing the whole neighborhood for hours with this scandal!" I apologized to her and then slipped out a side entrance.

There was another surprise waiting for me at the news kiosk in the Argentine Métro stop. "Good morning, Monsieur!" exclaimed the old lady from whom I bought my paper each day. "You really did it, eh? And where do you have the beauty hidden? You have to tell me!"

Around her in the kiosk was arrayed the journalistic response to our adventure. On page one of *Paris-presse l'intransigeant* I discovered a large photo of Marie Christine under the headline BEAUTIFUL HEIRESS KIDNAPPED. The coverage was much the same in the other periodicals. "The Perfume King said no," announced one. "Marie Christine chose love," said another. A third called me "Love's commando."

This sensationalized elaboration by the papers was, to say the least, an unintended consequence of the scene at Orly. It didn't require much imagination to envision how the wild stories were being received on Avenue Montespant. I hurried on, somewhat stunned, to my meeting with Father Rossi.

At Pigalle, I was grateful for that morning's steady drizzle; it had a calming effect on me as I walked in great uncertainty to my meeting with Father Rossi. He was, I knew, a colorful character, well esteemed by his parishioners. Marie Christine had told me of his quick humor and beneficent nature, but how would he receive our request for help?

"My boy," he said as we sat down, "you have real Latin blood. What could have possessed you to attempt to kidnap Marie Christine?"

Heavy and nearly bald, the priest addressed me with a serious expression and a firm voice. Still, I did see a certain gleam in his eye and a reassuring expression of mirth around his mouth.

"Do you think you're living in the sixteenth century?" he continued. "We're in the middle of the twentieth century! And you, riding horseback on romanticism, have tried to steal your beautiful lady when you don't even have a place to put her. At least in the old days the abductor would have arranged a hideout ahead of time!"

Father Rossi was having a wonderful time at my expense.

"Let's see," he said, "are you Catholic? Where did you go to school? Surely it wasn't in a school run by priests—they don't teach those things. I suppose you'll get married in the church, won't you? Are you baptized?"

Then it was my turn. As he leaned back with his hands folded over his prominent belly, I defended my Catholic upbringing. "Look, Father," I said, "regardless of what you may think, I was educated by the priests. You can deduce that I'm baptized. If you like, I can ask one of my teachers, Brother Juan Salvador, for a reference. I assure you it will be a good one, in spite of my Latin blood. And no, the Brothers didn't teach me how to kidnap people, but I did learn lots of other things with them. All I need—"

He raised his index finger to his lips as a sign I should be quiet.

"Don't worry," Father Rossi said, then added calmly: "I have a place for Marie Christine. In line with the romantic plot you've started, I've thought of a convent in Montparnasse."

Now he offered a mischievous smile.

"José Luis, don't repeat this to anybody, but I really enjoyed reading your story in the papers this morning. Not to mention how my parishioners have enjoyed it! All they've talked about today is the abduction and the daring Cuban, and how the authorities can't charge you with anything. May God forgive me!"

Then Father Rossi crossed himself and allowed himself an ironic grin.

Marie Christine and I managed to elude the crowd of reporters still gathered at the de Noblet's building and headed for the convent in Montparnasse, where the Mother Superior received us warmly. She took us to a small, modestly furnished room decorated only by a simple crucifix on the wall. I explained that we needed time to make preparations to be married, including the necessity of getting my papers from Cuba. "Take your time, my son," she said simply. "Marie Christine will be safe here with us."

Marie Christine stayed at the convent through the end of June, and then she moved, a few days before our wedding, to the Budins' Château de Vaumain in Oise, near the town of Gisors, where we were to be married. The château, with its high tower, emanated an almost unreal beauty. A semicircular balustrade marked the end of the formal front garden, where lovely statuary had been placed symmetrically between two ornamental pools. To the left of the main house was the kitchen garden, planted with vegetables and strawberries.

There were two large cherry trees and, a little beyond them, an apple orchard. In the château's cellars the family made a cider very similar to champagne and a Calvados that Uncle Jean (as we had come to know Maître Budin) offered us proudly at the end of each meal.

We tried to keep our marriage day, July 9, 1960, private, but the press somehow found out. The mayor of Le Vaumain, with a French tricolor sash across his chest, blinked constantly at their flashbulbs as he read the words of the civil ceremony. His voice trembled and his spectacles kept slipping down his nose. Surely he was asking himself why *he* had to be the one to marry us.

To no one's surprise, Marie Christine's parents absented themselves from both the civil ceremony and the church wedding, which was performed in Le Vaumain by a Polish priest named Torkaski. Although she was sad about her parents' renunciation, Marie Christine accepted the situation, as she knew they would not be reconciled to the idea of our marriage.

Noting that the press had barraged us with questions, Father Torkaski ended the ceremony with a confidential aside to Marie Christine and me. "I approve of your union," he said. "I find it very normal that two young people who are of age should marry without the consent of their parents." Then he came with us to the château to celebrate with champagne and wine at the party the Budins had prepared for us.

Most of the wedding presents were practical gifts of money, enough for Marie Christine and me to afford a brief honeymoon in the South of France. We spent two days in Saint-Raphaël and then continued on to Beauvallon, a small beach surrounded by murmuring pines.

For the balance of the summer, we took jobs at the resort in Beauvallon, helping the tourists with their chairs and umbrellas in return for our room and board and modest wages. Then in early October, we returned to Paris.

Because of a new regulation of the National Bank of Cuba, I could no longer receive financial help from my aunts. In the letters I received from my parents, my father wrote that he could not help me either, as he was just getting established in Venezuela and had little money. I therefore had to discontinue my studies—but this was the least of my problems. Now I was a married man, and I had to support myself and my new wife. I needed to make my own way in the world.

My first position was with a company called Comptoir Maritime International, where I learned the complicated operations of customs and international commerce. To my surprise, I seemed to have an aptitude for business. I worked feverishly at this, my first real employment, and after a few months won a promotion.

The only members of Marie Christine's family with whom we were close were her aunt and uncle, Pierrette and Jean Meynard. The two of them were kind and understanding and treated us with a love and tenderness I will never forget. Their daughter, Florence, who then was living with her husband in the Comores Islands, lent us her apartment on Lamennais Street near the Champs Élysées. We needed a home for the two of us, or rather the two and a half of us; we were expecting a baby.

Our daughter Marielle's birth filled me with an emotion I had never felt before. I still have a vivid mental image of Marie Christine propped up in her hospital bed, her blond hair falling over her loose hospital gown and our child sleeping tenderly in her arms. An ordinary picture, perhaps, but it seemed unique to me and I felt an indescribable happiness.

In 1961, Baron de Roüyn, an insurance company executive whom we met through Uncle Jean, found me a position with a better future as second-in-command to the director of purchasing at the NYCO Chemical Products Corp, in Aubervilliers. Its overall director, Pierre Lafage, was a young entrepreneur who introduced me to the vast national and international chemical market, and I thrived in his employ. Within a few months I was the director of purchasing and in charge of exports. Soon (and with the Meynards' help), Marie Christine and I were able to buy an apartment of our own on Rue Saint-Ferdinand.

We were each other's emotional center, wife, husband, and parents. For my new wife I felt a great tenderness and a desire to protect and shelter her against any further turmoil. There was something in Marie Christine's sweetness and gentle nature that made me want to take care of her. I very naturally took on many of the responsibilities of our life to make the transition for her as easy as possible.

Marie Christine adapted to her new role with ease, and never once gave any sign that she missed her old life of circumscribed luxury. Her high spirits were evident and her confidence grew. She laughed and played the guitar often and even seemed to enjoy the more routine aspects of caring for a house and family. In time, she took an interesting volunteer job in the archives of the Comédie Française.

These months were the happiest of our lives together.

BAD NEWS

Fidel's open hatred toward the United States—and Washington's reciprocal hostility to the revolution—intensified throughout 1960 and into 1961. Cuba had established diplomatic relations with the Soviet Union in May of 1960, and by September, Fidel had nationalized practically all U.S. holdings on the island. During this time the CIA was openly training Cuban exiles in the southern United States to launch an invasion and sabotaging mission in order to overthrow Fidel. On January 2, 1961, Cuba formally

charged at the United Nations that the United States was preparing an invasion. The next day, not three weeks before John F.
Kennedy would succeed him, President Eisenhower broke diplomatic relations with Cuba.

Most people in France—including myself—then perceived
the escalating tensions as the fault of the superpowers. I further
believed that Fidel's recognition of the USSR and his other, early
ties to the Soviet bloc were nothing more than a series of shrewd,
and necessary, defensive ploys in the face of the U.S. threat.
Since Fidel had to survive U.S. tactics against him, his only
alternative was the Soviets, as Cuba's economic and defense
needs were urgent.

In the midst of this crisis I received a fateful and deeply
disturbing letter from my mother in Venezuela. My uncle Sergio,
she wrote, had been arrested and detained in Cuba, accused of
being a counterrevolutionary. She had no other details.

This terrible news distressed me greatly. My heart went out
to my uncle, alone and in prison. In addition to my natural
feeling for him, I felt a moral debt. Uncle Sergio had financed my
education at the University of Havana at a time when my father
could not, and had been an important part of my childhood. He
was also the father of my cousin Silvio, who had been like a
brother to me.

But there was worse news to come. On April 15, 1961, Cuban
exiles under CIA direction staged aerial bombardments of air-
ports at Havana and Santiago de Cuba, killing seven people. Two
days later, some 1,350 exiled invaders landed in southern Las
Villas Province at the Bay of Pigs. In less than seventy-two hours,
however, the CIA-coordinated operation was totally crushed by
Fidel's forces.

The CIA had seriously underestimated Fidel's popularity in
Cuba, the deeply rooted nationalistic feelings developed since
1959, and the Cuban people's willingness to defend the revolution with their lives. In addition, the CIA and the fighting exiles
had expected widespread support from the U.S. Navy once the
attack was under way. But the assault could have succeeded only
by massive and direct U.S. military involvement, which the exiles believed they had been promised. In fact, President Kennedy
had also promised the U.S. public that he would never order
such a commitment.

In a subsequent letter my mother told me that my cousin
Silvio, once sympathetic to the revolution but now himself in

exile in the United States had taken part in the invasion. He had been among the very few attackers who'd avoided injury, death, or capture. Nevertheless, Silvio first had to survive a horrible ordeal in the swamps before making his way to Havana with the help of some *campesinos*. There he had taken refuge in the Venezuelan Embassy and shortly thereafter returned to the United States.

One of my two maiden aunts was briefly detained at the time of the invasion. She was among the estimated 100,000 Cubans similarly arrested at that time for the mere fact that they were not associated with the revolution.

These detainees were held without trial or any other legal procedure. The opinion of the Interior Ministry (MININT), denunciation by neighborhood committees, or accusations from co-workers were sufficient cause. And since the number of prisoners was so huge, they were interned in stadiums, schools, churches, or any other available space.

After her release, my aunt, her sister, my grandfather, and the rest of my cousins all managed to leave the island. Only my uncle, still in jail in Camagüey, and his wife remained. Uncle Sergio, whose crime it had been to circulate a few religious pamphlets, was tried, convicted, and sentenced to three years in prison, my mother told me.

Because of the news about my uncle Sergio, I was now following events in Cuba with much greater intensity, buying Cuban newspapers as often as I could, and pressing for updates on the political situation from Cuban officials passing through Paris.

In early May, I read in the French press Fidel's speech in which he said Cuba must develop a Socialist constitution. Given the U.S.-sponsored Bay of Pigs invasion of two weeks before— unequivocal evidence of the Norte Americanos' intentions toward Cuba—this seemed an unremarkable statement. For the many of us who naively still thought that Communism could never come to Cuba, it seemed that Fidel was only defending the revolution, not signaling his own agenda. But on December 2, 1961, he finally chose to be explicit. "I am a Marxist-Leninist," he declared to the world, "and I shall be a Marxist-Leninist to the end of my life."

The statement took me totally by surprise, although by now it shouldn't have. Fidel's brother Raúl was an avowed Communist, and I'd satisfied myself directly of Ché's political philosophy. But until Fidel himself said it, I had refused to accept the obvious truth about him.

Now that I faced it, my first feeling was one of betrayal. A bitter anger filled me at the sacrifice made by all the people who had died in the name of liberty and democracy, now subverted by one man's personal ambitions. At the same time, however, Fidel had ratified my longstanding doubts about his true intentions. If, like many others, I had been made a fool, I also could now lay to rest any guilt for having left the revolutionary struggle in 1958.

There remained the problem of my uncle's imprisonment. He had to be helped, and the responsibility for doing so rested squarely with me. As I was the only one in my family with connections to the Cuban government, my first step was to make discreet inquiries among my old friends from revolutionary days. Through them, I hoped to discover the dimension of Uncle Sergio's situation as a convicted opponent of the revolution.

I found them very reluctant even to discuss the problem, an attitude that was explained to me by Saúl Yelín, a friend from the revolutionary days visiting Paris who had lived in La Tía's apartment and who had recently become director of international relations at ICAIC, the Cuban Institute of Arts and Cinematography.

"José Luis," Yelín said, "in Cuba you can't have relations with anyone who is disaffected from the revolution. If you try, you lose your job immediately. There's no way to intercede for anybody, not even for your own parents and family."

Yelín explained this as a matter of principle. The world was divided into those who were revolutionaries and those who were not. And the battle against the revolution's enemies had to be implacable.

Yelín's words only confirmed for me how right my instincts had been to keep my misgivings about Fidel to myself.

The tension between the United States and Cuba was now at a peak. Under U.S. pressure, Cuba was expelled from the Organization of American States in January 1962, an attempt to isolate her from the rest of Latin America. In February of the same year, the United States announced a total trade embargo of Cuba. At the embassy in Paris, I learned that more than a quarter-million Cubans, many of them skilled technicians and professionals, were leaving the island or trying to leave by whatever means they could. On March 12, 1962, food and clothing rationing began, and in July, housewives in Cárdenas took to the streets with pots and pans to protest the food shortages.

Then, on October 22, 1962, President Kennedy charged that Soviet offensive nuclear missiles had been installed in Cuba. Demanding that the weapons be dismantled, Kennedy announced a U.S. naval blockade of the island.

That Fidel could allow atomic missiles in a country ninety miles from the United States and believe that the Soviet Union would support him seemed crazy to me. I knew he had delusions of grandeur, but now he had exercised them far beyond the confines of Cuba and put the entire world in jeopardy.

The threat seemed real enough to most Parisians. I could see the fear in people's faces and watched my neighbors stock their pantries against the possibility of World War III.

I expected the Soviets to back down, as in fact they did; the USSR was not so foolish as to risk a nuclear holocaust over an underdeveloped island country in the Caribbean. The Soviets had completely miscalculated the United States' reaction, and Fidel had misjudged the importance of Cuba to the Soviet Union. He had been treated as a pawn by the international powers. I imagined how deeply the Soviets' retreat had wounded his pride.

None of my attempts to learn of my uncle's situation met with any success. Compelled by duty and conscience to do something for him and frustrated at every turn, I was no closer to a solution in early 1963 when José Revellón, another of my former classmates at the University of Havana and a close confidante of Fidel's at the time, surprised me with an official invitation to visit Cuba. Marie Christine loved the idea; she was excited to see for herself the tropical land I had told her so much about. For her it was a vacation, a chance to spend time in an exotic country whose beauty was legendary. For my part, the invitation meant a chance to check on my uncle personally and, perhaps, to help him directly through my contacts inside the country.

FIDEL ON STAGE

That spring of 1963, Fidel made his first visit to the Soviet Union. In his official entourage were José Abrantes, Fidel's Chief of State Security, whom I knew from my university days when he'd been a member of the Communist Youth Organization; Comandante Derminio Escalona; and Captain Emilio Aragonés, organizing secretary of the United Party of the Cuban Socialist Revolution (PURSC) and the highest-level official of the mission. On their way back from Moscow, the three of them came through Paris, where I spent two days with them.

Aragonés was then a powerful man in Cuba. Since he was very close to Fidel and his decision-making, I decided he might be able to help me contact my uncle.

I took the opportunity of our introduction in Paris to tell him of my upcoming trip, and how I wanted to learn firsthand about the revolutionary process. Aragonés adopted the idea enthusiastically, saying that he wanted to help me see for myself the achievements of the revolution. Once I was there, I decided, I would also find the appropriate moment to enlist his aid in requesting permission to visit my uncle.

After the triumph of the revolution, Aragonés had begun displaying the insignia of captain in the Rebel Army, one of many so-called fighters to affect the rank. Known derisively as the Captains' Club, these men were the target of countless jokes and barbs from authentic revolutionary fighters.

In Paris, Aragonés disported himself freely. He made sure to buy bottles of perfume and other luxury articles by the dozen for future use—as he put it: "to win over the *compañeros'* wives." At night he went to the very best Parisian restaurants and nightclubs, squandering his country's scant hard currency. "Gentlemen, in Cuba we're talking shit!" Aragonés told us at one point. "The decadent West really knows how to live. You have to cut out the crap. I hope Communism never comes to France. It would ruin Paris!"

I was astonished by his behavior. He seemed more like a prerevolutionary politician than a member of the Revolutionary Government. Cuba was now a country whose people were required to live austere lives, and here was a man spending the Cuban people's money on superfluous things. His cavorting was certainly not what my friends and I had fought for; I hoped he was the exception among revolutionary leaders and not the rule.

In July 1963, I left for Cuba, a few days before Marie Christine, who went first for a visit with her aunt and uncle, the Meynards; they would care for Marielle while the two of us were away that summer. As I waited for Marie Christine in Havana, I found the capital had become a very different city from the busy metropolis of my university days or the happy, boisterous place I had visited in the summer of 1959. I felt the familiar awe at Havana's beauty but also a sadness at her evident decay. The buildings seemed neglected, dirty, and poorly maintained. There was little traffic now, and many fewer electric signs were turned on at night. The street lights were dimmed. There seemed to be a kind of grayness over everything.

I checked into the Havana Libre, where the crowd of revolutionaries mixed with several foreign delegations invited to the upcoming celebration of the July 26th Movement's tenth anniversary. Cuba was facing many problems, the revolutionaries told me: difficulties that could be traced exclusively to the imperialist Yanquis' trade embargo and mischief by the CIA. The only exuberance they showed was at any mention of Fidel, whose great leadership, they claimed, would soon overcome every obstacle.

Captain Emilio Aragonés received me with a hug at his office in the PURSC building opposite the Capitol. He asked after Marie Christine, whom he said he hoped to meet when she arrived in Havana. He then gave me an invitation to the speakers' platform for Fidel's July 26th speech in the Plaza de la Revolución. "Call me after the twenty-sixth," he said, "and we'll arrange your route around the island. I'll lend you a car and you can travel whenever you like."

My uncle's predicament was uppermost in my mind; indeed, I would never have returned to Fidel's Cuba were it not for Uncle Sergio's imprisonment. But since I was there, I wanted to see for myself what the revolution had meant for my homeland. I was very curious.

On July 26, by invitation from Aragonés, came my first opportunity to witness one of Fidel's famous oratorical addresses. A party car delivered me to the Plaza two hours before Fidel was scheduled to speak. In the warm forenoon of a Cuban summer day, a large crowd had already begun to gather. All city streets that gave immediate access to the area around the Martí memorial, where Fidel would be, were manned by security guards. Only drivers in authorized vehicles who could also produce an invitation and a parking permit were allowed through. I was among them.

Minutes before the ceremony was to begin, Fidel arrived in a 1960 Oldsmobile. From my seat I noticed he was wearing a clean, pressed uniform, unusual then for the Commander-in-Chief. He stopped to talk with Interior Minister Ramiro Valdés and José Abrantes, the head of State Security. Standing nearby were Comandante Vallejo, Pepín Naranjo, and Carlos Rafael Rodríguez, the PSP attorney and former Batista minister who had denounced the Moncada assault in 1953.

The lower part of the official platform was full of Asian, African, and European faces. On the upper rostrum, reserved for the higher echelons of the Cuban party and government, I saw Raúl Castro and Osvaldo Dorticós, President of the Republic, whose power was nominal and whose duties were largely ceremonial. Dorticós was known as *Cucharón*, the Big Spoon. He didn't cut like a knife or stab like a fork, people said. The Big Spoon was a figurehead.

The crowd had swollen to a half-million people or more now, filling the Plaza. I saw thousands of Cuban flags, hats, berets, and placards. Immense portraits of Marx, Engels, and Lenin covered the walls of the nearby buildings. Over the many loudspeakers blared patriotic and revolutionary songs.

Then the sweltering Plaza exploded into a great roar of "Fidel! Fidel! Fidel!" as he came out from the back, smiling and waving along a respectful waiting line of his highest leaders. Fidel removed his belt and pistol and sat on the left of the podium next to his brother Raúl. The crowd's thunder stopped only temporarily for the national anthem. It required Fidel himself to quiet the people long enough for him to be introduced.

This was to be a consummate performance of several hours' duration and a day of mood, not of substance. What Fidel actually said was not the point; in fact, when I later read the speech I hardly recognized the words. Throughout, I paid close attention to him from my place on the platform, about fifteen feet away. And no sooner did he begin than I felt a strange, profound sense of connection between the huge mass of people and their *Líder Máximo.*

Fidel stood before them, fully conscious of his magnetism. He controlled every movement and modulated his voice to perfection, manipulating the crowd as he chose.

He struck the manly pose, brought his hand to his beard as a sign of deep thought, turned his head to majestic profile—both sides. As he spoke, each gesture amplified his words, conveying solemnity with a wrinkled brow, anger and defiance with heaving breaths, and threats with his forefinger thrust upward to the sky.

His hands went to the bank of microphones before him. He'd utter a phrase and then pause in thought, adjusting the microphones. Another phrase, another pause.

I could *feel* him emphasize just the right word and then repeat that emphasis. Then, for dramatic effect, there would be a void, silence. That intense, brilliant gaze was directed from time to time at his entourage, seeking the approval that was never denied. Fidel accented his moments of agitation with a slight bouncing motion and an incessant movement of his right arm up and down.

Minutes, hours went by with the people in a trance. After several hours Fidel closed his speech at midafternoon with the standard *"¡Patria o Muerte!"*—"Fatherland or Death!"—and then *"¡Venceremos!"*—"We shall vanquish!"

It had been a mesmerizing example of oratory. There was more shouting and applause to end the ceremony. Fidel then donned his belt and pistol, held up his arm for a few seconds of farewell, and disappeared from public view. Behind the rostrum, where cold drinks were being served, I saw several of the foreigners congratulating him effusively.

As the Plaza emptied, I lingered to chat for a while with friends. Then, with my head burning, I returned on foot to the Havana Libre, deep in reflection over what I'd just seen.

The spectacle in the Plaza was palpable proof of Fidel's hold over the Cuban people. But any objective observer of the new Cuba could see that Fidel's influence went far beyond cheap demagoguery. He was polarizing the country, radically altering the very structure of its society.

Communism, so alien a notion for Cuba, was an established fact. Paranoid distrust of the United States, especially after the Bay of Pigs, flowed from Fidel into the hearts and minds of millions. With the continuing mass exodus of professionals, the wealthy, and many of the island's skilled workers, even Cuba's demography was changing.

Most startling was the change in how Cubans saw one another. Before the revolution's triumph, the blood bonds within the typical Cuban family were practically sacrosanct, a given, a matter of pride and honor. My family's special closeness may have differed somewhat in its emphasis upon shared duty and responsibility, but ours was fundamentally the traditional Cuban attitude toward one's blood relations.

Yet once I returned to Cuba, I found that Saúl Yelín, the ICAIC official with whom I had spoken in Paris, had understated conditions in the new order. In Havana, I heard stories of children denouncing their parents for counterrevolutionary activity; of parents denouncing their children to neighborhood CDRs (Committees for the Defense of the Revolution), which were organized block by block as watchdogs; and of spouses denouncing spouses.

Such accusations were hailed as the purest expressions of revolutionary dedication. One example I later heard cited approvingly was that of Jaime Crombet, president of the Communist Youth League, who had denounced his own mother as a counterrevolutionary and had her jailed—a deed considered to be of high revolutionary merit.

In this atmosphere, even a modest expression of normal human concern for my incarcerated uncle would have been fatal to any chance I had of helping him. Thus, after Marie Christine arrived in Havana and I met again with Aragonés to arrange our tour of the island, I mentioned my uncle Sergio as a revolutionary worry. After explaining why he was in the Camagüey prison, I said I wanted to see him so that I might help reform and rehabilitate him if he was unwilling to do so himself.

"I wish that every problem was like yours," the captain said when I finished, and immediately put me in touch with one of his assistants who would call the MININT office in Camagüey to obtain permission for me to visit my uncle.

Marie Christine and I left early the next morning for Camagüey. As we traveled, my mind was weighing what I'd seen and speculating anxiously about how I would help my uncle in the emotional climate of this new Cuba.

After two more hours we reached Ciego de Avila, the city of my birth. The city looked dirty and unkempt. Its main park, once one of the most beautiful and cared-for in the country, now had faded gardens, overgrown grass, and wild-looking unpruned trees. The houses needed repair and paint. Maintaining Cuba's cities evidently was not one of the Revolutionary Government's main priorities.

I showed Marie Christine the landmarks of my childhood, such as the house in which I was born and my grandmother's home. And yet, worrying about my uncle and dismayed at my seeing not even one remotely familiar face, I felt emotionally distant from all I beheld, as if it were from another life.

I knew that we couldn't risk visiting my uncle's wife; she was probably under CDR surveillance, and a visit to her would be interpreted as a counterrevolutionary act on my part. So Marie Christine and I went in search of whatever information I could get from an old family friend, Lucrecia, whom I'd known all my life.

She received me with cries of joy and surprise, and then asked right away, "Did you hear about your uncle?"

"Yes," I answered, "but I wanted to find out the details."

According to Lucrecia, Uncle Sergio had been denounced to the State Security by "that shameless Candito," a man he'd helped many times over the years. As soon as the revolution had triumphed, she went on, Candito turned on Sergio, perhaps hoping he could take over part of my uncle's coffee-toasting business if he went to prison.

She said my uncle's only act had been to collect pictures of saints with the idea of distributing them, but that Candito had charged him with all sorts of counterrevolutionary activity—outright lies.

"Now he's in the prison at Camagüey," Lucrecia said with fiery indignation, "and his poor wife has to travel there when they give her permission to visit."

Listening to Lucrecia's news, I realized that the task of helping my uncle was going to be even more difficult than I had imagined. He was, she said, very bitter at what had happened and he refused absolutely to have anything to do with the rehabilitation program for inmates.

Under the revolutionary penal system, both political and

common prisoners could ease their penalties if they cooperated in certain programs. Their studying Marxism or Fidel's speeches won favorable treatment. Their cases could also be advanced if they engaged in "socially useful" work on farms or road construction. Such activities might mean more visits from friends and relatives, more freedom of movement, and sometimes periodic passes to leave the prison. They could even shorten their sentences. On the other hand, those who resisted rehabilitation became known as *plantados,* and they received drastic and often brutal treatment. If you didn't bend to the revolution, it would break you.

I was heartsick as we drove away from Lucrecia's. My uncle had suffered greatly, and his combativeness—which I secretly admired—would mean further abuse for him in prison. Since I would not be allowed to see him alone, all I could hope to accomplish with my visit would be to find out for myself how he was managing to survive and, I hoped, to reassure him that he was not forgotten, that I had not abandoned him.

On our way to the Gran Hotel in Camagüey City, Marie Christine and I talked at length about my uncle's predicament. She was dismayed by the evident injustice meted out to him and understood and admired the closeness of my family. For the first time I acknowledged to her that the most important reason we had come to Cuba was for me to learn the dimensions of my uncle's trouble. And I cautioned her that she must say nothing about him to anyone.

The Gran Hotel, an old building from the 1930s, was remarkable for its generally good repair. Its rooms, with their high crossbeams and mosaic floors, were still comfortable. I did find it strange that there were so few people in the hotel's popular top-floor dining room, until it was explained to me that city residents no longer had access to the Gran Hotel. According to our waitress, the hotel was at that moment filled with important foreign guests who had been invited to the July 26th celebration— which also accounted for all kinds of meats and imported wines we found on the menu.

Marie Christine and I were almost finished eating when I felt the gentle pressure of a hand on my shoulder and heard a familiar voice. "Damn it, *compañero.* Now that you've made it, have you forgotten your old friends?"

I turned to see a bespectacled young man dressed in a white *guayabera.* He showed me a warm smile and friendly green eyes behind his glasses. At first I didn't recognize him, but when I stood up I realized he was a close childhood friend whose identity and true circumstances I must still protect. I will call him Luc. I hadn't expected to see Luc in Cuba in 1963, since he came from a very conservative and wealthy landowning family which had been seriously affected by the revolution.

Luc and I exchanged warm *abrazos* and then I introduced him to Marie Christine, of whom he had already heard much. The story of the abduction and our marriage had received wide circulation in Camagüey.

After dinner Marie Christine excused herself. She was very tired and returned to our room. As Luc and I had arranged, I went down to the lobby to wait for him and, after tendering Marie Christine's apologies, accepted his suggestion that the two of us drive through the city and relive old times.

We soon found ourselves at the Institute, my birthplace as a revolutionary. So many memories! Faces. Moments. The Institute, still imposing despite its present shabbiness, provoked vivid recollections of a distant, innocent era. It had been just ten years since I'd left this place for Havana, but it seemed as if a lifetime of experience had passed.

A YOUNG
REVOLUTIONARY

THE FIRST STEPS

Death came for democracy in the Republic of Cuba one week after my sixteenth birthday. On March 10, 1952, Fulgencio Batista, an ambitious general, overthrew the legitimate if unexemplary government of President Carlos Prío and installed himself (as he had done once before) as our dictator.

The international reaction to Batista's bloodless *golpe*, or coup, was indifferent; after all, this wasn't the first strong man to usurp a Latin American democracy, and he surely wouldn't be the last. But even on the island itself the response to Batista was muted, confined among most of the nation's leaders to ineffectual hand-wringing and, among the people, to a weary resignation.

Certainly few people were going to miss Carlos Prío. Although he had governed democratically since his election in 1948, Prío had headed a weak and corrupt national government—a major reason, Batista asserted, that he had felt compelled to make his *golpe*.

At the start of the dictatorship, it was the students at Havana University—historically the island's democratic conscience—who saw the brute illegality of Batista's power grab as reason enough to abominate it and to denounce it openly. A student would also be the first Cuban to lose his life resisting Batista.

For me, then a schoolboy in the provincial capital of Camagüey, the coup was a cataclysmic shock. I had been raised in a democracy; it was all I knew. I remember vividly that when the news came to my school that morning I reacted in uncomprehending, indignant anger, as did most of my classmates. But that March day of 1952 was, for me, also an awakening—first to thoughts and then to deeds.

Camagüey, capital of Camagüey Province and Cuba's third-largest city, is located about 330 miles east of Havana along the island's long spine. Then prosperous and politically conservative, Camagüey was known for its colonial red-tiled roofs, narrow winding streets of cobblestone, and the city's emblem—huge amphora-shaped pots called *tinajones*. Life in the city of my youth moved at a measured pace, a beat or two faster than the reserved tempo of the surrounding province, which was generally a wealthy region of cattle ranches, dairies, and sugar-cane and pineapple plantations interlaced with palms.

I was raised in a typical middle-class Camagüeyan household. We were Catholics. Parental discipline was firm. And the prevailing atmosphere at home was tranquil.

Both my parents were descended from old Spanish families that had immigrated to Cuba in the early nineteenth century. Their nationalism, and thus their children's, ran deep. My father, usually a quiet man but with a formidable temper once he was aroused, had business interests that included the distribution of industrial and domestic alcohol products, such as cooking fuel, distilled from sugar cane. I remember my mother in those days as a cheerful, active, and communicative woman who controlled household affairs, her husband's subtle delegate.

The extended family's emotional center was my paternal grandmother, María de los Angeles, a strong, affectionate woman from the Canary Islands. She was the focus of an exceptionally close family; when my father went away to college in the United States, he wrote to her every day for four years.

My two maiden aunts lived with my grandmother and grandfather in Ciego de Avila, a city of 35,000 located less than seventy miles west of Camagüey. My only uncle, my father's brother, Sergio, lived in Ciego de Avila, too, with his wife and sons, my cousins.

As a boy I spent my summer, Christmas, and Holy Week each year in Ciego de Avila, where I developed an especially strong friendship with my eldest cousin, Silvio, who was my brother's age, four years younger than I. On Christmas Eve, when the entire family gathered at my grandmother's, she always served us the classic holiday feast of roast suckling pig, *congrí* (red beans with rice), yucca with garlic sauce, Spanish almond nougat, and wine. The Christmas holiday ended each year at Epiphany, January 6, when my brother and I impatiently tore open our presents while our parents looked on.

I felt a special affinity for my grandmother, and as the eldest of her five grandchildren, I was her favorite. She frankly spoiled me and she treated my frequent bouts of misbehavior with doting forbearance.

Unlike my brother, who was mostly quiet and obedient, I could be a very annoying child; in the Spanish term, *bellaco*—fractious, uncontrollable. All types of mischief attracted me, especially if it involved the prospect of personal risk. Then and throughout my life, danger has excited my palate. Often such risks have arisen as a result of another, more important characteristic: a sharp sense of justice that was part of my family's values and my education.

Perhaps because I saw so little true injustice as a boy, my occasional glimpses of it always stirred me to action, as if unfairness were some rare, deadly germ to be stamped out. The slightest bit of meanness in my friends, for instance, would compel me to challenge them physically. If they teased a smaller child or abused one of Camagüey's rare street vagrants, I'd leap to the victim's defense. Justice was also a matter of personal honor. On the infrequent occasions that I believed my father had punished me unfairly, it was a point of pride for me to withstand his belt without crying.

My willfulness persisted until I completed elementary school and encountered the Marist Brothers' discipline at Camagüey's Marcelino Champagnat Academy. The Marists were inflexibly strict, particularly Brother Juan Salvador, who rigorously discouraged student inattentiveness with such character-building practices as assignments to the feared "Room," in which I spent many Fridays from four until seven in the evening, writing *I must not speak or play in class* over and over again.

I rebelled strenuously but to no avail. By the time I went on to complete my last two years of high school at the Camagüey Institute for Secondary Education, I had acquired an inner voice that kept repeating: "Nothing is possible unless you are organized and disciplined." Juan Salvador and the rest of the Brothers had made sure I was ready for what proved to be many years of schooling ahead—and not all of them in a conventional classroom.

Since politics were rarely discussed in my family, the Marists were responsible for most of my early political education as well. In civics class I learned the rudiments of democratic governance and was taught democracy's inherent superiority as a political system. When Batista later made his *golpe*, my reaction to the injustice was amplified by the Marists' teachings.

But it was my father who first influenced me regarding the evils of totalitarianism. Although he did not talk about politics in general, tyranny enraged him. He often spoke to me of the injustices of the Machado dictatorship from the mid-1920s to the early 1930s—the poverty, violence, and corruption. My father taught me to hate dictatorship.

The Institute broadened my perspective on my father's principles. It was an all-boys public school, one of several such tuition-free, college-preparatory high schools located in Cuba's major cities. The students were drawn from a wide variety of social and ethnic backgrounds with which I had no previous experience. Before coming to the Institute, I'd never known a black classmate, one from a poor family, or even a non-Catholic.

Unlike me and my old friends from the Marist Academy, many of these boys had come this far in their education only after great personal sacrifice. I got to know some of them very well, including a boy from a marginal district of Camagüey itself, a neighborhood into which I'd seldom ventured. When Marino first invited me to his family's house, a bleak structure on a dreary back street, I was struck by the contrast with my own comfortable background. Marino had been embarrassed by his family's humble house and later confessed to me that he'd been afraid of how I would react to it.

This and similar experiences with my classmates created in me a new curiosity. Until entering the Institute, I had known only a Camagüey experienced within the tight orbit of my family and friends. But now I began to see my surroundings with a different eye.

One of the incidents of my childhood that changed me most occurred one day while I was swimming in the Baraguá River near Ciego de Avila. I had taken a very long and deep dive and when I broke the water's surface on the far bank of the Baraguá, I looked up to see five sets of staring eyes. They were *campesino* children, sons of a small farmer.

Two of them squatted and regarded me without emotion. The other three stood with bare, distended bellies full of parasites (a common affliction among the *campesinos*), and splayed feet, the result of going shoeless. I spoke briefly with these boys, but what I remember of the encounter was their lifelessness, their blank eyes, their near nakedness, and their incredible filth. I was disturbed to discover that people in Camagüey Province could live so abjectly.

Another time, also near Ciego de Avila, one of my aunts' friends invited me to his hacienda to go horseback riding. My guide that day was the son of a *campesino* family who took me to his parents' *bohío*, or hut.

I had seen a *bohío* only from a distance, and I viewed these typical rural structures as just another picturesque part of the Camagüeyan countryside's eye-catching beauty. Up close, I discovered a different reality.

Most *bohíos* are constructed almost entirely from palm trees. On a rickety wooden frame, the palm-frond stems—*yagua*—are woven to make walls. The roof is fabricated from the fronds' individual leaves. In the rare instance of a quite deluxe *bohío*, split palm logs or wood scraps are used for the sides instead of *yagua*.

Since the *bohíos* of that time had no electricity, their interiors were often quite dark. The floors were nothing more than tamped earth. A *bohío* had no bathroom or running water, and ten or more relatives could be crowded into each of these single-room huts.

I made several visits to the *campesino* families of the hacienda, each trip a revelation and an episode of growing personal shame at the disparity between their lives and mine. Recollections of my family's lavish Epiphanies came to me with mocking clarity as I joined the farmer's children while they played with old, broken, or primitive toys.

I discovered that many Cuban *campesinos* were little more than field hands who earned exceedingly low wages. In most cases they were paid only during the three- to four-month sugarcane harvest. April to December of each year was *tiempo muerto*, dead time, when scant paying work could be found.

Even those *campesinos* who did own small pieces of land could not work their farms properly, for lack of credit or other financial resources. Eventually they fell too deeply into debt and saw their tiny holdings swallowed up by the big landowners, who often sent the feared Guardia Civil to evict them brutally from their miserable *bohíos*.

Since most *campesinos* had little access to schools, few could ever break out of the poverty cycle through education. And since medical care for these families was nonexistent in most cases, the children were infested almost from birth with parasites and routinely died from diseases they would have survived with proper medical attention.

As Batista began to consolidate his dictatorship, I noted with bitterness how easily he ignored the disenfranchised and wretched poor of the countryside and sought instead to neutralize his only potent opposition at the time, Cuba's university students.

At the University of Havana, Batista was denounced by the students within hours of his coup. A few days later he courted the Federation of University Students (FEU) with a grand bribe. In exchange for political peace, Batista promised, he would build a new and modern University City for the students, including free housing for all.

"The University will not surrender and is not for sale" was the FEU's emphatic response.

Such defiance couldn't help but impress us younger boys in the provinces. At the Institute, my classmates and I cheered on April 4, 1952, when the FEU organized a massive demonstration in the capital. A huge throng gathered before the bust of José Martí, Cuba's Apostle of Independence and the most revered figure in the island's history. Then the FEU demonstrators symbolically buried the country's model progressive constitution of 1940.

Nine months later, on February 13, 1953, the dictatorship claimed its first victim when Rubén Batista Rubio, a Havana University student, died of gunshot wounds inflicted by the police during a demonstration in the capital on January 15. The incident sent shock waves throughout Cuba; it was an early signal of the extreme measures Batista was willing to take to maintain his illegal rule. In Camagüey about fifty of us students at the Institute planned our own protest of the shooting. We nailed together a rough wooden coffin, intending to parade it through the streets.

I was astonished when the local police came screeching up in patrol cars and began firing their pistols into the air. What did the dictatorship have to fear from a ragtag parade of protesting schoolboys? I was also very embarrassed that we all scattered like rabbits at the first shots. My friend Jorgito and I were so surprised and confused that we hid inside the Caridad Church instead of demonstrating.

But this ridiculously failed protest nevertheless had a galvanizing effect on me. The policemen's drawn pistols were my first direct experience with the violent heart of the Batista regime. Moreover—and for the first time in my life—I felt, among us young boys of such different social, religious, and ethnic backgrounds, a Cuban solidarity. I was one of them. Soon we were writing proclamations, organizing meetings, and holding demonstrations on patriotic holidays, of which there were then at least ten a year in Cuba. Suddenly, I was not just *bellaco*; my sense of right and wrong had been transformed into a political awakening. A naïve act became the first step to my becoming a revolutionary.

I had just graduated from the Institute in the summer of 1953 when an obscure leftist lawyer from Cuba's eastmost province, Oriente, conceived a chancy plot that he and his companions believed might trigger a nationwide revolt against Batista. Fidel Castro, then twenty-six, had planned a surprise attack on the army's Moncada Barracks, a small fortress in Santiago de Cuba, the island's second-largest city and Oriente's capital, situated on the province's southern coast, approximately fifty miles directly west of the U.S. base at Guantánamo.

At 5:30 A.M. on July 26, 1953, Castro's column of twenty-six automobiles carrying 111 men and 2 women left Siboney Farm just outside Santiago and set out for the attack. Fidel's brother, Raúl, was responsible for taking the Palace of Justice, near the barracks. Abel Santamaría, Fidel's second-in-command, led another assault on the military hospital. Fidel himself directed the main attack on the Moncada Barracks proper, and he was the only one of the three to fail.

Eight men were killed outright that day, and most of the rest were hunted down within seventy-two hours. Batista exacted a ferocious vengeance; the captured were tortured and executed. Fifty-three in all were dead before the indignant public and the Catholic leaders of Santiago de Cuba demanded a halt to the killing.

On August 1, in the mountains just east of Santiago, Fidel himself and the remainder of his band were taken by surprise while hiding in a *bohío*. Any other army patrol most probably would have executed Fidel on the spot. But his captors, led by Lieutenant Pedro Manuel "Black" Sarría, took Fidel into custody instead, thereby altering the course of Cuban history. Fidel's life was then protected by Monsignor Enrique Pérez Serrantes, the Archbishop of Santiago de Cuba.

Among the many organizations that not only had failed to denounce Batista's *golpe* but had opposed any armed resistance to the new dictatorship were the Cuban Communists, the PSP. In fact, two PSP members had served as ministers without portfolio in Batista's first legal government of 1940–1944.

Nevertheless, in the dictatorship's post-Moncada crackdown, several prominent members of the party were arrested in Santiago, where they'd gathered to salute their Secretary General, Blás Roca, on his birthday. Lawyer Carlos Rafael Rodríguez, one of the two former Communist ministers, was among the detainees and spoke on behalf of his *compañeros*. Before a Santiago court, Rodríguez denounced the Moncada raid, saying: "The party had no connection with the adventurist exploits of gangsters and madmen." In time, both the party and Fidel would find it convenient to forget this insult.

In October 1953, three months after the failed assault, Fidel and the rest of the survivors were tried and sentenced to several years at the Presidio Modelo, a prison on the Isle of Pines, the large island off the south shore of Cuba's western provinces. During the trial, Fidel defended himself and delivered his famous "History Will Absolve Me" courtroom speech, which he revised in prison the next year and published in pamphlet form. "History Will Absolve Me" outlined the foundation of Fidel's political platform, from agrarian reform to his call for a return to Cuba's 1940 constitution. In the same month that he spoke to the court, I boarded the Santiago–Havana express bus in Camagüey for the ten-hour trip to the capital, where I was to begin my university education. My experience in Havana would also complete my transformation into a revolutionary.

REVOLUTION AT THE UNIVERSITY

From my earliest childhood, my family had pointed to me and said, "This one will be a doctor." In case I missed the cue, they'd given me stethoscopes, doctors' kits, toy labs, and anatomy books while I was growing up. Naturally, when I began my studies at the University of Havana, I enrolled as a medical student.

I had little enthusiasm for the subject, but I was thrilled simply to be in Havana, a city I had visited only once, and to be studying at the university. Here was a vibrant, exciting world with its long history of conflict, confrontation, and danger in the name of justice—and I was going to be part of it.

The capital was huge, with more than a million inhabitants, and I was overwhelmed by the contrast between this city and Cuba's countryside. In contrast to the small, slow-paced city of my boyhood, Havana was dazzling and enigmatic. Everything fascinated me; every detail seemed related to Cuban history or to what I had seen on television or in newspaper photographs.

I was going to live in Havana for at least six years, and from the moment I left the bus terminal it was love at first sight.

I walked for hours through the long, winding Malecón, or sea walk, which encircled the city along the intensely blue Caribbean. At the entrance to Havana Bay, I toured both the Morro Castle, a magnificent sixteenth-century fortress constructed to thwart pirates, and its neighbor with a bloody history, La Cabaña, built in the eighteenth century and used intermittently by various Cuban governments for political executions.

I was enchanted by Old Havana, settled by Spain in the sixteenth century. Its landmarks included the cathedral, the historic Plaza de Armas, which I walked through, and the promenade Alameda de Paula, which runs along the boat-filled bay. I spent long hours in busy, narrow Obispo Street, crowded with small shops.

In Central Havana, I sat on the granite benches of the lively Paseo del Prado, the main thoroughfare, guarded at intervals by great bronze lions and lined with laurel trees. A little farther away was the imposing Capitol building and picturesque Central Park, a small square of green surrounded by a large plaza that held a statue of José Martí. I enjoyed watching the vendors hawk everything from lottery tickets to peanuts, iced drinks, and coffee for 3 cents a cup. Crowded into the plaza were the old Pole selling cloth remnants, the shoeshine stand, the photographer with his box camera, the fruit seller, the knife grinder, and the stalls where fried foods were sold. It was impossible to be bored in such a kaleidoscope.

Farther west I found Havana's commercial district, centered at the intersection of Galiano and San Rafael Streets, where I saw the most elegant citizens of Havana mingling with the lowliest. Then came the Vedado area, where I lived and the university was located. I was amazed by its multistoried houses, unlike any in the provinces, and by the great hotels, the *Nacional* and the *Presidente*. The Vedado's main street offered me a splendid panorama of the Caribbean to the north. This section was the Havana of American movies—with Club 21, Cabaret National, and Cabaret Montmartre, where stars such as Maurice Chevalier and Edith Piaf appeared. What astonished me most was the university itself, a collection of neoclassical buildings fronted by Greek columns, founded in the eighteenth century and dominated by its gigantic 163-step stairway to the Rectory and ever-vigilant statue of Alma Mater. When I stood near her, I was filled with pride to be a student here.

The University of Havana provided no on-campus student housing and so I, like everyone else who came from the provinces, first had to search the surrounding Vedado district for an affordable room. On H Street, two blocks from the medical school, I found a two-story boardinghouse where, with eleven other medical students, I paid $52 a month for a shared bedroom and meals, only one of which each week was particularly edible.

The day I enrolled for classes, I was returning to the boardinghouse when I encountered a knot of students listening to a heavyset young man in his early twenties who waved his arms energetically as he addressed his audience in an excited voice. His subject: preparations for an upcoming demonstration, a march to take place on November 27, 1953, the anniversary of the day in 1871 when seven medical students were executed by the Spanish Crown for alleged sedition. One of the onlookers told me the speaker was José Antonio Echevarría.

This was my first glimpse of José Antonio, a twenty-one-year-old architecture student from a middle-class Catholic family in the port city of Cárdenas, some ninety miles east of Havana. Known familiarly as El Gordo ("The Fat One") or Manzanita ("Little Apple") for his rosy cheeks, Echevarría represented the higher aspirations of the student movement.

In a reform dating from the 1930s, the university had been declared autonomous; that is, to insure student freedom of speech the police and the armed forces were forbidden to enter the campus with weapons. Unfortunately, Havana's violent gangster factions, with the complicity of some student leaders, had since the 1940s used the university as their own sanctuary. José Antonio Echevarría would first be elected president of the Federation of University Students in 1954 on a platform that promised, among other things, to stop the gangsters' abuses.

I next bumped into Echevarría—literally—in early November. I was running up the small staircase of the School of Architecture as he was running down and we collided in a heap, our papers scattered everywhere. José Antonio and I made our laughing introductions, begged each other's pardon, and then he said, "Come on, José Luis, I'll buy you a sandwich. I'm starving!"

We walked to the L & 27 Cafetería, a popular student hangout, where everyone greeted Echevarría by one of his nicknames. At the counter, as we waited for our sandwiches, the conversation was filled with national politics and José Antonio's plans for the university. Echevarría spoke with great sincerity of the need to rid the university of gangsters and to fight Batista and his corruption. José Antonio was clearly intelligent, firmly religious, and very open. While I, at that time, could hardly match him as a thinker, our views were in total accord. When he asked for my help among the university's medical students, I enthusiastically agreed.

Resisting Batista was my first, but not my only, concern at that moment. Bored as I was by the minutiae of histology or the complexities of anatomy, I applied myself to them with rigor for the sake of my family. I was the oldest and the favored grandchild, the first to go to the university. Not only was I expected to set an example for my brother and cousins but I was, in a very real sense, the embodiment of the family's hopes for the next generation. My success in my studies was a serious responsibility.

I had barely begun my medical education when my father suffered some business reversals. My aunts and my Uncle Sergio immediately took it upon themselves to guarantee my continued studies, a gesture typical of my family's closeness but one that also caused me to feel deep gratitude and a moral debt.

Medical education at the university was demanding and thorough, although in a peculiar way. The quality of the faculty's classes was rather spotty. One of my professors graded exams by throwing them into the air. If your paper fortuitously landed on his table, you passed. If not, you were failed. Another, Professor Piloto, was so dilatory that the class delegate had to force him, at gunpoint, to administer his exam at all.

Yet the standard exams we all had to pass at the end of each semester were very, very exacting; the University of Havana enjoyed an international reputation for producing well-schooled doctors. Because most classes were so poorly taught, the only way to meet these strict criteria was to engage private tutors and then to study constantly. Here my Marist training was instrumental in my coping with a subject that interested me little. My background in *how* to study, together with liberal recourse to caffeine to keep me awake through long nights with dull texts, were my chief means of fulfilling my responsibilities.

Family duty notwithstanding, there was no way a rebellious and idealistic person such as I could ignore the highly charged political atmosphere all around me. Although active opposition to Batista was confined at that time to no more than 400 or so of the university's 10,000 students, no one on campus was unaffected by the polarizing atmosphere.

My grasp of the situation began with a general understanding of its context. Since the establishment of the Cuban Republic in 1902, political life on the island had been characterized by demagoguery, corruption, violence, and foreign interventions. Success in politics meant getting rich as fast as possible through the use and abuse of power. If a person obtained an important political post, his future and the future of his family and closest friends were assured. The distribution of *botellas*, government jobs that paid well while requiring no work, was a standard corrupt practice. Buying votes was another. Only at election time did most politicians pay any attention to the lower classes, including the *campesinos*.

While the politicians devoted themselves to getting rich overnight—and fending off their equally avaricious opponents— one national economic crisis followed another. Cuba also became increasingly dependent upon the United States.

We students were overwhelmingly anti-Communist. But we couldn't help seeing that the U.S. government, the self-proclaimed model of democratic rule, considered any attempt at Cuban social reform as an immediate threat to American economic interests, principally sugar production. Automatically, any reform gesture was labeled as Communist, even though Cuba's Communists historically did little to upset the status quo. The most modest reforms, many unconnected in any way with the PSP, were often the pretext for U.S. political and military intervention. In the same vein, when the Eisenhower administration promptly recognized Batista's government, we were angered and convinced that for the United States the security of North American companies and businessmen mattered much more than democracy.

By this time I had also come to see that the structure of Cuban society was ossified, with an extremely wealthy upper class closely connected to United States capital and an impoverished lower class of chronically unemployed rural and urban workers. Between these extremes there was a comparatively small, heterogeneous middle class. Its fundamental concerns were with the maintenance of its status and the emulation, as far as was possible, of the life style of the wealthy.

There was also an enormous difference between rural life and life in the big city. In contrast to the subhuman conditions I'd seen in the countryside, life in the capital appeared to be in no way inferior to that of the world's other great cities. Havana was macrocephalic, to use the economic term—the great head on the tiny body of Cuba. Here, side by side with its charm and beauty, I saw the latest in consumer technology (Cuba, for instance, built one of the first television stations in Latin America) as well as the most expensive and sophisticated goods of the U.S. market. For the tourists, especially, Havana afforded luxury, abundance, and comfort, as well as gambling, drugs, and prostitution.

Living far beneath this opulent veneer was a good part of Havana's population, relegated to slum districts like Las Yaguas, with its wretched hovels and hungry children. Throughout Havana there were pockets of such misery, ghettos of swarming tenements called *solares*, where hundreds of families crowded together in unimaginable filth. So densely packed were these buildings that the police often couldn't penetrate their mazelike interiors to answer calls.

Under Batista, as I saw for myself, the situation only grew worse. The rich thrived and the poor remained forgotten. Corruption, already institutionalized, spread uncontrollably while repression, crime, and cruelty became the weapons of the dictator's authority.

These problems, which we students discussed endlessly, united us in our common desire to eradicate them, to build a better Cuba. We believed in radical change through a democratic revolution that would forever end the gross poverty, corruption, official violence, authoritarianism, and foreign interference we saw every day. In a country so favored by nature, a country with more than enough natural resources to provide for all its citizens, it seemed only just that there be equal opportunity for everyone. This wasn't an academic position on our part. We fervently believed in this ideal and were ready to give our lives for it.

*   *   *

In the early months of the dictatorship, the sharpest expressions of the student rebellion were demonstrations in Havana. Beginning for me with the *manifestación* of November 27, 1953, these marches were nearly constant and always exuberantly reckless. We would first gather on campus at the Plaza Cadenas behind the Rectory. Then, at the appointed moment, the students would form themselves into rows and with linked arms march from Alma Mater down the great steps to San Lázaro Street.

All the way we'd sing the Cuban national anthem, often to the enthusiastic encouragement of the neighborhood's residents, who cheered us from their balconies. Sometimes student snipers were stationed above them on the roof to open fire if the police dared violate the campus's autonomy.

Usually the police would be waiting for us three blocks from the steps, at the edge of the university at San Lázaro and Infanta Streets, where they would reroute traffic and line up their patrol cars. After we had finished singing the anthem, we would bear down on them shouting antigovernment slogans. Once we were outside the university proper, they waded into us with their clubs and fists, firing their weapons into the air and training enormous fire hoses on us. In the end, they usually succeeded in dispersing the students, sending us running down adjacent streets looking for the protection of a sympathetic neighbor.

These were the days of relative restraint by Batista's police. Perhaps because Rubén Batista Rubio's death after the *manifestación* of January 15, 1953, had provoked such shocked reaction throughout the country, the authorities for a time contented themselves with breaking bones and making perfunctory arrests. But by 1955, an inexorable spiral of violence began in earnest.

I recall a typical incident from December of that year. Several of us who had been carrying that day's banner were cut off by the police. I ran down N Street with several officers in chase, threatening to shoot me if I didn't stop. At Infanta Street, I leapt for the window of a passing bus and shouted for the driver to stop and let me in.

Most of the bus drivers could still be counted on for such help—this bus stopped for me—but in the growing repression they soon chose to ignore fleeing students lest they suffer themselves if the police identified them as helping us.

Three blocks farther on, I saw several of the policemen savagely kicking and beating the vaguely human shape of a demented old beggar familiar to everyone in the area. In his troubled wanderings through this part of the Vedado, the old man periodically would shout, "Batista! The son of a bitch!"

Enraged at what I saw, I jumped from the bus, ran to the beggar, and then punched one of the policemen in the face, knocking him back several feet into a fried-food stand on the corner. Amidst the sounds of shattering glass and cries from the police and the food-stand owner, I knelt to help the old man to his feet. Suddenly, I felt a shooting pain in my head.

Some hours later I awoke in the student clinic at the Calixto García Hospital nearby. As my senses cleared I discovered that I had three broken ribs and that my face was bruised and badly swollen. According to those who'd witnessed the incident, my head injuries came from a policeman's club, and the broken ribs were a further courtesy from the officer and his friends, who had kicked me until they tired of their sport.

Several of us from the *manifestación* had been taken to the clinic that day. I recognized one boy from past demonstrations who seemed to be in good humor despite the bullet in his leg.

"Listen," said Camilo in a jaunty voice, "what's happened to you? You look like Frankenstein." This was my introduction to high-spirited Camilo Cienfuegos, a fellow revolutionary with whom I discussed politics passionately as we recovered from our injuries.

Camilo would soon leave Havana and reappear in the mountains with Fidel's small band. By 1958 he would rise to become the undisputed second-in-command of the Cuban revolution.

DIRECT ACTION

I got to know most of my *compañeros* in the student resistance after moving to a more comfortable rooming house on the fourth floor of a building on 21st Street, between L and M Streets, next to La Roca Restaurant, famous for its haute cuisine.

The new neighborhood was a magnet for revolutionaries. The first friend I made on 21st Street was José "Pepín" Naranjo, a likable and easygoing medical student and friend of José Antonio Echevarría. Pepin served as a sort of secretary to Echevarría at the FEU. While every bit as politically involved as the rest of us, Naranjo did not neglect his fun. He had a weakness for gambling and was always chain-smoking Chesterfields. Week after week Pepín played the lottery or chanced his allowance at the Cinódromo dog track in Havana. Once, when he was flat broke, he borrowed and gambled away my matriculation money.

Pepín knew José Antonio Echevarría through José Antonio's childhood friend Rolando Cubela, who was studying medicine at the university. Echevarría, who lived at Cubela's mother's boardinghouse near the university, had accepted Pepín as FEU's executive secretary at Rolando's suggestion.

Living next door to me was Fructuoso Rodríguez, also an FEU leader. Fructuoso, intelligent and courageous, enjoyed enormous prestige at the university for his bravery in confrontations with the police. A later photograph of him, lying brutally beaten on the sidewalk of San Lázaro Street, would be published in all the Cuban newspapers and magazines.

Across the street lived a woman we knew as La Tía, "The Aunt," my landlady Ina's sister, admired for her honesty and integrity. I was told many stories of her long involvement in political struggle. We students often visited her house, where she presided over our protracted discussions and impassioned debates on politics. Many of our actions were planned at La Tía's; she was always there to offer advice and help.

Beginning in 1954, when I'd moved to my new neighborhood, I also began to learn how to handle guns and explosives. Our policy was never to set devices in order to hurt or kill people but only to amplify our presence by shock and noise, to keep the capital city on edge, and to remind people that there was opposition to Batista's dictatorship. Empty theaters and deserted parks were favored targets for our bombs.

My world as a student *compañero* was all books and bullets. I took tests and also target practice, studied disease and cached weapons in anticipation of future actions, discussed course work with my tutors and disrupted Batista's police by setting patrol cars on fire. Although I'd been arrested several times at demonstrations, I was not the specific target of official interest until one morning in July of 1955.

I'd been up all night studying and then spent a full morning in anatomy lab. Exhausted, I came back to my room, stripped to my shorts, and fell onto my bed for a nap. Suddenly I was startled awake by a loud banging on the front door downstairs.

"Everybody out!" came an authoritative shout. "This is a

search! Move!" The house erupted with noise, and I could hear heavy-booted footsteps starting up the stairs toward me.

Instantly alert, I sprang for two Colt .45 pistols and a box of bullets I'd stashed in a towel under my wardrobe, intending to pitch the evidence out onto the street. But as I looked down I saw two patrol cars and several uniformed officers standing guard. Glancing up, I could see across the street both Pepín Naranjo and La Tía standing on her terrace, staring at me in astonishment.

The pounding boots were nearly at my door. Quickly I shoved the bundle back under the wardrobe. Then, as three belligerent *esbirros*—our derisive term for cops—burst into the room, I nonchalantly reached for a heavy paper bag resting on my nightstand. At first glance the bag appeared to contain just several ripe guavas. Underneath the fruit, however, were two boxes of bullets and a pair of hand grenades.

At that time I was nineteen years old, six feet four inches tall, and I weighed about 145 pounds. Standing there before the police in my shorts, holding what ostensibly was a bag of guavas, and feigning a look of innocent curiosity at their presence in the boardinghouse, I looked the complete fool.

"Out!" shouted one of them, stifling a grin.

I meekly strolled with my paper bag into the adjoining dining room, where several of the women of the house beheld me in round-eyed amusement. Carrying on the charade, I behaved as if the police had interrupted a boy's simple errand.

"They're for Mercedes, the cook," I explained. "I want her to make some preserves." I even offered one of the guavas to the police before moving on, with their irritated approval, toward the kitchen.

There I found Mercedes standing with a tall policeman who was ransacking her cupboards. When his back was turned, I emptied the bag into her sink. Then, with the startled cook gaping in surprise, I quickly grabbed the bullet boxes and grenades from the sink and tossed them into the big pot of rice Mercedes had just set on to boil.

Thunderstruck as she was, the cook did have the presence of mind to turn off the stove. She then walked mechanically to the next room and sat down, staring silently, waiting for what she expected to be an enormous explosion from the kitchen. No one in the house could figure out what on earth was wrong with her.

The police didn't think to search the rice pot, but they did find the Colts under my wardrobe and proceeded to arrest everyone in the house except Mercedes. At the soon-to-be-infamous

Bureau of Investigation, they held us for three hours before releasing everyone except my roommate, Domingo del Valle, and myself. We spent the night together in a cell.

During our interrogation, all we got were a few kicks. A year later, in 1956, the story would have had a very different ending. By that time a proven revolutionary rarely left local police custody alive. The next morning, July 26 and, by coincidence, the second anniversary of Fidel's assault on the Moncada Barracks, we were set free on bail arranged for us by Dr. Sánchez Ferrer, an attorney hired by the FEU. Later, we paid a 150-pesos fine for firearm possession.

My mother, to her horror, read of this latest arrest and called Havana in a terrible state of agitation. This wasn't the first time she'd seen my picture in the papers after one of our revolutionary actions, although she believed that she had kept my career in the resistance a secret from my father. In truth, they both were anxiously monitoring my activities, neither of them mentioning the subject to the other, and neither of them aware of how deeply involved I had become in the struggle.

A short time later, while I was working at a clerical job in the Congressional Library at the National Capitol, I conceived a somewhat more ambitious project: A plot to blow up the National Congress. After discussing the idea with José Antonio Echevarría and later with Fructuoso Rodríguez, I soon was bringing sticks of dynamite into the library a few at a time and secreting them in the back of bookshelves that I knew were never used.

We intended somehow to place these charges, to connect the right fuses and detonators (none of us then knew exactly how this was to be done), and then to carry out our sabotage in October. Unfortunately—or fortunately—the head of the library, a Mr. Molina, heard of my July arrest, and I was fired before we could strike. Over the next several weeks and under many pretenses, I returned to the library and slowly cleaned out all the dynamite.

Such schemes were characteristic of the early struggle against Batista. We were essentially self-taught revolutionaries, determined to overthrow the dictatorship and very much alone in those days in our willingness to act against it.

In November of 1954 the dictatorship staged a rigged presidential election. Two months later, Batista assumed the presidency officially in a ceremony at which Vice President Richard

Nixon of the United States was an honored guest. After Allen Dulles, head of the CIA, visited Cuba on a goodwill mission in April 1955, Batista and his followers felt more secure than ever.

In this mood, the government evidently thought it politic to make a gesture of magnanimity. On May 15, Fidel and Raúl Castro and the rest of their followers were released in an amnesty from the Presidio Modelo on the Isla de Pinos. (Abel Santamaría had been tortured to death.) During their tumultuous welcome in Havana—I was part of the cheering crowd— Fidel appeared decisive and full of energy. Although I was closely aligned with Echevarría and the FEU, I saw Fidel as courageous and daring for his Moncada attack, and I felt a solidarity with him as I did with everyone who opposed Batista.

Fidel greeted everyone effusively, hugging people and slapping them on the back. Prison had obviously given him new determination, but he could not stay in Cuba much longer without risking assassination. Already, there had been at least one attempt on his life, a poisoning plot, while he was in prison. Within a few weeks of the amnesty in 1955 he and some followers (including Camilo Cienfuegos) left for Mexico, where they began to prepare for Fidel's return.

Batista soon realized the amnesty would buy him no more domestic tranquillity than had his earlier attempted bribe of the FEU. Disaffection had now spread far beyond the university. There were more and more demonstrations, from Havana to Santiago. Strikes broke out. Bombings, sabotage, and other subversive acts multiplied.

Violence was met with even greater violence. Batista's prisons were filled with revolutionaries. Torture methods became more savage. Crime and assassinations spread throughout the country. Every day, Batista's enemies' corpses, riddled with bullets and disfigured by torture, were discovered in back alleys of all the island's major cities.

One result of the broadening opposition to Batista was the strengthening of Fidel's July 26th Movement. Another was the formation, late in July 1955, of the secret Revolutionary Directorate, an *ad hoc*, direct-action organization of students and workers that coalesced spontaneously around the leadership of José Antonio Echevarría and was dedicated to Batista's overthrow, the restoration of democracy, and social reforms for Cuba. The Revolutionary Directorate's membership was nominally secret, but most everyone, including myself, who had moved beyond simple protest of the Batista regime soon joined it or the July 26th Movement.

Fidel spent this period in Mexico, preparing to return with his fighters to Cuba. In late August of 1956, José Antonio, as head of the Revolutionary Directorate, traveled to Mexico and concluded with Fidel the so-called Mexican Pact, a secret cooperation agreement that specifically pledged the Revolutionary Directorate to armed action in Havana in support of Fidel's impending return.

In October, Echevarría traveled again to Mexico, where he and Fidel discussed, but could not agree on, tactics. Fidel wanted the Revolutionary Directorate to stage an uprising in Havana to coincide with his landing, an armed revolutionary action similar to ones planned in Oriente Province at Bayamo and Santiago de Cuba. Echevarría, however, believed that such an uprising in metropolitan Havana would be a pointless waste of lives. The Revolutionary Directorate wanted to hit the dictatorship at the top, to kill Batista himself.

At dawn on November 25, 1956, Fidel at last left Tuxpán, Mexico, and headed for Cuba. His attack group consisted of eighty-two men crammed aboard an aged yacht, the *Granma*. Fidel officially proclaimed himself this army's commander in chief.

After a protracted, wave-tossed crossing, the *Granma* reached Coloradas Beach on the south coast of Oriente Province the night of December 2. *"¡Libres o Mártires!"*—"Free or Martyrs!"—was the watchword of those on board. But the attackers' guide betrayed them, and the force was ambushed several times before Fidel at last managed to regroup the survivors, relying for help upon Crescencio Pérez, a local thief wanted by the rural police for numerous robberies and murder.

Pérez led Fidel and his revolutionary force of about one dozen bedraggled *compañeros* into the safety of the rugged Sierra Maestra in Oriente. In the meantime, the national and international press published false reports of Fidel's death, creating confusion and uncertainty among the July 26th Movement's supporters and the rest of Cuba as well.

On November 27, José Antonio Echevarría was beaten senseless by the police in a morning *manifestación*. That night, a rally was scheduled for 9:00 P.M. at the university. Intent upon stopping us, the police threw up an armed guard all around the campus. Only fifty of us managed to make it from our various boardinghouses through the police cordon and up to the Rectory. We were alone in the deserted university.

A speaker's platform, strung with electric lights, was erected in front of Alma Mater. Knowing the authorities would probably cut off the electricity the moment we began the rally, we had brought our own portable power generator.

In the fading twilight the police began moving toward us up San Lázaro Street. They had already violated the university's autonomy that year, and we couldn't be sure any longer if the Rectory itself was safe. Still undaunted, we waited in the ghostly silence until precisely nine o'clock, when we switched on the lights and began the meeting, as always, by singing the national anthem.

Then the shooting started. First from afar, and then ever closer and more constant, the bullets made a metallic zing as they ricocheted off Alma Mater and loud pops as they burst the electric bulbs above us. This was the heaviest gunfire I'd ever witnessed at a university protest.

As the fusillade intensified, we flung ourselves to the ground around Alma Mater, then inched our way back into the Rectory's open central colonnade. All the doors on both sides of us were securely locked. Protected from the officers' direct line of fire, we hugged the floor for several hours as their bullets continued to whiz over us from below, shattering nearby windows and smashing chunks of facade from the Rectory itself. The slightest motion by any of us instantly drew concentrated firing.

At midnight, Clemente Inclán, the university rector, finally was able to intercede with the police, and we were allowed to disperse. Twelve days later, however, a daytime demonstration drew an even more brutal police response. Scores of students were beaten and arrested. This would be the final "peaceful" demonstration at the University of Havana. The university was declared closed, and the students' fight to overthrow Batista moved into its final, most violent stage.

THE FIRST DECEPTIONS

Fidel Castro's rise as a revolutionary leader owes much to chance and to his uncommon good fortune. He was lucky to survive the assault on Moncada, as well as his subsequent arrest and the attempt on his life while in prison. Without Batista's amnesty, he might have remained merely a caged observer of the developing revolution. As it was, Fidel barely made it in one piece to the Sierra Maestra, and even then his immediate prospects as "commander in chief" of a dozen footsore guerrillas were doubtful.

Relations between José Antonio Echevarría and Fidel deteriorated to outright enmity following the *Granma*'s landing. After the Revolutionary Directorate had not instigated an armed uprising in Havana, Fidel wrote José Antonio a letter in which he accused the Revolutionary Directorate of cowardice and treason against the revolution. In his reply to Fidel, José Antonio told me, he angrily rejected the accusations. He also told me at this time of his conviction that Fidel intended to monopolize the revolution. "Slim," he said, using my nickname, "Fidel is egocentric. If he takes power in Cuba, I don't know where democracy will go."

In March 1957, while I was in Havana, my friend Julio García Oliveras, an architecture student like José Antonio, brought me a message from him: We were to contact Pepín Naranjo, who would provide us with arms for some imminent, though unspecified, revolutionary action. At Naranjo's house in Sancti Spíritus, I discovered that his parents had refused to allow him to return to Havana. Pepín nevertheless assured me that he'd be back. On March 11, again through García Oliveras, I informed Echevarría of the situation and promised him that I would stay at my rooming house on 21st Street to wait for Pepín and the weapons. But Naranjo never came.

Two days later, on the afternoon of March 13, the Revolutionary Directorate undertook two coordinated armed actions. At

3:22 P.M., fifty attackers began an assault on the Presidential Palace in Old Havana, supported by one hundred snipers positioned in buildings surrounding the three-story structure. Eight minutes earlier, a smaller force led by Echevarría had arrived in three automobiles at the Vedado studios of Havana's twenty-four-hour news station, Radio Reloj. By 3:25 P.M. they had shot their way inside, and José Antonio was at the Radio Reloj microphone, announcing, "People of Cuba! The revolution has begun! Our forces have taken the Presidential Palace and the dictator has been executed in his lair!"

Tragically, he was mistaken.

The attackers at the Palace had indeed found Batista's second-floor office and had lobbed four grenades into it, one of which exploded. However, moments earlier, the dictator had taken his private elevator up one floor to the Presidential Suite, where he was safe from any further action. The assault had failed.

Echevarría would never know this. Because his voice was too loud for Radio Reloj's broadcast equipment, his message of triumph was abruptly cut off. He and his men then shot up the studios and ran to the street where their automobiles waited. All three headed for the university, with José Antonio behind the wheel of one of the vehicles. On the way, however, he encountered a police car coming at him in the opposite direction. Someone in Echevarría's car panicked and opened fire on the police. In the midst of the resultant gun battle, José Antonio impulsively jumped out of his door and was machine-gunned to death on the spot. His bloody, mangled corpse lay on the street for hours.

José Antonio was killed only four blocks from my boarding-house. I was listening to the radio at that moment; I had known nothing of the objective for which Pepín was supposed to provide weapons and instructions. All I knew from the news report was that there had been a wild gunfight near the university and that people had been killed.

As I walked to the site of the reported disturbance I came upon José Antonio lying dead. That day I lost a lot of friends. But this was the first time I faced the reality of being a revolutionary: the slumped, vacant-eyed body of one of my closest friends. In the midst of my shock, I knew one thing was certain. I could not let this event go unrecorded. Fearing that the police might make José Antonio's corpse disappear, I ran back to my room, grabbed my camera, returned to the scene, and quickly took photographs of José Antonio Echevarría's body.

I spent the days following the failed attack trying to find hideouts for those who'd managed to escape immediate arrest. It wasn't an easy task; everybody was afraid. Many in Cuba today who claim they took part in the struggle in fact refused then to open their doors to a single revolutionary. While I was looking for a safe house for Fructuoso Rodríguez, for example, he had to wander from one park to another. Finally, with the help of friends, we found an apartment near 14th Street in the Vedado, where I hid Fructuoso and later brought his mother and very pregnant wife. It was the last time they would see him alive.

In these tumultuous times I learned a mode of behavior that stayed with me throughout my life. I had always been a reserved person, but during this period the lives of my friends and my own life depended on my silence. A careless word to the wrong person could mean death, and so I was always on guard.

After a brief trip to Ciego de Avila to visit my parents' new home, I returned to Havana to learn that Fructuoso had left the hideout. I tried to find him, without success. On April 20, the police at last caught up with him and three other Revolutionary Directorate founders in an apartment on Humboldt Street. There was no question of peaceful surrender. Juan Pedro Carbó was machine-gunned in the apartment hallway. Joe Westbrook fled to another apartment, where the police found him and shot him dead. Fructuoso and José Machado jumped from the window and were riddled in a police fusillade as they hit the ground. The police did not stop firing at their lifeless bodies until forced to by neighbors' protests.

In all, the attacks on the Presidential Palace cost thirty-nine lives. The Revolutionary Directorate came under the leadership of an unknown, Faure Chomón, who did not have the leadership talent of Echevarría or Fructuoso Rodríguez. In my opinion, Chomón was more committed to fighting than to the ideals we were fighting for. I also did not think he could regroup the fragmented Revolutionary Directorate into an insurgency capable of ultimately defeating Batista—which remained the first priority of every revolutionary.

That left Fidel and his July 26th Movement. Here I also had grave reservations. I shared Echevarría's suspicions that Fidel dreamed different dreams from those of the Revolutionary Directorate. He and his leaders were idealists, yes, but as his letter to José Antonio had revealed, Fidel also seemed determined to dominate the struggle personally. Would he also expect to dominate after the triumph? It appeared that he might, but without the July 26th Movement and Fidel, I feared, there would be no triumph. And so, despite whatever doubts I had about Fidel's agenda, I joined the July 26th Movement that spring.

My primary function in the Movement was to lead a cell that carried out sabotage and other subversive acts in the Ciego de Avila area. We built bombs to frighten and harass pro-Batista forces in the province and planted others to destroy critical rail junctions and various economic targets. We collected and hid weapons and then sent them to Fidel's guerrillas in the Sierra Maestra. We also raised money, secretly distributed proclamations, and served as a sort of partisan underground, helping and hiding members of the Movement as they passed through the area.

Communications with the forces in the Sierra were sporadic. All we really knew was that Fidel was in the mountains of Oriente with a few men and women. But in February of 1957, *New York Times* correspondent Herbert Matthews managed to get to the Sierra Maestra and to interview Fidel. Matthews independently confirmed for the first time that Fidel was actually alive, and the published interview went far to create the legend of Fidel Castro as the hero of the Sierra Maestra. It also confirmed the existence of a rebel army, although Fidel had tricked Matthews as to the guerrillas' strength by marching his motley fighters, all eighteen of them, past the reporter several times.

What Matthews did not report was that at this early stage of the Sierra Maestra struggle the operational head of the July 26th Movement was a devoted young Baptist named Frank País, general coordinator of the *Dirección Nacional*, the executive group of the July 26th Movement's leadership, headed by Fidel.

País was not a guerrilla. He was an urban fighter and also a gifted strategist and ideologue who efficiently directed the Movement's apparatus and oversaw all its programs while Fidel was fighting to survive in the mountains.

Under País, the collective influence of the *Dirección Nacional* was evident everywhere in the July 26th Movement. But after the National Police mysteriously discovered his hiding place in Santiago de Cuba and killed País there on July 30, 1957, the *Dirección Nacional* soon withered as a power base within the Movement.

Very soon thereafter, the July 26th Movement fell into a period of widespread disorganization. In Ciego de Avila, the once-smooth flow of directives, plans, personnel, and materiel became disrupted and confused, an experience repeated all over the island. It was clear to all of us just how vitally important Frank País had been to the July 26th Movement.

But Fidel was always the Movement's most visible leader and as such commanded the most attention by his pronouncements. One of these came just two days after the failed March 13, 1957, Revolutionary Directorate-led attack on the Presidential Palace. In the midst of the bitterness between Fidel and José Antonio Echevarría, it was not surprising that the Movement did not join in the assault, although Fidel knew it was coming and had been invited to join. What deeply irritated many of us was Fidel's contention in a CBS News interview that the attack had been "useless bloodshed." He also asserted that Batista's life did not matter and, as head of the July 26th Movement, denounced all acts of terrorism, as if the Movement did not carry out such actions routinely.

In the months that followed, I kept turning Fidel's words over in my mind. They wouldn't leave me, no matter how I tried to convince myself that the first goal was Batista's overthrow and that Fidel was the only means of accomplishing this. It was when I looked beyond the coming triumph of the revolution to the most important goal, the institution of social reforms within a democratic government, that Fidel loomed most ominously.

Following Frank País's death in July of 1957, the Movement's center of influence shifted dramatically to the Sierra Maestra. In Ciego de Avila, we began to hear less and less about the plans and strategies of the *Dirección Nacional*, in which every member's voice had equal weight, and more and more of what Fidel wanted to accomplish and how. At the same time, the tone of the conversations we held with July 26th Movement members from the Sierra Maestra who passed through Ciego de Avila was fundamentally different. Their favorite topic became Fidel's brilliant leadership, the wisdom of all he said and did.

It was obvious by the end of 1957 that Fidel had preempted the once powerful *Dirección Nacional*. If there was any doubt left about his plans, they evaporated in December with his abrogation of the Pact of Miami, a unity document that had been signed by his July 26th Movement that month, with the Revolutionary Directorate and all the other revolutionary factions in Cuba.

Now Fidel declared that the July 26th Movement's representative had not been authorized to sign the pact. At the moment

Fidel had no intention of being equated in any way with leaders of the other factions. Also, Fidel was then planning to call the general strike in Cuba for April 1958. This action was to be carried out under the exclusive aegis of his July 26th Movement; Fidel didn't want any other group sharing the credit for its expected success.

Taken together, Fidel's actions, the inexorable redefinition of the struggle into *his* revolution, and events in my own life led me to a complete reappraisal of my course of action. In October 1957 my grandmother, María de los Angeles, died after an extended illness, plunging me into deep sorrow. Soon afterward my father announced that the political upheaval and economic uncertainty in the country left him no choice but to leave. He decided to try to begin a new life in Venezuela, whose economic climate he thought was favorable to business. I was twenty-one years old. I had seen my grandmother die, my immediate family about to be scattered, and I had no confidence in Fidel.

Looking back on the extraordinary five years from the March morning in 1952 of Batista's *golpe* to my present crisis of doubt and sadness, I knew I couldn't turn my back on the struggle. But instinct told me this was no longer the revolution I'd joined. I decided to leave Cuba too.

I knew that the Sorbonne in Paris would accept my credits for course work completed at the University of Havana, as I had Cuban friends studying there, and so I decided to continue my studies in France. I told the Movement that I would work for it in France, and I delighted my parents, who knew how dangerous it had become for me to stay in Cuba. My maiden aunts took over financial responsibility for my schooling, and I acquired a false passport in the name of José Hernández Alonso, which allowed me past Batista's security to the Havana airport. Certain of nothing but my own uncertainty, on March 23, 1958, I boarded a Super G Constellation to New York and sailed on the *Liberté* to Le Havre, France.

IN CAMAGÜEY PRISON

Now, five years had passed since I arrived in Paris, still haunted by the memories of my slain *compañeros*. My youth had been willingly given over to a cause I believed in; in France I was able to be somewhat carefree. But the news of my uncle had brought an end to this respite. Back in Camagüey, I walked in the warm night with Luc; my reminiscing giving way to the current trouble.

In the midst of our talk, he dropped a little bomb.

"So you're finally going to visit your uncle?" he said.

"Damn it, you're with the police!" I exclaimed, really surprised. "That's the only way you could know about it."

"Absolutely right, Chico. I'm a cop—and a bad one, because you've found me out right away." He was laughing so hard I could barely understand him.

He managed to control his laughter and added, "Don't worry. I'm a chief at Camagüey MININT. I saw the telegram from the head office of PURSC authorizing your visit. I also took their phone call from Havana. You can't imagine how happy I was to learn you were in Cuba. I think it's terrific to run into somebody from the old days who's not part of this whirlpool." He stressed the final words.

Something tacit in Luc's words and manner assured me I could trust him. I told him what little I knew about the reasons for my uncle's imprisonment and made no effort to hide the sorrow it caused me. I also revealed Lucrecia's suspicion that Candito, Uncle Sergio's accuser, had been motivated by greed. Then I asked if I could see my uncle's personal file.

"I'll have them show you the court and MININT records," Luc said. "Then you'll know exactly what his present situation is. You can't tell anything about the future here. It depends on his behavior in prison and his attitude when he gets out."

Suddenly Luc fell silent. He continued to walk beside me, but he was absorbed in his own thoughts. When we reached the

Casino Campestre park he sat down on one of the benches and stared for a moment at the ground, his face in his hands. Then he picked up a branch and began to trace figures on the earth, completely self-absorbed.

"Luc, what is it? What's wrong?" I asked.

"José Luis, this life stinks," he exclaimed bitterly. "You have your uncle and I have my sister. She's been in prison since 1960. Do you remember how religious she was when she was young? Well, later she led a Catholic group that was plotting against the revolution. They gave her four years. She won't conform to prison and doesn't want to be involved in rehabilitation. My mother is suffering terribly. Every day she begs me to help my sister, but I can't. I can't! If I make even the slightest move to help her, they'll have my head."

His voice trembled and broke. Luc was anguished, although talking seemed to give him some relief. He took a deep breath and went on.

"You know my family was always very close, just like yours. Remember my father? Authoritarian, upright, a typical paterfamilias who made all the decisions and dispensed all the rewards. After the revolution they expropriated his lands. He couldn't get over it. Soon afterward he died of a heart attack. That and her own religious fanaticism started my sister down the road to counterrevolution."

"Does your sister have a family?" I asked.

"She's married," he answered, "and her husband isn't revolutionary either. They have a little girl who's four years old; my mother's crazy about her, but I wouldn't dare see her except when she's with her grandmother."

"Tell me something, Luc. What you're saying now: I don't suppose you talk about it very often?"

"Never," he said with apprehension. "I don't even know how I've told you about it now. Perhaps because you spoke so openly about your uncle's problem. Besides, today I feel more depressed than usual."

He looked at me with disturbed, questioning eyes. Then Luc squeezed my arm and almost stammered as he added, "I beg you, don't say anything, anything at all, please! It could do me a lot of harm."

"Don't worry, Luc," I said, trying to calm him. "You're my friend. I only want to help you. Or rather, I want us to help each other. Our situations are very similar."

"Who knows, José Luis, who knows!" he exclaimed.

"You mustn't repeat what I've told you, either."

"Don't worry," he said, suddenly standing up. "We should go now. I have to pick up my wife. She's waiting for me at my mother's house. Did I tell you she's three months pregnant?"

"No, damn it, you didn't say anything. Congratulations! If you need anything from France, write to me or send a message with somebody, and if you can, let me know how my uncle's case is coming along. I'm often at the Embassy. Forget you said anything to me," I said, noticing the concern in his face. "This is strictly between us. We'll solve our problems somehow, you'll see."

He was silent again on the way back. When we reached the hotel, Luc told me again how glad he was to see me, embraced me, and said, "You know, Slim, this was a catharsis for me, and it really helped. Thanks."

He slapped me on the arm affectionately. Then his face tightened as he climbed into his car and pulled away with screeching tires.

My trepidation was now a hundred times greater. In such an atmosphere of suspicion, how on earth would I help my uncle?

Early the next morning I went to the provincial MININT offices. Following the instructions of Aragonés's aide, I identified myself and requested a meeting with the appropriate official.

I was shown into a small waiting room. Its walls were covered with portraits of revolutionary martyrs, many of them my personal friends, serving in death as icons for a revolutionary regime they would not have endorsed. I saw José Antonio Echevarría portrayed in a heroic pose, as well as Camilo Cienfuegos, killed in a suspicious air crash only weeks after I'd last seen him at the Bacuranao Beach in 1959.

After half an hour a robust man came in and apologized for the delay. "I've received orders to allow you to visit your uncle and to provide you with any information you need about him," he told me. "Your uncle has given us a lot of problems. He's rebellious, he's allied himself with the most recalcitrant elements in the prison, and he refuses to join the political rehabilitation program. I read his dossier yesterday. Do you want to take a look before you see him?"

My uncle Sergio's trial had been brief; its transcript ran only a very few pages. I read in detail Candito's malicious statements.

He had accused my uncle not only of distributing religious pictures but also of being an "outstanding bourgeois counterrevolutionary and possible saboteur." There was no defense at all—just a brief statement asking for the generosity of the revolution.

In the MININT records, I also found out who my uncle's worst enemies were in Ciego de Avila. There were reports written by the CDR, by some of his neighbors, and by Candito. But the most serious charges were made by party and government officials in the city. One of these denunciations was signed by one of my uncle's closest friends, a person who had emigrated to another Latin American country shortly afterward. There were dozens of names of people who had once been very close to him and our family, former friends whose only possible motive was to show their revolutionary zeal.

At the prison, accompanied by a MININT official, I stopped first at the warden's office. Patiently I endured his long speech about the government's concern for political prisoners and for integrating them into the new society—a performance meant to impress my MININT escort as well as me, since the warden couldn't be sure who I was—and then I was taken down a series of dank corridors to a small room used, I was told, for special visits.

Minutes later my uncle was brought in, clad in a dark-blue shirt and pants and looking very edgy. I could see that he'd lost considerable weight and had aged dramatically behind bars. After I gave him a restrained hug, we sat down to an uneasy conversation with both my escort from MININT and a prison official sitting nearby.

Our talk was confined exclusively to family matters; I didn't dare ask him about his own situation lest he explode angrily in front of the two government men. Instead, I recounted to his gloomy smile the superficial news of my life and that of family members in Venezuela and the United States.

Uncle Sergio said very little in the perhaps forty-five minutes we were together, but his eyes conveyed a heartbreaking plea for help. As we sat there, the images of Silvio and my other cousins, my grandmother, my father, and my aunts passed through my mind, and melancholy filled me. The revolution had dispersed us to two hemispheres and continued to ravage those left behind. Looking at my uncle, scarcely a shadow of the lively man I'd seen not four years before, my sorrow mixed with a new, cold determination to rescue him somehow.

*   *   *

From the beginning, I had shared with Marie Christine only the most general facts of my uncle's situation. In part, it seemed pointless to burden her with a problem that only time, patience, and luck could resolve. But it was also imperative that neither of us give away any hint of my true intentions. Since for the balance of our tour of the island we would be seeing many revolutionary officials, I believed it safer and more sensible if I carried on the charade of communist revolutionary belief.

From Camagüey, as part of our official tour, we crossed the immense, sun-drenched plains toward Oriente Province and the Sierra Maestra. Our first destination was Santiago de Cuba, cradle of the revolution, where we would meet Captain Jorge Risquet, Second Secretary of the Provincial party, who had invited us to visit during one of his trips to Paris.

Risquet, like Emilio Aragonés, was a member of the ridiculed Captains' Club, a jovial and corpulent former PSP member who was distinguished in the main for his incompetence and opportunism. He was always ready to lecture on Marxism, Socialism, the revolution, and Fidel's many virtues and, so as not to make an exception of us, held forth *ad nauseam* on these topics during an otherwise excellent meal we shared in our first evening with him. Although I kept my feelings discreetly to myself, I was amused and annoyed to be lectured by a man who had not even participated in the revolution whose philosophy he was explaining at such length. Marie Christine was bored—and so was I.

Even though he was then out of favor because of his involvement in the sectarian crisis, Risquet was still an important official. I knew that in the revolution one's fortunes could rise and fall very quickly. In fact, today Risquet is one of the members of the Politburo.

We left for Havana as soon as we could get away.

Upon our return to the capital, I called the MININT legal department and spoke to a lawyer and friend from Camagüey. That night, he came to our hotel room for supper, and afterward, when Marie Christine had left the room, I explained my uncle's case to him.

"His situation is difficult," he said when I had finished. "If your uncle doesn't want rehabilitation, he'll have to serve his complete sentence. He'll leave prison with a negative report, and then it may be hard for him to leave the country. He's so well known in Ciego de Avila, he must have enemies who will stand in the way of getting an exit permit from MININT. I know of many similar cases."

The conversation only confirmed what I had come to see for myself. I would not be able to get Uncle Sergio's sentence reduced, and once he was released, he faced almost certain reimprisonment. My only choice now was also the most difficult and risky: Somehow I would have to arrange for him to leave secretly.

WITH CHÉ IN THE MINISTRY OF INDUSTRY

During this trip I renewed my acquaintance with Pepín Naranjo, whom I had not seen in four years. He was now first secretary of the party in Havana and had become one of Fidel's closest confidants. Toward the end of the trip, as Marie Christine and I were returning from a drive with Pepín and his wife, Fidel pulled up alongside us. He engaged Pepín in a bantering conversation and invited us all, informally, to join him at his beach house at Santa María.

I thought this was a great idea, another chance to observe Fidel at close range. But Pepín was more interested in the meal that was awaiting us at his own house. As I later commented to Marie Christine, Pepín liked the company of lobster and beer more than that of Fidel. Because Fidel had tendered an invitation, not an order, Pepín was able politely to decline, to my disappointment.

I also saw Ché Guevara again, continuing our relationship begun at the home of Suárez Gayol in 1959 and broadened during Ché's subsequent trips to Europe, where we had visited museums and bookstores together. Our conversations, dominated by Ché's soliloquies on issues and ideology, seemed to be an outlet for him. Because of his reputation for unapproachability, Ché probably had few opportunities for such spontaneous openness. To take him at his word, he simply enjoyed my company.

Ché was growing more renowned not only as a romantic

guerrilla but also as a revolutionary ideologue; among the leaders of the Cuban revolution, only Fidel was better known. Ché's
views on economic and political matters received broad international attention at forums such as the Economic and Social
Inter-American Council meeting in Punta del Este, Uruguay, in
August 1961. He had also stirred tremendous interest in 1960
and 1962 with two extended trips to the Soviet Union and other
Socialist countries.

In 1963, Ché was serving as the Revolutionary Government's
first minister of industry, a position from which he promoted one
of his central ideas, the immediate and massive transformation
of Cuba from an essentially agricultural economy to an industrial state, a process he had seen and admired in Japan. This
program ran directly counter to Soviet thinking, which was then
that Cuba should emphasize sugar production.

Much more radical, however, was Ché's rejection of traditional material incentives to spur worker productivity. In this
scheme, the masses were not to be motivated to work by the lure
of wages or any other material incentive. Quite the contrary. Ché
believed that a truly Communist society required the creation of
what he called the "New Man," whose self-interest was entirely
moral. It was a utopian dream, but Ché believed in it absolutely.

"If you're not busy, I'd like you to stop by here," he said
when I phoned him one evening to see him before we left. He
meant later that night and told me that his secretary, Manresa,
would be waiting for me when I arrived at the Ministry. "Tell
him to give you lots of coffee," Ché added. "You'll need it."
Evidently we were in for one of our marathon talks.

At 11:00 P.M. I was waved through the ground-floor reception
area of the Ministry, which faced the Plaza de la Revolución.
Enmita, Ché's bashful typist, showed me into Manresa's office.

Manresa had been in Batista's army, a blot on his record
that Ché ignored; he was equally unbothered by the veiled criticism he received for having chosen Manresa. People didn't realize that Manresa's work ethic, administrative ability, and loyalty
were virtues much esteemed by Ché. The two had been together
since early 1959.

While we waited for his boss to return from a meeting,
Manresa asked me several questions about the French political
situation and the way of life there. Apparently, Ché had promised that Manresa could accompany him on his next visit to
Paris.

Around midnight Ché's voice came over the intercom. Manresa left to give him a folder full of paperwork and returned a few seconds later to show me in.

Ché greeted me with a friendly hand on my shoulder. Then he growled to his secretary: "Damn it, Manresa! That's enough red tape. The bureaucracy we've generated is going to devour us. It's a cancer gnawing at the bones of the revolution. Death to the bureaucrats, damn it!"

After glancing through the letters in the folder, reading some, signing others, Ché handed them back to Manresa and dismissed him for the night. Then he pulled out his shirt, unbuttoned it halfway to his chest, and sat down in a comfortable armchair with his feet propped up on a small table. Ché was breathing easily this night; for once the cursed asthma was not bothering him.

By now I was generally familiar with Ché's extreme views, his idealistic certainty that real men and women everywhere could be made perfect by living the "New Man" ideology. But before this night, I had never felt the intensity with which he held this vision.

"Human beings," he said to me, "must be stripped of egoism and individualism. You must develop to its maximum man's revolutionary consciousness and make his materialistic appetites disappear. He should be satisfied with the absolute reward of doing his duty. In Socialism there is no room for material incentives. They are the chief corrupter of consciousness."

Under my prodding, Ché conceded that the material incentives of the old order could not be done away with immediately. But he was fully convinced that the true power of socialism lay in the creation of a pure, generous New Man, and he feared that the contemporary discussion in the Soviet Union over the relative merits of moral versus material incentives for the people—a debate that would be decided in favor of the latter—threatened the purity of Soviet Socialism.

"You'll see that the moral incentive will triumph," he went on. "For Cuba, the real revolutionary battle now has to be won day by day. We have to gain ground, foot by foot, in our struggle against weakness and bourgeois values. Profound and irreversible victory is ideological. The degree of resolution with which the revolution acts in this regard will determine whether it takes more or less time for the New Man to emerge, along with the hope of freedom that he carries under his arm."

Most of that night's conversation went on in this vein. Perhaps because Fidel had declared Cuba a Socialist state, Ché now felt he could be more direct with me, more brashly open about the direction he believed Cuba must take and how the country would achieve a pure form of Communism. When we parted, I was struck not so much by the content of what he argued as by his unshakable faith that, in time, a New Man would in fact emerge. I also could not imagine how profoundly this concept soon would alter the course of the revolution.

THE REVOLUTION ON THE MOVE

In Paris, Marie Christine, Marielle, and I resumed our contented family life, and I returned to my position at NYCO with as much career enthusiasm as ever. But my spirit was trapped in that prison with my uncle, and my mind was crowded with thoughts of what I'd seen in Cuba that summer.

I felt myself changed. I had gathered a huge amount of information in Cuba, most of which confirmed my doubts about Fidel. I had seen with my own eyes Fidel's compelling magnetism, the accelerated deterioration of the Cuban economy, the corruption and lax working style of the revolutionary leadership, and the radical reordering of society itself. In the months following our trip, I analyzed and dissected my impressions, trying to make sense of the transformation—and hoping that such insights might provide me with a solution to my uncle's dilemma.

The new government was still experiencing domestic difficulties. Resentments I had first noted in 1959—those between the Sierra Maestra veterans, who believed *they* had carried the revolution, and the urban guerrillas, whose role the Sierra fighters thought was minimal—persisted. An even deeper antagonism, however, existed between these two groups and the PSP members who were working their way into Fidel's government. The old Communists' late-blooming revolutionary fervor earned them the fighters' derisive epithet *oportunistas*.

On March 8, 1962, Fidel had sought to erase these divisions

by subsuming the wildly pro-Soviet PSP, his own July 26th Movement, and the Revolutionary Directorate under the umbrella Integrated Revolutionary Organizations (ORI). However, Aníbal Escalante, a PSP member and the ORI national coordinator, had his own agenda. Escalante had always wanted power, and he distrusted anyone who wasn't an old-line Marxist like himself. Within the recently created ORI, he began to displace the real revolutionaries with his old party cronies. As the situation was later explained to me by Emilio Aragonés and others, everyone at the time knew that Fidel was aware of Escalante's intent; his own Sierra Maestra veterans had come to him for many months with stories of the PSP plot.

But Fidel knew how to make Escalante's power-grab work for him. He watched the plot unfold, listening to the complaints of his *compañeros* from the guerrilla days and gathering evidence against the PSP until the politically opportune moment for action. Less than three weeks after the creation of ORI, Fidel struck, denouncing the PSP attitude. On March 26, 1962—the beginning of the so-called "sectarian crisis," during which Fidel appeared to be attacking the narrow, ideological orientation of the PSP members.

"Sectarian" meant Escalante's sector of PSP thinking, and the supposed "crisis" was in the sector's threat to undermine the Revolutionary Government. In fact, and for his own purposes, Fidel simply allowed Escalante and his clique to self-destruct.

In the months that followed, dozens of PSP members were removed from their posts and sent into various states of power exile. Escalante, their leader, was given a ticket to Moscow, where he went to work for a time at *Pravda*, the official newspaper of the Soviet Communist Party.

Conscious of his overwhelming popularity, Fidel had chosen just the right moment to consolidate absolute power in Cuba and, while still a good Marxist-Leninist, to underscore to an international audience his sovereignty vis-à-vis the revolution's "Soviet friends."

Some months later, in October 1962, the missile crisis hit. When the Soviets had backed down and dismantled the bases, Fidel was furious. In Paris, I had not met a single Cuban official who did not condemn the USSR's actions. And in Cuba itself, people had demonstrated in the streets, shouting, *"¡Nikita Mariquita, lo que se da no se quita!"* ("Nikita Mariquita, what you give you don't take away!")

Privately, Fidel was continually accusing Khrushchev of cowardice, of having pulled a dirty trick, of betraying Cuba. In truth, his fury and indignation were born of injured pride. He had been informed only after the decision to remove the missiles had been made. The Soviets may not have cared what Fidel thought or wanted, but by ignoring him in front of his people and the world community, they had injured his most sensitive spot, his immense ego.

Of course, the missile crisis had been a serious reversal for the Soviets too. They would not seek another confrontation with the United States until the odds looked better. Instead, they chose to stress their politically opportune message of peaceful coexistence, a line developed in 1956 that advocated the possibility of the peaceful transition of a society into Socialism—that is, without violent revolution.

Fidel, stung by the embarrassment of the missile crisis, now scorned Soviet foreign policy. He wanted nothing to do with peaceful coexistence and pursued his own radically opposing line of exporting revolution, a cardinal point of *his* foreign policy.

But there was a contradiction here. The Soviet Union was beginning to be Cuba's principal trade partner. And the Soviets could, if they so desired, force Cuba to adopt their political, economic, and ideological lines. For the time being, however, it was convenient for them to allow Fidel some latitude while strengthening their economic ties to Cuba. Soon Fidel would be so dependent that his autonomy would be rhetorical.

And so, during his long trip to Moscow in the spring of 1963, Fidel had been entertained royally and had received every ego-soothing attention, even though not a single old PSP member was in his entourage. With the exception of the durable and valuable Carlos Rafael Rodríguez, they had all been placed in marginal, unimportant positions. ORI had been dismantled and PURSC established, with Captain Emilio Aragonés as its organizational secretary. But this restructuring did not bring Cuba any closer to an efficient economic management.

As we'd witnessed on our trip, Cuba's economy was obviously stagnating, although in this area the revolution had achieved one measure of democratization—that of poverty. Whereas before 1959 the poor of Cuba had lived at or below the subsistence level while the wealthy pursued often lavish life styles, now the whole country enjoyed a rather low standard of living.

Ration books for most foods had been implemented on March 12, 1962, and were hardly enough to last the month they were supposed to, according to the friends we'd visited. Shortages of food and other consumer goods had encouraged a *campesino* black market and an informal barter economy. They also gave rise to the long lines we'd seen at overcrowded restaurants, where it was common for diners to bring plastic bags or nylon totes to carry home leftovers or an extra plate of food. This was against regulations but could be managed by giving the waiter a generous tip.

Clothing, shoes, and household articles were rationed, too, but even with a valid coupon, there was no guarantee that you could secure the item you wanted. Either you waited in long, slow-moving lines, hoping the article would still be available when it came your turn, or you relied on an insider network to keep track of what was available where. TVs, air conditioners, radios, refrigerators, and the like were unavailable, period. They were no longer being imported. Because of raw-material shortages, processed goods such as detergent, soap, and dairy products were also frequently impossible to find. The most welcome gifts we'd brought were things like razor blades, deodorant, and soap—and when we left, we gave away whatever we'd traveled with for our personal use.

In his speeches and private conversations, Ché Guevara had honestly admitted that there was a crisis of production in Cuba. Fidel would not. He attributed the scarcities to considerable growth in consumption, the inherent difficulties of underdevelopment, and the U.S. economic blockade. Although I realized that the blockade was strongly affecting the Cuban economy, I wondered to myself what relationship it had to the disappearance of vegetables, milk, butter, cheese, and many other foodstuffs Cubans had always produced for themselves. I had no recollection before the revolution of these items being massively imported, as I understood they were now. In the midst of all this, Fidel kept promising the people dizzying development—"a standard of living higher than in Sweden," he said. Since reality wouldn't go away, however, his projections for "a shining future" kept getting pushed back. First, things were going to be great by 1965. Now the target was 1970.

The revolutionary leaders' work habits were striking. In the summer of 1963 I'd had difficulty finding them in their offices during normal working hours. Most of them imitated Fidel's style, which was to travel constantly around the island to attend personally to matters often of no consequence, or about which he, or they, knew nothing.

Fidel's frequent interventions in internal economic affairs had created chaos. He almost always left orders that contradicted either his own previous instructions or those of national or provincial governmental agencies. But as far as any revolutionary official was concerned, Fidel could never err. Even his most far-fetched inspirations, which occurred to him all the time, were implemented because, as I'd heard again and again, "Fidel knows what he's doing," and "He knows more than we do."

At his initiative, lands were cleared of pangola grass, a plant used as cattle feed, only to have the same fields planted again in a few weeks—with pangola. Expensive, high-tech hydroponic gardening technology was introduced for vegetable farms, even though there are vast acreages in Cuba of land so rich that all you had to do was sow them to guarantee a harvest. Of course, to get results you did have to respect the seasons. But to meet governmental quotas, Cuban farmers were often told to plant out of season, meaning that only 20 to 30 percent of the crop would ever be harvested.

Fidel had decided that Cuban agriculture was overdependent upon sugar-cane production, and he ordered that crops be diversified. But instead of encouraging the cultivation of crops suited to Cuba's climate, he had introduced fruits such as apples, pears, peaches, and grapes. Naturally, the plants were sickly.

If I hadn't tasted the acidic grapes, seen the stunted apple trees, and inspected rice plantings in arid lands, I would never have believed such foolhardy projects had been undertaken. They were the random stumblings of a blind man, experiments everywhere with no prior planning or consultation with experts. And if experts *were* brought in, their advice was ignored unless it agreed with Fidel's ideas. Everything was approached as if it were some kind of diversion, a game in Wonderland. As long as a project was ideologically correct, it did not have to yield results.

Nothing in Cuban life matched in importance the ideal of seeming to be a good Communist revolutionary. To be considered as such it was necessary to accept whatever the revolution ordered. This correct revolutionary attitude was the first criterion in the selection of administrators; competence didn't count. With the removal of PSP members (themselves practiced in party discipline but not in disciplined management) to marginal posts, some comandantes from the Sierra were reincarnated as ministers, directors of agriculture, or heads of important projects. Unquestionably brave and totally loyal to their leader, most were relatively uneducated and otherwise ill-suited to manage peacetime enterprises.

Similarly, capable people in one field were named to head undertakings in other areas they knew nothing about. A physician, for instance, was appointed director of a state farm. An athlete was placed at the head of a cultural institution. And an attorney was charged with the operation of an iron and steel facility.

The mismatch of talent to task led to various tragicomic episodes, particularly when it came to the foreign purchase and importing of basic goods. Several of these fiascos had been the talk of Havana during my 1963 stay there.

In one instance, five strange-looking machines, without operating manuals or even any known destination, were unloaded one day in the port of Havana. Nobody could guess what they were for, although one camp argued they must be a new type of bulldozer and another held that they were potato-picking machines.

Both were wrong: Cuba, a tropical country, now owned five snowplows. The machines had been offered to a foreign trade official in the Soviet Union who had purchased them without inquiring what they were for. According to one of the heads of the Mambisa Navigation Company, who told me this story between fits of hysterical laughter, the machines were quietly pushed into a corner of a dock warehouse. He took me to see them for myself. There they remained for a long, long time.

One story I heard had to do with the worldwide shortage in 1962 of cooking oil. A Cuban official bought on the international market what he had been told was lard. He hadn't bothered to inspect the shipment. When it was distributed, housewives complained at once of its "funny smell." No wonder—it was whale oil.

But it took a member of the Captains' Club, Captain Antonio Núñez Jiménez, then the minister of agriculture, to engineer one of the most wasteful episodes. Núñez Jiménez sold Fidel on a proposal to make Cuba an important producer of copra oil from coconuts. Eager to foster Cuban industrialization, Fidel was persuaded that seeds could be imported from Ceylon (now Sri Lanka) and that the plants would grow well in Cuba. The copra oil itself would be manufactured in a factory that would also be imported. Núñez Jiménez personally supervised the trade agreement. And a few months later a ship full of coconut seeds docked in Havana.

That's when disaster struck. That night a militiaman guarding the ship heard a thud and then looked down to see a huge

snake crawling along. Shouts and shots ensued, alerting everyone in the area, which was quickly cordoned off by the revolutionary police. Investigators soon discovered that the ship was
alive with poisonous serpents which were not found on Cuban
soil and were hardly a desirable import. Apparently they had
burrowed among the piles of seeds at embarkation. There was
nothing to do but to guide the infested freighter out of port
where it was thoroughly fumigated and its cargo of coconut
seeds dumped overboard.

Four years after the revolution's triumph, there was a shortage not only of essential goods and amenities but also of people
qualified to prevent these sorts of mishaps. Unfortunately, many
of Cuba's most skilled citizens were no longer there to help.

The first mass exodus from the island in 1959, of nearly
75,000 people, had been composed mainly of the well-to-do and
those connected with the Batista dictatorship. Few of these exiles
had been candidates for integration into the revolutionary process.

But the second wave of emigration, from 1960 to 1962, of
about 190,000 Cubans, had included many professionals, technical specialists, and craftsmen. A significant portion of these people were hounded out of the country. "Those bourgeois," as the
revolutionary leaders called them, for many reasons might have
accepted if not embraced the revolution. But they had met suspicion and hostility at every turn. Their initiatives had been vetoed
and their advice ignored. Those who left Cuba in disgust and
frustration with this harassment were then sneered at as "worms."

The cost of such ideological purity was high. The revolution
had squandered a critically important economic resource: its
capable citizenry. On the other hand, the exodus did reduce the
number of domestic consumers and thereby eased, however min-
imally, the demand for ever-scarcer goods and products.

Those disaffected Cubans who had chosen to remain or, like
my uncle, were caught in the country, paid a higher price than
the exiles. Executions and torture in prisons continued, but the
greater terror was the summary judgment and imprisonment
under supposed revolutionary justice, which lacked any legal
foundation. As I'd discovered, a person could be jailed indefinitely. If his or her case finally came to trial, no adequate defense
was permitted. Neither guilt nor innocence nor extenuating circumstances were considerations. Verdicts and sentences always
reflected the perceived self-interest of the Revolutionary Government, which meant that Cuba's prisons were filled to overflowing.

*   *   *

Some of the Revolutionary Government's programs were very laudable and popular. Early in 1959, Fundamental Law, a revised version of the model Cuban constitution of 1940 had been introduced; it benefited the revolutionary citizen, although not those who disagreed with the new regime. In the same year, the Urban Reform Law reduced rents by one half. The ITT subsidiary was taken over, and telephone as well as electric bills were pared back. The first Agrarian Reform law passed in 1959, and a second reform law was proposed in 1963. Professional medical care became available to everyone. The government also launched successful campaigns against diseases from polio to tuberculosis. Unemployment was eradicated, and meaningful social security benefits were introduced for the first time. Also for the first time I saw no official racial discrimination; blacks and whites went to the same beaches, hotels, and social clubs.

In this respect, the revolution had kept its promise. The child mortality rate plummeted, life expectancy started to rise, and the *campesinos* were no longer dying of curable diseases, as they had before.

Possibly the noblest of all the revolution's achievements was the national literacy campaign, begun in 1961. Fidel declared education free. Army barracks from the Batista era were turned into schools, and new universities opened around the island. As Marie Christine and I toured Cuba in 1963, I saw for the first time in my life *campesinos* reading books, magazines, and newspapers. The content of what they read may have been tightly controlled, and the material they were encouraged to digest— Communist tracts, Fidel's speeches, and the like—may have lacked breadth and vitality. But certain classics of world literature were made available at low prices. The revolution quickly erased the darkness of illiteracy from Cuba.

A good many Cubans had benefited from these changes. In spite of the shortages, the *ad hoc* justice, lack of understanding, and the Revolutionary Government's many failures and mistakes, the great majority of the people I'd met were very confident of the future. I was not so optimistic.

A FATEFUL DECISION

In early 1964, I learned from Luc that my uncle had been released from the Camagüey prison the preceding December. Luc's letter, sent to me via diplomatic courier and thus guaranteed by his position at MININT to be read by no one but the recipient, explained that my uncle's rebelliousness might soon land him back in prison. His enemies and the CDR in his neighborhood were denouncing him again. Worse, the MININT office in Ciego de Avila would not allow Uncle Sergio to leave the country.

Luc's wife had given birth to a son, Luc told me, and the boy had a cardiac condition and needed special medicines. Luc wrote that his joy in fatherhood was further dampened by concern for his mother, who had been admitted to the hospital suffering from nervous depression. She would not even respond to her new grandchild.

I found Luc the medicines his child needed that afternoon and sent them to him, again by diplomatic courier, with a letter telling Luc of my resolve to get Uncle Sergio out of Cuba. I asked his advice and warned him to destroy the note.

A short while later came his reply. "You can solve your problem only in Cuba," he wrote, "and, incidentally, help me to solve mine. I have the solution."

Whatever answer Luc had in mind, I was determined to help my uncle. There were two basic alternatives. One, I'd somehow supply my uncle with forged exit papers. Two, and much more dangerous, I could try to get him out secretly. Neither course, if successful, would require more than a couple of months to initiate. But in either case, I couldn't return to Cuba as a tourist or even as an invited guest. I was going to have to reintegrate myself into Fidel's revolution; we would have to live in Cuba.

I was sure it would take no more than a year at most for me to penetrate the system deeply enough to help my uncle. During these months, Marielle could live with her grandparents in Venezuela; they would be thrilled to have her. When I'd succeeded in my plan, I would arrange to have her sent back to France for Christmas and return with Marie Christine to Paris on the pretext of picking up our daughter to bring her back to Cuba permanently.

I'd thought it through very carefully, based on what I'd seen in France and in Cuba. Since my wife and daughter were French, it would be natural for us to spend a one-month holiday in France. There was absolutely nothing keeping a credentialed revolutionary from vacationing in his wife's country, provided of course that the country enjoyed diplomatic relations with Cuba. I knew of revolutionaries who had studied with me in Paris, married French citizens, and returned to France for holidays regularly.

I did not feel at ease hiding my true intention from Marie Christine, but I felt even more uneasy about the possibility of jeopardizing our security in Cuba by telling her the truth. Although she had visited the island for two months in 1963 as a tourist, she had a very idealistic view of the country. She'd stayed in deluxe hotels and lived the way visitors or officials did. She could not know the real Cuba, where scarcity and political control were a part of daily existence, and could in no way have anticipated the difficulties most people lived with. Since the knowledge of what I had planned would make her nervous and full of trepidation in Cuba, the best way to protect her and myself was to be sure she knew nothing. I knew she was incapable of deception, and I could not ask her to live a double life; she would break.

Marie Christine had always trusted my decisions because her experience had been, until then, that our life together had been the best for both of us. My overprotectiveness of her was a characteristic of our relationship; she had been very sheltered, she depended on me, and I wanted to take care of her. I wasn't the only one. Marie Christine had a quality of innocence and trust that made everyone who met her react that way.

And so, when I approached her with the idea of living in Cuba, she assumed I was capable of making the right decision about our future. The questions she raised were: How long would it be before we were together again after her taking Marielle to visit my family in the United States and Venezuela? How long would we then be separated from Marielle? Was Cuba safe and good for us? Could we leave Cuba for holidays? What would Marielle's education be like in a Communist country? Where were we going to live, and where would I work?

With all these questions she was not doubting my decision to live in Cuba but only expressing her concerns. She never criticized the decision. She was anxious—no doubt about that—but her trust in me prevailed over everything else.

I told her that I wanted to live in Cuba because I was homesick; I was a revolutionary who had fought for the revolution, and I wanted to participate in it. I said we'd be together as soon as I could find a place to live and a job. We would be separated from Marielle until we were settled—at most, one year. Then we would send Marielle to France and travel there to bring her back to Cuba. I explained that Cuba was a safe country for us because I was a revolutionary and I had fought for the revolution. And so there would be no problem getting out of Cuba for holidays; it was a very accepted, normal thing to do, and others had already done it. I also told her that we could periodically review this move if we weren't happy. She was a French citizen, free to do anything but fight against the revolution.

Despite all that I had seen and analyzed, I could in no way envision how great a gamble I was about to take. Because I had taken such risks as a revolutionary and had been involved in so many truly life-threatening situations, I was used to prevailing over seemingly insurmountable obstacles. Our one summer in Cuba had disclosed to me many examples of individuals who were victims of the revolution's policies, but it had not been long enough for me to understand, as a visitor, how pervasive the system was, how impossible it was for anyone to act freely in the face of it—even with the resources of self-assurance and conviction.

I was far too confident of myself. I believed that my plans would develop exactly as I had envisioned them, and I did not doubt myself at all. Once I'd worked out all the details in my mind, I had no misgivings. Now, when I look back at my youthful reasoning, I cannot believe how naïve I was, while I was trying to protect my wife.

Marie Christine left that summer with Marielle for Los Angeles, where they were to meet my aunts and cousins. Marie Christine had not met them and very much wanted to do so. I could not be admitted to the United States on a Cuban passport, but she was eager to get to know the people she'd heard so much about—and to introduce them to our daughter. Then she and Marielle would continue on to Caracas and my parents' house.

We agreed that Marielle would live for a time with her grandparents after Marie Christine joined me in Havana.

I had long observed the Cuban revolutionaries' fascination with Western consumer technology and luxuries, especially automobiles. New cars—the flashier, the fancier, the faster the better—enthralled them. And so, when I sold our apartment, I used some of the proceeds to buy a new Mercedes 320SE, white with a red leather interior. The Mercedes, a top-of-the-line trinket in which I even installed a new Blaupunkt radio with automatic scanner, would be my calling card back in Havana. I hoped the machine would open doors—or gates—where our proletarian VW bug would never take me.

I did drive the VW on one last extended trip while I waited for Marie Christine's papers to be processed in Cuba. Then I shipped the VW and the Mercedes to Cuba and at last was prepared to embark on my risky mission.

A strange, vague presentiment, an unexplainable mixture of doubt and sorrow, oppressed me at this time. Although I fully intended to return to France once my uncle was free, an inner voice warned me of trouble ahead.

During the days prior to my departure, Paris turned sad and melancholy for me. I was leaving part of myself behind. I had been happy there with Marie Christine and Marielle. I had known the generosity and love of people like the Budins and the Meynards. Christian, Bernard, Jocelyn, and his sister Prisca, friends with whom I had shared so many happy moments, would now become part of my memories during the unknown life I would lead in the coming year.

Before leaving Paris, I saw Aragonés and Osmany Cienfuegos, accompanied this time by Raulito Roa, later to be the Cuban ambassador to the U.N., and Comandante Rolando Cubela, then president of FEU, the student federation. I had known Cubela at the university, where he had been a friend of José Antonio Echevarría and one of the most popular leaders of the Revolutionary Directorate after 1959. He had been kept out of the higher echelons of the revolution due in large measure to Fidel's old hostility to the Revolutionary Directorate. During my visit to Cuba in 1963 we had often met, and he'd seemed depressed, preoccupied; since then, his political fortunes had not improved. He did have one privilege: His position as president of the FEU gave him the opportunity to travel abroad frequently.

On February 15, 1965, I arrived in Madrid to catch the Cubana de Aviación plane for Havana. Because of irregular flights and the large number of passengers, my stay in Madrid was extended for two weeks. Cubela was in Madrid, too, staying in the Plaza Hotel with his good friend Enrique Rodríguez Loeches, Cuban ambassador to Morocco. One night Cubela invited me to supper. Later we were joined by the lawyer Jorge Robreño, better known as *El Mago* ("The Magician"), who Cubela said was living in Madrid temporarily with the permission of the Cuban government. I wondered at this; Robreño was not a diplomat. But I supposed that if Cubela accepted him, there was no reason to doubt his political position.

Rolando was more talkative that night than usual. He chatted happily about our years at the university, mentioning incidents I had forgotten.

I saw Cubela and Robreño several times after that in my two-week stay. Robreño was excessively friendly to me, more than one would have expected given the nature of our acquaintance, and the same was true of Gallareta, a diplomat from the Cuban mission who often came with him. Both insisted I visit their houses, and these signs of attention and concern made me suspicious, as did their effusive conversations about the virtues of Fidel and the revolution.

I was, nonetheless, far from imagining that I was caught in the middle of a CIA plot to assassinate Fidel, and that the actual killing was to be done by Cubela himself. He had made contact in Madrid with Manuel Artime, one of the organizers of the Bay of Pigs invasion. Robreño; Gallareta; and another conspirator, "Crazy Man" Blanco; all were involved in the plot, and they were behaving as they did with me in order to divert any suspicion about their true intentions.

Finally, on February 28, 1965, I left for Cuba. As it turned out I traveled with Cubela, who was carrying in his luggage the telescopic sight he planned to use for the assassination. When we landed in Newfoundland the plane had mechanical difficulties and our stopover lasted two days. Cubela and I shared a hotel room in a small city almost buried in snow. I remember him as completely withdrawn—undoubtedly he was thinking about the assassination and all its dangers. He scarcely spoke as he stared out into the distance. In one of our few conversations he referred to the disloyalty of some *compañeros* after the triumph of the revolution: "Watch out for people. Not all your old friends are still sincere; values have changed a lot," he said in an absent-minded way.

At that time, it seemed to me that Cubela was really the one who had changed. In no way did he resemble the good-natured medical student of a few years back.

Of course he knew something that I, despite my revolutionary knowledge of loyalty and betrayal, could not begin to imagine.

BIRTH OF THE STRANGER

ACCEPTING A MERCEDES-BENZ

As soon as I arrived in Havana, I went to the Hotel Capri, where Emilio Aragonés had reserved a room for me. That same day I visited his office and found Comandante Manuel Piñeiro, also known as *Barba Roja*, "Red Beard."

"How's that ambassador you have over there?" Piñeiro asked me, referring to Antonio Carrillo. "Is he still spending his money on fur coats for his wife?"

"Leave Carrillo alone," Aragonés protested to Piñeiro. "When you have it in for somebody, you're a pain in the ass."

"That man is a bastard," Piñeiro exclaimed with a sneer.

"All right, all right, let it go," I interrupted.

I had known Antonio Carrillo since our student days, when we were both studying medicine. At the university he'd been called *Amarillo*, or "Yellow," because, it was said, *amarillo* was the color Carrillo turned whenever he faced any danger. José Antonio Echevarría had delighted in hatching schemes to scare Carrillo, just to see if his skin really would change color.

Antonio Carrillo is also extremely shrewd and very ambitious. During the dangerous days of the clandestine struggle, Carrillo's family, which was politically connected to Batista, had arranged for him to leave Cuba for Spain. When he returned, he hid under the aegis of Celia Sánchez, Fidel's longtime companion, and also cultivated his old friend Pepín Naranjo, the patron of Carrillo's diplomatic career as ambassador, first to Morocco, then to Iraq, and finally to France, where Carrillo had replaced Ambassador Harold Gramatges in 1963.

I'd seen that in his campaign to gain absolute control over every function of the Paris embassy, Carillo had targeted one diplomat after another for elimination, and then replaced the fallen official with a handpicked Carrillo loyalist. But when he'd targeted Jesús Cruz, the head of Cuban intelligence in France, for back-channel elimination, he had crossed Cruz's superior, the powerful Comandante "Red Beard" Piñeiro. Although I would later learn that Carrillo had also sent bogus reports condemning my own behavior in Paris—reports that Commander Piñeiro had intercepted—at this moment I wished to avoid implication in anyone else's intrigues. My time for confrontation with Carrillo lay ahead.

In Paris, Ché Guevara's behavior had provided a telling contrast to Carrillo's and to other Cuban officials'. On a visit in early 1965, accompanied by Manresa as well as Emilio Aragonés and Osmany Cienfuegos, Camilo's brother, Ché was staying at the Hotel Vernet near the Champs Élyseés, where he liked to walk. He summoned me to his hotel room, where I found Ambassador Carrillo outlining a busy schedule of activities for Ché. Although he was well aware that Ché scorned all pomp and protocol, Carrillo obviously hoped to monopolize his time with official occasions. As he ticked off the list of events, Ché abruptly interrupted him.

"That's fine," he said, "but I prefer to spend my time in Paris without commitments. I'll go to this lunch you planned for today because it would be very rude for me to cancel now, at the last minute. But keep the rest of the program for other officials who like this kind of fuss more than I do.

"And don't worry," Ché added in his mocking way. "There'll be quite a few of them."

Carrillo was taken aback but quickly collected himself and said, with an affected smile, "Look, Comandante, I understand perfectly. But as ambassador I feel obliged to make sure you spend your time here as pleasantly as possible."

"The pleasantest thing for me," Ché answered, "is to do whatever I feel like when I'm not working."

He walked into the bathroom, as Carrillo and I rose to leave. Just then, however, he stuck his head out from behind the bathroom door. "José Luis is invited to lunch, too, isn't he?" Ché asked. He wanted company for what he foresaw would be a tedious afternoon.

"Of course, Comandante, of course," Carrillo answered quickly.

We arrived for the private lunch at the Embassy at 1:00 P.M. and were shown into the formal reception room by Roxana, Carrillo's wife, who was dressed as if this were an occasion at the Élysée Palace. Ché eyed her disapprovingly. When she asked if he'd care for a whiskey or perhaps an aperitif, he answered, "Thank you very much: I drink mate. If you don't have that, I prefer Cuban rum. Right now, all I am is hungry."

No one else drank, either. Within five minutes we were sitting around a grandly set table with plates of fine Czech china, silverware, and crystal glasses of various sizes. Osmany Cienfuegos sent comical glances toward Aragonés and then to me, arching his eyebrows several times as a sign that he anticipated a stiff and dismal lunch.

And it was dismal. Ché, clearly uncomfortable and impatient, spoke little. He answered questions in monosyllables or very short phrases. Immediately after we had finished our coffee he excused himself, saying he wanted to walk through the city. Offering his rather dry thank-you's for the lunch, he headed for the elevator with Aragonés, Cienfuegos, Manresa, and me close behind.

Carrillo, determined not to let Ché shake free, followed him to the elevator door. But Ché guessed his host's intentions and signaled us to hurry into the elevator with him as he said with finality to Carrillo: "Well, Mr. Ambassador, see you soon!" The door slammed shut in Carrillo's face.

"I don't like bourgeois ambassadors," Ché said as we descended to the street level, "especially if they're opportunists besides."

Ché took us on a long walk around the Left Bank and in and out of several bookstores before we broke up, agreeing to meet again at seven that evening. A dinner had been planned, but Ché decided he wanted to stay in that night with his new books. Only after Osmany insisted did Ché finally agree that we could go out without him, but he did set two conditions: There was to be no drinking, and the night was to end early.

Away from Ché, Aragonés became more himself. "It doesn't matter if it's expensive," he said as we tried to decide on a restaurant, "as long as it's good." Aragonés chose a Latin Quarter establishment called the México Lindo.

Ché's strictures notwithstanding, we ate—and drank—and were entertained by a guitar trio until three o'clock in the morning. The bill was astronomical and my three companions apprehensive. Ché was not going to be pleased.

When we got back to the hotel, the clerk told us that a bearded man, looking very annoyed, had come downstairs several times looking for us in the bar. Aragonés, Cienfuegos, and Manresa were no longer just apprehensive; now they were scared. Assuming that my presence might mitigate Ché's irritation, they insisted I accompany them to the room.

The ancient elevator creaked in the predawn stillness. As

silently as possible, the three made their way to the door, opened it carefully, and walked in, in their stocking feet. Ché, whose face was to the wall, appeared to be asleep. But as I exited this scene of grown men, revolutionaries, not daring to move a muscle, I heard Ché's grave, imperative voice.

"You finally finished stuffing yourselves with that shit," he said.

I smiled inwardly as I quietly closed the door.

Now, in Havana, my first priority as I waited for an apartment to become available and for Marie Christine to join me from Venezuela was to learn as much as I could about the complexities of bureaucratic life in order to know which strings to pull to help my uncle. I also needed to find out where my old friends were now working and whether or not their positions were powerful. In this the Mercedes-Benz was an important tool. My white 320SE with red leather seats was the only one in all of Cuba, and I had guessed that I would never be anonymous as long as I was in it.

I soon realized that at least in this respect my understanding of the leadership's mentality was totally on the mark. Almost every night I met for coffee and conversation with senior revolutionary officials such as Comandante Pedro Miret, a veteran of the Moncada assault and then minister of agriculture as well as acting military commander at La Cabaña, Ché Guevara's old post in the early days after the triumph. Miret, I knew, was obsessed with Mercedes-Benz automobiles. He owned a black 220 sedan and asked me countless questions about my 320. Through Miret, word of my Mercedes ultimately filtered up to Cuba's number one car enthusiast, Fidel, who let it be known via Miret that he was very interested in trying out my new car.

Fidel was then living more or less permanently with Celia Sánchez Manduley at her apartment on 11th Street in the Vedado district. Very thin, a heavy smoker, and a believer, like René Vallejo, in *santería* as well as a devotee of Santa Bárbara, whose image she worshipped at home, Celia Sánchez had been very close to Fidel since the early days in the Sierra Maestra.

Theirs was a deep personal relationship in which she saw to the many details of Fidel's life, and he trusted her absolutely. I don't think Fidel ever made an important political decision without consulting Celia. And I think she was a good partner for him—his "human face," some people said. A revolutionary with a point to press did well to cultivate her support; she could be a very effective advocate before Fidel.

A month after my arrival, Fidel summoned me with my Mercedes to Celia's apartment. At the corner of 11th and 8th, Miret told me to ignore the traffic light, which indicated we should turn left, and directed me to continue straight ahead on 11th, albeit very slowly. A guard armed with an FAL rifle stopped us. But when he recognized Comandante Miret, he saluted him and let us pass.

Fruit trees and carefully tended lawns lined that block, a contrast to Havana's general shabbiness. The tight security was evident everywhere. Guards stood at each intersection and on the roofs, and there was a permanent garrison in the middle of the block. We parked on the right, near a group of soldiers chatting in front of some locked garages.

When Fidel emerged from the building, he was followed by Celia Sánchez and Pepín Naranjo, who was then the first party secretary for Havana Province and Fidel's personal aide. The chief of Fidel's personal guards signaled to us to get into an Oldsmobile 60 with him while the "Galician," one of Fidel's drivers, got into the Mercedes.

The day was suffocatingly hot, but Fidel was wearing a long-sleeved uniform and a jacket over his shoulders. Later I learned from Comandante Vallejo that some years before, Fidel had been quite ill with pleurisy (a disease he was still very prone to). Also, because of a metabolic dysfunction, he did not feel high temperatures.

Fidel said good-bye to Celia and sat down in the front seat of the Mercedes, next to his driver, while I watched Naranjo get in the back. Several bodyguards got into the two other Oldsmobiles and off we went, a four-car motorcade with Fidel leading the way.

Once we reached the Vía Blanca highway, the white Mercedes began to pull away very fast from the three escort cars; Fidel apparently wanted to play a joke on his bodyguards. No matter how much we accelerated we couldn't catch up to him. Forty minutes later, and well behind Fidel, we reached our agreed-upon destination, a camp Fidel maintained near the town of Güines.

The retreat consisted of three tents, all the same size, set up in the shade of some leafy carob trees. Some distance away there was an open-air kitchen with stools and rustic benches. It was impossible for a stranger to get within half a mile of the camp: Fidel's personal bodyguards were stationed all around it. They were armed with high-powered rifles and the two-way radios they used to communicate with camp headquarters and with each other.

In the kitchen, when I went for a cup of coffee, the guards and Fidel's driver talked enthusiastically of the Mercedes. A few minutes later Pepín came to the front of the tent farthest from the kitchen, a Chesterfield cigarette in his hand, and signaled for me to come over. We embraced—we hadn't been together since 1963. He was the same Pepín of university days, down to his trademark cigarettes.

Inside the tent there were two army cots made up with carefully pressed white sheets. There was also a table covered with books and papers, a black-and-white cowhide stool, and a refrigerator, on top of which rested a large plate of fruit. To one side hung two of Fidel's olive-green uniforms, decorated on the shoulders with a rhombus on a red-and-black background with a star in the center. Fidel himself stood next to the tent refrigerator, drinking a glass of water. He wore scuffed open-toed leather slippers, his shirt was unbuttoned, and I could see his chest, smooth except for a clump of hair in the middle, and his stomach, already prominent and somewhat flabby.

Setting the glass on the refrigerator, Fidel extended his right hand and placed his left around my shoulder. "Shit, it's always hard to find somebody taller than me. How are you, Llovio?" he said, patting me on the back.

He walked to the cot, indicated that I should sit down on the stool near him, and lighting a huge cigar, he began: "So, tell me, did the Frenchwoman come or did she stay in France?"

"Right now she's visiting my parents in Venezuela," I answered, "but she'll be here soon."

"And have you found a job?" he continued, looking at the cigar with pleasure as he turned it around in his fingers.

"Aragonés promised to take care of that for me," I said.

He got up, went to the table, and began to search through the papers.

"If you have any problems, talk to Pepín. But tell me, how are things in France? What's new with the General?"

Fidel was now searching the table frantically. "Damn! That's what I was looking for," he exclaimed to Pepín, who had just walked in with a folder in his hand.

Fidel opened the folder, took out some papers, and said to Naranjo: "Send a cable to Carrillo. Tell him to buy a Mercedes just like Llovio's but in a dark color. I like it very much."

As I stood to say good-bye, he said, "Okay, we'll be seeing each other. Don't worry about a job—there's lots to do. You came at the right time."

Naranjo walked outside with me.

"He loves the Mercedes," Pepín said, as if to reassure me that my car had met with the highest approval.

All the Communist revolutionaries are great talkers, but they are also careful watchers and listeners. The grapevine is the lifeline of the upwardly mobile revolutionary. I knew word would spread of our motoring adventure with Fidel, and that it would be noted far beyond his immediate circle that my white 320SE was seen parked outside Celia's and Fidel's apartment in Vedado and in Fidel's private camp.

A SECRET PROPOSAL

A few days later Luc came to Havana to attend a MININT National Information Assembly. We arranged a secret meeting at a public park in Havana's Miramar section. There, Luc told me he wanted to get his family out of Cuba too. He looked even more haggard and strained than he had in the summer of 1963. Evidently he had given our predicament a lot of thought and concluded that the safest way to help our families was to secure the proper documents—the applications for exit visas and the authorizing seal—at MININT headquarters in Havana. Although MININT had these seals in each of its provincial offices, only a seal from MININT's national office could guarantee that no provincial officials would interfere. Luc knew exactly how disorganized the MININT offices were, and he assured me that I would have no problem getting my hands on these materials. That would be my job; he'd see to the rest.

We managed to have one more meeting, at the Bellomonte lookout over Guanabo Beach, in order for him to bring me the names of those MININT officials who would have the documents in their offices.

"I've brought you the list," Luc said, handing me a sheet of paper. "Tell me if you know any of them." Then he produced some documents. "Here's an example of an accepted application. It's filled in with the necessary information. Notice that there's a seal at the bottom of each page and a number on top. That's the authorization."

I looked at the documents slowly until I had memorized them. Then I read the list of names.

"I know a few of these people," I said. "I won't have any problem approaching one of them. The hard part is getting the forms and the seal."

"Do you have access to the MININT building?" he asked me.

"I can get it," I answered. "I know a lot of people there. But I have to choose the best spot, study it carefully, and be very clever not to arouse suspicions."

"You have until July to do it," Luc said urgently. "Three months. I'll see you in Santa Clara for the July 26th celebration. Don't call me before then, even if you get the forms and the seal. Fidel is preparing a mass exodus of the disaffected to the United States. That may complicate things, but don't worry; I've anticipated everything. It all depends on your getting the stuff. If we do manage to get our families out," he added, "we shouldn't see each other again."

He paused, looking off into the distance. He seemed oppressed, broken, as if nothing really interested him any more. "Only a situation like this would make me risk anything so dangerous," he said. "Really, you can't imagine how I'm suffering. I can't stand the tension anymore."

"I understand, Luc," I said. "Don't worry about me. I'd die before I said anything about this."

"The same goes for me. If I betray you, I betray myself as well. Now give me back the documents. You shouldn't keep them. Everything will work out, Slim. It's been lucky having you to count on," he said, looking into my eyes. We embraced, and then he walked away with tired steps.

Despite Luc's depression, our meeting had filled me with confidence. I was certain that we should both succeed and that I would soon be back in France.

Several days later Uncle Sergio called me in Havana. Because he was a counterrevolutionary, I could not be seen with him if I was to help him. To protect both of us, I arranged that we meet at a friend's house. I looked forward to seeing him, although I was also apprehensive. One part of me wanted to tell him the truth of my mission and to reassure him. My cautious side, however, told me that candor would be imprudent. I was afraid of some involuntary indiscretion on his part, either in Cuba or even later on in the United States. He might easily say to someone in the family, "My nephew helped me get out," and when his words reached a Cuban agent—as they inevitably would—that would cost me my own freedom and jeopardize Marie Christine as well.

Uncle Sergio looked even older than he had in prison. The lines on his forehead were much deeper, and they accentuated the bitter expression on his face. He spoke nervously, with his hands clasped, and he constantly rubbed the palm of one hand with his thumb.

The conversation went as I had dreaded it would. "You can help me get out of the country. It isn't hard for you to do," he argued. "You can appeal to your friends. You know almost all the revolutionary leaders."

"I can't use my friends for a matter like this," I answered. "Everybody runs away from this kind of proposal. It's absolutely forbidden to intercede for anyone who wants to leave the country."

"But you must be able to do something," he insisted. "You have friends—"

"Listen to me, Uncle Sergio," I said, interrupting him. "I can't do anything, and I can't trust anybody. The idea of friendship has changed a lot in this country. I'm sorry, believe me. I can't promise you something when I know it's impossible."

His mouth twisted into disappointment. His arms fell to his sides in a gesture of impotence, and he sat there looking at me in astonishment, as if he were seeing me for the first time.

I was anguished. It is one thing for someone you respect and love dearly, as I did my uncle, to turn on you, to move from trusting you to despising your cowardice. But for me to shove the knife of despair into a proud, defiant man of principle, now broken both physically and spiritually, was almost more than I could bear. For a moment, I felt the incautious urge to embrace him, to console him, to give him the support he so desperately expected to find in me.

But I could choose between redemption and responsibility for his safety. I just barely managed to control myself. Aloof and proper in the survival posture of a correct-thinking Communist revolutionary, I walked away from what would prove to be our last meeting.

My only solace after the painful encounter with my uncle was the belief that we all soon would be reunited outside the country, the nightmare behind us. Until then, I would be spiritually alien in my own country. There was not one person I could talk to, including Luc, for safety's sake.

The chronic emotional stress of such mental estrangement creates a powerful urge for physical refuge. I needed to be somewhere away from Havana for a time, and I left in a mood of gloom and anxiety for the nearby port city of Cojímar.

Cojímar was special to me. In my youth I had been there many times—often, as now, in need of its peace and tranquillity. In 1963, after visiting my uncle in prison, I'd gone to Cojímar for just such a visit, a moment alone to gather my strength.

Others, too, had savored Cojímar's tonic effect on the spirit. Sitting at the bar at La Terraza restaurant with my *mojito*, I thought back over my excursion there in 1954, when I'd made the acquaintance of Ernest Hemingway at almost exactly the spot where I was now lost in my reminiscences.

Then I had been at La Terraza with a girlfriend. Standing next to me at the bar was a tall, corpulent man with a proud face and heavy beard, talking in a powerful voice to a group of three or four people around him.

He had a very poor command of conversational Spanish and appeared to be under the influence of drink. As he spoke, he gestured dramatically. With one flourish, his elbow caught my glass and sent it crashing to the floor.

He apologized, asked the bartender to give me another drink on his bill, and unconcernedly returned to his audience. In a few moments he was waving his arms again, and again off went my drink.

This time I stood up, visibly annoyed. Aware that any further apologies were useless, the garrulous raconteur put his arm around my shoulder and smiled so spontaneously and warmly that my anger disappeared at once.

My companion and I soon joined his circle of listeners. He told stories of lions and tigers and jungle adventures that were absolutely fascinating, although I wondered if his inspired retelling didn't owe as much to the liquor as it did to the actual details of what he'd done and seen.

At the end of the night, I was fairly well sodden with rum myself. When we introduced ourselves, I barely made out his name and remembered only that the others had called him "Papa."

Hemingway had just published *The Old Man and the Sea* and would soon win the Nobel Prize. But at the time I met him, he was not particularly famous in the Spanish-speaking world. We saw each other in Cojímar from time to time that year. During one of our conversations over dinner Hemingway told me that the ambience of the port city put him in touch with his work, made it easier for him to write.

Ours was a casual friendship, one centered on our mutual fondness for Cojímar, a place we both saw as sanctuary. In 1965, four years after "Papa" had died, I found myself again in Cojímar, sitting there alone at the bar with my *mojito*, thinking of him and of my own, unfinished journey.

A FAREWELL

As it turned out, I didn't have to worry about where to live. Emilio Aragonés offered me one of several luxurious houses and penthouses in the best neighborhoods of Havana. All I had to do was select what I wanted, he said. Instinct told me not to take advantage of this largesse, however. Nor did life in the grand style suit my purpose. If I were to choose an extravagant home, my life style might be the focus of others' envy. The last thing I wanted were enemies in the revolution who might stand in the way of my uncle's leaving the country or jeopardize my own situation in Cuba. Besides, I had no need for a large house and its superfluous accessories.

In the end, I chose a small, pleasant two-bedroom apartment on "I" and 23rd Streets in the Vedado. It had a refrigerator, gas stove, and air conditioner, all in good working order. Also, it was near hospitals and the district's luxury hotels, with their privileged utility grids—valuable protection against the blackouts and frequent water shortages that most other areas of the capital were long accustomed to under the revolutionary regime.

One night in April 1965, several months before Marie Christine would join me from Venezuela and while I was still pursuing at MININT the delicate matter of the exit papers and proper
seals, there came an insistent ring at my door. I answered it to
find a man from MININT.

"José Luis Llovio?" he asked.

I nodded warily.

"You'll have to come with me. Someone you know wants to
see you. Excuse me, but he's asked me not to mention his name."

I got ready to leave with him, mystified at his mission. His
relative politeness to me and the extreme care I'd taken not to
rouse suspicion at MININT convinced me that I was in no danger. But as we traveled the Pinar del Río road west, I had no clue
where I was being taken, or why.

After a time the driver turned onto a narrow dirt road,
where a guard recognized him and waved us along. Five minutes
later we pulled up to a dimly lit wooden cabin. A man stood at
the door, silhouetted by light. I couldn't recognize him.

"José Luis," he said in a familiar voice. "Want some mate?"

It was Ché.

At that moment, Ché had been missing from public life for
nearly a month, and there had been some uninformed international speculation that he had run afoul of Fidel, or Raúl, or even
President Osvaldo Dorticós. Inside Cuba, the disappearance had
created much less curiosity; "the demands of the revolution"
was a blanket explanation for most unexplained comings and
goings.

But I, like everyone else in contact with the revolutionary
leadership, was fully aware that Ché had been having troubles.
In Algiers for the Economic Seminar on Afro-Asian Solidarity the
past February, Ché had delivered a speech sharply critical of
Socialist countries' policies toward underdeveloped nations. He
had not singled out the Soviets, but the address nonetheless had
generated great controversy. It was the first time that a Cuban
leader, besides Fidel himself, had dared publicly criticize other
Socialist countries. Ché's directness in Algiers had caused such
perplexity in Havana that, contrary to practice, no text of this
major address had been officially published.

"How are you?" he asked as I walked inside with him. The
interior, lit by a single dim bulb, was covered in dust and nearly
bare of furniture. It didn't appear that Ché, or anyone else,
actually occupied the cabin.

"You must be wondering why so much mystery," he then said, correctly interpreting the look on my face. "But I really don't want anyone to know where I am."

Ché was preempting any thought I might have entertained of asking him where he'd been, what he was doing, or where he might be headed next. He volunteered that he'd seen Alberto Granados, his fellow Argentine and boyhood friend, then living in Havana, but would say no more to me than "I've prolonged this secret flying visit so I could talk with you a little while. We won't have the chance again for a long, long time."

His asthma was bad again that night. The dust hung in the air around us, and the thick atmosphere, eerily lit by the bare electric bulb, sent him gasping at intervals for his inhaler.

"I heard you found a place to live," he said, motioning for me to sit. After pouring us both a glass of mate from his large thermos, he added, "When's your wife coming?"

"I expect her in July," I answered.

For whatever reason, he then felt obliged to repeat his insistence on the secrecy of this meeting. "I don't want you to say anything to anybody," Ché said firmly. He was now seated on a rickety stool. "We've always had good arguments, and we've been united in our battle of words. That's what I want today too."

This remark somewhat overstated my role in our many conversations. I had not openly disagreed with Ché or ever contradicted him. Mostly I'd listened and asked questions. It was this habit of questioning he found challenging, as most Cubans wouldn't dare query a revolutionary leader on delicate matters.

"They tell me," I began, "that you delivered a fiery speech in Algiers. Is it true you gave the Socialist countries hell?"

"Listen!" he shot back in what I recognized as feigned exasperation. "You never get tired of asking the most fucking annoying questions, do you? You haven't stopped hounding me with them since I met you."

Ché was now smiling, stretching his legs. "I didn't tear anybody apart," he said evenly. "I only told the truth. The Socialist countries are obliged to help underdeveloped nations and to help them disinterestedly. That's the price they must pay; the Soviet Union more than any other, because it was the first Socialist country in the world. All the Soviets' agreements about peaceful coexistence, their flirtations with the capitalists, are a death blow to the liberation of underdeveloped countries. None of it helps to wipe out exploitation of one man by another. On the contrary, it fosters it. The Soviets are behaving just like the imperialists. They're losing their essence, which is man. I mean *man* in the broadest sense, because as far as I'm concerned, *man* means humanity."

Ché rose and paced, a familiar scene in our encounters. He moved from one side of the room to the other, his arms crossed behind him and his mind only partially on me as he began to think out loud.

"I don't understand why they refuse to supply weapons to the liberation guerrillas [in Latin American and Africa]," he continued. "That's how they oppose the liberation of oppressed people, just like that! They don't supply weapons! And then the Chinese keep wanting Cuba to join them in their stupid disagreement with the USSR. And the Yanqui imperialists are taking full advantage of it."

Ché was referring to the deepening ideological rift between the Soviets and the Chinese, who, under Chairman Mao, had violently rejected the doctrine of peaceful coexistence and accused the USSR of pursuing bourgeois economic policies.

"Everybody's looking out for his own interests," Ché went on. "There's always a condition, an *if*, and as long as there's an *if* there'll never be a disinterested proletarian internationalism that's really Communist."

I'd never seen him like this before. Ché was distracted, querulous, upset.

"Right now," he said portentously, "the Soviets are on the verge of approving an economic reform based on material incentives." This was exactly what Ché had confidently predicted the Soviets would not do in our previous discussion at the Ministry of Industry. "Do you know what that means?" he now said. "It's a step backward for the establishment of Socialism. The USSR will be back where they started at the beginning of their revolution. They'll destroy man's noble, unselfish aspiration to be socially useful."

Ché, for whom revolution was a first principle of life, was struggling not to overreach himself in his criticism of the Soviets. He could never say in public what he was saying to me, lest it somehow damage the Cuban revolution. But he was clearly torn.

"The Soviets," he went on, "have been good to Cuba. They

gave us weapons so we could defend ourselves, and that's what we've done. But we don't need their rockets! Like cowards, they gave them to us only to take them back again the first time the Yanquis let out a yelp."

Then he returned to his puzzlement. "Why aren't they helping other revolutionaries?" he asked. "They've changed a lot since the October crisis. They're on the defensive. But we won't back down! We'll go on helping all the liberation movements. If they want a rifle they'll have it, even if we have to make it out of thin air. Our only hope is not to give up even one iota of our principles."

He held up his pinched thumb and forefinger. "Not even this much! The Cuban revolution must become the symbol of irreversible struggle for all the peoples of Latin America, Asia, Africa. Our internationalist duty is—it must always be—not merely to help but to encourage the guerrilla core anywhere in the world. That's where it will all begin."

The Soviet example notwithstanding, Ché believed his New Man could emerge in Cuba. What seemed to obsess him were the many threats to an independent, authentic Cuban revolution. And, for emphasis, he stated and restated his fundamental ideological truths.

"The Cuban revolution has to transform the mental structures of man," he said, addressing himself now to me. "It has to educate him toward internationalism and nobility, free him from materialism. At the moment, when man thinks only about himself and not about the collectivity, about his country, about humanity itself—that is when the revolution will lose the struggle.

"The authentic revolutionary is generous, he owns nothing, he loves humanity, he dies for the revolution! I have no material possessions, and I'm happy to be useful, working, and helping forge the revolution. I've fought in Cuba, my adopted country. I could fight in Argentina, my native country, or in any other country where I was needed. My motivation would be the same: to do my duty."

In this sense, Ché himself was the New Man, and since he found fulfillment being "useful, working, and helping forge the revolution," it is perhaps understandable that he could foresee legions of New Men thus happily living for one another, moved only by moral incentives.

Such vigorous idealism, together with Ché's open disdain for much of the Soviets' orthodoxy, had made him many enemies among old PSP members.

"I can't be a politician—I don't know how," he explained. "I love the truth. I love to speak it, to recognize it. And that's why many people criticize me behind my back. To be a politician, you have to take many factors into account, manipulate them, lie if it's necessary. I'm no good at that. I'll never be any good at that.

"I feel tied to Fidel, to this country, to the revolution wherever it may appear," Ché reiterated. "I'm not the only one. There are many who think as I do. I consider them my brothers.

"The others, the counterrevolutionaries and those so-called revolutionaries committed to orthodox, rigid ideas—I hate them with all my heart."

While most of the PSP members remained outside the key government posts they'd held before the sectarian crisis, the old Communists continued to exert indirect influence in Cuba through their protector, Raúl Castro.

I was very surprised to hear that there was such ideological controversy about the Soviets in the upper reaches of Fidel's government. Nor had I heard that the PSP had been attacking Ché over it.

"I'll fight the counterrevolutionaries with a gun; I'll use words against the rest," he continued. "But believe me, it's easier to fight a counterrevolutionary on the battlefield with a rifle in your hand than to fight a sectarian and opportunistic 'revolutionary' who doesn't have the courage to say to your face: 'This is what I believe.'"

Again, Ché's honesty was leading him to say what he never would utter in open company for fear that he could harm the revolution. There was anger in his voice.

"The interests of Soviet ideology—and I mean Soviet, not Socialist—are promoted in Cuba by the same men who have done so much harm to the revolution. They are men without morality and without prestige and yet they become more and more powerful."

Then the old optimism reasserted itself, Ché's bedrock faith in the revolution, which for him was synonymous with Fidel. "Fidel's carrying on a silent war inside a whirlwind," he averred, "and he'll come out of it the winner, I'm certain. Cuba can't be a mere pawn. It won't yield to either side [the Soviet Union or the United States]. It will stay on the side of reason, close to true revolutionary sentiments. Cuba will not be anybody's satellite.

We'll continue making our own judgments and we'll maintain our own personality, our own originality."

Ché had once been among the revolution's most ardent admirers of the Soviets. In fact, since returning from his first trip there in 1961 he had proclaimed the virtues of the Soviet system on national Cuban television.

"Why," I asked at a convenient break in his discussion, "have you praised the disinterested aid of the Soviets so much in the past?"

"Because the Soviets helped this country a great deal," Ché retorted. "And I think they'll keep on helping her. Without the USSR, the revolution would have ceased to exist a long time ago. But Soviet aid becomes more and more dangerous for Cuba. Whoever keeps you wants to rule you. Do you think the USSR would continue helping us if Cuba allied herself with the Chinese now? How can we maintain our own revolutionary position if we depend on a single source of aid? In politics you have to be able to give something if you want to get something. It's always been that way.

"Well, in spite of the influence of Raúl and other pro-Soviet forces, I'm certain Fidel will uphold the principles of the Cuban revolution. He'll arrange it so we won't have to depend on the USSR or on any other country. In the long run I think that Raúl himself, when he thinks deeply about Cuba and frees himself from his orthodox prejudices, will realize that the best course for this revolution is to keep on being Cuban and independent—a new road, an example for oppressed countries. As for the other forces, the old Communists, I tell you they'll survive only as long as Raúl protects them. Without him, they'll be sunk. They can't stand me, and I don't care. I can't stand them either. I don't think they're sincere revolutionaries. They're too sly. They're too damaged by Stalinism to be useful."

Acerbic as ever and still the energetic revolutionary, Ché also seemed disillusioned to me. His voice conveyed a sense of impotence; he was changed.

"Well, José Luis," he said toward morning, "this is just a temporary farewell. Remember, you mustn't tell anyone that you've seen me. Seal your lips. And you mustn't say anything about what we've discussed, unless we save it for my memoirs." He gave me a strange smile. "By then we'll both be old enough."

As we walked outside to a jeep that had been brought for

him, Ché seemed to be giving himself a lecture while ostensibly speaking to me.

"You have to believe in the revolution about everything else," he said. "Beyond criticisms and discrepancies, what matters is to be a faithful and unconditional servant of the revolution. That's what I've been up to now and what I'll always be in Cuba, or any other place on earth where they need me. I could never stand in the way of any revolutionary process, least of all in Cuba."

I thought to myself that that was the strangest remark of the night. Was there more to this "secret flying trip" then what I could suppose from our conversation?

"Why do you say that?" I asked.

Ché caught the intent of my question. He stared away for a moment, then looked at me in the half-light, his eyes shining. He put his hand on my forearm and then spoke.

"Don't think there's any problem between Fidel and me. There isn't. I have my ideas and I know that he understands them and even shares them. But he's a politician. I'm not. He is the Commander in Chief of this revolution. He's obliged to act politically in order to protect it. He can't evade certain circumstances.

"I've recently talked for hours with him. I've talked to him like a brother and I've told him frankly, with no ambiguity, everything I feel, my most intimate thoughts. I've given him my arguments and I've pointed out to him what I think are the dangers to the revolution, both internally and externally.

"You can talk to Fidel. It's more difficult with the other leaders because they hold on to narrow concepts that leave no margin for the preservation of our revolution's originality. I want you also to understand that I have no problems with Raúl, although I can't have a dialogue with him.

"But I no longer have confidence in the USSR. It's true they help us, but we're only an unavoidable problem for them. They can't step back, because they'd lose prestige among the underdeveloped countries [if they dropped Cuba]. In Algiers, I warned them. I explained the correct course of action. Now I hope they're receptive to my message. And I call it *my message* because it really was mine alone.

"Everything will work out, you'll see. Fidel will know how to make the Cuban revolution the guiding light for the underdeveloped countries. Our path will be independent. If it isn't, we will become like the rest of the Socialist countries. I have nothing against them, but I think they must become more aware of the importance of man. Before they think about their own advantage, they have to help others. They have to be generous without imposing conditions."

Ché then sank into a kind of lethargy. He appeared spiritually spent. For the first time, I pitied him. He seemed to me to be truly a Don Quixote whose limitless confidence in human beings kept him from thinking objectively and dispassionately about the real prospects for the Cuban revolution and, sadder still, about his own situation.

"Well," he then said, stirring from his momentary daze, "I'm counting on your discretion. I trust in that, you know. As always, I've enjoyed talking to you."

Ché was contemplative for a brief while as we stood by the jeep. Then he made his final remark to me. "You know something?" he said. "Being a revolutionary is very hard. But staying one is harder."

We parted in silence. Ché followed my car back down the dirt road to the main Pinar del Río route and then turned off into the night.

When I arrived home, it was nearly dawn. But I made some strong coffee and sat down to record that night's disconcerting conversation. I had thought that, especially at the top, the revolution was monolithic, and now I saw that it wasn't. I decided to try to piece together my past conversations with Ché, to understand how his ideas had developed. And so I took out my notes from five and a half years of intermittent discussions with him and searched through them for clues about what I'd heard from him in that dusty cabin.

From the beginning of our acquaintanceship Ché had been absolutely consistent in his adherence to the ideal of the New Man, his hatred for imperialism, and his blind faith in the revolution. But in my notes I could trace an indirect yet distinct tone of doubt and then concern about the Soviets, dating from the 1962 missile crisis and intensifying with his final trip to the Soviet Union in 1964.

Now that I knew where his thoughts had led him, I could see in our earlier conversations Ché's realization that Soviet economic planning was not so highly developed, and that aid from the Socialist bloc was not so unselfish.

He had been more explicit over the years about the crisis of production in these countries, just as he'd acknowledged the same problem in Cuba. But Ché was constitutionally incapable of seeing the roots of these problems in the system itself. Or did he believe idealistically in Marxist-Leninist theory but not in the system that implemented it?

The difficulties thus far in sustaining rational industrial production, he had insisted, resulted from "the application of certain noxious and dangerous mechanisms that imply movement backwards as far as the development of man's consciousness is concerned"—meaning that material incentives corrupt revolutionary consciousness.

Ché had emphasized this on another occasion. "If the economy in the Socialist countries isn't working," he'd said, "it's for very specific reasons. The superiority of the system itself is undeniable."

And what, I had asked at still another time, of the lax work habits we'd both seen in Cuba? Ché's response: "The root of the *campesinos'* and the workers' lack of interest must be sought in the attitudes of the leaders, who become bourgeois by granting themselves privileges at the people's expense and become a bad example to them."

Ché knew as well as anyone in Cuba that the tone and substance of the revolutionary leadership was set by Fidel. But to Ché, Fidel was the revolution and so could not be criticized. Ché referred to everyone *but* Fidel when once he told me: "A leader should be austere and self-denying. He should earn respect through his values, his dedication to work, his modesty, his proper use of the resources that the state places at his disposal. Our leaders are losing these habits very quickly. I may have many defects, but no one will ever be able to say that I am more privileged than the people, or reproach me for laziness or lack of responsibility in my work."

Ché could never see that the system demanded that one *seem*, not *be*, a true and loyal revolutionary. In fact, from everything I'd heard him say, he could never view Fidel except as the embodiment of the revolution. Thus, Ché was correct in foreseeing the possibility that Cuba would follow the Soviet path, but he was wrong when he thought Fidel would prevent it.

As Ché prepared to set out on his undisclosed mission, he had obliquely acknowledged that he was a stumbling block between Cuba and the Soviets. So, faithful to the end, he was leaving Cuba. This romantic, idealistic, fanatically revolutionary man was removing himself from the process to which he had given so many years of struggle and, out of paradoxical loyalty, separating from the man he'd once described in a poem as his "burning prophet of the dawn."

THE ASSIGNMENT

For someone whose world view was formed in pre-Communist Cuba and then in an open Western society since 1958, it was impossible to comprehend immediately how much Cuba had changed by 1965. For all my care and caution, my calculating steps such as buying the Mercedes, living modestly, and maintaining my revolutionary correctness even to the point of emotionally injuring my uncle, I couldn't foresee or grasp the real dangers around me. Specifically, I was still too ignorant of the new order to be at all alarmed when José Abrantes, the MININT deputy minister for State Security, mentioned at lunch one day that I should consider working at the Ministry of Construction, then headed by Osmany Cienfuegos.

"I'm particularly interested in having you work there," Abrantes said. "But first you ought to take some time to get back in touch. Life is very different here than in Paris. You should visit your friends, go to their houses, go to their parties, make new friends. It's a good idea for you to have a social life."

I knew I had to take some sort of job—for the time being, Aragonés had been supporting me with PURSC funds—and so Abrantes's suggestion that I first devote myself to mixing socially fit very conveniently with my own scheme. The more acquaintances I made within the revolutionary bureaucracy, I reasoned, the more protected I would be in case something went wrong with my plan—and the more trustworthy I would seem.

And so I took Abrantes' proposal as something very ordinary, not suspecting any devious intent or how dearly I would be made to pay for my naïveté.

The Ministry of the Interior, MININT, was one of the most strategically important agencies in Cuba. Not only was it responsible for the police, exit permits, and other functions, but MININT had the heavy duty of fighting the enemies of the revolution. State Security was charged with that mission—and Abrantes was its chief.

Ironically, my plan to help my uncle and his wife leave the country, which I had anticipated to be full of risk and danger, turned out to be quite simple. I had no problem acquiring the application and the seal. I knew many high-ranking officials in MININT and met with them frequently in their offices in Havana. The administrative disorganization in government offices was so extreme at that time that all I needed to do was keep my eyes open. Soon enough I found what I needed, mixed up with other documents on various desktops at MININT.

In July 1965, I traveled with these materials to Santa Clara and delivered them to Luc at the Los Caneyes motel, where Marie Christine and I had stopped for breakfast two years earlier on our tour of the island. There wasn't much to say to Luc this time. His job was to sneak the doctored exit papers into the MININT immigration offices in Camagüey. The official machinery of the state would then execute our plan for us. Unfortunately, it would be too risky for Luc to attempt to inform me if my uncle and his wife were finally free. No news, in a sense, would be good news, but many months of anxiety lay ahead for me.

Santa Clara was chosen that year as the site of the main July 26th Movement anniversary, so Luc and I had a legitimate reason for being there. After we parted, I remained in the provincial capital to hear Fidel's address.

The annual celebration is rotated among Havana and the various provincial capitals, where the local citizenry savor their turn as hosts to the main July 26th gathering. It always means, at least for a short time, relative abundance, as Fidel concentrates Cuba's resources on the chosen site. In honor of the holiday, construction is ordered begun on schools, hospitals, movie theaters, museums, and other public facilities. Although the ambitious building programs are sometimes impossible to execute, the projects are always declared finished in time for the celebration. Fidel, or some high official acting on his behalf, will travel to one of the new projects, trailing contingents of foreign guests and as large a press corps as can be lured or directed to cover the splashy inaugural ceremony. Propaganda is one machine that does work in Cuba.

The main streets and parks of the host city are spruced up, again for television and Fidel's foreign visitors. Efficiency suddenly returns to every sphere of service. Hotels and restaurants are better run. The employees are responsive, rooms improve, and menus are diversified. The entertainment schedule is upgraded, and the best orchestras, performing groups, and artists appear in town.

In Santa Clara, as elsewhere each year, the center of the city was equipped with temporary wood- and palm-thatched kiosks selling beer, rum, pork and goat meat, tamales, cracklings, fried green plantain, and other traditional Cuban foods that were normally unavailable.

Fidel always speaks at the main July 26th celebration, and in Santa Clara in 1965, the foreigners seated on the podium to hear him were a sorry assemblage, roasting in the direct sun with their red faces under Cuban straw hats, vainly flapping newspapers, magazines, and placards for any breath of air.

The speech before the huge crowd was extremely long. And it was Fidel's classic July 26th address. As usual, Fidel's magnetic oratorical style had the crowd under his full control.

Although these speeches vary in their details, they generally follow a single pattern: First, Fidel talks about the attack on the Moncada Barracks, commemorating anew the bravery of that day's heroes and emphasizing their close political kinship with Cuban martyrs of the 1930s revolutionary movements, as well as with the *mambises,* those who fought in the nineteenth-century War of Independence. Then he expresses his great satisfaction and pride in the people of the host province, the members of the party and its mass organizations, and all those who've helped the revolution reach its goals.

He dwells on advances in health and education, recounts all the recently completed projects in the host city's vicinity, and reads a long list of economic statistics that prove progress is being made all over the country, even when the reality significantly differs. His next theme is past difficulties and present threats; he tells of the need to work harder and to be ready for battle and the defense of the revolution's achievements.

At this point, Fidel turns to his confidence that difficulties will be overcome, and he promises prosperity in five, or ten, or twenty years. He takes up any convenient international issue as a means of furiously attacking the CIA, imperialism, and the United States' embargo. Every year, he contrasts the hated Yanquis with the honorable Soviets, and speaks again of the "shining future": always the future.

Then Fidel shouts "*¡Viva!*" several times for the valiant fighters for independence, the heroes of Moncada, proletarian internationalism, Socialism, the USSR, and Marxist-Leninism. Finally comes the passionate and resounding "*¡Patria o Muerte! ¡Venceremos!*" and the automatic thunderous applause.

As soon as Fidel finished the 1965 edition of the speech, I left immediately for Havana. In a few days Marie Christine would finally arrive from Venezuela—and I was longing to see her after three months of solitude, and to hear every detail of her travels with Marielle.

THE STRAITJACKET

According to Pepín Naranjo, Fidel was among the many Cubans who had followed with interest the 1960 press reports of Marie Christine's abduction and our marriage in France. "I admire the courage of the French girl," Pepín quoted Fidel as saying. "She exchanged a palace for this Cuban craziness."

I met her at the Havana airport with elation that my long loneliness was now over and a sure sense that the months ahead, while trying, would end with our safe and happy return to France and with Uncle Sergio's freedom.

But I found my wife quite tense and apprehensive. With our daughter remaining behind in Caracas, where she'd stay, at least for the time being, with my parents, Marie Christine was now cut off from all familiar surroundings. Furthermore, she was coming to Cuba in 1965 as a new resident, not a tourist. When she had visited Cuba, it had been a tropical island full of revolutionaries, exciting and exotic, but I could see now that the prospect of actually living in such a place was frightening her. I could certainly understand it.

She was also a woman finely attuned to mood, especially my mood. In Paris, I hadn't anticipated the added strain of masking my intents and concerns once I was in Cuba, directly under the stress of seeing to my uncle's escape. Now on our apartment terrace in Havana my mind would wander and she would ask perceptively, "What's happening to you?"

Still, Marie Christine made a rapid adjustment to yet another sea change in her life. I introduced her to La Tía and her circle of friends, people who soon became a sort of surrogate family for Marie Christine. Because she spoke Spanish perfectly and because of the quiet charm that drew people to her, Marie Christine easily integrated into my social circle. And her isolation eased somewhat when I was able to find her work at ICAIC as a French teacher. Her salary was good and the position, together with her nationality, gave her access to the only reasonably well stocked stores in the city, those shops reserved for foreign technicians and professional workers.

Of course I knew that she knew something was wrong with me, and I was tempted over and over to reveal what our move to Cuba was all about. In retrospect, I can see that my trying to spare her my anxieties had the practical effect of increasing her own. I'll never know how much more difficult it would have been for her to know the truth. But right then I was ingenuously certain that the charade would soon come to an end. My silence would protect her by shielding her from the tension of living a double life, a tension I knew she could not withstand. To survive until we could leave seemed only a matter of caution and patience to me.

In a short while I would be violently disabused of that notion.

The call came from State Security only days after Marie Christine's arrival in July 1965. I was to go immediately to a house in the Kohly district of Havana where a MININT official was waiting for me. As in the previous April when Ché had summoned me via a MININT officer, I had no idea what was afoot—except that I couldn't imagine it had anything to do with my uncle, or I would have been arrested immediately.

On that score, I was correct. The official, a sepulchral-looking fellow with yellowish skin, slanted eyes, and an exaggerated martial crew cut, met me in his olive-drab uniform, perfectly pressed and spotless. His polished boots shone like patent leather. I recognized him as one of Abrantes's aides-de-camp, and so I guessed that whatever was about to take place would be related to my previous conversation at lunch with Abrantes, although I couldn't imagine how.

He asked me to sit and began to speak, without preamble.

"*Compañero* Llovio," he said, "the revolution needs you."

That phrase, when used by a high-ranking official, marked this as a matter of greatest importance. It is used only when a directive is being passed down from Fidel.

"Your proven revolutionary record," he went on, "makes us confident that we can trust you with important secret work. If you accept, you'll have to do exactly what we tell you. Under no circumstances will you ever be able to share it with anyone. Don't ask me why. I can't say any more."

He stood before me.

"Now tell me, will you accept the task that the revolution entrusts to you? Think it over. I'm going to leave and I'll be back in fifteen minutes to hear your answer."

As soon as he left, I suddenly began to have the same sensations that I had felt during my clandestine days. The taste of danger flooded my palate. My senses felt acutely sharpened, my temples throbbed, and my muscles clenched. My mind blocked off everything that did not concern the immediate threat. It was a kind of feline transformation, an instantaneous mobilization of my reflexes.

I had no idea what the task would be, but I knew that my answer would have to be yes. To say no to what was essentially an order, not a request, from Fidel would be political suicide and would mean my ruin. We would never get out.

When I felt the official's presence behind me—the weight of his stare on the back of my neck—I didn't turn around. Whatever followed from this meeting would demand of me every resource of ingenuity and courage I had. I put a cigarette in my mouth, and as I was going to light it, his cigarette came over my shoulder and drew near the flame.

"Have you decided, *Compañero* Llovio?" asked the official.

I faced him. "My decision was made from the very moment you asked the question," I replied. "Didn't you realize that?"

He obviously thought my answer insolent. His eyes flashed with hatred that quickly disappeared and was replaced once again by the same cold expression. "All right then, you know the rules of the game," he said. "Absolute obedience and discretion. No one can know anything about this work, not even your recently arrived wife. Understand?"

I saw, of course, the underlying implication of his last statement. He knew everything about my life. But all I said was: "That clarification is unnecessary." This man was acting as if these orders were coming from him, but I knew he was the lowest executioner.

He opened a glistening leather briefcase and took out a folder full of papers. After leafing through them for a few seconds, he began to read a long list of names: Osmany Cienfuegos, Pedro Miret, Emilio Aragonés, Rolando Cubela, and those of many other leaders close to Fidel as well as several fighters from the Sierra and the urban struggle. Then he stated the places I had recently frequented, with a brief description of what I'd done and the time I'd spent in each of them.

That they had been spying on me was obvious. But I listened to him without moving, totally without expression. Even though he was only obeying orders, I could tell he was enjoying these moments thoroughly. His desire to intimidate was clear. His voice had an inquisitorial, rather sadistic tone, and from time to time he shot a quick glance at me from the corner of his eye to study my reactions, as if he was searching for some questioning gesture or look of surprise on my part.

I could not afford to seem in any way affected by his tactics. When he paused, I spoke up. "That minute analysis of my activities during these last few months—is that the undercover work you want from me, or is there something else?"

He looked somewhat startled, but, showing his good psychological training, he instantly recovered. "Your work consists of mingling even more with these people whom you know so intimately. You will go to their parties, their meetings, you will go on outings and trips, and you will inform us in writing, every forty-eight hours, of all the details: what they say, do, plan to do. Of course, your information will be correlated with that of other *compañeros* who have also been honored with this mission entrusted to them by the Commander in Chief. You show a deep revolutionary spirit by accepting the assignment without objections or questions of any kind," he added, his eyes fixed on mine.

"Memorize this list of names. If others are to be added, we will inform you immediately."

That was the end of our meeting.

As irritatingly self-assumed as I may have seemed to the MININT officer, I was totally confused. This exchange did cast a new light on my conversation with José Abrantes. Now I realized there was nothing at all innocent about his suggestion that I work at the Construction Ministry, headed by Osmany Cienfuegos, one of the main objects of my reporting. I also understood why he had urged me to lead a full social life, as this would be my opportunity to mingle with those officials who were under investigation.

It seems that MININT, at Fidel's direction, had been interested in the life style of the revolutionary leadership for at least four months. But why? Fidel didn't need spies to tell him his government was filled with hedonists; that was evident even from my casual experience with them in Paris.

I wondered if this was some sort of trap, or test, set for me. But I could not imagine why that would be. As I drove away from the house, none of my speculations seemed to account for this assignment, and rational analysis began to give way to Socialist paranoia, a condition I would come to know intimately. I sensed that I had been placed in great danger, with no choice but to do as I was told.

Yet my having said yes produced in me an anguished feeling of disgust. I felt like an inanimate object, a thing that could be manipulated and treated with absolutely no thought or concern for my principles or feelings. *Welcome to the revolution,* I thought.

To the revolution there could be no greater honor than working on its behalf; but to me, my moral code, deeply instilled in me from the beginning of my life, would be shattered by this assignment. At this moment nothing practical was in my mind—I could not analyze circumstances or implications. My head was full of only one realization: I was about to do something I had never in my life expected to do. If I refused, I would jeopardize my uncle, my wife, and my daughter: everybody I cared for. For the first time in my life I lost my self-respect. I saw myself as low and contemptible, a creature without value.

When I was close to home, a wave of nausea made me stop the car beside the Malecón. I got out of the car and went over the wall, trying to control my retching. I felt shooting pains in my forehead, my temples, the back of my neck, and I had a strong bitter taste in my mouth.

A soft breeze cooled my face, but I still could not take a deep breath. I seemed to be inside a straitjacket that was holding me tighter, tighter, tighter. . . .

A nightmare was about to unfold. I was powerless to stop it—and utterly alone. If I could not tell Marie Christine about my plans for my uncle, how much more would I have to hide from her now. No way out, I saw. No way out.

Slowly I forced myself to control the wildness in my mind. I had to think about what it could mean that I was being asked to do this. Why would Fidel be spying on his closest friends?

LA DOLCE VITA

At that moment Fidel's behavior was a mystery to me. The more I tried to understand it, the less logical it seemed. Only years later was it obvious that I had been assigned a minor role in a vast network of interconnecting schemes and machinations Fidel had set in motion in 1965. Shrewd and diabolically complex, these strategems reveal Fidel's many-sided genuis for manipulation as well as his political acumen. Like many others, I was an innocent bystander, a loose thread now woven by chance into Fidel's Byzantine tapestry.

Sometime in early 1965, Rolando Cubela's CIA plot to assassinate Fidel had been discovered by his old friend Ambassador Antonio Carrillo in Paris. Thus alerted, Fidel did not have Cubela arrested at once but only had him watched; MININT needed time to discover who Cubela's co-conspirators might be. During this investigation, Fidel himself met several times, alone, with Cubela, a typical example of Fidel's temerity.

Fidel was able to act very freely in Cubela's case because, internally, Cuba was then in a time of relative political stability. Fidel's power had been consolidated four years earlier with the victory at the Bay of Pigs. A CIA-backed guerrilla insurgency in Las Villas and Matanzas provinces—an uprising supported by many local *campesinos*—had also been smashed. The counterrevolutionary activity of Cubans in exile had become more and more disorganized and ineffective, largely as a result of infiltration by Cuban Intelligence. And so Fidel could act with confidence.

CIA plots against the revolution and his life were nothing new to Fidel. Yet this one—headed by Cubela, a popular founding member of the Revolutionary Directorate and current president of the FEU—came to light just as another problem, one that permeated the entire revolutionary leadership, was threatening to seriously damage Fidel and the revolution itself. It is typical of Fidel to see such difficulties as opportunities, which is how he handled them.

Fidel called the crisis in Cuba's revolutionary leadership *La Dolce Vita*, "The Sweet Life," after the title of the Fellini film, then playing in Havana. He likened Fellini's tale of morally corrupt and effete Italians to the dissolution among his own officials, a phenomenon that dated from the beginning of the revolution.

There had been a progressive breakdown in the standards of conduct of most of the leaders, revealed in their irresponsible work habits, their use of state resources for private gain, their profligate spending while traveling abroad, and their parties, which generally became orgies. Fidel's own behavior fostered these conditions. In absolute contrast to the spare, self-abnegating life of virtue Ché preached and practiced, Fidel maintained several residences. He spent lavishly on himself and gave away as gifts luxury houses, cars, and such expensive items as waterproof Rolexes, the preeminent emblem of personal power in the early years of the revolution. He indulged his every whim, ate well, and was known in leadership circles for his womanizing. Not surprisingly, everybody followed the leader.

The dangers of *La Dolce Vita* were many. The great mass of Cubans who eked out their lives below the privileged elite, those who stood in line with their ration cards, endured shortages, lived in deteriorating houses, and were sustained, in the main, on Fidel's promises, couldn't fail to notice the heedless indulgence in which the country's leaders reveled. Very little caution was exercised in hiding the spoils of official life.

Abroad, these same high-living Cubans were becoming a source of embarrassment, too. As I'd seen in Paris, the majority of them showed neither restraint nor taste in their diversions. They went on lavish shopping sprees. They ignored the city's museums in favor of its brothels. And they passed over the everyday fare of Paris's working-class restaurants for its gaudiest and most expensive tourist meccas.

But these were only *La Dolce Vita*'s most blatant excesses. What had to worry Fidel even more was the high-ranking revolutionary leadership's more extreme administrative and moral degeneracy, which was leaving his key men open to exploitation and extortion. A set of photos, an incriminating recording—these were standbys of the espionage trade.

My task for MININT showed me how different this corruption was from what I had seen in a capitalist society. Unlike the politicians of Western democracies—men and women who are not necessarily expected to fulfill campaign pledges and whose occasional ethical lapses come as no great surprise to their constituents—hierarchs in Cuba are supposed to function more like priests of the state religion, Communism. They are the keepers of the revolutionary flame, high-minded and moral figures whose behavior should be an example to the people. When such leaders are exposed as dissolute, it is not a pardonable error but a transgression, as if they really were priests who had violated their sacred vows.

Here I was in a country where scarcity was a daily fact, and yet the ostentatious display of luxury by the leaders was flagrant and pervasive. The members of Fidel's leadership did not just have everything; they monopolized goods and services, defining themselves by their possessions. Day after day I saw them lead a privileged existence irreconcilable with the pieties about austerity they spouted on every occasion.

Because the people did not have any official channel through which to obtain additional food, a color TV, or an air conditioner, money acquired a disproportionate importance. The only way for them to have what the state gave the elite was to earn money in the informal economy by being illegal entrepreneurs, supplying goods and services not offered by the state, and in almost all cases stealing from the state to nourish the black market. Then they could afford to buy what they wanted, even though they risked being caught engaging in forbidden activity.

In the face of this situation, Fidel could not attack the corruption of the people without trying to eliminate that of the leadership. Cubela's case gave him the opportunity to launch a campaign against corruption from within. And so he assigned the investigation to Ramiro Valdés, founder and then head of the Interior Ministry, MININT.

Ramiro Valdés represented, with Raúl Castro, the most inflexible, coercive, and repressive strains within the Revolutionary Government. A small man, physically off-putting, with a dry, penetrating voice and a goatee, Valdés was known as narrow-minded, pretentious, and bitter. He surrounded himself at MININT with functionaries who knew all the slogans and shared his vindictiveness.

MININT officials believed themselves to be the front-line guardians of the revolution. Thanks in part to organizational help from the KGB, they comprised an efficient internal organ of repression devoted to controlling every aspect of every Cuban's life. Now the MININT State Security apparatus had reached down to me, in its directive from Fidel, and made me part of its information web.

The Ministry of Construction, where I'd begun to work in July 1965, was like the rest of Cuban bureaucracy: totally disorganized. My job was completely mechanical, and I gave it no thought. It was what happened after work that obsessed me. Almost every evening I had to assume my revolting assignment. My reports detailed who spoke to whom and where; what happened when and for how long; what people ate, drank, and smoked; who paired off with whom and how often.

As frequently as possible I absented myself from parties and gatherings, pleading illness or any other plausible excuse. But this ploy had limited utility. I had to make a credible show of Communist revolutionary zeal for my work, and I had to report all I saw. At every social occasion, I had to assume that one or more of the others present were similarly engaged. I knew that our reports would be scrutinized for omissions and inconsistencies.

In addition to the problems with his leadership that I and others were forced to document, Fidel was facing other internal problems as well. Under pressure, he chose October 5, 1965, as the date for the official establishment of a Communist Party in Cuba. Since the island was already a Marxist-Leninist country, it naturally followed that a domestic party would someday be launched. ORI (Integrated Revolutionary Organizations) had been a transitional body, torn apart by the sectarian crisis in 1962, Fidel's masterstroke against the old PSP. And ORI's successor, PURSC, was never meant to be a permanent organization but only a step toward the ultimate consolidation of a national Communist Party.

But Fidel's timing was curious. Many people might have read the move as a step backward into the Soviet fold, a reorganization emulating the orthodox Soviet model. Why would Fidel, who so assiduously promoted Cuba's independent image, risk creating such an impression? Why wouldn't he wait, as he might have, until 1966 or 1967 or even later?

One possible explanation is that a party structure would be a useful tool for solidifying and sustaining his power. A second motive might have been the legitimizing effect an official Communist Party lent Cuba as a model revolutionary country. Fidel not only excoriated Soviet foreign policy, but he was a stern critic as well of the Latin American Communist parties that, like the old Cuban PSP, had hewed slavishly to the Soviet line. With his own party in place, Fidel might now show by example that a Marxist-Leninist government could also be independent and truly revolutionary. The fact that this was an illusion, Fidel's posturing only at Soviet sufferance, did not make any difference to him.

Behind these involved geopolitical considerations, however, there lay a much simpler and very practical problem. Fidel had discovered that one of PURSC's very highest-ranking officials had become involved in a secret sexual scandal of such potential embarrassment to the revolution that the entire PURSC leadership was paralyzed, in crisis. Any leak of the story would have had disastrous consequences for the revolution's image. Whether or not this secret scandal forced Fidel's hand, it is true that he disbanded PURSC and established the Cuban Communist Party at a peculiar time coinciding with the suspected party official's removal to a lower administrative position.

Because of such scandals, MININT was interested in the life style of the leadership. Its principal focus of attention was how the leaders used their power for personal purposes. MININT was on the lookout for those instances when restaurant bills, rented houses at the beach, or liquor tabs were paid by the state—which was always the case. Its officials were also eager to know how the leaders spent the state's hard currency on foreign goods.

As the days and weeks of my documenting these excesses lengthened into months, it became plain to me that Fidel was orchestrating an unprecedented and massive underground examination of his leadership. I guessed, at first, that he would move against the worst offenders before the upcoming Tricontinental Conference in January 1966, so that the revolution could put on a clean face for its foreign guests. Osmany Cienfuegos, minister of construction and widely known as one of *La Dolce Vita*'s most enthusiastic practitioners, excitedly announced to me that Fidel had put *him* to work as an organizer of the conference.

Osmany was a decided contrast to his late older brother Camilo, a true hero of the revolution. An architecture student at the university when I had met him in the 1950s, Osmany had played an insignificant role in the student struggle. He'd belonged to the Young Socialists, an association that had aroused suspicions among the university fighters. José Antonio Echevarría

and the rest had kept Osmany and other Young Socialists outside any significant action, for fear of betrayal. After the revolution, Osmany was a founding member of the Captains' Club,
provoking general wonderment the first day of the victory when
he appeared in a captain's uniform.

Osmany traded on his brother's name both before and after
Camilo's death in 1959. And he exploited his many government
posts to such an extent that he could not be ignored by Fidel's
investigation.

I was ordered to report on him specifically, and thus was in
nearly constant contact with Osmany throughout the second half
of 1965; in the office, at parties, and in his penthouse apartment
in a luxury building on the Malecón near the Riviera Hotel.
During our times together, he often complained about MININT
operations—"especially," he said, "those carried out behind the
backs of the revolutionaries." Osmany had gall. "It's a sign of
lack of confidence that reminds me of the Soviet Union under
Stalin," he'd say to me when we'd meet at his apartment. "Their
work makes them feel all-powerful," he declared.

I did not report Osmany's words, just as I never informed
MININT of my private conversations with the officials I was
assigned to watch, but only those incidents that occurred in the
presence of a third party who might be informing on me as well.
This was my small revenge on MININT for giving me an assignment I despised, and it relieved to some extent my guilt about
informing on people, some of whom considered themselves my
friends.

The demands of preparing for the Tricontinental Conference
were such that MININT was distracted from its investigation
toward the end of 1965. The pressure on me from State Security
eased considerably in these weeks. To my enormous relief, I
thought my assignment was nearing its end and that my stay in
Cuba would soon be over.

As host of the conference, Fidel hoped to showcase Havana as
the capital of world revolution. In a frenzy of activity he prepared for the meeting. Four hundred delegates and forty observ-
ers from eighty-two Asian, African, and Latin American countries
came to Cuba in January—among them the principal guerrilla
leaders from these lands—for a demonstration of solidarity and
to work out a common front. The conference provided Fidel with
an international platform, an opportunity to emphasize Cuba's
leadership in the underdeveloped world and to draw attention to

Fidel's independence from the Soviets and the Soviet policy of peaceful coexistence.

But when the conference closed, MININT began leaning on me all the harder, destroying my hopes. Mysterious telephone calls I could not explain to Marie Christine came at all hours. At times I was instructed to report daily, sometimes immediately, on what I'd seen.

Life at home, when I could be there, was tense. Marie Christine did her best to cope with my deepening isolation from her and my secretiveness. She spent more and more time at La Tía's, her only spiritual refuge. Unsurprisingly, we had stopped communicating.

Spontaneity was impossible for me, even in our rare moments of quiet togetherness. What I showed my fearful wife was the stranger that was developing in me, a detached shell of a person who functioned defensively against the tides of doubt and confusion that were always overtaking me. He was my twin self, defending me by telling me how to react, how to behave, cautioning me against the dangers that surrounded me and my own naïveté.

So began an unceasing interior dialogue between us: I, trying to express my natural feelings, to live by the code of my values; he, recognizing that my old life was obsolete and threatening now. In my marriage the Stranger watched, saying nothing, as Marie Christine's powerful and implicit trust in me slowly withered.

I learned from a MININT officer, Figueredo, that in late January 1966, Osmany Cienfuegos was discovered in his car at the corner of the Malecón and G Street in the Vedado, semiconscious from smoking marijuana. If Fidel had hoped to keep a lid on the practices of *La Dolce Vita*, this incident surely demonstrated to him that he could not.

A month later Rolando Cubela and several of his confederates were arrested in connection with their assassination plot. About this time, when I suddenly stopped hearing from MININT, I assumed that perhaps the assignment had been canceled. I had already taken the precaution of destroying all my personal copies of the reports, which I had kept against MININT orders. I had hoped to be able to analyze them at some later date when I might understand the reasons behind and consequences of the investigation. Now I felt I could not afford to have incriminating evidence of any kind in my possession.

Again I allowed myself a glimmer of optimism. I reasoned that no matter what came of the MININT investigation, my role in it would remain confined to that of a listener and watcher for State Security. Although I knew from my first interview that I, too, was being monitored, I believed that the strict correctness of my behavior through it all was my personal insurance policy against calamity. I was living modestly, indulging in none of the excesses I witnessed at the social gatherings I had to attend. I had nothing to hide, I thought, unaware that *everyone* in a Communist revolutionary society has enemies. Ignorant of the purpose of these reports, it didn't bother me that I was being watched. What could anyone say?

LIKE K

Late one gray and blustery afternoon in March 1966, as a north wind hammered at Havana, I put Bach's Brandenburg Concertos on the record player and climbed into the shower. Bach's soft melodies and the soothing shower spray relaxed me. In a good humor, I dressed and then left to pick up Marie Christine at La Tía's.

I had decided to leave without having dinner. But when I arrived downstairs, I noticed that the stormy weather was keeping people off the streets and out of the usually crowded pizzeria in our building. Besides, it was early in the month; most Cubans had just received their monthly food quota and didn't yet have to go to restaurants to eat. I decided to take advantage of this rare opportunity for a quiet meal.

Inside, I chose a Neapolitan pizza from the menu and then sat down to wait. In time, my pizza arrived and I was just about to take my first bite when I heard squealing tires and the sound of a car door slamming. Elsewhere, people might look up at such a commotion, but the wild recklessness of local traffic had inured Havana's citizens to such sounds.

What did get my attention—fast—was the sudden thrust of something cold and hard against my back and the low, authoritative voice behind me saying, "Citizen Llovio, get up as quietly as possible and come with us. By order of the Commander in Chief, you're under arrest."

As always, adrenaline flashed inside me. I turned around on my stool to see an official pointing a Colt .45 at me. Behind him there were two other men, their guns partially hidden under their shirts. This was serious.

I rose slowly, trying to process what was going on and, for a moment, ruing my uneaten pizza. Then I walked toward the door, followed by the terrified eyes of the restaurant staff and the few customers. I was ordered into the back seat of the waiting car, and we pulled away at full speed, followed by two other official cars.

Minutes later, we were in the Víbora district at the Villa Marista, a Marist seminary and rest house confiscated by the revolution and turned into State Security headquarters. Then, as now, Villa Marista is a detention center for suspected counter-revolutionaries.

Still under armed guard, I was taken through a hall full of officials, who made way for us in absolute silence, into a small room where I was fingerprinted quickly and photographed. In an adjoining room, I gave over my watch, emptied my pockets, and then was told to strip. In place of my street clothes I was given a pair of loose cream-colored overalls that buttoned in the front to my waist.

Through this whole process I was numb, overwhelmed. I had no rational powers of reflection or any focused thought of what it was all about. I just did as I was told.

A guard led me down a hallway lined with small identical doors, and then into a narrow stairway that connected to a reception area. At the desk a second guard wrote my name and other information in what looked like a thick account book. Immediately after that, my guard took me through an iron-reinforced door and along a corridor of cells. At the next-to-last door on the left, my door, we stopped and he told me to go in.

It was a tiny room, about ten feet long and six feet wide, very cold, and lit by a wire-enclosed low-watt bulb above the door. To my right there was a sink and beside it a European-style toilet, a depression in the floor between two small cement platforms for one's feet. It was connected by a pipe up to a tank with no flush-chain, a measure designed to prevent suicide attempts. In the rear of the cell was a cot with a pillow. The walls were covered with graffiti.

There I would pass many hellish hours and days before I was given any inkling of why I had been arrested. Held completely incommunicado, I had no idea what sort of ordeal Marie Christine was enduring, alone, without any knowledge about what had happened to me. I wondered if Luc had been discovered, but then discounted that possibility; the phrase *by order of the Commander in Chief* was reserved for only the most serious offenses against the revolution. Also, it had been eight months since I'd given Luc the documents in Santa Clara, and I had to assume that by now he'd acted, successfully, to get my relatives and his out of the country.

What kept turning over and over in my mind was why I had been arrested at Fidel's request. Somehow, in a way that had me baffled, my assignment for MININT seemed responsible for my plight.

I soon lost all sense of time, abetted by my jailers' practice of extending or contracting the hours between meals until, with no sun or nighttime to tell me the approximate hour, I was turning into a sort of zombie. I had to fight my physical and mental decline, and so I began exercising in my cell for hours a day.

Sleep was fitful and erratic. I never got used to the incessant clang of metal doors, a sound common to all prisons. The monotony of the racket was interrupted only by the occasional screech of my own rusty cell door, the noises in the hallway at mealtimes, or the sounds as one of my fellow prisoners (with whom I could not communicate) was brought in or out of the cellblock. I knew an interrogation should be coming, but the wait seemed infinite.

One day as I nodded near sleep on my cot, I was suddenly startled awake by the sound of my cell door being opened. A guard leaned in and ordered me out into the hallway, where the electric light dazzled my weakened eyes as if I were looking directly into the sun. We retraced my route into the prison until we reached the corridor upstairs, where the guard opened one of the small doors and ordered me inside, shutting the door behind me.

This room was even smaller than my cell, and was furnished with a rough table and two chairs. I waited there alone for a long while before a plump young officer with a folder under his arm burst into the room. He said his name was Omar and sat down. Placing the folder on the table between us, he rested his short forearms on either side of it, gave me a fixed stare, and then said in a sharp voice, "Citizen Llovio, you are accused of having conspired against the security of the state. It is necessary for you to answer my questions and confess to the truth of what you have done."

Omar pulled the folder toward him and added, "Before we go on, do you have anything to say?"

I did, and my words took Omar by surprise.

"Yes, officer," I said. "Of course I have something to say. I am a revolutionary. I would never do anything against the revolution. I have blind faith in revolutionary justice, in Fidel. And for that reason I do not accept this accusation. I assure you that someone will pay for this."

It was a bravura front, a show of outrage that I hoped would not be betrayed by my face, which might have reflected my true sense of helpless anxiety.

Omar did not respond. He only looked at me slowly and carefully, trying to evaluate me and, I'm sure, to see if he was in any danger from me. If he found anything that worried him, he didn't show it. He opened the folder and deliberately leafed through it until he came to what he was looking for and began to read out loud.

Omar recited reports very much like the ones I had filed for MININT, except that they included me in their minute retellings of events. There were no lies or accusations in the papers, only the dry recitation of my actions at various times and places. There was not even a case for guilt by association in what he read, because I had been at these affairs by order of MININT.

This is impossible, I thought to myself as he finished reading the reports. *Where am I accused of anything wrong?*

Omar, however, seemed more than satisfied that I had been deeply involved in *La Dolce Vita*, a phrase I then heard for the first time. He went into a ferocious harangue, castigating me as one of the irresponsible and corrupt who enjoyed themselves and wasted state resources while heroic *compañeros* were even then sacrificing themselves far from home in the liberation struggle for other people.

He was nearly hysterical, a dangerous mood for a man of clearly extreme tendencies. As his face reddened and twisted into a fierce expression of contempt for me, he threw up his arms and then violently pounded the table with his fists, almost shouting his praises of Fidel and his condemnations of me.

I sensed that I had to respond. Abruptly I, too, slammed my fist onto the table, stood up to take advantage of my height, and then leaned down over him, putting my face up close to his.

"Look, officer," I said coldly, "'I don't need to listen to lessons from anybody about how a revolutionary should behave. And listen to this! Long before you even dreamed about the existence of this revolution I had already been arrested several times for the cause. If you're sitting there now in that chair, wearing that uniform and doing the work you're doing now, it is because of the grains of sand that men like me brought to the victory. I don't feel guilty about anything, and I would rather you keep me in my cell until you change your mind than to sit here listening to your political sermons."

With that I walked out the door and headed toward the guard at the reception desk. Omar shouted furiously behind me, demanding to know what I was doing. Then he came after me, catching up as I reached the guard, whom I asked to return me to my cell.

The guard was confused and looked at Omar without knowing what to do. But Omar, having regained some control of himself, recognized that he'd lost control of me. He only nodded his head to the jailer, and I was taken back to my isolation.

I kept track of time as best I could by adding up my meals and dividing by three. It felt as if I were spending years in there, worrying about Marie Christine and wondering what sort of game my captors were playing with me, a game without rules and one I didn't understand.

During my incarceration, I found out that Rolando Cubela and his co-conspirators had been brought to trial, Fidel's occasion to make *La Dolce Vita* and the assassination plot work for him. First, he saw to it that an official statement was published on the front page of *Granma*, now the country's only newspaper and the organ of the Cuban Communist Party, named for the yacht that had brought Fidel from Mexico in 1956. The statement emphasized Cubela's "moral decay" and blamed it for making him vulnerable to an approach by the CIA.

Then Fidel intervened at the trial.

Cubela's prosecutor was Commandante Jorge "Papito" Serguera, attorney general of the Rebel Army at the start of the revolution and a very able attorney. Fidel waited until Serguera had laid out the full, damning case against Cubela in the well-publicized trial and then sent the prosecutor a letter asking that none of the accused receive the death penalty.

The letter was a great stroke of showmanship; Fidel projected a magnanimous image for both himself and the revolution. But the letter's main purpose was to connect the assassination plot with *La Dolce Vita*.

I think [Fidel wrote] it is much more useful for the Revolution not to eliminate the individuals who engaged in such an act of treason but to eliminate the vices that contributed to the birth of such behavior. What must be done is to pull up by the roots cronyism, favoritism, the various forms of parasitism, the enervating tendencies to accommodation and even corruption, the lack of methodology in selecting cadres, the lack of criteria in distinguishing the revolutionary from the counterrevolutionary, tolerance of faults, attitudes, and vices that are incompatible with the revolutionary spirit but that still persist in some people, in some sectors, on some work fronts.

Cubela's determination to kill Fidel, and his dealings with the CIA, were only tangentially connected with *La Dolce Vita*. But by asserting their close interrelation, Fidel could now exploit Cubela's past association with the Revolutionary Directorate. While connecting the plot with *La Dolce Vita* was a superficial attempt to stop the corruption that stemmed mostly from his own example, Fidel had a secondary objective: to weed out of his government onetime Revolutionary Directorate members—a goal that was fully realized.

His motives for this move can be explained, at least in part, by revenge as well as paranoia. The Revolutionary Directorate as such no longer existed. And its members who had distrusted Fidel the most, such as José Antonio Echevarría, were now dead. There was no one left who might defy Fidel. Still, the memory of the Directorate's old independence of spirit seemed to pose a psychological rather than substantive threat to Fidel's absolute power.

Yet when it came to fixing punishment for the hundred revolutionary leaders who had been detained in *La Dolce Vita* arrests, Fidel himself directed the process on a case-by-case basis. Now Cubela's avowed treason against the revolution gave Fidel a strong justification for permanently removing veterans of the Revolutionary Directorate from power. From 1966 onward, the defunct organization's remaining former members exercised practically no influence in either the Cuban government or the party.

Others accused in *La Dolce Vita* came in for a range of punishments, some stern but most quite lenient. But many leaders who were not expendable or whom Fidel held in favor had been warned in advance of their danger if they didn't mend their ways. Still others had been quietly dismissed before the mass arrests of early March. One of them, Emilio Aragonés, would reemerge in time as president of the Institute for Fishing, where he'd find limitless opportunities for self-indulgence.

Osmany Cienfuegos didn't fare badly, either. He was relieved of his Construction Ministry duties and sent to direct Cayajabos, an agricultural project in Pinar del Río Province, for five years. But this "punishment," like that handed to Aragonés and many of the others, was relative. Osmany was still able to travel abroad and lived just as dissolutely as before, except that now he had to be somewhat more discreet.

All this I discovered only later. In the first days of my imprisonment, the fate of *La Dolce Vita*'s perpetrators and the fact that I had been implicated was still unknown to me.

UMAP

The revolution sought to enlighten my days of confinement at the Villa Marista by providing me with selected works of Marx and Lenin, as well as the text of Fidel's "History Will Absolve Me" speech, his famous defense oratory at the Moncada trial in 1953.

Considering my circumstances, the speech contained one passage of exquisite, if unintended, irony. Speaking of his own difficult days behind bars waiting for his moment of judgment, Fidel waxed indignant. "Never," the transcript reads, "has a lawyer had to exercise his profession under such difficult conditions; never have so many overwhelming irregularities been committed against an accused. In this case, they are the same person. As a lawyer, I haven't even been able to see the indictment. And as the accused, for seventy-six days I have been locked away in solitary confinement, totally and absolutely incommunicado, contrary to all human and legal prescriptions."

I was reading Fidel's words one day when an officer opened my door and peered in. "Come with me," he said.

The officer took me to a room equipped with two barber chairs where a man in his fifties, dressed in olive-green pants and a white smock, was waiting for me. He told me to sit and placed a towel over my shoulders.

I caught my reflection in a narrow mirror—gaunt, emaciated, with sunken eyes. My skin was sallow, my hair shaggy. I had sprouted a scraggly beard. The barber's old and rusty implements didn't do much to improve my appearance; he left my face burning. Then I was taken back to my cell, where Omar appeared five minutes later.

"Get dressed," he ordered. "Your wife's here to see you. You can't tell her anything that's happened here, and you are forbidden to speak in French with her. I'll be there for her whole visit."

He took me out of the building, across a small courtyard and down a path lined with areca palms, into a large room furnished only with a sofa and two armchairs covered in faded red vinyl. Omar left me there for a moment and returned with my wife.

It had been a month since we'd seen each other. Marie Christine was pale, with deep circles under her eyes. I could see how great her anxiety was, and dreaded the impact my appearance no doubt had on her. As for myself, my clothing made me feel ridiculous. In those shapeless overalls I looked like a clown— and I was ashamed.

With an effort I rose and kissed my wife on each cheek, pained by Marie Christine's helpless, startled expression. Tentatively, she asked how I was, how I felt, never taking her eyes from mine. Omar sat by impassively.

Of course I could discuss nothing of my treatment in the Villa Marista. Sensing that we had to speak only in generalities, Marie Christine kept to a minimum the distressing details of what she had endured. She could not tell me that when I hadn't come for her at La Tía's on the afternoon I was arrested, and then did not answer our telephone, she'd gone to our apartment with Julio Gómez Planas, a captain in the Merchant Marine and an old friend of mine. There they had discovered a large seal on the apartment door, an official-looking sign that read: "These premises under investigation by State Security." Very frightened, Marie Christine had then returned to La Tía's.

The next day, friends of ours had informed José Abrantes of what happened. He'd professed that he knew nothing of the matter. But shortly afterward the seal was removed from our door. Inside, Marie Christine confronted a scene of devastation. Our belongings were strewn everywhere; the whole place had been looted. Almost all my personal possessions—clothing, records, books, and of course my pistol—were stolen. MININT did allow Marie Christine to get our Volkswagen back. Unsurprisingly, the Mercedes-Benz had disappeared.

At the Villa Marista I asked her what she had been told about my arrest. After some faltering, Marie Christine repeated the reasons she had been given by an officer from State Security: my licentious behavior in *La Dolce Vita* and the damage it had done to the prestige of the revolution. At her words my muscles contracted in intense rage. I clenched my fists with desperate impotence and swallowed bile while my eyes burned with tears of rage.

Unembellished as it was, her story still conveyed Marie Christine's desperate uncertainty. I was incensed by the ransacking of the apartment and the lies State Security had told my wife. There was no longer any doubt in my mind that I had been deliberately singled out for punishment, even though I couldn't fathom the motives. Since this plot apparently would be taken to the extreme of undermining my marriage, I had to prepare myself for the worst ahead.

Omar interrupted us before we were finished, declaring that our time was up. I kissed Marie Christine again, hoping to give her some strength and reassurance. She only kept her questioning eyes on mine, signaling nothing but her exhaustion, anxiety, and fear.

I could imagine what was going on in her mind and how these events had affected her trust in me. For the first time I doubted my decision to shield her from the knowledge of the real reason we'd come to Cuba, a decision whose consequences I was facing now.

One hundred and five meals had been pushed through my door—thirty-five days, by my calculation—when one morning I heard a commotion in the corridor outside my cell. Soon an officer carrying my street clothes came in and ordered me to dress. Then the guards led me to an area where about thirty other detainees, also in street clothes, were crowded together in front of a dozen or so high-ranking officers. The whole group was very agitated.

"Quiet!" said one of the officials. "They're going to tell you your destination."

Another officer began pacing back and forth as he pronounced our fate. "By order of the leadership of the revolution," he barked, "you will leave in a few minutes for Camagüey. You've been called up for three years of obligatory military service in the Military Units to Aid Production. You will receive military training and you will contribute to the development of the country by working in production. Each of you will receive the same salary as any other recruit, seven pesos [or dollars] a month and four packs of cigarettes a month."

The Military Units to Aid Production (UMAP), conceived by Fidel, had been officially established in November 1965, although I and my fellow Cubans hadn't known it. During a secret Armed Forces Ministry (MINFAR) ceremony at the Chorrera Fort in Havana, Fidel himself had delivered a speech that outlined his reasons for creating this new military structure. Cuba needed UMAP, he said, to absorb men of draft age who were not politically fit for regular army service because of any number of political deficiencies: lack of integration into the revolution, active membership in any religion, laziness, homosexuality, or a criminal record. Individuals with these flaws, according to Fidel, were not to be sent to UMAP as punishment or to serve a sentence but as part of "the process of ideological rehabilitation."

At UMAP, an effort would be made to bring them closer to "the goodness of the revolution." They would be taught the value of work and would receive vocational training, so that when their period of service was over they wouldn't "lapse into social parasitism." Fidel asked for MINFAR's complete cooperation to realize "this important task [to] combat indolence in certain sectors of the young—their numbers are growing constantly—who had strayed from the straight path of the revolution."

Behind the ideological arguments for UMAP, however, stood the unstated practical reasons for their establishment. In the first place, MINFAR was being radically restructured. Fidel was building a modern, professional Cuban military, which meant its officers would have to be educated. Since there would be no place for the generally unschooled Rebel Army veterans, usually of *campesino* background, UMAP was the ideal alternative. It would solve the growing problem of "old" uneducated officers in the delicate position of being unemployed but still in the army.

Then, too, there was a constant need to mobilize personnel for farm labor, particularly in underpopulated agricultural regions such as Camagüey, where UMAP would be located. UMAP provided just the answer for Camagüey's labor shortage, a young, conscripted, free work force under military discipline.

After the mystery of my arrest, a month of solitary confinement, the confrontation with Omar, and Marie Christine's bitter
revelations, I was stunned but not surprised by my three-year
sentence to forced labor in UMAP. Confusion ruled my daily life.
The incredible and the illogical were everyday events. Since I
couldn't hope to get out of Cuba now, I had to focus on survival. I
knew I had the will to make it through the coming ordeal, but I
wasn't sure if I had the wits.

The guards loaded us onto a rickety old bus at the Villa
Marista and we embarked on a grueling eighteen-hour drive to
Camagüey. No one spoke. We were all lost in our private thoughts
and anxieties, including our guards, teen-aged recruits from Obligatory Military Service, who, though armed with rifles and bayo-
nets, seemed more frightened of us than we were wary of them.

In the middle of the night we arrived at MINFAR Camagüey
Staff Headquarters, a large house on the central highway opposite the city's old Copacabana nightclub. After herding the thirty
of us under a ceiba tree, our guards took us behind the headquarters building and locked us into an abandoned shack—four ma-
sonry walls with a nonfunctioning toilet and a splintered door.
We shared it with the rats, cockroaches, and spiders until morning, before being fed a breakfast of weak coffee and watered milk
and then loaded back on to our bus for the UMAP camp near the
city of Nuevitas, in northernmost Camagüey Province.

An armed sentry guarded the camp at its entrance, and the
entire installation was surrounded by a fence of reinforced concrete pillars strung with barbed wire. I saw three buildings. One
small structure housed the MINFAR personnel in charge of the
camp, distinguished by their olive-drab uniforms. The two much
larger buildings were for the UMAP recruits; our uniforms were
light-blue denim shirts and olive-green pants. As soon as we
arrived from Camagüey, each of us was issued two of these
uniforms and given a receipt for our street clothes, receipts that
were to prove useless, as the officers of the unit stole our clothes
and divided up what they wanted among themselves.

At about ten that morning, one of the officers ordered us to
line up and had us march back and forth for three hours until
lunchtime, when the UMAP workers returned from the fields.
We, the new arrivals, were very tired, but compared to the
workers we were in excellent shape. These young men, seventeen
and eighteen years old, were not criminals, but that fact had not
deterred those in charge from meting out the most severe treat-

ment. The workers' faces, their walk, their general appearance indicated the most profound exhaustion. They were filthy, and their hair and shirts were soaked with sweat. These men had cut sugar cane without a break for seven long hours, machetes in their hands and a burning sun on their heads.

In the ramshackle, filthy, fly-ridden hut used as a dining room, we were served a lunch of a few chickpeas swimming in hot broth, some gummy rice, and a piece of sweet potato. All of us, weak and hungry, devoured the meal avidly.

Then, at two, the recruits went out to the fields again to work until eight. We continued marching from three until seven-thirty, when we were transferred to one of the sleeping barracks, a utilitarian structure with prefabricated walls and a high peaked ceiling of asbestos cement that made the room unbearably hot. A few meters away were the outhouses, wooden boxes with holes in the middle of the floor that filled the air with a putrid smell— and swarms of flies.

As I finally lay down to sleep, I felt as if I were viewing everything through a tunnel or in a film. I could think only of how Marie Christine would fare without me, and I was still reeling from the blow to my plans for returning to France. My planned one-year stay in Cuba was now stretched to at least three years. Overwhelmed with these thoughts, I did not even try to make sense of my new circumstances.

MILITARY UNIT 2096

The next day, the new arrivals were divided into groups of four and then shipped out of the camp to our assigned units around the province. My group was bussed back through Camagüey and then toward Ciego de Avila, my birthplace. The familiar scenery and landmarks I'd known since my youth rolled past. Everything looked more or less the same, but there was no emotional resonance in what I saw. The Stranger in me, still inchoate, was taking command of my senses.

Our destination was military unit 2096 near the old Violeta sugar mill, renamed the First of January sugar mill by the revolution. The camp was very similar to the one at Nuevitas, although it seemed newer and in better condition. Four companies of 120 recruits each, a full battalion, were stationed there.

Upon our arrival the UMAP commander, Francisco González, eyed me and my three companions curiously from time to time as he tried with great difficulty to read the orders he held in his hand.

I, in turn, was discreetly examining him, this man who was to be my commander. I thought he seemed brutish, and his sunburned skin, rough hands, and manner of speaking all told me he was of *campesino* origin. From where I was standing I could read the return address on the envelope he was holding. Unlike the instructions that generally accompanied new arrivals, ours were all directly from Havana. Although I didn't know their content, they clearly merited his close attention.

When he was at last finished with the documents, González spoke to us about the many discipline problems the authorities had encountered with UMAP recruits: how they didn't adapt well to regimentation and how he was counting on us, because "even though you are being punished, you are revolutionaries and it is your duty to cooperate with the cadres in command."

Then the four of us were divided into pairs. The only one of the other three I'd known before coming to UMAP was Raúl Fernández Sáens, a veteran of the revolution's Second Front and

With my mother, around 1940

With my uncle Sergio *(left)*, **my cousin
Silvio** *(near right)*, **and his brother
Ramón** *(right)* **in the early '50s**

CUANDO LLEVABAN LA OFRENDA FLORAL... He aquí un numeroso grupo de estudiantes cuando transitaban por la calle San Lázaro esquina a M, llevando una ofrenda floral que tenían proyectado depositar en el Mausoleo de los Mártires, frente al Castillo de la Punta. Al llegar la manifestación estudiantil a dicha esquina la fuerza pública los dispersó, por medio de mangueras de agua de los flushres de los bomberos que tenían situados estratégicamente en esos contornos. Los manifestantes corrieron unos en distintas direcciones y otros trataban de avanzar inútilmente, quedando disueltos finalmente, mientras que la ofrenda floral quedó destrozada en el pavimento. (Foto: P. PÉREZ.)

Newspaper photo, clipped by my mother, of me in a demonstration against Batista

Echevarría, at his election as president of the FEU

**Filmstrip I took to document Echevarría's death,
March 13, 1957**

A new life in Paris, 1958

Attempting to ski in the French Alps the day I met Marie Christine, March 3, 1960

Headlines in France:
MARIE CHRISTINE CHOSE LOVE

Marie-Christine
a préféré l'amour

Elle est l'héritière d'une des plus riches
familles de France. Lui, étudiant à Paris, était
il y a encore quelques mois un des chefs de
l'insurrection de Fidel Castro.
Ils s'aimaient, mais les parents de la jeune fille
étaient opposés au mariage. Alors, le jeune
amoureux prépara l'enlèvement de sa belle...

Marie Christine with Marielle on the day of her birth

Marie Christine *(left)* **with Pierrette Meynard and Marielle, 1961**

Marie Christine in Prague on her way to Havana, 1963

**Listening to Fidel at the July 26th rally in the
Plaza de la Revolución, 1963**

**View from the Havana Libre, 1963. Right foreground is the
Radiocentro theater, which I remodeled after UMAP in 1967.**

**In a Madrid restaurant, February 1965, on my way to Cuba.
Robreno** *(second from left),* **Loco Blanco** *(third from right),* **and
Rolando Cubela** *(second from right),* **who were planning the
assassination of Fidel, although I** *(center)* **didn't know it**

Marielle in Caracas
while living with my
parents, around 1965

The barber Nivaldo
Alayón, my companion
in UMAP, today

With Maggie the year we met, 1969

Papito Serguera *(left)* **and Alfredo Guevara at our wedding in Havana on January 23, 1971**

once an aide to Raúl Castro. Fernández Sáens was serving his fourth "punishment" for his usual weaknesses—women and drink—but this was his first in UMAP. Earlier, he had served time in ordinary, nonmilitary rehabilitation camps for fallen revolutionaries. Fernández Sáens left with his partner for Manga Larga, an area known for its ferocious swarms of mosquitoes and gnats; the insects at Manga Larga were so thick that a farm animal, left tied up outside for too long, would die from their biting attacks.

I was a little luckier. Along with Nivaldo Alayón, a barber from the village of Güines (where Fidel kept his camp), I was sent to the unit closest to headquarters, about four miles away, where conditions were at least more bearable.

We were received at our unit by Lieutenant Mora, the company head. Mora had earned his rank fighting in the Sierra Maestra with Fidel, whom he had joined in 1957. But because of his lack of education—he could barely read—he had for the past two years been transferred without success from one regular unit to another. Mora represented the fighting *campesino* of the Sierra who had been marginalized for lack of schooling, "punished" like so many others, and made an officer in UMAP, one of the dumping grounds of the Revolutionary Armed Forces. Another, I knew, was the Cuban prison system, where the *campesinos* were sent as guards and administrators.

Lieutenant Mora sent us out to cut sugar cane each day, every day at 4:30 A.M. At ten in the morning we received a fifteen-minute break. Lunch was from noon until two, and then we were returned to the back-breaking work until 7:00 P.M. All day we worked under the scorching sun in temperatures above ninety degrees. There was no choice but to work, and no malingering was allowed by our ever-present armed guards.

My UMAP file, the one Lieutenant González had had so much difficulty deciphering, must have been very complete, including details of my education, for within a week I was named head of medical services for the unit. Someone in the capital must have reviewed my years of medical study in Havana and Paris and concluded I was qualified to practice medicine in the region. In this they were more or less correct. I had indeed completed five years of medical school but I had little practical experience as a physician.

My new assignment meant extra work for me, since I wasn't relieved of labor in the fields, but I took comfort in the thought that I would at least have the chance to protect sick recruits. From my first day on the job, I examined teen-aged boys with temperatures as high as 104 degrees, boys with signs of gastroenteritis, with measles, with lesions on their hands from the machetes. No matter what their condition, they were sent to work in the fields.

This situation was at the root of one of my first confrontations with the authorities. One night during my first week at the camp, a young man of about eighteen came to see me. A machete had accidentally cut through his boot, his leg was red and swollen, and he had a very high fever. Everything seemed to point to severe infection, but still he had been forced to keep working. I prescribed the appropriate antibiotics and ordered absolute rest, with the leg raised and covered with cold compresses.

The next day, when we lined up for roll call and our sergeant noticed the recruit's absence, I explained the seriousness of his condition and said that he could not work for three days.

"Nothing is wrong with him," the sergeant shouted, prowling back and forth. "He's faking so he won't have to work, but he can't fool me!"

He went into the barracks shouting and cursing. I looked at my fellow recruits, but they were used to his outbursts and didn't move. Then, without thinking, I broke ranks and walked toward the barracks. The officers and recruits stared at me in amazement. I found the sergeant beside himself with rage, tearing up the paper on which I had authorized bed rest for the recruit. The sick boy's blanket and sheet, along with his other belongings, had been thrown to the floor.

I walked up to the sergeant and said very firmly, "This recruit is in bed because he's very sick. I've authorized his rest according to regulations. You cannot force him to work under these circumstances. If you don't agree, we'll wait for the company commander. Or, if you prefer, let's go right now to battalion headquarters. If you still object, then we'll go to Camagüey Staff Headquarters. I don't care where we have to go, because you're breaking regulations and I am not going to permit you to abuse anybody, not now, not ever."

The sergeant looked at me in confusion. The situation that had seemed so ordinary to him had now suddenly turned into something he could not explain. I had reacted with spontaneous fury at the injustice. But I also knew that if I let him intimidate me now, the same thing would only happen again.

"I'm going to wait here for Lieutenant Mora, to explain what's happened," I added. "As chief of medical services I must be respected or I resign from the post."

This last sentence had its hoped-for effect. Without saying another word, the sergeant strode out of the barracks and ordered the rest of the recruits to leave while the sick man and I stayed in camp.

Lieutenant Mora arrived sometime after eleven. I told him what had taken place and emphasized that he—not the sergeant—was responsible for such excesses. When he saw how determined I was, the lieutenant decided to give in. "Don't worry, it won't happen again," he said. I could tell he intended to keep his word.

Even without Mora's abuses, life in the camp was grueling. Once in a while, the twelve-hour days of cutting sugar cane alternated with twelve-hour days of digging yams, cleaning sugar cane, or weeding the unit's vegetable fields. I was constantly exhausted, often too tired for thought, let alone any deep reflection on my future.

Marie Christine wrote me twice during the first several weeks of my internment, newsy letters that told me nothing of her inner life. But my imagination was unceasingly engaged in thinking of her—and of us.

When I finally got out of this nightmare and returned to Havana, should I tell her the truth about all that had happened—why I'd come to Cuba, what I had been doing for State Security—and risk endangering her by what she knew? It would be impossible for her to hide her knowledge if she were ever pressured by officials to disclose it; she was naturally sensitive and anxious, and her face always revealed her true feelings. The very qualities of sincerity and openness that I loved in her could be what betrayed her, and I would rather risk our marriage in the short term for the chance to be reunited in France as soon as possible. On the other hand, it sickened me to think of her alone with her failing trust in me. She was utterly innocent in all of this, and she deserved the truth. But the truth was now more dangerous than ever.

This inner debate, back and forth, was relentless. In the end I decided again not to tell her the truth—the risk to her was simply too great.

My decision not to confide in Marie Christine may seem incomprehensible, but for five years under Batista, I had lived a life in which I knew that one remark to the wrong person could cause the death of my friends—or my own. I had seen several friends betrayed and killed under such circumstances and I knew there was no way that Marie Christine, with her background, could imagine how easy it was for someone to win revolutionary favor by reporting what she said. In order to survive in such a society, one had to live a double life, in complete control of every word and gesture, without trusting *anyone*. I knew my wife very well; she would break under the strain of this secrecy, even if she could maintain it. She could not be expected to invent the kind of facade she would need to bear the burden of the truth.

I also knew the probable consequences of my decision—the distance it would place between Marie Christine and me, and the confusion and uneasiness she would continue to feel at having lost her trust in me.

The only relief in my near-total emotional void was the barber, Nivaldo Alayón, who had taken the bunk beneath me in our barracks. Except for his constant worry about his wife and daughter, then living alone in Güines, Alayón was happy-go-lucky and quite popular among the recruits. He was helpful and good-natured and I, too, liked him very much. One advantage of my new assignment was that I was able to use my relations with unit headquarters to get Alayón out of the hard field work. Lieutenant Mora agreed to let him practice his barber's trade instead, as well as help in the kitchen and sometimes as my nurse.

Unlike the vast majority of UMAP recruits, Alayón was an older man, a circumstance that led me to suppose he must have gotten into serious trouble to warrant such punishment. In time, he explained what had happened.

According to Alayón, he had been close friends with Comandante Arsenio García, a hero of the Moncada assault who had been accused of sexual promiscuity and "not working with revolutionary spirit" during *La Dolce Vita*. Alayón's local CDR, as well as the Güines MININT, then falsely accused Alayón of contributing to García's corruption.

The comandante possibly was dissipated, like most of the rest of the revolutionary elite, but his greater crime had been his repeated denunciations of MININT brutality and persecution. This had set García against Ramiro Valdés, minister of the interior, and his *campañero* from Moncada, who had therefore marked García for elimination during the *La Dolce Vita* investigation.

Like many of the UMAP recruits, Alayón was considered by the Revolutionary Government to be the detritus of Cuban society. UMAP was supposed to be a sinkhole for misfits, which is how we were treated, but in my unit most of the boys were decent people. The younger ones, who came from different cities throughout the country, appeared to have gotten into trouble because of revolutionary apathy, or because they had chosen not to hide their religious beliefs. Many were the victims of the vengeance of some enemy in their CDR. We were told that UMAP was a dumping ground for Cuba's homosexuals and members of religious sects such as the Jehovah's Witnesses or adherents of Abakuá, a Cuban blood cult. I'd soon see the treatment inflicted for those "crimes."

BRUTE FORCE

Five weeks into my sentence, First Lieutenant González summoned me to local headquarters. En route we stopped for lunch at the Manga Larga unit. As I got down from the vehicle, I saw one of the recruits returning from the fields start running toward me, calling my name. It was Raúl Fernández Sáens.

"Slim! What is this?" he asked in frightened tones as we walked into the unit's courtyard. "What's going on here? I'm sure that Fidel and Raúl don't know anything about this."

Fernández Sáens looked very pale, thin, and sickly. His voice trembled and he constantly mopped sweat from his forehead and neck as he talked.

"Yesterday," he told me, "they made two recruits dig ditches from eight at night until five in the morning. And they were naked! Can you imagine? They were eaten alive by mosquitoes. It was horrible to see them suffer, but nobody could do anything. And all because they refused to cut sugar cane at four in the morning."

Raúl was almost out of control. His lips were dead-white and flecked with dried spittle. His eyes bulged and shone with an eerie brilliance.

"That's nothing," he continued. "The officers here use the rope punishment for any breach of discipline."

"What the hell," I replied, "is the rope punishment?"

"They whip prisoners with agave rope as if they were animals," Raúl answered. "Slim, it's like being in a Nazi concentration camp. Fidel doesn't know. He can't know!"

He stopped short for a moment and looked furtively around us. Then he went on: "The officers are so brutal here because they're afraid. They don't know how to control the situation. They are very stupid. They shouldn't have sent these officers to deal with such difficult people—counterrevolutionaries, religious fanatics, common criminals, killers—"

"Killers!" I interrupted him in astonishment.

"Yes, Slim," he said. "There are three convicts here with long sentences. One of them killed his wife. Another kicked a prostitute to death. The third one killed a fourteen-year-old girl after raping her. All these men came from Príncipe prison, and they say that Ramiro Valdés is sending more everyday, emptying the prisons and sending these killers to UMAP. I would never have thought he'd do such a crazy thing, but after what I've seen here, I can believe anything. Anything. Anything!"

Fernández Sáens seemed on the verge of hysteria. If only a few weeks in UMAP had driven him this close to the edge, I wondered if he could ever survive a full sentence.

"Look, Raúl," I said, in an effort to calm him, "try to stay out of trouble. We're just pawns. We can't do anything for the moment. But this will all work out, you'll see. For now, the only thing we can do is wait. Be patient. Don't despair."

After lunch I saw him again from a distance. Fernández Sáens stood at the unit gate staring at me as I got into the truck, and then silently waved good-bye with his mouth half open and a lost look in his eyes.

About half an hour later we reached headquarters and I headed for González's office, curious about why he wanted to see me.

The room was dirty and desolate-looking. On the cement floor I could see hardened traces of the Ciego de Avila region's distinctive red soil. When González saw me come in, he got up from his cot.

"*Compañero* Llovio," he said, "we're going to transfer you here to battalion headquarters. From now on you'll sleep in the hut alongside headquarters. It has five cots, which you will use for a hospital for the officers and recruits. You'll also treat the *campesino* population around the camp."

He gestured toward some boxes. "They are full of medicines.

In the shack you'll find some storage closets. A doctor named Rodríguez will be transferred within a few days and he'll be meeting with you to give you instructions before he leaves. Do you have any questions?"

"Yes," I answered, thinking quickly, "I want to know if my decisions regarding the sick will be respected."

"They will be," the lieutenant responded. "I know all about what happened in your unit. And I hope you know how to make those decisions, because the recruits are very smart. They'll always look for some way to get you to authorize time off, and you know our primary function is to produce."

"Yes, Lieutenant," I said, "but not at the cost of the men's health."

"Remember that almost all these recruits are antisocial, religious, counterrevolutionaries—and still the revolution's done quite a lot for them," he said. That was the end of our discussion.

As I was leaving the office by the back door, reflecting on the good fortune of my transfer—no more work in the fields—I saw one of the most degrading and depressing sights I've ever witnessed. In the center of the courtyard, tied by both hands to the top of the flagpole, there hung a boy of about twenty, his body swaying in the breeze just below the raised flag. Without thinking, I headed toward him.

"Hey, where are you going?" Lieutenant González called after me. "It's not permitted to approach those Witnesses."

"Take him down, Lieutenant," I answered curtly, stopping and looking back at him.

González stood in the doorway with his legs wide apart, his olive-green shirt unbuttoned, his belt unbuckled. Meanwhile, the UMAP recruits had rushed outside the barracks and to the windows.

"This is outrageous," I said in indignation. "The revolution preaches respect for human dignity. I'm going to take this man down even if you try to stop me. If anything happens, I know that the recruits will testify to exactly what occurred. I don't believe that Camagüey Staff Headquarters will accept such barbarity to correct the behavior of these boys. You may have fought against Batista, but that doesn't give you the right to use his methods."

I turned around, went to the pole, and started to lower the recruit slowly, trying to hurt him as little as possible. When he reached the ground he fell into a faint. Dr. Rodríguez appeared at that moment, and with his help I picked up the boy's limp body. To a burst of applause from the barracks, we took him to the infirmary. Lieutenant González had disappeared.

The recruit's wrists were raw and bloody. The rope had almost cut off circulation to his hands, and they were numb and purplish. He was crying with pain. After giving him a strong sedative, we proceeded to treat him.

"If he had been left hanging for two more hours, he would have lost his hands," said Rodríguez.

Dr. Rodríguez was a regular army doctor, about forty years old, extremely thin and nervous. I never did learn why he was in UMAP. Evidently not a revolutionary, he was discreet, respectful, not interested in looking for trouble.

"Why was the boy punished?" I asked him.

"Look, we'd better walk to the *batey* [village]," he said. "I'm not comfortable talking here. I'll tell you the story on the way to the settlement."

Although the infirmary was not part of the unit, I asked him if he thought it wise for us to leave.

"Don't worry," he answered, "from now on you're under MINFAR discipline, not UMAP. There are more privileges. In fact, you'll be given a five-day pass every month to return to Havana."

I could hardly believe that after these hellish weeks I might see my wife alone, at home, and in fact I cautioned myself not to get my hopes up.

As we walked toward the *batey* and I thought about these things, Dr. Rodríguez was explaining what we'd just seen. "That boy is a Jehovah's Witness. They don't believe in anything worldly. Their country, for example, doesn't mean anything to them. That's why they refuse to salute the flag and have been punished in the way you've seen. And they refuse to work in uniform, because they say they belong only to the army of God. Some parents will not even send their children to school.

"They are very rebellious and do a lot of proselytizing, but they are also severely punished. The officers consider them the worst kind of counterrevolutionaries and they use brute force to break their spirit. A while ago there was the case of another Jehovah's Witness who was very cruelly disciplined. They tied a rope around his arms, and the other end around the neck of a horse whose genitals had been treated with carbon bisulfate. The horse bolted, dragging the boy hundreds of meters. His wounds

were serious, and I had to send him to the hospital in Ciego de
Avila, where he spent two months."

"And afterward," I asked. "What happened to him?"

"He was discharged from the unit," Rodríguez answered.

Then he offered a personal assessment. "I think the officers
in the UMAP don't have the intelligence to deal with infractions
of discipline by these young men," he said, "and their powerless-
ness turns them into animals. Every time something like this
happens I wish I could run away, forget my time here.

"I'll tell you one thing. I thought you were crazy when I saw
you walking toward the flagpole. I don't understand why Lieutenant González gave in so easily. He's a brutal man."

I didn't understand either.

In the little store at the *batey* where we stopped to buy some
cigarettes, I noticed the local *campesinos* kept their distance.
When I mentioned it to Rodríguez, he told me: "You'll have to
get used to it. They're always like that. The UMAP has a bad
reputation. They think we're all criminals."

When we returned to the infirmary, a sergeant waiting there
informed me that Lieutenant González urgently wanted to see
me.

González was waiting in his office. As soon as he finished
signing some papers, he looked up at me. "Listen, Doctor," he
said. "You're not right in the head. It looks like you've forgotten
that I'm the one in command here. In case you didn't know it,
military discipline means obedience. My orders must be respected,
understand?

"You got away with it because I don't know who the hell you
are. The order for your transfer to headquarters came from Havana, and I don't like having any big shots in disguise under me.
You and I have to reach an agreement: Medicine is your business; the military is mine. But regardless of all that, I'm the boss.
Those Witnesses are counterrevolutionaries organized by the CIA
to overthrow the revolution. We have to crush them. If it were up
to me, I'd shoot them all."

As I was learning, I couldn't let any such violent assertion go
unanswered. "Lieutenant, I've made mistakes and I must pay for
them," I said with proper revolutionary humility. "Like you, I
fought for the victory of this revolution to bring an end to injustice
and to create a new Cuba. I'd never permit anything that de-
grades human dignity. Not then, not now. I object to abuse, and
an abuse was committed against that boy. If the same situation

were to occur tomorrow, my reaction would be the same, you can be sure of that. I'm sure your superiors think as I do."

After the stick, I offered the carrot.

"There's no reason for anyone to hear about what's happened," I said in a reassuring tone. "I'm willing to forget about the incident as long as you understand the stupidity of repeating this kind of reprisal against the recruits. Anybody can make a mistake. I made one; now you've made one. But the revolutionary knows how to correct his errors, just as Fidel does, right? I assure you that I'll do everything I can to help you if things like this don't happen again. And I'm a man of my word."

Lieutenant González radically altered his attitude toward the sick recruits after our chat, although only when I was around. From then on, he did not interfere with me and even seconded some of my suggestions that earlier he would have summarily vetoed.

This was his way of surviving, too. If I, whom he now feared, encouraged a more humane policy in the camp, then Lieutenant González was amenable. If I had used the same methods of intimidation to promote even harsher policies, he would have just as happily obliged me. It was the system.

But my beginning to know how the system worked did not prepare me for the shock of learning what it did. While I was somewhat less naïve by now than people like Raúl Fernández Sáens—and thus was better able to cope with the horrors around me—I was still not jaded enough to have imagined the way the revolution chose to deal with those whom Fidel judged to be "a social disease."

One such group was Cuba's homosexuals. From the beginning MININT had hounded them and persecuted them, including many prominent Cuban artists and performers. With the advent of UMAP, the harassment intensified. MININT officers would patrol known homosexual gathering places, areas in Havana such as the Rampa district and the neighborhood around the Coppelia ice cream parlor, where they rounded up anyone who looked like a homosexual and shipped these people off to UMAP. The reason I had not yet encountered these detainees is that they were segregated in their own camps, where they were subjected to the full ferocity of revolutionary rehabilitation.

In Lieutenant González's battalion, the homosexual camp was the Malesar unit, where I was sent one day to hold a clinic for the recruits. "Doctor," said the lieutenant in charge, a middle-aged *campesino* named Machado, "you've chosen a bad day for your visit."

I had arrived just as the 120 recruits in the unit were being turned out in a raid for contraband. Machado was apoplectic, furious with the camp political instructor for not ordering the recruits into formation during the search and angrier still with the men themselves, who were milling around the camp in a din of agitation.

"Look how topsy-turvy this unit is!" Machado exclaimed to me. "I'm fed up with these faggots! If this job didn't have high priority for the revolution, I'd have resigned a long time ago."

Machado stopped his tirade long enough to grab his political instructor, whom he told to restore order outside. Then the lieutenant returned to his complaints.

"Last night," he said, "they had a party in the barracks. Do you know what for? A goddamn wedding, that's what! I wish you could have seen how they decorated the barracks. Shit! It looked just like a church! And a bride and groom, all painted up, with a wedding dress and everything! I don't know how these motherfuckers manage to get all that crap into the unit."

Machado ranted on in this vein for several minutes longer, screeching his denunciations of the homosexual recruits but also conceding what was to him a mystery: "There's always some trouble with these people," he said, "but the funny thing is that they're excellent workers. We've been the best battalion in the company for the last five months."

I told him I wanted to get on with my clinic and excused myself to head for the barracks. The visit was supposed to be a brief one, but I ended up spending more than four hours treating the recruits and listening to their stories.

They were in deplorable physical condition. Many were covered with insect bites, some so severe that they had become infected. Extreme sunburn, eczema, and several types of fungal infections were evident too. Most appalling were their bruises from the beatings they'd received.

To my surprise, the recruits knew of me; they had heard of the episodes with Lieutenants Mora and González. Because I had successfully defied the camp authorities, the men of the Malesar unit trusted me and took the opportunity of my visit to reveal what was being done to them.

They told me of petty brutalities, such as suspension of their visitors' privileges, public humiliations, and interference with their mail. More serious were their stories of being denied meals, forced to work at night by lantern light, and the requirement that they go to the fields even when sick. Then I heard about the ugliest abuses. They said they were routinely beaten in the cane fields, were made to stand at attention in the sun for eight hours, or were placed overnight, naked, in pits of foul water while the mosquitoes fed on them. Several gave me very accurate descriptions of the rope punishment.

My afternoon with the Malesar recruits served to bolster my conviction that the barbarity I'd already witnessed was not isolated but part of a pattern throughout UMAP. If what I saw was being repeated at camps across the province, as I believed it was, these outrages would eventually come to light as more and more recruits returned home from their service with tales of what had happened to them.

I decided I would try to denounce the cruelty so prevalent throughout the camps, but I knew I would have to proceed very carefully. For the time being I began to take careful notes on everything I saw: who had been abused, by whom, when, and in what exact fashion. This, of course, was a far more palatable exercise than my MININT assignment in *La Dolce Vita*, even though it shared the same basic absurdity. UMAP was Fidel's brainchild and MINFAR's and MININT's direct responsibility. Everyone knew what was going on. Still, I did take some bitter delight in looking forward to the scuttling and backbiting, all the feigned surprise among the worried officials of Fidel's government, when the UMAP scandal broke.

Once I'd been transferred to headquarters and was no longer required to work in the fields, I hoped that my rising fortunes in the battalion meant that my UMAP sentence was being eased, that perhaps some anonymous ally in Havana was pulling strings on my behalf. Although I did not receive the sure signal that this was the case—early permission to visit Havana—within some days, it was declared that from nine to five on one day we could receive visitors in the camp. I looked forward to Marie Christine's visit with eagerness and worry. She was not free to tell me anything in her letters, and I only hoped that MININT was not feeding her more false information about me—but of course I didn't know.

Alone, Marie Christine drove the entire distance from the capital over Cuba's deteriorating and unfamiliar central highway. I remember in detail the windless Sunday morning I watched her approach the camp behind the wheel of the VW, driving slowly but still throwing up a cloud of red dust behind her.

As soon as I saw her walking toward me, I knew from her expression that things were very bad indeed. She was pale and had lost a lot of weight. In the distance, she regarded me uneasily, as she had two months before at the Villa Marista. Her kiss was hesitant and cool.

We could speak more or less in private at the camp, and in French, but this hardly lessened the tension between us. As Marie Christine and I walked together, I could tell her nothing of what I'd seen in UMAP, and she was equally aloof. The atmosphere relaxed when she took out photos of Marielle, pictures that had been included in letters from my mother in Venezuela. When Marie Christine related how well our daughter was doing in school and among my family, the strain left her face.

But soon we had to talk about my situation. Her appearance only reinforced my previous decision. As desperate as I was to regain my wife's trust and esteem by telling her the truth, I still could not risk jeopardizing our escape. Marie Christine would understand if I told her not to share this knowledge with anyone, but what if she nevertheless confided it to La Tía in a moment of despair? And what if La Tía was then interrogated?

Marie Christine could not add anything to what she'd already told me in connection with my arrest. She couldn't remember the name of the MININT official with whom she'd spoken, and she offered nothing further on the reasons he'd given for MININT's actions against me. When I said as consolation that the government might soon recognize it had made a mistake in my case, she brightened, which made me feel even worse about myself; I knew how unlikely it was that justice would prevail.

Nevertheless, to myself I continued to cling tenaciously to the belief that somehow I would get out of UMAP and then very soon afterward we'd get out of Cuba. But all the while my wife was with me at the camp, I suffered a helpless, self-recriminating despair that lasted long after she drove away down the long dirt road in a cloud of red dust.

MISSION IN HAVANA

Because I no longer worked in the fields, I now had the luxury of time to reflect, and I turned my thoughts once again to all the possible motives behind my arrest and sentencing. I wasn't merely curious. Unless I grasped the meaning and dynamics of what had happened, I might never be able to devise a way for Marie Christine and me to break out of this net of intrigue and deceit.

It seemed to me consistent with revolutionary logic that my crime and punishment had been foreordained. That is, my assignment by MININT necessarily gave me the appearance of taking part in *La Dolce Vita*, in that I was present at so many of the occasions being reported on, so that at the moment of reckoning I would also have to pay the price. Otherwise, my true function in the government's plot to spy on its own leaders would have been exposed. Therefore, my arrest and sentence in Camagüey must have been arranged beforehand by the same people who had given me the assignment in the first place. My punishment was simply a part of the plan, a stratagem cleverly designed by MININT to hide one of its machinations. In this case, I was probably not alone.

I knew that because of my status as the chief of medical services, I would soon be granted a pass to go to Havana, although I did not know when. When I got there, I wanted to make the most effective denunciation of UMAP possible.

If I chose to break my news initially to the political leadership, I risked being accused of going over the heads of my military superiors in what would be considered an army matter. Also, the first question any political leader of the revolution would ask me was whether I had previously brought the matter before the proper MINFAR official.

I didn't expect MINFAR to act on my news; I'd have to find a sympathetic and powerful personage somewhere else to set events in motion. But before that, I would make the proper and obligatory approach to MINFAR. For my contact I chose Comandante

Pedro Miret, not because I trusted him but because I could reach him easily on a brief trip.

As I'd expected, about six weeks after my assignment to battalion headquarters I was granted a five-day pass to Havana. When I got there in July 1966, I found that Miret had not only weathered *La Dolce Vita,* he'd prospered in its aftermath. He had been promoted to become the army chief of staff. However, like many of the rest who'd been spared, he was now maintaining a much lower profile. All the lively old haunts of the revolutionary elite were quiet. "Consciousness through Repression"—the grim slogan of the revolution's hard-liners such as Raúl Castro—seemed after *La Dolce Vita* to be taken very seriously. Now Miret only rarely set foot in the Havana Libre, his old hangout, and suggested when I called him that we meet in Cadenas Plaza behind the Rectory at the University.

Pedro had been hearty, jovial at the sound of my voice on the telephone. But at the plaza, when I began telling him about conditions in UMAP, he turned impatient, annoyed, and, I thought, fearful.

"That's what they're saying in Havana," he told me, "but it's all fairy tales. Don't pay attention to what people say, because you can get into trouble. This is counterrevolutionary propaganda."

Thus the game.

Miret was unquestionably aware of where I'd been and of the brutality of UMAP. Yet he clearly wished I had not ambushed him with my direct report. As long as he had a fig leaf of ignorance, he was safe; my insistence exposed him to danger. As I talked, I thought about how Socialist paranoia ruled his every move. Once a tiger on the revolutionary battlefield, he was now another fearful mouse in Fidel's Revolutionary Government. Miret knew how to survive.

"How can you possibly doubt what I'm telling you?" I asked, mustering all the incredulity I could. "Don't you realize what I've lived through? Pay attention to me! I've detailed each one of the cases with all the data necessary to start an investigation. It's not fairy tales. What's going on there must be stopped."

There, Pedro was caught.

"All right, all right," he agreed in resignation. "Make your report. Take it to MINFAR. Leave it with the receptionist. Someone will look into it."

Disconsolate now that the stain of UMAP had been shown to him and aware that in any later controversy I would have to report this conversation, Miret gave me a bleak look. "And how's your wife?" he asked lamely.

My wife was much the same. For our five days together, we both wore a facade of forgetfulness, as if nothing at all had happened. I think back in admiration at Marie Christine's courage. She had driven half the length of Cuba to visit me in May, only to find the blank shell of the Stranger inhabiting her husband's body. In Havana, I learned, she had been shunned by some of the people we knew. I heard that others had come to her with gossip and malicious remarks about me, and that she'd answered every one of them, firmly: "My husband is free to act as he chooses; nobody has the right to judge him."

Such staunch loyalty to me, in view of Marie Christine's manifest and wholly understandable doubts as to my integrity, made me feel all the more guilty, morally diminished when I was with her. She could never bring herself to ask exactly what my participation in *La Dolce Vita* had been, or why I had been away so many nights. The closest she came was one evening on our terrace as we watched the sun set.

Apropos of nothing we had been discussing, Marie Christine suddenly turned and looked deeply into my eyes. "Have you told me the whole truth?" she asked, holding me in her gaze.

The few seconds of intense silence between us said more than my answer could.

"Yes, I have," I told her.

Marie Christine knew I was lying.

After speaking with Pedro Miret, I had the quiet satisfaction of knowing that my denunciation was like a ticking time bomb for the military. He would have trouble defusing it, and he couldn't tell when it might detonate in his face. Then I went to visit Alfredo Guevara.

Guevara, president of ICAIC, the Cuban Cinema Institute (and no relation to Ché), was a personal friend of mine, one of the few revolutionary leaders I believed was sincere. Well-educated, with an acute polemical intelligence, Alfredo had been a Marxist since his time at Havana University in the 1940s. He was also very close to Raúl Castro and Fidel, to whom, it was said, Guevara had given his first book on Marxism.

Alfredo was passionate about his Communism and about his esthetics, and he was happy to blend the two in all ICAIC projects. Art in the service of political ends seemed proper to him.

But Guevara was also fearlessly independent in his thinking. When Blás Roca, the old PSP secretary general, had objected to the screening of capitalist films (including *La Dolce Vita*) in Havana, Guevara had defended the policy and slugged it out with Roca in an extended debate in the newspapers. In the end Fidel had endorsed Alfredo's view.

Earlier, when Aníbal Escalante at ORI had tried to place one of his PSP cronies as "political commissar" at ICAIC, Alfredo had come to Fidel with a "him or me" ultimatum and won. Until the sectarian crisis had swept Escalante and his PSP crowd out of power, ICAIC was the only Cuban governmental agency to escape their meddling and interference.

I saw Alfredo several times during my short stay in Havana and broached UMAP to him in the course of one of our usual chats. It was late in the afternoon at his ICAIC office, and we had been casually discussing a whole range of matters when I turned to the topic of where I'd been for the past many months.

Alfredo reacted as I'd expected he would to my detailed account of UMAP's excesses. He told me he had heard many similar stories and was glad to have my eyewitness testimony to bolster the case against UMAP, which he was already actively opposing.

I assured him that I'd passed my information through channels at MINFAR and stressed that my sole purpose in repeating what I knew to him was my great fear of the damage UMAP could do to the revolution. Alfredo agreed with my assessment. I later learned that, within days, he repeated all I'd told him to Raúl Castro. I returned to Camagüey with the hope that my denunciation would soon put an end to the torture in UMAP and lead to my permanent discharge, when I could go back to Havana and try to rebuild my life with Marie Christine.

THE "OLD WOMAN"

By midsummer 1966, UMAP was an organism riddled with disease, festering with brutality which seemed to feed on itself. Comandantes Casillas and Silva, respectively the UMAP's military and political chiefs as well as members of the Central Committee, went so far as to take a direct hand in the violence. I had been told by several people in headquarters of an occurrence they had witnessed at the Malesar unit, when Comandante Silva had lent his official presence to a rope punishment in front of the entire unit.

Elsewhere, there were scattered attacks by UMAP recruits against their oppressors, incidents that culminated in savage reprisals. In at least two cases the rebellious ones were shot as an example in front of their fellow recruits.

I continued to treat the injuries and disorders, keeping as many of the sick and lame out of the fields as I could and recording everything. I managed to get Nivaldo Alayón, my barber friend from Güines, transferred to the comparative ease of headquarters duty, but I could do nothing for Raúl Fernández Sáens. Try as I might, Lieutenant González adamantly refused to intercede for Fernández Sáens, an indication that his case was still being directed from Havana.

Around this time I made the acquaintance of a UMAP officer, Sergeant Labra, a one-time PSP member with a surprisingly encyclopedic knowledge of Marxism. Labra did not disclose why he had been sent into UMAP. Our conversations dealt mainly with Marxist-Leninist theory, a subject I was determined to study. It seemed a good idea to master the revolution's supposed ideological underpinnings if I was to navigate our way out of it.

Labra's greatest personal ambition, he said, was someday to win membership in the party. For me he was an invaluable guide to its historical literature.

He directed my reading of Communism's seminal documents and the order in which I should digest them. At night I'd go over my notes with him, slowly steeping myself in the fundamentals. Arid or unappealing as many of the ideology's precepts were, I did find the tutorial with Labra intellectually stimulating, a welcome chance to stretch my mind.

In August 1967, Lieutenant González informed me of another new assignment: I was to take charge for a month of the polyclinic located at the First of January sugar mill. Until a doctor could be brought from Havana, I, with two nurses and a lab technician, would comprise the entire medical team for 14,000 officers, recruits, and *campesinos* in the area. The volume of work would be overwhelming. Nevertheless, I would be working outside the unit and, for the first time, would see the effect of the revolution on *campesino* life: What had happened to the people for whom we'd fought ten years earlier?

Two or three weeks after my move to the polyclinic, an incident occurred that helped break down the wall of suspicion between the *campesinos* and me—or, rather, between the *campesinos* and what I represented to them. One morning around seven, I was sitting in the doorway of the polyclinic studying a volume of the *Selected Works of Lenin*—which I did every day from six to seven-thirty—when I noticed a young man and a female approaching. The woman looked starved. She dragged her thin legs and leaned on her companion, who was much younger than she. Her long, loose dress hung shapelessly around her body. Her gray hair was greasy and disheveled, and it almost completely covered her dead-white face.

The boy, about twenty, was wearing torn trousers and a patched, stained *guayabera*. The leather handle of his machete stuck out from under his shirt.

"What's wrong?" I asked as I came forward to help them.

"I feel very sick, Doctor," the woman stammered through cracked lips.

She then fainted. Quickly we moved her into the examining room. Her body was cold and sweaty. Her blood pressure was sixty-five over forty, and her pulse was fifty per minute. At my side the boy kept repeating nervously, "She was bleeding down there. Bleeding!"

When I raised her dress, I saw large bloodstains on her thighs and dried blood on her pelvis. A fetid odor filled the room.

I cleaned her quickly and put on my gloves to examine her. The remnants of placenta adhering to her uterus indicated a recent miscarriage. I made an urgent call to my lab assistant, telling him to prepare for a transfusion. While he did the blood analysis, I gave the old woman an injection of Coramine to revive her. Then I called the hospital at Ciego de Avila to ask for an ambulance.

Fortunately, her blood type was the same as mine. We began the transfusion immediately. After an hour, when the ambulance arrived, the *campesino* woman had regained consciousness. The young man sat beside her, and as they drove away he said over and over again, "Thank you, Doctor. Thank you."

I often slept in the infirmary on nights before my regular consultations so that I could begin office hours early. One such morning in September, I heard a knock on my door at five. The sun wasn't even up yet. Sleepily, I made for the door, assuming it was some emergency.

When I opened the door, however, I saw a single *campesino* grinning broadly at me. In one hand he held a large, squawking chicken and, in the other, a jute sack bulging with vegetables. He was permanently burnt by the sun and his face was deeply wrinkled. The grin was huge and it exposed two lonely, large, yellow teeth.

"Pardon, Doctor, for making you get up so early," he stammered, still grinning. "I brought you this present to thank you for what you did for the old woman."

"The old woman?" I asked, somewhat confused.

"Yes, Doctor," he replied. "She's better. She lost the baby but she laughed at death because you gave her your blood. She came with me. She wants to thank you too."

I opened the door a bit wider to see the old woman I'd treated the month before. She was sitting contentedly on one of the benches at the doorway, crooning to a little girl asleep in her lap.

"Doctor," she said, looking up from the child, "I want to thank you. I was in the hospital more than three weeks, you know? They took out everything. I can't have any more babies. But the doctors there told me that if you hadn't given me your blood, I wouldn't be here at all."

Her appearance and expression were a far cry from the haggard, half-dead creature I'd seen in August. When I'd first set eyes on her, I'd gauged her age as considerably more than fifty, too old to conceive, much less bear, children.

"Old woman," I asked as her doctor, "how old are you?"

"About forty," she answered, and then explained that she was the mother of ten surviving children, the oldest of whom was now twenty-four and the youngest the little girl on her lap.

Her gifts did create a problem, because it was strictly forbidden for us to accept any sort of compensation from the *campesinos*. But I quickly saw that my protestations were offending them. There was only one solution.

"Okay, let's do this," I said. "Next Sunday I'll come to your house and we'll eat the chicken and vegetables with the whole family. And we'll celebrate your recovery, all right?"

They joyfully accepted my proposal, and the following Sunday, I set out on the four-mile walk to their village, Trucutú. Just in case, I took along my doctor's bag and prescription pad.

Village was perhaps too expansive a term for Trucutú. It was actually no more than a small settlement of single-story houses and a few *bohíos*, all thinly covered with Ciego de Avila's omnipresent red dust. The short clinic I held that day was a novel and wonderful event for its inhabitants. One of the things that struck me most was the complete absence of that ubiquitous sight of my youth—*campesino* children with bellies distended by parasites.

My hostess, whose name was Caridad, and her husband, Diosdado, were proudly waiting for me at the door, surrounded by all their children. Inside their modest prefabricated house of post-revolutionary construction, we first enjoyed a glass of *saoco*, a mixture of coconut milk, rum, lemon juice, and sugar, together with a plate of pork cracklings. Then came the introductions. Boys and girls, aunts and uncles, cousins, in-laws, and friends all trooped through the small dining room to meet me and then to linger around the house and its porch.

Everyone talked at once in a gathering bedlam. Hopelessly at a loss to sort out who was who and what was their connection to Caridad and Diosdado, I just sat back and listened to the happy noise, occasionally distinguishing Caridad's voice from the direction of the patio, where she was plucking chickens and tending to her large pot of boiling water.

In time the babble gave way to guitar music and folk songs. At four in the afternoon we all sat down to Caridad's delicious chicken-and-vegetable stew, a very special meal for me after six months of consuming the UMAP diet of thin gruel and bad rice. But my real nourishment that day was psychic. For the first time since I'd arrived in Camagüey in April, I was relaxed, at home with boisterous farmers unburdened by ideology or revolutionary dogma.

Soon I was a regular visitor to Trucutú, ostensibly holding consultations as my reason for going there but in fact almost fleeing to the little settlement as an oasis of simple friendship. The contrast between my days in Trucutú and the rest of my life in UMAP was overpowering. I'd almost forgotten the honest pleasure of direct conversation.

Diosdado and I got along famously. "I have worked this land all my life," he told me. "My father was born and died right here, with a hoe in his hand." Then he offered a connected observation. "I don't care about politics," he said, "and nobody else around here does, either."

Although the revolution had transformed the *campesinos'* lives by improving their health dramatically, fighting their illiteracy with education, and building them houses, it was also committed to the eradication of their independent ways. Fidel saw the small farmer as too individualistic. Even though he'd made good on his pledge for agrarian reform, he intended that Cuba's *campesinos* inherit the earth collectively, according to good Socialist doctrine.

An early mechanism aimed toward regimenting *campesinos* such as Diosdado was the National Association of Small Farmers (ANAP), to which most of them belonged. In principle, ANAP was a quasi-governmental agency established to advise and assist farmers with credit, fertilizers, and tools. But in practice, ANAP was most concerned with controlling what the *campesinos* planted, where they planted it, and when.

One day Diosdado demonstrated for me the ground-level impact of these policies. "There's a lot of work for nothing now," he said as we walked out into Trucutú's fields. "On that land there," he continued, indicating with a wave the countryside in all directions, "you can grow the biggest bananas and the sweetest pineapples. Then those people come. They don't know anything! They tell me I can't plant pineapples or bananas. Now I have to plant yams.

"But that's not all. They make me plant out of season, when the moon is wrong. Then what do you get? Yams the size of limes!"

He showed me to a vast acreage planted with potatoes and yams. In the middle of the fields Diosdado squatted along a row, dug his fingers into the soil, and pulled up a couple of yams.

"See what I'm telling you? Limes!" he exclaimed, holding the tiny yams in his rough hands. "See, these were planted in July, because they're always talking about filling some kind of quota."

Like most of the rest of Cuba's small farmers, Diosdado avoided trouble by doing what he was told, no matter how stupid the centralized planning was. In quiet, apathetic disaffection, the *campesinos* obeyed the letter of the official directives.

But on the small plot Diosdado could plant as he liked for his family's consumption, he worked diligently according to his knowledge of the land to produce the sort of rich harvest that Camagüey soil traditionally yielded. His surplus, and that of thousands of other *campesinos*, naturally found its way into the barter and black markets, where Cuba's impatient customers bid up the prices of all the farm products they could no longer find in state stores. The black market grew so huge that a peso drain from city to countryside ensued.

This skewed Cuba's teetering economy even more. Some middlemen in the black market became very rich, and an unknowable but substantial portion of the rest of the country's currency began collecting in old cans and under mattresses as the *campesinos* hoarded their share of the profits. Before Fidel thought up more effective ways of coercing or tricking the farmers to do his will, an important source of freedom and power—money—was systematically lost to state control and flowed into the hands of those Fidel least wished to see gain any more independence, the *campesinos*.

THE REVOLUTION
DISCOVERS UMAP

I visited with the *campesinos* as often as I could in the months that followed, my only relief from UMAP's cruel environment until its bubble of anonymity burst, at last, in December 1966. As far as I know, no single event or revelation triggered the national and then international wave of protest against the year-long barbarity of the camps. Instead, the recruits' tales of savagery against them leaked out of Camagüey to their families and friends and neighbors, who then started flooding Fidel and Celia Sánchez with outraged letters. Fidel finally had no choice but to register his own shock and then to act, in classic Fidel fashion.

He swept Camagüey Staff Headquarters of its senior officers, including Comandantes Casillas and Silva. These two, however, suffered no further sanctions and even kept their Central Committee membership. Captain Quintín Pino Machado, a former ambassador, and Captain "Guerrita" Guerra Matos, ex-president of INDER—the National Institute of Sport, Physical Education, and Recreation—were sent to Camagüey headquarters as the comandantes' replacements. This was not a promotion for them but a punishment; no one, not even those in charge, was in UMAP voluntarily.

Below this level, few UMAP officials were affected. Those

such as Lieutenant González, who had continued to direct the brutality when I was gone, now visited each unit to read a prepared statement. "The Revolution," it said, "unaware until now of everything that was occurring, has taken action to remedy the situation and will demand an accounting from those responsible for such outrages." González even added his own flourish of indignation, denouncing corporal punishment as "contrary to the principles of the Revolution." The fact that he had until this day been one of those "responsible for such outrages" was no impediment to his condemning them now.

Early in January 1967, Pino Machado and Guerra Matos, both of whom I knew from the early days of the revolution, summoned me to Camagüey Staff Headquarters. When I walked into his office, Guerrita rose from his chair and came forward, limping from an old wound he had received in the Sierra.

"Slim, how are you?" he said cordially. Then he explained his presence. "Here I am, fucked up again," he said. "I put my foot in it and they sent me to this rat's nest. What do you think of this mess? I've never been in such a hot spot!"

Just then, an aide called me to see Captain Machado. I found Quintín standing in the middle of his spacious office. His short, thickset figure and fat-cheeked reddish face with its babyish features gave him the appearance of an overgrown boy. After a brief chat, he ordered us a succulent meal, throughout which he jabbered incessantly, as was his well-known habit. Later, while we were drinking our coffee, he got down to business.

"What do you think of UMAP, Slim?" he asked. "Do you agree with it or not? What do you know about torture in the camps? Are there killers among the recruits?"

I framed a revolutionarily correct reply consistent with my denunciation of UMAP to Pedro Miret and Alfredo Guevara. I assumed Quintín knew of it. "UMAP doesn't work," I said. "It doesn't solve anything and only harms the revolution's prestige. Its original purpose was good, but in practice it is a disaster. And the proof is the punishments and tortures that I've witnessed personally. There are killers among the recruits, and among those who aren't recruits too."

I ended this little speech with the obligatory disclaimer. "I'm certain," I said, "that they hid everything from Fidel."

Quintín had followed my movements with unblinking eyes. He got up to offer me another cup of coffee.

"I agree with you. You're right," he said. "Fidel and Raúl

were deceived by false reports from Casillas and Silva. In the last three days I have also talked to seven of your 'punished' colleagues. I've asked them the same questions. But their answers, all of their answers, were evasive and self-justifying. I sent them back to their units. From now on I want you to be my adviser. I'll give you a letter ordering your transfer. Go back to your battalion and pick up your things. When you come back here I'll explain your new duties to you."

I was under no illusions about my new status, which I had earned simply by my having denounced UMAP at a time when it was deemed politically correct to do so. At battalion headquarters, Lieutenant González couldn't hide his surprise at my immediate transfer. In his usual bluff manner he bid me his version of a friend's farewell. "In spite of our disagreements, Doctor, I'm sorry you're leaving," he said. "I was growing fond of you. And now who's going to take care of the infirmary, huh?"

I didn't say good-bye to anybody else except my friend Nivaldo Alayón. When I told him about my transfer his face grew solemn.

"I'm leaving you in good shape," I said. "You're working as a barber and you don't have to go to the fields. You have peace and respect. All that seems like progress to me if we remember that night with the cockroaches and the rats, don't you agree?"

Alayón was in no mood for jocularity. "What I want is for you to take me with you as soon as you can—that's what I want," he said very seriously. "Now that you're leaving, they'll start torturing again. Just thinking about it makes my hair stand on end. Please, don't forget me. Don't forget me."

Now, when I was definitely leaving that place of so much outrage, oppression, injustice, violence, and contempt for human beings, I paradoxically felt a certain nostalgia. I was saddened to leave Alayón behind. Greater still was my sorrow at leaving Diosdado, Caridad, and the rest of the *campesino* friends in Trucutú. They had been my sanctuary, my connection to real feelings and open thoughts. For a short while these people had offered me those most essential gifts, genuine emotion and friendship. All too soon I'd realize that such naturalness, even within oneself, was an unaffordable luxury in Fidel's Cuba.

At Camagüey Staff Headquarters, I was billeted on the top floor of the mansion in a room with a green-tiled ceiling, two cots, a table, two chairs, a dysfunctional bathroom, and a French lieutenant named Lavandeira. A veteran of Ché's invading column from the Sierra Maestra, Lavandeira was a tall, thin, blond man with an aquiline nose and small green eyes that eerily complemented our ceiling. Behind the thick lenses of his old-fashioned tortoise-shell glasses, those little green orbs darted constantly. After a couple of days in his company, I concluded that the lieutenant appeared to be unstable.

While Quintín and Guerrita were busy dismantling UMAP, issuing face-saving directives and investigating "those responsible" for the UMAP scandal, Lieutenant Lavandeira had come from Havana to Camagüey as the Armed Forces Ministry's designated expert on homosexuality. I was assigned by Captain Machado to be his representative on a research project involving Lavandeira and a team of specialists from the psychology faculty at the University of Havana.

The Cuban government did not officially acknowledge the existence of homosexuality, although the leadership was obviously concerned about it. Since soon it would no longer be possible for Cuban homosexuals to be rounded up and shipped off to UMAP, Lavandeira had been sent to find a means of rehabilitating these men. The cure, he told me, would be simple. "There is only one medicine," Lavandeira explained excitedly, his eyes, like a pair of frozen peas, flitting in their sockets. "And we have it at hand. It is Marxist philosophy, accompanied by hard labor that will force them into manly consciousness and gestures."

Lavandeira was headed for trouble.

Initially the recruits tried to cooperate with him, but the lieutenant made such inane, prurient inquiries of them that his interviews soon turned farcical.

"How do you feel with a man?" he asked. Or, "Does it hurt?" Another favored question: "Do you have an erection when you're with a beautiful woman?"

Finally, at a collective meeting of 120 homosexual recruits, presided over by the team from the university, some of the bolder recruits couldn't contain their laughter. Others burlesqued Lavandeira's intense manner with deadly accuracy. The lieutenant quickly turned frantic in front of the crowd. "Be a man!" he shouted, shaking with messianic fervor. "Be manly! Marxism will save you!" At that moment, the chief psychologist stepped forward and abruptly ended the meeting.

Lavandeira did not remain long in Camagüey. He had emotional outbursts and returned to the capital where he spent time in the psychiatric ward of the Military Hospital.

That, however, is not the end of his story. In revolutionary Cuba, no career is irredeemably scuttled. Today the lieutenant is regarded by the revolution as one of Cuba's preeminent psychologists, a reputation in the highest circles of government that utterly confounds the professional faculty at the University of Havana.

UMAP ensnared other unlikely victims as well. Antonio Carrillo, the former doctor and ambassador to France, whose star had been ascendant in the revolutionary firmament ever since he'd reported his best friend Rolando Cubela's assassination plot, by now had become a deputy minister of foreign affairs. He also continued to wield considerable derived influence from his identification with Pepín Naranjo and Celia Sánchez. But Carrillo grew too certain of his power. As I heard the story in headquarters in Camagüey, he had dared to hide his nephew, a recruit AWOL from UMAP, and had then gone to MININT to arrange his nephew's discharge from the service.

Unfortunately for Carrillo, his old nemesis, First Deputy Minister Manuel Piñeiro, handled the matter. Piñeiro refused Carrillo's request and then sent the details of the case to Fidel and Raúl for their consideration. Carrillo was doomed. He was dismissed from the Foreign Affairs Ministry, according to the official explanation presented at worker assemblies throughout the ministry, for "holding petit bourgeois attitudes incompatible with the ideology of the Revolution." Then he was sent as an ordinary physician to a small polyclinic in Rancho Boyeros, outside Havana.

Having cleaned up the camps and buried the acronym now synonymous with scandal, Fidel was still left with the problems for which he had established the UMAP in the first place.

His solution was to create the Youth Column of the Centenary, named in commemoration of the uprising that had sparked the island's War of Independence in 1868. The Youth Column, later renamed the Youth Work Army (EJT), was for neither criminals nor homosexuals. Its ranks would include members of dissident religious groups and all the rest of the young Cubans thought to be unsuitable for regular army units.

By June this transformation was complete. Recruits over thirty-three years of age were discharged from UMAP altogether, including my friend Alayón at my instigation. The criminals were all back in their cells. The unchecked brutality, so damaging to the revolution's image, had been ended. Now Camagüey had a conscripted farm labor pool, and the army's *campesino* veterans were conveniently redeployed. Cuba's homosexuals still "did not exist," but at least no new "solutions" to their unacknowledged presence were being attempted.

On June 22, 1967, I was released as well. My file, forwarded to Havana, included a commendation "for impeccable conduct, discipline, and a revolutionary attitude" toward my errors. After fourteen months in this Orwellian system, I was "free" to resume my life.

An uneasy instinct told me that the ordeal really wasn't over, that *La Dolce Vita* and UMAP would cast a long shadow. Nevertheless, full of determination to be rid of Cuba's revolution and to save my tottering marriage, I headed for Havana.

I could not allow myself to dwell on the far-fetched irony of my situation: that I had come to Cuba to rescue my uncle in Camagüey from a revolution I had helped to make, and had done so only to find myself trapped, in Camagüey, by a very different revolution. What is more, my deceptions in this cause had destroyed Marie Christine's loyalty and trust in me, just when I needed them most. I was caught in a web of accusation and innuendo, unable to speak the truth or to undo the harm that had been done to her.

My focus in the midst of this drama was entirely on escaping it. Originally, in my naïvely simple plan, I had intended to return permanently to France with my wife and daughter, perhaps as early as Christmas 1965 but no later than the end of 1966. We would have had Marielle sent from Caracas to Paris, and then, under the pretext of returning to France for the holidays (where we supposedly would be fetching our little girl home with us again to Cuba), Marie Christine and I would fly over to freedom.

My arrest, however, had put this strategy indefinitely on hold. I knew that after UMAP the organs of the revolution would watch my every movement for signs of recidivism. Until I was completely restored to the bosom of the revolution, I had no chance of being allowed a trip abroad.

As I had no clandestine connections, either, we wouldn't be able to sneak away. Nor could I register to emigrate. If a revolutionary is foolish enough to request an exit visa, he faces immediately internment as a subversive. What other motive, asks the revolution, could a revolutionary have for wanting to leave?

Seeking asylum at some embassy was also not an option. According to the usual procedure, we would have had to go to a Latin American embassy in Havana, and in 1967 only Mexico among Latin American nations still maintained an ambassador in Cuba. I didn't know anyone I could trust in the Mexican delegation, and we couldn't risk simply presenting ourselves for proposed political asylum. The Cuban government would be automatically notified by the embassy. Then, if asylum for any reason was refused, we might spend the balance of our years in a Cuban prison.

Finally, there was the alternative of hijacking an airplane or a boat. I figured out a number of ways that this could be accomplished, but was stayed by the formidable risks involved. Each plan I thought over entailed the probability of killing someone, perhaps even someone I knew. All these stratagems would endanger Marie Christine's life too. It seemed to me that I'd jeopardized her enough already; and I couldn't chance leaving our daughter an orphan.

Consequently, I set aside hijacking as an absolute last resort and resolved to make time my ally. I had little choice.

In the first few weeks following my release, my relationship with Marie Christine stabilized into one of formal politeness. There was always tension between us, but I hoped that for the time being we'd achieve a tacit means of persevering together.

While I waited to be assigned a new post in the government, we lived modestly on her salary. MININT, although no longer the constant source of incredible strain it had been during *La Dolce Vita*, nevertheless contacted me often, its political officials signaling by their demeanor and carefully worded conversations that I had not yet lost my taint. They hinted repeatedly that Marielle's continued absence with my parents in Venezuela made them very suspicious of my commitment to building a new life in revolutionary Cuba. When they became explicit with me—as when one State Security officer said, "You need a regular life; why haven't you sent for your daughter?"—it didn't require any special interpretive skills to understand their meaning.

Under duress, in July 1967, a month after my release, I told Marie Christine that Marielle could now join us in Havana. Joyful as she was at the prospect of seeing Marielle, Marie Christine remained ambivalent about me, particularly after this decision. I had consistently dismissed the idea of Marielle's joining us, hoping at first that my holiday escape plan might be put into action, and then reasoning that Marielle should be spared the hazards in which I'd involved her mother. Not privy to my thinking, Marie Christine plainly wondered what had changed my mind.

As a result, I managed even to poison our pleasure in our reunion with our only child. Marie Christine, perhaps subliminally, may have reached her crisis point with me at this time. There could be no doubt in her mind that my pattern of aloof deception was persisting.

Marielle had been a toddler when last I'd held her in Paris. Now she was a lively six-year-old with a blond ponytail and a command of Spanish nearly equal to her French. An uneasiness that told me my bringing her to Cuba was only another fateful step into the quagmire edged my happiness with apprehension, but I did feel a pure paternal pleasure in showing Havana to my daughter, strolling through bookstores with her, seeing her off to the French school where we'd enrolled her that autumn, and on our many trips together to the beach. In her adulthood, Marielle's special recollection of these days would be our time at the shore.

THE MOMENT FOR GUERRILLAS

Cuba's gathering domestic crisis, the tangle of official corruption and hypocrisy—from which I was struggling, and failing, to extricate myself—together with the island's worsening economy did not worry Fidel enough that he neglected his wider role as a world leader. Fidel's commitment to promoting revolution to the underdeveloped world was the first objective and cornerstone of his foreign policy. As reflected in the grand scope of the January 1966 Tricontinental Conference in Havana, Fidel initially had hoped to ignite a pan-global insurrectionary conflagration all at once.

After the conference, however, he began to realize that the first arena for action had to be Latin America. Part of his revised thinking was strategic. Even with the Soviets' massive economic aid and Moscow's willingness to wink at Fidel's international adventuring, Cuba's resources were finite; the country had neither the financial nor the human resources to support revolution everywhere. Moreover, Fidel had learned a specific lesson from Ché, whose secret destination after my last conversation with him had been Congo (Brazzaville), where he'd fought for nine months in 1965 with Pierre Mulele's rebels against the army of Moise Tshombe.

According to Comandante Papito Serguera, Rolando Cubela's prosecutor and then ambassador to both Algeria and Congo (Brazzaville), Ché had made detailed written reports of his observations in Africa, a secret unpublished diary. In their conversations, said Serguera, Ché had lamented the primitive conditions in Africa. He'd had no luck as a Marxist-Leninist missionary among Mulele's guerrillas, concluding, in Papito's paraphrase, that "brutal underdevelopment, the product of the most heartless colonial exploitation, has left these peoples far from the threshold to revolution."

The decision to concentrate at first on Latin America was by no means a retrenchment for Fidel. This new emphasis did not mean he was indifferent toward liberation movements on other continents. In time, he would concretely demonstrate the fullness of his intentions outside the Western Hemisphere with Cuban weapons and Cuban blood.

But in 1967 he decided to take advantage of geographic proximity, a common language, and shared heritage to build a unified Latin American movement. He talked of Latin America as being "united by the heart of Bolívar": Simón Bolívar, the continent's fabled liberator of the nineteenth century. Fidel, who regarded himself as a man of destiny as well, would be his era's liberator, transforming the Andes into a larger-scale Sierra Maestra.

Exploiting these conditions and promoting the radicalization of Latin American leftists would enhance Fidel's power—and burnish his prestige—in several ways. Once on the road to guerrilla warfare, the region's rebels would need help from somewhere. If they turned, most logically, to Cuba, any aid would come with ideological strings attached, resulting in the rebels' direct and open defiance of U.S. hegemony in Latin America, another challenge to the hated Yanquis. Just as important, however, was the strategy's ideological thrust in the opposite direction of Soviet policy. Fidel meant by any means possible to emphasize the Cuban revolution's independence on the world stage.

For many years, Latin American Communist parties had adhered to Soviet pragmatism. The Soviets had believed that each national situation demanded its own unique solution—a view that did not discount the possibility of a peaceful transition to Socialism. Rather than abet armed revolt, they discouraged it. Under the umbrella of peaceful coexistence, these parties sought to become institutionalized, part of each nation's legitimate political landscape.

Fidel unequivocally rejected this analysis. His experience in the Sierra Maestra had amply demonstrated that a guerrilla movement could achieve power in Latin America and establish an alliance of peasants and workers without any leadership from the party. In other words, revolution meant armed conflict, and it was not the exclusive privilege of a national Communist Party to give it. Quite the opposite: In his opinion, the party should be led by the guerrilla. In Cuba, Fidel had seen how the old PSP had opposed armed insurrection and therefore lacked prestige with the Cuban masses. Looking around him in Latin America, he saw the same brand of bourgeois behavior among Communist leaders there.

In private, Fidel was reliably reported to have expressed his uniform contempt for those parties that, as his words were reported back to me, "prefer to follow the lead of the USSR instead of being guided by the experience of a sister nation, harassed and threatened by imperialism." Yet he wasn't ready to test the outer boundaries of Soviet indulgence. To both the world audience and the inner counsels of the Soviet bloc, the letter of solidarity had to be observed, even if the spirit and substance of Fidel's world view ran directly counter to Moscow's.

Given this requirement for tact, Fidel settled on a means of publishing his recipe for revolution so that everyone would recognize its source without its being revealed. His tool for this would be the young French leftist Regis Debray, a scholar of Marxism and student of Latin American affairs who was undeniably bright, a fine wordsmith, and, conveniently, then on the faculty at the University of Havana. Fidel ordered State Security and Cuban Intelligence carefully to investigate Debray. Once they had sifted through every knowable detail of his background, the Frenchman was invited to join Fidel in a series of lengthy sessions in which Fidel freely expounded his ideas. Then Debray, who had no personal experience with guerrilla warfare, polished and packaged Fidel's thoughts as his own in *Revolution Within the Revolution*, published in March 1967.

Fidel-Debray's essential points were these: The guerrilla operating in the countryside is the focus of the revolution, and the movement to which he belongs is self-directing, independent of extant political machinery; urban fighters are the bourgeoisie of guerrilla warfare; and physical stamina is the most important requirement of the guerrilla, since survival in the mountains is his first necessity.

The timing of *Revolution Within the Revolution* was crucial, the key move in a complex maneuver to advance the Cuban agenda. It appeared in print four months before the August 1967 opening in Havana of the first conference of OLAS, the Organization for Latin American Solidarity, a Cuban-sponsored gathering of Latin American leftists of all stripes where Fidel planned to press his doctrine. He could be sure that by August everyone attending the OLAS meeting would have read *Revolution Within the Revolution*.

Osmany Cienfuegos, brought back from punishment to Havana by Fidel to help organize this important conference, told me that Fidel was tireless and minutely painstaking as he shaped the Cuban delegations's official report to the conference, a document that thoroughly capsulized *Revolution Within the Revolution* without being overtly confrontational. It never once mentioned the USSR or China, or even alluded by name to any of the Latin American Communist Parties, representatives of which all attended the OLAS meeting.

The delegation's report and Fidel's closing speech to the conference amounted to an open, albeit oblique, repudiation of the Soviet doctrine. The document proclaimed that the notion of proletarian revolution in Latin America was absurd, because Latin America had no appreciable proletariat. The policy of working toward peaceful transition to Socialism on the continent, it said, was utopian. The report emphasized that the revolution's core, its mountain guerrillas, needed to be guided by Marxist-Leninist ideology, but it rejected any party role in revolution by neglecting to mention the party at all.

After reiterating the rest of Fidel's ideals, the paper closed with a clear statement of Cuba's willingness to offer all material and human aid to the Latin American movements with the unspoken proviso that Cuban aid would flow only to those that met the revolution's standards of eligibility.

Osmany and others I knew who attended the closed sessions of the conference told me that the delegation's report had rankled the Latin American Communists. Apart from the Cubans' deviationism, the local Communists rejected the revolution's unilateral determination to interfere in their countries' internal affairs whenever it wished.

I personally heard Fidel irritate his brother Communists even further in his closing speech. "Let no one think he will take power peacefully in any country on this continent," he said. "We cannot understand what kind of peaceful transition they refer to, unless it is a peaceful transition in agreement with imperialism." With his typical wordiness, he continued: "The essence of the question is whether the masses will be led to believe that the revolutionary movement, that Socialism, can come to power without a struggle, that it can come to power peacefully. And that is a lie! And any person in Latin America who asserts that he will come to power peacefully is deceiving the masses."

Fidel took Soviet foreign policy to task, too, indirectly attacking the USSR's aid programs to Latin American capitalist countries. "We are talking," he said indignantly, "about financial and technical help given by any Socialist state to the Latin American oligarchies." His opinion of such policy? "This is absurd; dollar loans to an oligarchic government that is repressing and assassinating guerrillas!"

The speech contained all the elements of bloat and repetition characteristic of Fidel's addresses. But those who could cut through the bombast understood that Fidel was clearly threatening to launch a radical offensive on the continent.

The audience for this address had been packed with Cubans; Fidel needed bursts of applause for proper punctuation. But the approval was not universal. The Cuban leader was assaulting the sacrosanct.

"We no longer accept any self-evident truths," he averred. "A whole series of clichés must be abolished." Since his ideology pivots on clichés, this last line held some thin humor for me. But it did not amuse the various party secretaries at the meeting. They stood with the rest at the end of the address but did not applaud. Looking around me, I saw several very long and disapproving faces, most prominently that of Rodney Arismendi, secretary of the Uruguayan Communist Party, who looked as if he'd just swallowed a lemon.

Fidel lost little time in making good on his threats. Guerrilla training camps were opened to radical leftists from several Latin American countries, including Venezuela, Nicaragua, Honduras, Colombia, and Bolivia. Urban fighters from Argentina and Uruguay came to Cuba for training too.

He also increased direct military and financial aid to the hemisphere's many leftist insurgencies, including the export of Cubans as advisers and combatants to Venezuela, Guatemala, and El Salvador. In the months immediately following OLAS, Fidel launched a guerrilla juggernaut in Latin America, a continent-wide offensive orchestrated directly from Havana. His goal was nothing short of repeating the Cuban revolution everywhere until the United States, not Cuba, was the embattled and isolated pariah of the New World.

THE DEATH OF CHÉ

Ché Guevara's nine months in Africa had been filled with frustration and disillusion. Pierre Mulele's troops had totally lacked discipline. Their rituals—such as hacking their defeated enemies to pieces, and cannibalism—had revulsed Ché. He'd told Serguera that he felt compassion for these brute tribesmen, "but revolutions are never made with compassion." Overall, as Serguera would explain to me in early 1968, Ché's detailed reports on the many obstacles to politicizing Africa for the time being had disabused Fidel of a pet conception: "tribal Marxism," his belief that Communist ideology was adaptable to the conditions of primitive society.

Other circumstances had further impeded Ché's efforts in Congo (Brazzaville). Relations between Cuba and China had reached a critical point in January 1966, when China had refused to increase rice shipments to the island. In February, Fidel had denounced a Chinese "conspiracy" to distribute anti-Soviet literature within the Cuban army and bureaucracy.

These conflicts had repercussions in Congo (Brazzaville). The Chinese had supported Mulele's rebellion, but now pressured him to get rid of his Cuban "volunteers." Meanwhile the Soviets, hoping to defuse the crisis, also wanted Ché and his eighty men out of Africa. Fidel could not refuse the USSR's wishes.

As for Ché, his return to the rigors of guerrilla warfare in Africa came at a time when his public profile was at its highest. In April 1964, the West European press had focused on him in Geneva, where he'd spent nearly a month as head of the Cuban delegation to the U.N. conference on commerce and development. In November of that year he had been given prominent coverage as the senior Cuban official invited to join the Moscow celebration of the Soviet Revolution. In December, he had been in New York to address the U.N. General Assembly and appeared on *Face the Nation*.

Then, late in 1965, Ché had vanished into Africa, provoking wild international speculation as to where he was, what he was doing—and even if he was still alive. The mission to Congo (Brazzaville) had been kept highly secret.

Knowledge of Ché's activities in Africa had been restricted inside Cuba to Fidel, Raúl, and members of the Politburo. All that the rest of the nation, including myself, then knew came from Ché's farewell letter to Fidel, which Fidel had read publicly at the founding ceremony for the Cuban Communist Party in October 1965, eight months after my arrival in Cuba.

"I feel I have fulfilled the part of my duty that tied me to the Cuban Revolution on its territory," Ché wrote to Fidel. "And I say good-bye to you, the *compañeros*, your people who are now my people."

He praised Fidel effusively. "Taking stock of my past life," the letter said, "I believe I have worked with sufficient honor and dedication to consolidate revolutionary victory. My only really serious fault is not to have trusted in you more from the first moments in the Sierra Maestra and not to have understood quickly enough your qualities as leader and revolutionary."

Naturally Ché made no mention of the antagonisms he had bluntly shared with me in our last conversation half a year before. "Other lands," he wrote in explanation for his departure, "call for my modest efforts. I can do what is denied you because of your responsibilities at the head of Cuba, and the time has come for us to separate.

"Know that I do so with a mixture of joy and sorrow. Here I leave the purest of my hopes as a builder and the dearest of those dear to me. . . . I leave people who took me as their son, and that wounds a part of my spirit. On the new fields of battle I will carry the faith you taught me, the revolutionary spirit of my people, the feeling of carrying out the most sacred of duties, to fight against imperialism wherever it may be. This amply comforts and cures any sorrow."

Ché renounced all his official ties to Cuba, thus absolving Fidel from any responsibility, or potential embarrassment, should misadventure strike. But he left no doubt as to his loyalties. "If my final hour comes under other skies," Ché wrote toward the end of the letter, "my last thought will be for this people and especially for you. I thank you for your teaching and for your example, to which I will try to be faithful until the final consequences of my actions. . . . Anywhere I go I will feel the responsibility of being a Cuban revolutionary, and I will behave as such. I do not leave my children and my wife anything material, and that does not sadden me. I am glad that this is true. I ask nothing for them, for the state will give them enough to live and to go to school."

He closed the letter with unaffected simplicity. "There are many things I could say to you," he wrote, "but I believe they are unnecessary, and words cannot express what I want them to; it's foolish to scribble on pages. Until our final victory. Ché."

Nevertheless, Ché had secretly returned to Cuba from Africa five months later, in March of 1966, at about the time of my arrest. Until September, Ché and fifteen of his handpicked fighters (among them my old friend Jesús Suárez Gayol) had trained clandestinely at a military facility in far western Pinar del Río province. Then Ché set out on his final journey.

Traveling first to Brazil, he acquired papers identifying him as Adolfo Mena, a "specialist" employed, in fitting irony, by the Organization of American States, which four years earlier had ousted Cuba from its membership. In a white shirt and tie, his hair slicked back and carefully parted in the middle, Ché flew in disguise from São Paulo to Bolivia, where he landed at the Cochabamba airport on November 1, 1966.

To me, it is incomprehensible that Fidel and Ché chose landlocked Bolivia out of all the possible places for him to begin his new war of liberation. True, Bolivia had among the least efficient armies and internal security forces in the hemisphere. And true, its geographical location in the very heart of Latin America was ideal for radiating a victorious revolution outward into neighboring countries.

But there was a confluence of less propitious factors facing Ché in Bolivia. First, he would operate in unfamiliar terrain; the impassable Bolivian jungle is very different from Cuba's mountain forests or the African savannah. Second, although Ché believed that the *campesinos* would suppport him, an objective rather than ideological analysis would have told a different story. These people are vital to Latin American guerrillas for their knowledge of the countryside and the news they can bring of the army's deployment and movements. But in Bolivia the *campesinos* were too afraid of the army to risk any guerrilla activity, including Ché's. In addition, the *campesinos* were Indian and Bolivian; Ché and his followers, who were white and almost all foreign, would not inspire their allegiance.

Finally, no guerrilla could be certain of the vital support of the cities' populations. And Ché's only possible ally, the Bolivian Communist Party, toed the Soviet line of peaceful coexistence and believed in a Socialist victory without shooting.

Whatever Fidel had to say about the guerrillas' political independence in revolution, he was well aware from his own experience in the Sierra Maestra that fighters in the countryside need a supply of weapons, ammunition, food, and medicine from the city in order to survive. He also had to know that he could not effectively manage a supply line for Ché from faraway Cuba, especially since Bolivia has no coastline to allow for surreptitious resupply.

While Ché was still alive, Fidel never officially acknowledged his *compañero*'s presence in Bolivia. But from the middle of 1967 onward, rumors about Ché's whereabouts and actions flew all over the island. Toward the end of September of that year, the Voice of America at last, and authoritatively, placed Ché in Bolivia and reported that the guerrillas were surrounded. Subsequently, the Voice of America reported Ché's death, but neither the Cuban people nor the Revolutionary Government believed this was anything but propaganda.

I vividly recollect the night of October 15, 1967, when Fidel came on television with the inevitable news. As I watched him, I could see the strain in his face and sensed from his manner that Fidel was sorrowful—and angry. He seemed hardly able to bring himself to announce the loss and defeat. "We must begin by stating," he intoned, "that we have become convinced that this news—that is, news related to the death of Comandante Ernesto Guevara—is unfortunately true."

Fidel recounted the details of Ché's death, including its background and photos of the bullet-ridden corpse. What affected me as much as the news itself was the way Fidel handled it.

"In all the time we knew him," Fidel said, "he displayed an extraordinary lack of fear, an absolute disregard of danger." He went on to comment: "We must say that we were always concerned that this temperament, this reaction to danger, could lead to his death in any action. No one was ever completely certain that he would adopt even minimum precautions."

At a very inappropriate moment Fidel was implying that Ché had been reckless, possibly to blame for his own death and the guerrillas' defeat because of his irresponsible leadership of the insurgency. The criticism, while veiled, struck me as gratuitous and self-serving, similar to Fidel's earlier dismissal of the Revolutionary Directorate's 1957 assault on the Presidential Palace as "useless bloodshed."

He repeated these same arguments, using different words, on October 18 during the solemn memorial vigil in the Plaza of the Revolution. Thousands of people attended, and the scene was dominated by a colossal photograph of the "heroic guerrilla" covering the side of the MININT building.

Nicolás Guillén, the national poet, read a long poem dedicated to Ché's memory. Later, Fidel broke the grief-stricken silence of the plaza with his own encomium to Ché. "One of the closest, the most admired, the most beloved and, without doubt, the most extraordinary of our revolutionary *compañeros*" was Fidel's description. "A man of complete integrity, a man of supreme sense of honor, of absolute sincerity. A man of stoic and spartan living habits. A man in whose conduct not one stain can be found."

Fidel was listing the revolutionary attributes whose absence Ché had so lamented in the rest of the leaders of the Cuban revolution.

In the years that followed, my image of Ché broke into irreconcilable opposites. He was a friend of mine. And I never lost respect for his integrity. He was always faithful to his convictions, living with absolute fidelity, vehemently, almost mystically—to the extreme of dying for them. He had consistently rejected all material gain, even power, the prize that few people have been able to refuse.

And yet, in the real world, each of this dreamer's ideas failed the test of use. The implementation of his economic system and parallel theories of industrialization ended in disaster for Cuba. His confidence in Fidel's ongoing political nonalignment was mistaken. The most cherished fruit of his ideology, the New Man, would be crushed by the social machinery of the system that was supposed to nourish him. Most tragic of all, Ché's doctrine of guerrilla warfare, put into practice, would lead to his own death.

On balance, his austere life of thirty-nine years proved to be, even by his standards, a failure. He would be reduced by the revolution to a sentimental standard, a political icon unscrupulously exploited by the man most responsible for Ché's departure from Cuba and for his fatal Bolivian adventure. Ché's violent demise in Bolivia was the illogical campaign's most logical outcome, its own predictable ending.

A CHAMELEON IN EMBRYO

Within a few weeks of Ché's death I received a telephone call from Alfredo Guevara, who told me that it had been arranged for me to go to work at his film institute, ICAIC. My job would be to oversee the renovation of the old Warner's movie theater, renamed Radiocentro, across the street from the Havana Libre. I'd be compensated at 40 percent of my previous salary at the Construction Ministry, part of my post-UMAP "proletarianization," the process whereby punished revolutionaries such as myself were placed in salubrious daily contact with Cuba's working class.

It was a blessing, after such bad fortune, to think of working with one of the few Communist revolutionaries I really respected. At about the same time, Marie Christine's aunt and uncle, the Meynards, invited her and Marielle to join them in France for the Christmas holiday. For a few days afterward I dared hope that all three of us might be allowed to go, but an approach through an intermediary to José Abrantes, the head of State Security, dashed my vain expectation. Abrantes indicated to my representative that it was not wise just yet for me to request vacation time outside Cuba.

Marie Christine and Marielle, both French citizens, were not so restricted. With my encouragement, Marie Christine wrote the Meynards that she and our daughter would be pleased to come home for Christmas. After what I'd put her through for the past two and a half years, Marie Christine certainly needed a couple of months away.

Their departure was set for December 17, 1967, and I tried to see our coming separation in the best possible light. My wife and daughter were my only bridge to the world; nothing mattered to me but my plan to end our nightmare in Cuba. Once Marie Christine knew everything, I told myself, we could happily sew back the torn threads of our lives. For now, it seemed a positive step to relieve her stress for a few weeks. When she returned with Marielle in mid-February after their holiday, we'd be that much closer to our eventual escape—together.

Marie Christine, however, had no access to this optimism, or any way of guessing what I wanted or what I would do next. At the airport, as she boarded their plane, she stopped and looked back at me in silence, our daughter standing quietly beside her. There was no reproach, not a hint of accusation in Marie Christine's blue eyes. Rather, I saw a look of confused, innocent grief, of wrecked faith in a love she believed had been betrayed. As she took Marielle's hand and turned away from me, I recoiled at the incredible, senseless anguish I'd caused my wife.

I couldn't even imagine how my life would feel without the vitality and childish energy Marielle had brought in the few wonderful months of domestic happiness since her arrival.

Marie Christine's bewildered expression haunted me for days. Back in our apartment, now empty and unfamiliar to me, I brooded each night on that silent scene at the airport and let my mind wander disconsolately to all the other bleakness in my life. I could barely stand the loneliness.

I fought it as best I could by trying to bury myself in work at ICAIC. Since I knew next to nothing about architecture, building materials, or any of the technical considerations attendant upon remodeling a theater as vast as Radiocentro, I had plenty to do.

My only other diversion was in disciplined research into Communist ideology, and in this the Marists' training once again rose to my rescue. Along with this ongoing study of Marxism, I also began to examine the content of revolutionary laws, foreign policy documents, and Fidel's speeches, which I read closely, copying significant passages into my notebook. I hoped to define Fidel's internal logic in these oceans of words and to compare what he said publicly with his private thoughts as they were reported to me. I also noted with special care each of his increasingly dramatic deviations from orthodox Communist ideology. Speculating about Fidel's intentions was the dominating theme of conversation among revolutionaries; I couldn't survive in this society without educating myself about him.

Fidel is not a serious political philosopher. But any shrewd revolutionary, I was discovering, had to be familiar with the *Líder Máximo*'s every pronouncement, for we all had to take part in worker assemblies and CDR "study circles," where everything Fidel said was digested and codified into revolutionary thinking.

Since certain of Fidel's inspirations had very brief half-lives and might have to be altered or forgotten by his devoted followers as he veered from one position to another, the trick in following him was to make one's mind a tape recorder, with a RECORD button, a PLAY button, and an ERASE button. In this way, one did not come to grief or risk being denounced for being ignorant of Fidel's latest insights, or for seeming to dissent by revealing any critical faculty.

It was wise to be cautious. Those Cubans, for instance, who still observed holy days such as Christmas did so with circumspection; the only approved year-end celebration was New Year's Day, the anniversary of the revolution's triumph in 1959. As 1967 passed into 1968, I was actually glad for the first time about the drabness of the holiday season in Havana. Without *Felices Navidades* ringing in my ears, it was easier to keep my mind firmly fixed on the middle of February, when I'd have my wife and daughter back.

I wanted at least to speak with them while they were so far away, but it was tacitly forbidden for revolutionaries to place international telephone calls except on official business. If I tried, the operator would say, "The circuits are congested." In addition to the political reasons, Cuba could not afford the outflowing dollars of thousands of Cubans phoning their relatives; every Cuban family had members outside, and the debt would have been enormous. Nor was the mail a reliable way to stay in touch. The first letter I received from Marie Christine, written before Christmas, didn't reach me until late January.

Its tone was reasonably cheery; she was enjoying herself, and I was thankful. A short while later, Alfredo Guevara came back from a trip to Europe and brought word that he'd seen Marie Christine in France and that she was doing fine.

When two months had elapsed, I was waiting for the telegram that would give me the details of my family's return. Instead, there was silence. Week after week went by with no word from or about my wife and daughter. Every day I raced home from work, expecting to find a message. With no other way of contacting Marie Christine, I was at the mercy of the slow and haphazard Cuban post office, which I bitterly blamed for its maddening inability to deliver a simple cable from France.

Evidently something was wrong, but I had no idea what. No one I knew was going to Paris then, and so I couldn't even send an inquiry that way. I tried to phone from La Tía's, but, as expected, the operator would not put through my call. Absolutely frantic, I had no way to find out what I desperately needed to know: What had happened to my wife and daughter?

I would never know what date Marie Christine's second letter was written. I discovered it under our apartment door one night in mid-March 1968. Eagerly, I tore open the envelope and found not an explanation for our extended separation but an epitaph to our marriage. Coldly, categorically, in a voice that I didn't recognize, Marie Christine informed me that she was not returning to Cuba. She had finally wearied of life with me in Havana, and she said she no longer had confidence in me. She could not understand why I chose to live in the midst of absolute insecurity in every sense of the word. And she was not about to let her daughter be raised in such an unwholesome environment. Therefore, Marie Christine wrote, she would keep Marielle with her under the protection of French law.

The letter crumpled in my fist. I stood dumbstruck. Nothing in my life, no death or treachery or ill fortune, had ever so suddenly and completely unmanned me. Then I fled, my lungs straining against a suffocating pressure inside me, out to the street and into the car. I slammed the old Volkswagen's throttle to the floor and went hurtling out of Havana toward the coast. I didn't know where I was going or why, and the faster I drove the more tangled and violent my emotions became. Finally, as if by instinct, I arrived at the Cojímar exit and, like an automaton, guided the machine off the Vía Blanca and through the town to a halt at the park by the port town's sea wall.

It was cold and black as ink all around me. I got out of the car into the raw north wind and walked through it toward the sound of the ocean. When I reached the sea wall, I stood alone for a long, long while, listening to the waves below me furiously thundering against the rocks. Rain and sea mist soaked my clothing, but for hours there I felt nothing but my desperate inner tumult. I raged against my impotence, and myself. There was nothing to hold on to, no anchor anymore. It took every bit of strength I had left to collect myself slowly through the night and then to begin soberly to consider my new reality. Sometime just before dawn I returned shivering and spent to the red Volkswagen in the park, and then drove slowly back to Havana.

Once I regained my wits that day, my overriding emotion was contrition. My naïveté alone had led to this estrangement. I had greatly underestimated the power of the system over me and had seen myself as invulnerable to any possible difficulties. Because I was perceived to be a Communist revolutionary, I'd thought I would not be touched, and it was this blindness that had destroyed my personal life.

In this mood, I wrote Marie Christine a return letter, basically an appeal to love, in which I recounted all that we'd shared together. Because my life depended on it, I still couldn't tell her the truth, and thus I had little rational reason to believe I could move her to reconsider; Marie Christine had been definitive and unequivocal. Nevertheless, I had to try to tell her what I had been incapable of showing her: that I loved her and that she should trust me enough to keep trying too.

Through a French national then temporarily posted to Havana, I arranged to have the letter hand-delivered to my wife. I also gave Marie Christine's telephone number to Saúl Yelín, my old friend from the university days who himself still worked at ICAIC. He was going to Paris soon and promised to speak with her.

Yelín returned to Cuba with the final, bitter word from Marie Christine. "She has filed for divorce," he said, "and intends to obtain sole custody of your daughter."

Like a prizefighter beaten senseless but still standing, I couldn't react to the ultimate blow of Yelín's news. The fight was finished for me. My marriage was over. It would be impossible for Marie Christine to regain her trust in me.

But there remained the separate issue of our daughter. If I forfeited my custody rights in France, I had no way to see Marielle once I succeeded in leaving Cuba. Determined by any means possible not to lose my daughter, too, I went to Carlos Chaín, deputy minister of foreign affairs, who arranged for me to meet with the ministry's legal director. I hoped to thwart what I regarded as a legal kidnap attempt.

At the ministry, Olga de Miranda was very precise with me. She explained that I could not contest a French litigation from Cuba. I would have to appear in court there myself or, at the very least, engage an attorney to represent my interests.

So much for the power of my intentions, a lesson it had taken me far too long to learn. José Abrantes, chief of State Security, was unmoved by my second indirect plea for a dispensation to travel to France. The state, concerned only with my well-being as a revolutionary, saw nothing compelling in the imminent loss of my wife and child. What is more, I had no hard currency to hire an attorney and no way to raise the requisite funds. The telephone was taboo, and the glacial pace of the Cuban mails made moot any thought of finding financing, hiring a lawyer, and then briefing him in time to answer Marie Christine's suit. She would gain her divorce and the legal custody of Marielle without a word of dispute in the French court from her husband, a Cuban Communist revolutionary.

I had to face the finality of Marie Christine's absence from my life and force myself to go on. I knew that somehow I would see my daughter again, but I could not even entertain the hope of winning back Marie Christine when I eventually left Cuba. It was over between us; the damage had been done. Now I had to focus on my own situation and without emotion figure out how I was going to leave the country. I could not think beyond that, and my need to see my daughter again only added more urgency to my desire to escape.

I decided the only way I would be able to come up with a solid plan for leaving Cuba was to get away from everything and think. And so I checked into the Hotel Riviera in the Vedado district and then disappeared into my room. For three days I didn't speak to anyone. Besides my own thoughts, my only company for seventy-two hours would be the most contemplative music I could find on the room's radio.

First, I had to deal with my attenuated psyche. Every nerve in my body felt raw. For two weeks my mind had been racing on an agitated adrenaline high, while my spirit had shriveled in despair. A long bath and then sleep quieted me considerably. When I woke it was dark and I was hungry. After a meal consumed for sustenance, not savor, I settled down to deliberate.

Now that Marie Christine had left me, I could no longer get out of Cuba on the pretense of a holiday in France. Again I

considered the hijack alternative, as now I would not be risking
Marie Christine's life as well as mine. While attractive to me at
such a desperate hour—it might even get me back to France to
plead my legal case in person—it was unacceptably risky. In my
youth I had often chanced death or imprisonment without considering the consequences; now I felt it was my duty to Marielle
not to take a chance with my life. Also, the thought of standing
armed before a planeload of innocent people and possibly being
forced to pull the trigger was horrifying to me.

I saw that there was only one route open to me now: to
promote my way up the revolutionary ladder—to rise slowly and
steadily through the bureaucratic ranks so that I could be suffi-
ciently high in the government to be designated for an official
trip abroad. At that moment, I would ask for political asylum in
whatever Western country would grant it. Even if I were sent to
a Socialist country on a trip, I could take advantage of a stopover
in a Western nation.

Slowly I was losing myself in a web of speculation about a
plan whose most vulnerable point was me. I would have to
bend my spirit, subjugate my real thoughts and emotions, sharpen
my perceptions, set out on immutable courses of action, and
rework my behavior to turn myself into the exact duplicate
of a peacetime Communist revolutionary. I had to dedicate myself body and soul to this spiritual surgery and identify fully
with the rules imposed by the system in order to deceive that
system.

Circumstances, not impulse, henceforth would rule my actions, and this would require a self-discipline exponentially
more stern and rigorous than the mere capacity for concentrated
study.

Shrewdness, calculation, and tenacity: All would be necessary. To fool the system so that it would mistake me for part of
itself was not going to be easy. And the greatest danger lay not
within the Cuban system—treacherous as it was—but within
myself. All that I thought of as myself—my confidence and spontaneity as well as the impulsiveness and naïveté that had led to
this crisis—would have to be suppressed with ruthless finality if
I was to survive. That old instinctive reaction to injustice, which
most recently had erupted during UMAP, necessarily had to be
stamped out of me. I had bluffed my way past Lieutenants Mora
and González, but I recognized these small victories of human
dignity for what they were: mostly luck.

On that day the Stranger, already a small voice within me, took charge. Every thought, every motivation of my own and other people's would henceforth be subject to the Stranger's implacable, objective censorship. No more could I be the man I had been up to this day. My true self was now the minority voice within me, in retreat, as the Stranger ruled.

I did not undertake this ultimate deception lightly, although I could foresee only some of its consequences. A silent war had begun, I pitting myself against the structure of the system, determined to defeat the intentions of the party, State Security, the CDR—all the mechanisms designed to subjugate my will. Twenty-four hours a day I would have to be on guard, not only against the organizations and society within which I lived but against myself. If I betrayed my true intent, if in even one step I revealed my ultimate goal, everything would be forfeited.

The road would be not only long, overgrown, full of difficulties and setbacks; it would also be responsible for showing me the wrenching consequences of a false life. There is no more crushing loneliness than to be a man whose life is dominated by the fiercest mistrust, who has to be wary of betrayals and appear to be who he is not. Surrounded by innumerable acquaintances but without a single real friend, I would become a solitary being, with only my conscience for a confidant.

A SOCIALIST CAREER

TWO PARTINGS

ICAIC was an ideal platform from which to launch my career as a Communist revolutionary. Alfredo Guevara was favorably disposed toward me, and he was solidly connected with Fidel and Raúl. Moreover, Fidel well understood the propaganda value of a healthy, aggressive ICAIC and therefore smiled on nearly all Guevara's initiatives.

In ICAIC's original productions, political themes were naturally dominant, but the dialogue was generally fresh, the artistic quality high, and the music well chosen. With Fidel's blessings many films were entered in international festivals, where they won several awards. Alfredo Guevara's film makers knew how to put an entertaining face even on the most boring themes of the revolution.

The Institute was further unique in the governmental bureaucracies because it actually accomplished something. Alfredo was a capable administrator. One of ICAIC's responsibilities was to build new movie theaters all over the country, and Alfredo saw to it that these capital programs were completed according to a more or less sensible schedule. ICAIC was also charged with renovation projects, such as the Radiocentro rehabilitation that I oversaw. The Institute managed the country's cinema houses, too, and provided them with old films confiscated by the revolution from American film enterprises in Cuba, imported pictures, and original productions, mostly short subjects.

The Cuban Institute of Radio and TV (ICRT), by contrast, was more typical of the government as a whole. Headed in 1968 by Comandante "Papito" Serguera in yet another of his incarnations, ICRT offered very weak programming heavy with Socialist films and Hollywood productions from the 1930s and 1940s.

Nobody much cared for the Eastern European movies, whose plots were mostly limited to World War II, the consolidation of Soviet power, or the heroic daily struggle of the proletariat. On the other hand, the television audiences were familiar to the saturation point with the studio warhorses that Papito trotted out night after night. Even classics such as *Casablanca* eventually palled on Cuban viewers, who knew the film as *The Millionaire* for the millions of times it seemed they had watched it.

My job at ICAIC was my first very small step toward my goal. I was resolved to acquit myself well and so I plunged into mastering the many new skills required to oversee the renovation of the Radiocentro theater.

In spring 1968 the theater was ready to reopen. Fortunately, all the new equipment somehow worked without major problems. Our first test feature, imported from Japan, was the saga of a blind samurai named Ichi, who, by his hearing alone, could locate a buzzing housefly and sever its wings in mid-flight with his sword. Ichi made no pretense to cinematographic art, but at least he was more entertaining than party favorites, imported features such as documentaries about racial abuse in the United States, or some day-in-the-life of a Red Army soldier during World War II.

Every new film, no matter what its origin, was shown to the ICAIC Commission of Censorship, a body entrusted by the revolution to review movies for undue sex, violence, or scenes of ideological deviation. What the revolution thought was good for the people, however, differed from what the revolution thought was good for itself. After the Radiocentro restoration, I was moved up at ICAIC to become second head of capital investments, a position with more power and, just as important for my plan, more perquisites. It involved the supply of materials to construct new movie theaters and the supervision of that work. But the part that was useful to me was my responsibility for establishing screening rooms, theaters of fifteen to fifty seats where the revolutionary leadership could quietly gather to enjoy the best of ICAIC's archives, as well as the trickle of new foreign films *before* the Commission of Censorship had snipped away their most provocative episodes and questionable political content.

The U.S. economic embargo and Cuba's chronic shortage of hard currency severely restricted ICAIC in the types and variety of films it could acquire offshore. Never was there an adequate supply even of lowbrow escapist fare such as the tale of Ichi. When we had no choice but to fill the cinema bills with Soviet-bloc features, Cuban moviegoers didn't go. When we occasionally offered censored versions of films such as *Picnic* or *Some Like It Hot*, or a French or Italian production, the movie houses filled to capacity.

Such box-office evidence of the people's preferences was tantamount to a referendum on the revolution's cultural policies, but the revolution insisted on being the nation's sole arbiter of taste. Its hostility to culture on every level was institutionalized at the Education Ministry, parent to the National Council for Culture, which in turn controlled all forms of art and entertainment besides movies, radio, and television. Not only did the ministry stint on substantive support for the performing arts, museums, literature, and the rest, but—with the single exception of Alfredo Guevara, whose propaganda machine was very highly valued—the Revolutionary Government tended to place the least competent leaders in charge of Cuba's cultural affairs.

In September 1968 the French chancellery in Havana served me with the divorce papers. In them Marie Christine described me the only way she could: as she had seen me, transformed from the man she'd married into someone whose behavior she could not understand. One charge—that I forced her to leave Cuba—was patently untrue. Another—that I'd made no attempt to communicate with her or my daughter since December—was false but, I wondered, perhaps true in her experience. I had written Marie Christine that very emotional response to her letter in March, and I had sent letters every month since then to Marielle. Yet it is possible that my wife and daughter were somehow prevented from reading them—or did not even receive them.

After looking over the divorce papers, I addressed myself to the dry little French clerk who had been waiting for some reaction. "You know, sir, that the case is lost," I said without emotion. "I can't fight it from here. Call me when you have the final decision."

The voice came from my new emotional wilderness, where Marie Christine was now a faint object growing dimmer in the distance. The emergent Stranger side of my nature forcefully abjured waste, especially the useless pining for lost love.

But my true self obdurately kept my daughter Marielle's image in my mind. My true self and the Stranger struggled with each other—sometimes, when I was alone, I discovered I was carrying on their debate aloud—the one rebelling at every effort to suppress Marielle's memory, and the other arguing logically that she was my weak point, a flaw in the otherwise cold objectivity necessary for survival. In a normal world, the habit of talking to oneself in two voices is suggestive of psychic maladjustment. For me, these spirited colloquies, always conducted out of my apartment, at the beach or in the countryside when I was alone, were a means of *preserving* my sanity, the only relief from total emotional withdrawal.

In those days I drew closer to La Tía than I ever had been before. She'd been close to Marie Christine and was extremely surprised and dismayed at the loss of my family. Although I could never risk endangering her—or myself—by sharing the truth, her company and that of her friends were my sole sources of unforced geniality. In her openhearted warmth and generosity, she was now my only genuine emotional connection. I gave her my ration book and ate dinner at her house every day, a welcome if limited haven for me.

Sometimes my mood was lifted by secondhand news of my family in Venezuela, who knew they could not write to me directly, as a revolutionary could not communicate with the outside world. Most evenings, however, I came home to an empty place, where I read or listened to music. Very rarely, the insipid uniformity of my existence was punctuated by brief liaisons, emotionally barren affairs with revolutionary females of willing physicality but enervating ideological virtue.

Despite all, my mask stayed in place. Knowing that my stature in the system depended more upon my political profile than on my efficiency, I showed up to be counted at every meeting and mobilization. The system kept close track of attendance at these gatherings, and each "merit" earned for participation raised an individual toward selection as a "front-line worker," a designation I soon added to my revolutionary résumé.

In 1969 my devotion to duty was rewarded with a second, unanticipated promotion at ICAIC, when the Institute's chief of capital investments left and I was named to replace him.

Since in these years Fidel was abolishing all economic controls, there was no budget to run or any other activity logically associated with my new title. In essence, I continued to build new theaters and restore old ones according to what Alfredo Guevara desired. Still, the new job was another small step up the revolutionary hierarchy.

As part of my responsibilities I traveled to provincial villages to inspect the progress of construction or reconstruction of movie houses. On one of these trips, as I was passing through the First of January sugar mill, I was taking a shortcut to inspect a new cinema when a man hurried past, jostling me. Turning to look at him, I felt as if an electrical shock had flung me back against the wall. He for his part looked terror-stricken.

It was Luc. He had aged a great deal, with prematurely white hair, and his face reflected back at me his fear that someone might see us together. In a few curt sentences, he told me the results of our old project. In the case of his family, he had used the papers and seal I had taken, and his mother and his sister were out of the country. As for my uncle: "Your cousin Silvio came from the United States to pick him up at Camarioca [during a boat lift in 1965]," Luc said, "but someone in the Ciego de Avila MININT intentionally lost his documents and they didn't let him leave. Luckily I discovered the plot in time, and immediately wrote his name on the list of emigrants with priority because of the good houses and cars they were leaving behind. In less than twenty-four hours he and his wife left for Miami on one of the Freedom Flights."

I was very comforted to know that my uncle and aunt were free; the burden of a great uncertainty was now lifted. My return to Cuba, with all its consequences, had not been in vain. And yet I couldn't help thinking about this: I had been right in believing it would take me less than a year to help my uncle and his wife, but so wrong in evaluating the risk to myself. Three years later I was trapped, with no one to help me and no concrete prospects of change.

No doubt Luc felt the same relief about his family as I did about mine, and yet our conversation was rapid, dry, and cold. Unfortunately, the dangerous episode we had lived through now made us a danger to each other. I never saw him again.

THE NEXT GENERATION

One indication of Fidel's commitment to excellence was his appointing Papito Serguera to head the Institute of Radio and TV (ICRT). But more egregious by far was his choice of José Llanusa as minister of education, suzerain of Cuban art and learning.

José Llanusa came to the Ministry of Education qualified to run it on the basis of his blind loyalty to Fidel and his having been a good basketball player. When he'd been president of INDER, the sports institute, he had been a success; reason enough to make him education minister.

Nearly every evening around six, Fidel and Llanusa could be found together at the INDER basketball courts, dribbling and shooting. Sometimes there were enough other players for an informal pickup game. As if by magic, spectators would begin filing in, all cheering wildly whenever Fidel scored a basket. Llanusa would react just as ecstatically. Such dedication was the quality Fidel most wanted to instill in the young people of Cuba, and José Llanusa was a principal in the revolution's efforts to regiment and rededicate Cuba's youth.

By 1968, scarcely nine years after the triumph, a new generation was coming of age on the island, adolescents with no connection to the struggles and vicissitudes of the 1950s. Most were more difficult to inspire, less dedicated to the revolution. Many were indifferent to its glories, and others, a small minority, had turned outright to delinquency and crime. Such disaffection gave Fidel good cause for alarm; within a few years it would harden into an irreversible generational alienation.

My first direct encounter with the delinquency phenomenon came one afternoon in a MININT office in the Vedado, where Havana's growing number of problem kids were often detained in periodic roundups. Before this time, I had often noticed them in my comings and goings, the groups of idle teen-agers hanging around the Coppelia or in front of the Hotel Capri, as well as the infinitely more disturbing sight of very young girls prowling luxury hotel lobbies, proffering foreign visitors nights of tropical pleasure.

As explained to me by Ángel Vila, a MININT personal security officer who had invited me to the office to show me personally these *lumpen*, U.S. imperialism was chiefly to blame for Cuba's plague of delinquency. The youngsters I met that day offered a somewhat different explanation for their antisocial behavior.

"You don't go to school?" I asked a group of sullen, defiant arrestees at the office.

"School! What for?" a teen-aged boy answered me in a sarcastic tone. "What good is school if what I want I can't buy, even if I had the money? I'm not the son of any boss. They're the ones who have everything. I have to find mine on the street."

"That's right!" exclaimed a pretty girl, quite young, with a wad of gum in her mouth. "You come with me to the school where I used to study and you'll see. Just by looking I can tell you which ones are the children of the bosses. They have the nice clothes. Their parents get everything. But me? I have to settle for new pants once a year."

She gave me a lewd look. "Know how I get what I want?" she asked, wriggling her body with her hands on her hips. "I have my ways."

The rest of them, mostly children, laughed uproariously.

"Right on!" shouted another boy, calling her *asere*, slang for "friend" or "buddy." "I stopped going to school a year ago when I realized it wouldn't get me the clothes or the shoes I want. I'm better off getting them myself on the black market, selling ten and keeping one. If they hadn't caught me, I'd have my pockets full now, *asere*. Full!"

Officer Vila felt his point had been amply demonstrated during this interview. "You see, Llovio," he said as we left the MININT office, "all these wretches think about is consumer goods. American cigarettes. Clothes. Tape recorders. Idiocies! And meanwhile, the Cuban people are working!"

I nodded my sympathetic assent.

"Those sons of bitches are the most recalcitrant," he added on the street, jerking his head back in the direction of the detention room. "You have to be tough with them."

The "children of the bosses" the young prostitute was referring to were the offspring of the revolutionary elite. Out of envy and anger at the advantages their privileged schoolmates enjoyed, and in frustration at the meanness of their own families' everyday lives, she and others like her were turning to expedience, taking for themselves what the others were given or the state could not provide. If caught, they might be returned to their parents once or twice. Otherwise, their unintegrated, antirevolutionary ways would earn them a one-way ticket to Camagüey and the Youth Column of the Centenary, or some other legitimized forced-labor camp.

Not that the young were waging the fierce, focused revolt of my school days. Their restlessness was generally tame. Nevertheless, the Revolutionary Government radicalized the measures by which it hoped to stamp them into its mold of conformity.

The government attributed extraordinary power to music, believing that Western pop music was an imperialist tool of

ideological deviationism. Suddenly one night in 1968, Latin sing-
ers such as Julio Iglesias and José Feliciano and the songs and
the music of many other popular foreign artists like Frank Sinatra
(officially derided as a "fascist and mafioso") simply and abruptly
disappeared from Cuban radio programs. Papito Serguera had
pulled the plug. All that was left of the entire capitalist world's
music was collapsed for Cuban audiences into a single nightly
program called *Nocturno* on Radio Progreso, which alternated
international hits with Cuban music. The other radio stations
bombarded their listeners with boleros, guarachas, cha-cha-chas,
and other old national rhythms. As a result, more and more
Cubans simply switched their dials to Miami music stations.

Then there were the issues of attire and grooming. Although
members of Fidel's conquering Rebel Army had worn long hair,
the students in Cuba who adopted the practice were now seen as
antirevolutionary and under the Western influence of the sixties.
Countless young men were refused admittance to school until
they had their hair cut. In some cases official summonses were
sent to their parents as sanctions for countenancing this unruliness.

Similar actions were taken against girls who wore miniskirts. According to revolutionary regulations, school uniform
skirts had to fall below the knee.

José Llanusa drew up several resolutions condemning style-
conscious teens for their "deviant conduct of a provocative nature." He went so far as to protest some of Alfredo Guevara's
ICAIC educational documentaries because they contained foot-
age of Cuban students in long hair or miniskirts. At one documentary screening, I listened to him angrily deplore such scenes
as morally corruptive to "revolutionary, austere, and self-
sacrificing Cuban youth."

Papito Serguera at ICRT was equally exercised. He prohibited the offending fashions for all television actors. Ever excit-
able, Papito even stationed a barber at ICRT's front door and
ordered all long-haired male personnel to submit, then and there,
to a trim. For the first two or three days of this tactical assault
on decadence, Comandante Serguera personally supervised the
barber's work.

In a September 28, 1968, speech delivered at the University
of Havana, Fidel characterized Cuba's young people as on the
front lines in their studies and in their preparation for the struggle ahead. He said they were always ready for any sacrifice,
ready to give their all. As for the delinquents, he said, "The

revolution will educate them, or reeducate them. It will deal with the cases as they should be dealt with. But it will reeducate them above all with work, which is the best education."

In fact, labor was his universal prescription for the young. Beginning in the late 1960s all young people in school were ordered to spend forty-five days each year mobilized into "Schools of the Countryside," a transparent excuse for putting them to work on state farms. Not only did Fidel get the workers he needed, but the extended physical separation from family furthered his campaign to supplant blood loyalties with a more proper first faith in the revolution. Individualism, fostered by family love, was to be lost in the collective consciousness promoted in the schools of the countryside.

During the same period Fidel, in the name of enhanced educational opportunity, ordered an aggressive increase in new regional school facilities and then filled them with students from all over Cuba. Much was made of the generous scholarships given to the young people so that they all could take advantage of the modern learning centers. But the true advantage accrued to the revolution, which sought to wean the students from their parents and to locate them conveniently adjacent to the fields where their labor was needed.

On top of this, almost all students were organized each year to take what Fidel called "a real vacation"—weeks-long supervised excursions to the beach or mountains in the company of one another and away from their families.

Most university graduates had to perform a social service; that is, work for a minimum of two years in the region of the country where they were needed most—and where they really did improve the quality of life in the countryside. This regulation mainly affected graduates in medicine, whose service was often extended for four or five years. Then, when they were done, the graduates were placed where the state thought best.

Finally, there was no way to avoid some sort of incorporation into the military. Once he reaches the age of sixteen, every male in Cuba is liable for immediate conscription. Boys and girls alike, when they finish high school, find their chances for further education or employment made difficult if they don't join the Civil Defense, where they receive military training and take part in periodic mass mobilizations for "combat readiness," should, as Fidel continues to warn, the hated Yanquis decide at last to invade.

Fidel evidently believed that regimentation and thought control would yield for Cuba a new generation of good Socialists. He had seen the same tactics work on the revolutionary elite. But the formula, when applied to the young, lacked two critical ingredients. First, the many Sierra and urban fighters and old Communists in Fidel's government were accustomed by training and inclination to unquestioning discipline. The young people were not. Second, the leaders around Fidel would swallow anything for the many privileges he could bestow upon them, while most of Cuba's young people regarded his repeated calls for sacrifice and self-denial as untenable. Predictably, they saw the future as now and did not care for its look.

The revolutionary youth of Cuba were caught in the middle. Some of them were believers in the system, while others maintained a facade in order to survive. Whatever the veneer, the inner life of Cuban youth ranged from indifference to self-absorption. The generation clash between the revolutionary leadership and the young people was well under way.

FIDEL AT WORK

The work I was doing in 1968 took me through the countryside, where it was easy for me with my official access to see the effect of Fidel's economic policies on the life of Cuba. What I observed were the results of the economic and political decisions Fidel had conveyed to the public in the July 26th speech I had heard at Santa Clara the previous year.

"By the first quarter of 1969," he had said then, "not one inch of briar [or] thickets of uncultivated land will remain in the country."

Fidel's epic scheme was for a phalanx of bulldozers and dynamite crews to sweep the island end to end from east to west, claiming for the tractor and planter behind them every arable hillock and copse in the country. "Working in terms of this new concept," he'd declared at inauguration ceremonies three months later, "the use of this machinery will yield at least five times as much as it would have yielded under the old work concepts, when the heavy equipment was distributed by provinces."

At this ceremony, held October 30, 1967, not far from the city of Bayamo in Oriente, Fidel announced that his new legion would be called the Ché Guevara Trailblazers Brigade in honor of his fallen *compañero*, dead less than a month.

The scene on television had a martial air to it. Arrayed in military formation were 150 pieces of heavy machinery: bulldozers, tractors, and tank-haulers, their uniformed crews standing at attention.

"Perhaps," Fidel said in his proudest voice, "the most revolutionary aspect [of this project] is the fact that the brigade will be led by officers of our Rebel Army and will be manned chiefly by soldiers who acquired experience in the operation of these machines while serving in our tank and motorized units."

I noted among the troops many *campesino* faces; Fidel had discovered another way to employ these fighters outside the regular army. They certainly looked ready for battle—and, in fact, they were.

The brigade scoured the Cuban landscape for eighteen months, leveling everything in its path, from weeds to thorny *marabú* bushes to royal palms. The men worked incessantly, twenty-four hours a day in eight-hour shifts, pushing the ill-maintained machinery until most of it was unsalvageable scrap. During a trip to the village of San Luis, south of Pinar del Río, where a new movie theater was under construction, I saw the extensive graveyards of equipment, including French Richard CD-6 tractors.

The advice and the laments of some peasants who tried to stop the outrage had no effect. The leaders of the brigade, military men after all, were following the letter and spirit of Fidel's October 30 speech. "Forward, *compañeros*," Fidel had urged. "Let nothing and no one stop you, regardless of hard tasks, regardless of difficult obstacles."

Fidel had been so certain of his idea's brilliance that he ordered a complete record of it. "The story of this brigade will be written day by day," he told the soldiers. "Movies and documentaries will be made showing all the regions where you go to work."

He went on to say: "And we are sure that the experience we are acquiring here will also be useful to other peoples tomorrow. We don't keep our achievements secret. Rather, we want to give our experience to other peoples."

According to Fidel, "The story will be written and all of you will be proud of this story; the people will be proud."

Let it be written, then, that the Ché Guevara Trailblazers wreaked on their country an unprecedented ecological and economic catastrophe, witnessed by the entire nation. The least serious offense was the vast swaths of lands, thousands of acres, that were scraped bare in preparation for planting that never occurred. INRA, the Institute for Agrarian Reform, together with the party, mobilized the population to plant, but the great majority of the cleared land quickly reverted to weeds and *marabú*.

Much worse was the indiscriminate razing of forests and orchards. For several years to come, common tree fruits such as avocados, mangoes, guavas, and many others almost disappeared from the domestic market. They became, as was sardonically whispered by the people, "pieces that belong in the natural history museums."

There is no way to reckon the cost of the destruction the Trailblazers caused across Cuba's countryside. But since, as evidenced by ICAIC documentaries, the brigade even dynamited stands of the royal palm—Cuba's national tree—it may be supposed that less familiar or majestic species were not spared. Clearly, much of the wild habitat was affected, because many animals, including birds such as the *tomeguín del pinar*, the *bijirita*, the *sinsonte*, the *negrito*, the *mariposa*, and the *sunsún*, were practically driven into extinction.

The Ché Guevara Trailblazer Brigade was only one of the many examples of Fidel's empirical spirit, his willy-nilly experimental approach to agriculture. One project displaced another on the basis of the supposed superiority to its predecessor. Fidel's so-called "Special Plans" were allotted the best lands and unlimited resources, to the detriment of established agricultural practices. Fidel obviously distrusted the ability of his own state-run farm structure to implement his ideas. Instead, he wanted them nurtured under his direct supervision.

One exemplar of Fidel's thinking was La Mulata, a special plan in the rocky coastal terrain of southwest Havana Province. Fidel believed that the region was ideal for growing citrus, if only it were fertile. To this end, he ordered that mountains of humus be extracted from the Zapata swamp, some kilometers away, and then brought to La Mulata. Dutifully, the earth was transported on Berliet trucks and spread over the impermeable rock surface at La Mulata. The citrus trees were planted all right, but the plan failed to take into account the power of Caribbean rainstorms, which promptly and repeatedly washed away the humus and trees until, after several years, Fidel finally gave up.

Fidel never ran short of such ideas or of promises for the future. "We know we are capable of many things," he told the nation on January 2, 1968, in his anniversary speech at the Plaza de la Revolución in Havana. "We know that in sugar there will be no one able to compete with this country in any way. But we will also be important meat producers for the markets of the world, in quantity and quality. And we will be important producers of tropical crops. In citrus fruit, we will be among the first-ranking countries of the world, and the same will happen with coffee and with bananas and pineapples."

While Fidel made promises, Cuba's agricultural production was diminishing steadily, and the country continued to suffer increasing food shortages. Nevertheless, we all were asked to redouble our efforts to help in the great cause—to implement Fidel's special plans and to compensate for the low productivity of state-run agriculture. The party organized enormous mass mobilizations for "productive work" or "voluntary work," either on weekends or for months on end, through the various mass organizations such as the neighborhood CDRs, the Federation of Cuban Women (FMC), and the unions. Their leaders harangued the populace, including housewives, to go to work in the countryside in trucks, station wagons, or any other available means of transportation.

To be a Communist revolutionary, I took part in these adventures too. On numerous occasions in the early spring of 1968, I signed up for voluntary work, principally during the annual "Girón Journey," two weeks of field labor supposedly in commemoration of the Bay of Pigs victory, but intentionally made to coincide with Holy Week in order to eradicate any trace of religious tradition in Cuba.

With sixty or so other office workers I made the "Journey" to southern Havana Province and Fidel's "April 19th" special plan near the town of Quivicán. The living conditions there were atrocious. Shower and washroom facilities were inadequate and primitive, and the latrines were filthy.

Nor did we accomplish much of anything. In our eight- or nine-hour scheduled workday, we might have made some contribution despite our ignorance of agriculture. But our effective time in the fields was reduced by more than half because of transportation foul-ups and all the other symptoms of poor planning. Either the "April 19th" managers couldn't decide what to put in the ground, or there weren't enough tools, or they had nothing for us to plant, period. Something always went awry.

"I don't know why they send you to work here," a local farmer on horseback told us one day. "You don't know anything about the country and you ruin everything that is planted, everything we were going to plant. The city man's for the city, and the country's for us, the *campesinos*."

The "Journey" dislocated resources and wasted everyone's time, just as our more routine "voluntary work" came to naught. At least once a week, those of us at ICAIC went to the area around Cubanacán, where our movie studios were located, to work lands forming part of the Havana Belt Project. Fidel's grand plan was to cover this cultivated strip surrounding the capital with coffee bushes, fruit trees, and a shrub called *gandul*.

Working large, open tracts on either side of the local highways, we scratched out ten- to twelve-inch-deep holes in the stony soil for transplantation of young coffee bushes, wrapped in black polyethylene bags. Fidel's goal: to plant more than 100 million coffee bushes in the Havana Belt, more than the new plantings in any of the principal coffee-producing countries such as Mexico, Brazil, and Colombia.

Naturally, the results were pitiful. Of the 100 million or more transplants, only 14 million survived. The rest failed because they were planted in too shallow a layer of topsoil. When their roots hit the stony subsurface, they grew sideways instead of straight down, causing the bush itself to grow horizontally, a condition called gooseneck. Moreover, because the lands were fully exposed to the sun, a coffee variety that was resistant to sun—Caturra—had been chosen for transplant, but it produced a very low-quality coffee that was undrinkable unless blended with other varieties.

The other main crop, the *gandul*, is responsible for an absurd chapter in the history of the revolution. After a long search for the ideal feed for cattle, a survey whose choices ranged from corn to alfalfa, kudzú, and other grasses, Fidel had happened to read an article that praised the high nutritional value of the *gandul*, a shrub prized for its beans by the people of Haitian descent in northern Camagüey province. Whether or not the rest of the shrub was palatable to any animal was not known.

Fidel became enthusiastic about the *gandul* and immediately ordered test plantings to begin. The experimental Indio Hatuey Farm in Matanzas was one of many facilities that quickly initiated these studies, and just as quickly produced negative results. Cows did not seem to like *gandul*. But the party hesitated to contradict the compulsive enthusiasm of its leader, and it held back the data, hoping for eventual success.

Impatient with these delays and certain that he had found the best feed, Fidel in April 1968 ordered a massive planting of *gandul* alongside the coffee I was helping to plant in the Havana Belt. As the huge crop took root, so did the incontrovertible evidence that no cow would ever touch it. Despite all the effort put into the experimental project at Matanzas, *gandul* proved about as savory to cattle as sawdust. Animals in fields planted exclusively with the shrub and surrounded by electrified fences grew thinner and thinner. The cows preferred starvation to Fidel's brainstorm.

The revolution could not account for this acutely embarrassing failure. When, in 1969, the *gandul* would have to be rooted out, the leaders would decide that Fidel must have been deceived somehow, thus explaining the disaster. For a scapegoat, Havana's first secretary of the party, a man named Betancourt, would be chosen, and removed to the other end of the island in order to serve in a minor capacity in an obscure municipality in northern Oriente Province.

But Fidel would never forswear gimmick agriculture. Each of his caprices would be trumpeted to the people, hailed for its ingeniousness, cited as a concrete example of his farseeing vision, and then blamed on someone else when it failed.

By contrast, Fidel's war on the foundation of Cuban agriculture, the *campesino*, necessarily was a silent one.

Like Ché, Fidel despised private industry of any sort. And he shared with Ché the belief that Cuba's independent *campesinos* had to be eliminated. In a speech on July 11, 1964, Ché had put it quite clearly: "We continue to speak of the small farmer, the poor, small farmer, and we never say that the farmer, no matter how poor and small he is, manifestly generates capitalism. It is obvious, but we don't say it. I hear people rejecting this: 'Oh, it's necessary to respect the *campesino* because Fidel once said that the *campesino* has been a pillar of the Revolution.' It is very true that the farmer has been a pillar of the Revolution, that he was always in favor of it, that he fought in the Sierra, that he was one of the first to join the Rebel Army. In spite of all this, he must be eliminated."

After the revolution had triumphed, Fidel had no choice but to make good on his promise to redistribute Cuba's farmlands to the *campesinos*. But through the edicts of ANAP, he had done his utmost to control what they planted, when they planted, and how the harvest was distributed. Having thus instigated chaos and shortages, Fidel was ready to move subtly to disengage the *campesino* from the land itself.

Beginning with the Second Agrarian Reform Bill of October 13, 1965, no private farm in Cuba had been allowed to be larger than five *caballerías*, or about 165 acres. Small as these individually held parcels were, they had still offended Fidel's revolutionary sensibilities. He'd ignored the fact that the *campesino* landowners were really the only productive sector of the agricultural economy. All Fidel saw were little dots of individualism in the middle of the huge state farms. He wanted to erase them, and the tool he chose, introduced in 1967, was what he called Microplans.

The small farmer was offered a house in the closest village or community, together with electricity, furniture, a refrigerator, and a television set, *if* he would give his land in usufruct to the state. In other words, the revolution would be free to plant whatever Fidel wanted on the land, and in exchange, the retired farmer would live comfortably, receive an income for life, and have at his disposal several acres of his own to feed his family— and the black market.

The arrangement appeared to benefit the *campesinos*. It meant less work, fewer responsibilities, and a guaranteed income. The great majority of those who held land inside the state farms happily accepted the deal. Even those who at first were too tied to their land to give in to such an attractive offer eventually accepted it. If they did not, they knew they would find themselves bereft of the meager aid provided by ANAP and the party.

Later, Fidel promulgated two more regulations directed at all the *campesinos* in the country. The first required that they turn their entire production over to the state, replacing the de facto ban on sales to individuals with the tooth of the law. The second statute forbade *campesinos* to hire workers to farm their land. Because the law stipulated that the farmer who did not work the land lost it, Fidel had the bulk of the *campesinos* at his mercy. Those farmers who, in spite of everything, had held out against the Microplan now faced the prospect of losing their farms because they couldn't make them produce on their own.

Nearly two thirds of the *campesinos* whose farms had been within the boundaries of the state farms "voluntarily" bowed to the Microplan. Only those whose families were large enough to generate the labor required to work their parcels managed to hang on. Of course, they became even more critically important in supplying the store shelves that the state farms could not fill.

Fidel enjoyed his sly victory in silence. He had finally succeeded in freeing himself of a good many private farmers, but he had also caused further hemorrhaging in the sick agricultural economy. The small farmer, without the incentive of his own harvest, did not care very much what the state did or did not do in the fields. It was done, or rather undone, haphazardly. And the rest of the country continued to pay a high price for the latest improvisation.

THE RIFLE OF JUSTICE

Fidel had the genius to appear beneficent toward the *campesinos* while at the same time trying to crush these small landowners. But arguably his greatest political gift, evinced earlier in *La Dolce Vita,* was for turning adversity into tactical advantage.

Since the early 1960s, Cuba's patent and paramount problem had been the country's declining economic output, largely because of the United States' blockade, which progressively eroded the quality of life on the island and drove Fidel ever further into the Soviets' debt. In his speeches he ceaselessly and, for the most part, accurately blamed Cuba's economic woes on the blockade. "The people," I heard him say to his entourage, "must be be taught infinite hatred for the Yanquis, who are responsible for all our misfortunes. So whether it's true or not, whether it can be proven or not, the Yanquis will always be responsible for any mishap we may suffer. The people will always respond to this argument."

After the 1962 missile crisis, the USSR, too, had come in for criticism. Fidel didn't denounce the Soviet Union by name, but no one could fail to grasp his meaning when he lambasted the policies of "Socialist countries."

Yet even as he carped over the supposed causes, Fidel was quick to recognize a means of capitalizing on the production shortfalls. With material rewards increasingly difficult to provide, he enthusiastically embraced Ché's theory of the New Man and declared material incentives to be antisocialistic. Ché had first expounded the theory at least three years earlier, but now, with scarcity, came the handy economic moment to make it national policy.

Instead of ensuring that the industrious, ambitious Cuban, by dint of labor, could earn the wherewithal to purchase a new car or a phonograph, as he had in the past, the revolution now showered "front-line workers" with certificates, awards, stamps, and flags. These were the symbols of New Manhood, a higher state of revolutionary consciousness which would respond purely to patriotism and moral responsibilities. The New Man would glory in the inherent satisfaction of undertaking "historic tasks" rather than in lowly material gains.

Unsurprisingly, the burdens of being heroic (assumed exclusively by those beneath the revolutionary elite) began to sap the people's vigor. Apathy infected society at all levels up to and including the state bureaucracy—even the rank and file of the party itself. The mass mobilizations, the mobs who gathered to hear Fidel speak, the crowded rallies, the study circles in the workplace and in the CDRs, all were a veneer of staged excitement that masked but did not solve Cuba's malaise.

Fidel was as heedless of economic reality as he was defiant of the laws of nature. Cubans already received free schooling, quality medical care, and social security, and paid no personal taxes. The cost of basic foodstuffs, acquired with ration cards, was low and had not risen since 1959. But from the early 1960s, all wages were frozen, no raises (even upon promotion) were allowed, and overtime compensation was abolished and replaced with merit points toward becoming a front-line worker.

As a result, those who could resorted to the informal economy, such as the barter and black markets. Some trafficked in goods stolen from the state. For Cubans with no access to these alternatives, hopes for acquiring consumer goods often turned on their luck in contests held in the semiannual worker assemblies, when their unions distributed such Soviet-bloc housewares and gadgets as were available.

Thus, as I witnessed at ICAIC assemblies, whatever fans or watches, TVs or washing machines the union had acquired were allotted by vote of the assembly. Aspirants were nominated, and then their merit records were read aloud to the group. Amidst cheers and applause the workers voted one another these prizes, based in small part upon their productivity but mostly on their political records: how many meetings they'd attended, how many hours of voluntary work they'd put in, or how many party tasks— tacking up posters, distributing handbills and the like during the workday—they had undertaken.

Of course, most everyone left the worker assemblies the way they'd arrived: empty-handed. They went home with their ration cards and their few pesos to continue eking along without. Once in a while the chronic shortages they endured turned acute, as when, in December 1967, the milk quota for adult *Habaneros* was abruptly canceled. Soon thereafter, there were rumors that egg and bread supplies might also be curtailed, which provoked not only a nervous unrest in the capital but led to long lines of anxious shoppers driven to the stores in a disorderly attempt at hoarding.

Unbeknownst to all but a very few of the leaders, Fidel had already set in motion a plan to exploit the mounting restiveness, an attack on his old enemy, private enterprise. He also sought, as he usually did in times of public apathy, to raise the level of tension in Cuba. In late 1967 he secretly assigned MININT, the Ministry of Internal Trade, the National Bank, the CDRs, and other organizations a massive task. According to what several officers involved in this project told me, its objective was to compile a massive, detailed study of private business in Cuba, including secret data on individuals' financial affairs. The survey was complete by March 13, 1968, in time for Fidel's annual speech to commemorate the death of José Antonio Echevarría.

Fidel's March 13th speeches were always stormy, full of vehement denunciations and drastic announcements. This one was no exception.

Speaking by tradition from the steps of the university, Fidel assailed the evils of consumerism, the public appetite for what he called "enormous trinkets" and "superfluous paraphernalia" (categories into which his Mercedes, specially ordered from France, might be placed).

"Isn't it plain," he asked, "that this country must invest its last cent, that it cannot invest in anything superfluous?"

The question, near the start of his speech, reaffirmed the revolution's determination to subordinate all for the sake of building heavy industry in Cuba. Then, as usual, Fidel doled out to the superpowers primary blame for the fitfulness of progress toward this goal.

But Fidel was intent, that day, on opening a new front, a strategic initiative that would be called the Revolutionary Offensive. First, he candidly owned to the food-market troubles in Havana. "Concretely," he said, "we want to refer to the circumstances of the protest—yes, of protest—of a certain discontent, confusion, and dissatisfaction raised to the matter of the availability of consumer goods."

He spelled out several possible explanations for this unrevolutionary response to the shortages, including Cuba's "international relations"—i.e., Cuba's disagreements with the USSR. But the Cuban people should look to themselves for answers, too, he said.

As always, Fidel prefaced his criticism with praise, one of his standard psychological ploys. "We are still a people characterized by great enthusiasm and decision at decisive moments," he said grandly, "a people capable of giving up life itself at any hour, on any day. Capable of any heroism."

Then he went on to describe an unhappy defect, referring to his constituents as "a people that still lacks the virtue of tenacity, the demonstration of this courage and heroism not only in the dramatic moments, but on each and every day. That is, there is a certain tenacity and perseverance still lacking in that heroism."

So what was retarding the emergence of New Manhood?

"There is no doubt," Fidel offered, "that certain institutions have lasted much longer than they should have, that certain privileges have lasted much longer than they should have. And these privileges and institutions feed those currents we are talking about, and they keep those weaknesses alive among the people."

Fidel in no way meant to refer to the corrupt example of his own senior leadership. No, he was pointing his revolutionary rifle down at Cuba's private sector, that "small segment of the population living off the work of others, living considerably better than the rest, sitting idly by and looking on while others do the work; lazy persons in perfect physical condition who set up some kind of vending stand, any kind of small business, in order to make fifty pesos a day."

As the *campesino* farmers were essential to supplement state food production, so did Cuba's small businessmen meet some of the demand for goods and services that the inefficient state-run economy did not provide. Fidel had concentrated on the big picture with projects like the construction of a 40 million-dollar fertilizer factory, the largest such facility in Latin America. But the mode of construction was so slow and idiosyncratic and Fidel had ordered so many "innovations" incorporated into the plans that the British company from which the technology was acquired finally canceled its guarantee. Once the plant did open, it never produced even half the fertilizer projected according to its original specifications.

This inefficiency did not matter; the fertilizer factory was ideologically correct in its last detail. Not so the private restaurateur, the seller of brooms or cosmetics, or the tradesman who, for a price, could fix your sink, build a cabinet, or repair an automobile. They were all individualists, sabotaging the people's vitality and spirit, and they were about to be erased.

Fidel quoted at length from the governmental study of private enterprise, speaking with contempt of its profits, the lack of hygiene in some establishments, their owners' alleged antisocial associates, and their overall deficiency in revolutionary militance.

Then he brought his hammer down.

"They are squeezing out the last drop," he said in a threatening tone. "While privilege lasts, they will cling to privilege up to the last minute. And the last minute is at hand! THE LAST MINUTE IS AT HAND! Clearly and definitely, we must say that we propose to eliminate all manifestations of private trade, clearly and definitely!"

Less than nine months earlier, in his July 26, 1967 speech in Santiago de Cuba, Fidel had also made critical reference to small business, but he had then assured the entrepreneurs that they were safe from state interference. "So the owner of the open-air stand pays no taxes and receives the same social benefits as real workers," Fidel said disapprovingly. "These are factors which we must be fully aware of."

Nevertheless, the roadside-produce man or similar self-starters were put at ease. "This does not mean that the Revolution is going to do away with these stands," Fidel had said. "Such vendors and merchants should not be alarmed."

Yet within hours of his March 13, 1968 speech, Fidel ordered the full fury of the revolution unleashed upon the small businessman; the Revolutionary Offensive had begun. That night, thousands of party members secretly on alert throughout the country spread out to confiscate all private businesses in the early hours of the following morning: bars, groceries, garages, small stores, the shops of self-employed artisans and other independent workers, from carpenters to masons to plumbers. The operation was dizzying. Two days later, not a single private business was operating in Cuba except for the few remaining private farmers, the owners of freight trucks, and cab drivers.

The Offensive was both extreme and opportunistic. The raiders, empowered to confiscate personal possessions, did so with an intense zeal to demonstrate their revolutionary commitment. Even cats and dogs belonging to business people were seized. From then on, these pets were state property.

The president of the CDR on my block typified the fervor with which capitalism was rooted out. Quite pleased with herself, she told me how her team had stripped the neighborhood manicurist of her nail polish and cuticle scissors; how the seamstress was relieved of her needles, thread, and mannequin; and the local hairdresser of her scissors and hair dryer.

A preemptive assault on Cuban alcohol consumption was a corollary aspect of the Revolutionary Offensive. Fidel was not content simply to shut down the privately owned bars, popular because of the variety of beverages they offered, but he also closed down state establishments, ushering in a period of Prohibition. Only a few hotels and tourist cabarets, such as the Tropicana in Havana, were allowed to remain open.

Cubans are not particularly heavy drinkers as a people; unlike the Soviet Union, the island has never faced any chronic or acute difficulties with alcoholism. But producing even moderate quantities of beer or rum, the national drink, was beyond the state planners. Therefore, this particular supply-demand equation was fixed by outlawing demand and by low production.

It was only among the revolutionary elite, or because of contacts in the black market, that one could enjoy a commercial alcoholic beverage. In response, the Cuban people concocted their own alternative refreshments, from home brew to rice wine to punches prepared with isopropyl alcohol stolen from pharmacies and hospitals.

The Offensive did achieve its major goals; private business was finished off. It failed, however, to reinspire the population as Fidel envisioned. Life in Cuba became only duller and more onerous without the amenity of an occasional bottle of beer or cocktail, the convenience of a corner laundry, the expert assistance of the self-employed handyman, or the casual availability of croquettes, *pan con tortilla*, and cold drinks from street peddlers.

As the conditions of daily life worsened, the flow of official requests to emigrate increased; another wave of discontented Cubans made the difficult choice of exile. Fidel's official emigration policy was freedom to leave for everyone. In some ways, the exodus was beneficial to him because it carried out of the country those most likely to form the nucleus of opposition. On a practical level, it also reduced food demand and left much-needed housing vacant.

But life was not very easy for anyone trying to leave. When such a person presented his documents to the Ministry of the Interior, he had to include a letter from his work center. Asking for this letter was tantamount to giving up his job, since when his intentions were revealed he was automatically unemployed. Moreover, the family's children lost the right to study and were expelled from their school or university. The local CDR exhaustively inventoried the homes of people who wanted to leave the country, to prevent them from giving away or selling any of their possessions—which would instead become the property of the state. If at the moment of departure the inspection of the inventory showed the absence of even a single item, the exit permit was canceled. And if the prospective emigrant had a bank account, he could not use the money in it; he had to hand over the entire amount to the state when he left.

Life for these people, stigmatized in their own country, turned into a continual anxiety. "Those who prefer the 'dolce vita' of the Yanquis and who are getting their passports and papers ready must also participate in the effort being made by the people, because they are not going to continue living as parasites," Fidel said. And so, those who had applied for exit visas were obliged to work in agriculture or construction, the only possible ways they could feed themselves until it was time to leave. This meant efficient, disciplined, and free manpower for Cuba—from 1968 to 1970, prospective emigrants were not paid. Since these people wanted no trouble, their work was impeccable for the up to four years they might have to wait. There were hundreds of brigades composed of the so-called "worms," the "stateless," the "sellouts" —terms that Fidel used, according to the circumstances and the times, to describe those who chose to leave Cuba.

Those who decided to remain in their country continued under duress to behold the agonizing stillbirth of the New Man.

One of the many "evils" Fidel perceived was tipping, "a

corrupting element in the hotel and restaurant sector," he said, and "a bourgeois leftover that undermined the real conception of revolutionary service." It had to be torn out by the roots, and so, on the party's instructions, a great propaganda campaign was initiated as if it had come spontaneously from the workers themselves. The national union of the restaurant and hotel sector, "echoing the desires and aspirations of its workers," organized meetings to demand that tips be abolished. The revolutionary restaurant and hotel worker "voluntarily" rejected the extra money because, said the union, "his consciousness led him to offer good service disinterestedly." Consequently, waiters were given a slight increase in salary. But from that time onward, their greatest incentive would be a distinctive medal with two capital letters inscribed on it: M.S., for *Mejor Servicio* ("Better Service")—which was meant to be reward enough.

The consequences of this measure were endured for many years. The lines outside the restaurants doubled in length, and the wait was sometimes two or three hours. The waiter didn't care if more or fewer customers came in; he didn't care whether he served more or less efficiently, since his salary would not be affected.

Of course, the revolutionary elite were not so inconvenienced. For them, there was a special telephone number to a woman named Marina at the Tourism Institute in Havana. One call and she would reserve the best tables in the most elegant restaurants.

Cuba's bus conductors were another of Fidel's targets. At that time, every urban bus had a conductor, in addition to the driver, whose job was to collect the fares. The system was rather archaic, but it was necessary given the chaos caused by lack of transportation. Because the Revolutionary Government needed labor for production, it eliminated conductors, replacing them with a crude collection box placed beside the driver. Each passenger was supposed to deposit 5 cents in the box in "conscientious and revolutionary" fashion. The drivers, who up until then had received a salary based on the number of runs they completed, were now put on fixed salary based on a predetermined number of trips. In a visit I made to a friend who had fought with me at the university and now worked at the bus company in Havana, I witnessed the disastrous effects of both measures.

"Llovio, this is sheer chaos," exclaimed Osmel Francis, the director of the enterprise, putting both hands to his head. "People are not paying the fares. They take advantage of the disorder at the stops to come in the back door and not pay. But that isn't all. Look in that wooden box."

Inside the box were hundreds of screws, nuts, washers, and other items that the "heightened consciousness" of the Cubans had deposited instead of a 5 cent coin.

"There is no way to straighten out transportation," Osmel explained. "We have problems acquiring new buses, but when we do buy them, it becomes difficult to maintain them. They carry a heavy load, and it doesn't occur to those imbeciles in Foreign Trade that the vehicles need replacement parts. Sometimes they don't even import them, and other times, even when they receive the request ahead of time, they take forever to send the parts to us. Many buses are paralyzed for lack of a simple part. I've had to cannibalize some so that the rest can function, but that's the joke about robbing Peter to pay Paul. There's no way out of it; we can't cope."

Urban transport had turned into a real torment. The stops were jammed with people, especially during rush hour. Often the bus they had waited for so long, so anxiously, passed them by, or the buses stopped but were so crowded that there were problems getting off and on. Every day there were violent confrontations between passengers or terrible insults hurled at the helpless drivers. The Revolutionary Government bought Spanish, English, and Hungarian buses that in less than a year were junk because of poor upkeep, overuse, and the lack of systematic maintenance.

Canibalismo, "cannibalism," a new word in Cuban slang, was applauded by the leaders as one of the great "inventions" of workers to avoid delays in service or production; no one stopped to analyze the damage it did to the country's economy.

As for the bureaucracy, Fidel was worried by the alarming increase in unproductive workers within the superstructure of the country. Propaganda in *Granma* and the other mass media exalted the work of commissions engaged in the "struggle against bureaucratism." These commissions, conceived by Fidel, meticulously reviewed the work lists of the ministries, the provincial delegations, and their enterprises to determine which positions were unnecessary or superfluous.

According to their instructions, the commission members were to consider accountants, economists, statisticians, and controllers as unnecessary and superfluous. These people were "excessed" and sent home with the guarantee that they would continue to receive their salary until another kind of work could be found for them—on the condition that it be work in production. The process was carried out by an organization that was so inefficient itself that many of the "excessed" spent months and even years collecting a salary without working. A decade later, during an inspection of the Ministry of Labor by the State Finance Committee in Havana Province, more than 1,000 cases were discovered of "excessed" workers who had been collecting their salaries without working since the late sixties!

Others of those "excessed" workers became laborers—privileged laborers, since they drew the same salary as they had before. Naturally, these arbitrary decisions provoked new malcontents and new requests to leave the country; others adapted to their situation and decided to accept the convenience of a good salary for a job that had lower status but also less responsibility.

Still unsatisfied with this antibureaucratic effort, which wiped out statistics, accounting, and mercantile relations, Fidel decided to eliminate university courses and technical training in these specialties. With a stroke of his pen he abolished the very foundations of economic controls. Convinced that he was right, he attacked. "What do we want with this pack of parasites if the only thing they know how to do is add, subtract, multiply, and divide and then earn a salary from the state and easily obtain the food that others sweat for?" For him, "revolutionary consciousness" was enough. There was no need for the most basic economic analyses, the simplest production controls.

Once Fidel had destroyed financial relations, he began his war against money.

"We should move toward the abolition of money," he affirmed everywhere, and he began to give away all he could through the so-called gratuitous goods and services, which were in effect for almost ten years. In the late sixties, schoolchildren received food, clothing, and shoes free. Their books were free as well, although they were supposed to return them at the end of the year so that others could use them. University students received a monthly stipend. Once a year, all workers received trousers, a shirt, and a pair of work boots without paying a cent. The public telephones, "exploiters of the nickel," operated free of charge. Sports events and work center parties were also free.

These goods and services, according to theory, were supposed to help combat individualism and to promote the freest exercise of revolutionary consciousness. The people should have responded with a collective and joyous rededication to hard work toward an Elysian future. If anything, however, the shower of largesse only deepened the Cuban public's apathy.

The students soon took universal free education for granted, as if it were their birthright and not a benefit won at considerable social cost. They demonstrated their revolutionary consciousness by lackadaisical attention to their studies and an abusive indifference to their texts, which they either kept at the end of each school year or returned in deplorable condition. In the workplace, employees also found no connection between their productivity and their compensation and rewards. Their revolutionary consciousness was expressed by even greater indolence and a consequent further erosion of productivity.

Such a response from the Cuban people was entirely predictable to anyone passably conversant with the rudiments of economic law and the laws of human nature. But if any of Fidel's leaders recognized his folly, none was foolish enough to say so. It would require the sterner Soviet sensibility to show Fidel the error of his ways.

FIDEL, GIVE THE RUSSIANS HELL!

The year 1968, so personally devastating to me and, due to Fidel's disastrous new domestic policies, a year of debacle for Cuba, also witnessed a stunning reaction to Fidel's international posture. After an extended strategic lull, the conciliatory Soviets suddenly stirred in anger. And Fidel for the first time was made to understand the terms of the bargain he'd struck with Cuba's "Soviet friends."

When Fidel has big problems, he begins by attacking small things. In his first speech of the year, January 2, 1968, at the Plaza de la Revolución, Fidel appeared to me to be tense, out of

sorts. He announced in irritation that such celebrations would
have to be curtailed in the future, because "every year we [have]
been investing great amounts of energy and time, great amounts
of equipment as well as a great amount of fuel, which were
wasted as a consequence, in the organization of the parades for
this day, not to mention the considerable damage done to the
approaches to the Plaza by heavy military equipment."

But Fidel had more than parades on his mind. Cuba was
going to have to tighten its belt all around, he announced, and he
went on to say why: The Soviets would not grant the revolution's
request for an increased oil allotment.

By going public with this information and mentioning the
USSR by name, Fidel was seeking to underscore the revolution's
brave independence. Also, he needed a scapegoat to blame for
the fuel scarcity caused, in truth, by the inefficiency and
wastefulness of the Cuban economy.

The Soviets, for their part, were withholding fuel as an
indirect means of forcing greater productivity in Cuba. The USSR
had plenty of oil but was unwilling to continue underwriting the
Revolutionary Government's profligate policies. Also, by restrict-
ing Cuba's oil allotment, Moscow sought to pressure Fidel
toward conformity with its foreign policy, particularly the doctrine of peaceful coexistence which he had so far furiously rejected.

The draconian new regulations limited private drivers to
twenty-five gallons of gasoline per person per month; Fidel was
making a great show of national sacrifice in the face of Soviet
pressure. Of course, the new rules changed nothing. They ac-
corded those who drove state vehicles special ration coupons
that allowed them enough gas to continue the unrestricted use of
official vehicles, even trucks and tractors, for personal business,
supposedly a banned practice. These people, well below the revolutionary elite, only emulated the leaders, refusing to join in
revolutionary self-sacrifice despite Fidel's exhortations to do so.

The day after Fidel's speech, high officials such as Osvaldo
Dorticós, President of the Republic, and Faure Chomón, then the
minister of transportation, were seen taking ordinary buses to work.
But on that day only. Likewise, the average state truck driver who
cheered Fidel's speeches until he was hoarse also then took his
family to the beach in his state flatbed. At the end of the month,
if he hadn't used up his gas quota, he gave away what was left
or funneled the fuel at personal profit into the hungry black market.

In early 1968, Fidel also tried to rebuke the Soviets more

directly. In a high-tech reprise of the sectarian crisis of 1962, State Security was ordered to watch a group of old-line members of the PSP who still hewed to the Soviet line, who wanted closer relations to the Soviets, and who worked surreptitiously to that end with the help of the Soviet embassy in Havana. State Security's meticulous surveillance, carried out with the latest technology—zoom-lens cameras, tiny hidden microphones, mail intercepts, taps, and shortwave monitors—disclosed to no one's great surprise that the PSP veterans, ever true to their training, were apparently conspiring against the primary policies of the revolution. According to the front page of *Granma* on January 28, 1968, these plotters had been summoned to an extraordinary meeting of the Communist Party Central Committee, whose purpose was to "unmask a diversionist and traitorous microfraction."

The microfraction was specifically alleged to have distributed clandestine, anti-party propaganda. As well, they were accused of having "unauthorized" relations with Soviets, Czechs, and other Eastern bloc officials; that is, they had discussed their views and intentions with the foreigners outside the rigidly prescribed channels for official contact.

The whole "traitorous" affair had the manufactured smell of the 1962 sectarian crisis. Fidel was attacking the Soviets by proxy. At bottom, the microfraction's unforgivable crime was to concur in the Soviet analysis of Fidel's policies. They believed, according to the report read by Raúl Castro at the January Central Committee meeting, that a budgetary system based on moral incentives had failed "to recognize the laws of social development." They also held that "voluntary work is resorted [to] in order to meet goals of production and this, when it doesn't produce enough to meet the costs, results in production of inferior quality." The microfraction, as Raúl read to the meeting, further claimed "that [economic] plans are made, remade, and everyone at every level intervenes in their preparations, so that one has to work three or four times more than necessary." How ironic that it was the PSP members, of all people, who were telling the truth about Cuba's economic problems.

This apostasy centered again, as it had in the sectarian crisis, on the person of Aníbal Escalante and earned him an extended rustication to the citrus-humus experiment at La Mulata. Other members of the microfraction were sentenced to several years in prison without the Central Committee's being empowered legally to hear or act on the matter at all.

Yet Jorge Enrique Mendoza, *Granma*'s director, wrote a docile endorsement of the episode. "I was greatly impressed," he said in an editorial, "by the spirit of justice, seriousness, conscientiousness, militancy, faith and revolutionary firmness that characterized this meeting of the Central Committee."

The case's harsh and arbitrary disposition was a message to the Soviets—and an object lesson for me. Clearly, the system arrogated to itself the right to use at will any means available to investigate any person, regardless of his or her political or administrative position. Even more emphatically than in *La Dolce Vita*, State Security's handling of the microfraction demonstrated to me the utmost need for greater caution and circumspection in everything I did and said.

By March of 1968, Fidel's simmering anger at the Soviets and his well-established insistence upon Cuba's independent revolutionary course, no matter how it might conflict with Soviet policies such as peaceful coexistence or the USSR's dispute with China, found further expression in his speech launching the Revolutionary Offensive. Standing on the university steps, he berated unnamed Cubans who took Soviet aid for granted, a laxness he characterized as a "let's-cross-our-arms attitude [that has] led to certain sit-back-and-take-it-easy mentality."

He mentioned the "microfractional elements" so recently smashed in the Central Committee and discoursed on "a certain ideological weakness [that] can still be observed in the masses of our people, a certain defect of political education."

Fidel also declared himself dissatisfied with the received ideological wisdom of the so-called manuals, Soviet-sponsored booklets translated from Russian into Spanish, whose texts contained the basic principles of Marxist ideology in schematic, condensed form. The manuals, distributed throughout the island, were in this address called "antiquated, anachronistic, incapable of offering solutions to the real problems of the masses." Fidel emphasized this criticism. "We must also say that the manuals contain a large number of clichés and stereotyped phrases and, what is more, some falsehoods," he said.

Finally, if anyone in early 1968 retained any doubt about Fidel's iron resolution not to heel to the Soviets, his March 13th speech reminded the world audience that Cuba practiced Socialist solidarity according to its own formula. "All of you," he said, "know perfectly well the decision of our Central Committee not to send a delegation to the meeting of the Communist Parties that was held in Budapest."

The torrent of anti-Soviet rhetoric had an effect among the revolutionaries. In the three years since members of the leadership had been shocked by Ché's outburst in Algiers, they timidly and slowly had begun among themselves to venture their own uncomplimentary views of the USSR. By the pivotal August of 1968, as the Soviets prepared to mobilize what would become a 650,000-man army of occupation in breakaway Czechoslovakia, the probability of this action preoccupied the highest levels of the Cuban party and Revolutionary Government. Once the invasion took place, army officers, ministers, directors—a clear plurality of Cuba's senior leadership—shared with one another their outrage at this violation of Czech sovereignty and recalled in disgust the similar events in Hungary in 1956.

The Cuban people opposed the invasion too. While everyone waited in anxious anticipation for the *Líder Máximo* to place his own passionate imprimatur on these attitudes, the old slogan "Fidel! Fidel! Give the Yanquis hell!" spontaneously changed to "Give the *Russians* hell!"

But there had been faint signals that Fidel might not be so ready to give the Russians hell, that his independence of spirit in no way matched that of the Czech people. For several weeks earlier that year, *Granma* had run reports from the Soviet news agency Tass detailing the dangerous political currents loose in Czechoslovakia. At the time I had been unable fully to understand the underlying meaning of these dispatches, but on August 23, 1968, three days after the Czech invasion began, Fidel taught me a lesson in how to read the clues to his thoughts.

I had gone to a gathering at an official's house to hear Fidel on television. Fifteen or so people were there, many of them high officials. Before Fidel appeared on the screen, they all were certain of what he'd say. "He'll really give it to them!" predicted one vice-minister. "The Soviets are as imperialistic as the Yanquis!" another man said. "You'll see how Fidel pays them back for the missile crisis and the gasoline."

These officials, familiar with Fidel's fierce defense of Cuban sovereignty, his steady avowal of independence, his advocacy of the liberation of the oppressed, and his indignant insistence upon the return of the Guantánamo military base by the United States, were certain, as indeed I was, that their fearless leader would now decry the Czech invasion. But we were wrong.

"It is our duty," Fidel announced on the screen, "to analyze the facts objectively and express the opinion of our political leadership, the opinion that represents the judgment of the members of our Central Committee, of the leaders of our mass organizations, of the members of our government, and that we are sure is profoundly compatible with the tradition and sentiments of our people."

Fidel's synthesis of Cuban opinion was that Czechoslovakia, before the invasion, had been a country under siege by retrograde elements to which it had nearly capitulated. Demands for political reform and a free press were symptoms of the sickness. And, according to Fidel, Yanqui imperialism, with its CIA and Pentagon, was behind it all; they were the ones responsible for the Soviet invasion.

Around me in the room, every jaw dropped in unison.

"We acknowledge," Fidel said in summation, "the bitter necessity that called for the sending of those forces into Czechoslovakia. We don't condemn the Socialist countries that made that decision."

The revolutionary elite soon recovered. The moment those in the room with me had absorbed how they were supposed to think, they instantly forgot their words of two hours before. "Fidel has guts!" I heard a person say. "He's turned the tables on the Yanquis!" Everyone chorused support. "I knew the CIA was involved in Czechoslovakia," said another man. "They should shoot all those counterrevolutionaries," remarked a third.

I agreed with everyone, wondering to myself how those who had somehow missed hearing the speech would handle the next morning's conversation at work.

IN DEEPER WATER

If a person went to work the morning of August 24, 1968 ignorant of Fidel's support for the Soviet invasion of Czechoslovakia, he or she might well venture the wrong opinion or utter a slogan already inoperative. Then a colleague, noting this deviationism, would in all likelihood use it to hostile purpose.

Vigilance in policy matters, however, was not nearly so difficult for me to master as were the intricacies of the power game itself, the constant striving for advantage among revolutionary officials. Driven both by greed for more privilege and by paranoia, this high-level struggle was characterized by ruthlessness and Byzantine plotting. To survive like anyone else but also to further my secret agenda—that is, to move up the power pyramid in order to escape the system—I had to be alert for enemies, prepare myself to thwart them, and be ready at any moment for ugly surprises.

There was everything and nothing personal in the combat. One's foes were individuals or members of a rival revolutionary clique, called a *piña* in Cuba, but the plotter wasn't motivated by *whom*, only by what political status his rivals held. This is one reason friendship had so little meaning in the new Cuba.

In my case, my position as ICAIC's chief of investments, a meaningless post save for my direct and confident relationship with Alfredo Guevara and the resulting latitude of action, inevitably made me an obstacle to a colleague's ambitions for advancement. Beyond doubt, someone would envy my relations with Guevara and challenge me sooner or later.

That someone was Benigno Iglesias, who provoked my first skirmish in the power struggle that would occupy me henceforth. Benigno was known behind his back as *El Cura*, "The Priest," because of his active prerevolutionary participation in Catholic youth organizations and his then-avowed desire to train for the clergy. However, once Fidel declared himself a Marxist-Leninist in 1961, Benigno had stopped professing his faith in the Christian God and begun worshipping at the altar of revolution.

El Cura wended his way smoothly into the party, and his rising trajectory had by 1969 brought him to the post of party secretary general at ICAIC, as well as to the directorship of the institute's Film Screening Enterprise. Because the latter was responsible for overseeing the technology of movie shows, projectors, screens, sound systems, and the like, our functions overlapped.

Benigno, like most other latter-day converts to the new faith, found me as a revolutionary with credentials an intimidating, threatening presence. He had no personal history of contribution to the revolutionary struggle. And I was close to Alfredo.

At first Benigno only irritated me with petty interference such as his insisting on a say in capital investment decisions properly left to me. I tried to be shrewd with him, avoiding direct confrontation so long as my revolutionary reputation was not affected or my attitude interpreted as one of "revolutionary softening." If at any moment it appeared to others that I could be intimidated, my hard-won prestige would evaporate. But Benigno kept pushing until I had no choice but to push back—hard.

The occasion for our showdown was a late-1969 party membership drive at ICAIC. I had long been worried by the prospect of having to join the party. In Cuba, as in other Socialist countries, being outside the party is a distinct political liability, both in terms of prestige and rank and because the outsider has no direct pipeline to the possibly vital details of party cell deliberations. In my situation, where my objective was to escape the system, party membership could be a great disadvantage.

In the party, absolute discipline is expected at all levels. If, for instance, a party member is directed to relocate from Havana to Santiago de Cuba or the Isle of Pines, he goes without question. In a worst-case scenario, I might be sent to the provinces for years, making any thought of escape hopeless.

Party members also have much less freedom to maneuver within the revolution. It was fine for me as a nonmember to have informally discussed UMAP with Alfredo Guevara, thereby assuring that the matter would go directly to Raúl Castro. Had I been a party member at that point, such a conversation would have been highly irregular. Alfredo would have directed me to make my denunciation through party channels.

The most immediate threat to my own plans was the current procedure for joining the party. The first step was to receive a letter, as I did in 1969, in which the prospective nominee was directed to fill out a fifteen-page questionnaire dotted with niggling demands for details of the most personal nature, and a written autobiography, also expected to be richly self-revealing. These two requirements alone guaranteed a reprise of La Dolce Vita and UMAP, episodes I had to bury in order to move up—and, someday, get out.

Next came a general assembly of one's fellow workers where, from a slate drawn up of those who'd completed their questionnaires and biographies, nominations for selection as an "Exemplary Worker" would be made from the floor. Presiding over this gathering would be El Dúo ("The Two"), party members from outside one's workplace selected to co-chair the meeting together with one's own party general secretary.

Once the nominations were in, the summarized biographies of those under consideration would be read aloud. Then there would be an open discussion in which anybody's doubts about the nominees were aired. *El Dúo* would subsequently express their opinions of the candidates, and finally, the nominations would be submitted to a general vote. *El Dúo's* remarks notwithstanding, the results of the vote were definitive. If they were positive, the Exemplary Worker moved on to the next step in the process.

Then the party itself investigated the candidate. Inquiries would be carried out through the nominee's local CDR, his or her previous neighborhood defense committees, the party cell, friends, co-workers, and anyone else who might have the slightest shred of personal information about one's past. The private life of a party member belongs to the party.

When this stage was completed, a joint meeting of *El Dúo* and party members from the candidate's workplace cell would be called. The Exemplary Worker would be obliged to review in revolutionary self-criticism every negative aspect of his or her life. Thoroughness in this self-flagellation was essential, since everyone in the room would have before him a very complete dossier of fact, rumor, and allegation collected by the party.

The Exemplary Worker might be asked such questions as why he didn't discuss his wife's reported adultery, a particularly damaging sort of allegation, since cuckoldry in the unwritten macho rules of Cuban Communism is fatal to male prestige. (Interestingly, a woman in the same circumstance is expected to respond only to questions about her own behavior. Before the joint meeting, her husband's affairs are never mentioned. In Cuba, only women commit adultery.)

I had no intention of subjecting myself to this procedure. After filling out my questionnaire and biography, I went to the party general secretary for ICAIC, Benigno Iglesias, and pointed out very strongly to him that despite the privilege of being considered for party membership, it seemed inopportune for my processing to take place barely two years after my UMAP punishment. My request was perfectly legitimate, and Benigno was quick to declare his understanding. "You have nothing to worry about, Llovio," he said. "I'll speak with *El Dúo* about considering your case separately."

About 200 ICAIC workers attended the nominating assembly held at a movie theater near Ayesterán Street, about three blocks from the ICAIC offices. "I nominate *Compañero* Llovio!" said the first worker to speak. "I believe that this *compañero* has the qualifications for an Exemplary Worker because of his responsible attitude toward his work, his participation in political activities, and because, to the best of my knowledge, he was very active in the revolutionary underground."

If the party Priest had been as good as his word, one of *El Dúo* should have risen at this point to explain discreetly that the *compañero* was not ready for party processing just yet. Instead, he turned to me and asked mechanically: "*Compañero* Llovio, do you agree to be analyzed for Exemplary Worker?"

So Benigno had double-crossed me. I glanced at him sitting at the table with *El Dúo*, tapping his pencil lightly in feigned indifference to the predicament he'd put me in. "Yes," I answered *El Dúo* evenly—I had no other choice—as my thoughts raced ahead to the next act in Benigno's little drama.

Over a dozen workers had seconded my nomination as Exemplary Worker, and since my name was entered first, my case was also first to be discussed. After the summary of my biography was read, the questions I had hoped to avoid began raining down.

"What was the extent of the *compañero*'s participation in *La Dolce Vita*?" asked a member of the audience. "What was the specific reason for his punishment?" wondered another.

Benigno took the lead in this grilling. Why had I spent so many years in France? Why had I married a French heiress? Why had I allowed my daughter to leave the country?

His objective had been to neutralize me, to embarrass me in front of my co-workers, and to block what Iglesias assumed I wanted most, party membership. But the strategy failed. Despite his insinuating questions, the assembly voted in favor of my nomination.

After the ballot, he whispered with *El Dúo* for a few minutes. Then one of them rose to address the assembly.

"*Compañeros*," he said, "in the opinion of *El Dúo* and the party at ICAIC, *Compañero* Llovio is not qualified at this moment to be elected an Exemplary Worker. As representatives of the party at this nominating session, we believe that more time should elapse before the *compañero* is processed, although he has shown evidence of correcting his errors committed in the past. Therefore, we have decided to ignore this assembly vote and to move on to the next case."

A charged silence fell over the assembly. Hoping to finish the uncomfortable business as quickly as possible, Benigno himself stood up and exclaimed, "*Compañeros*, we all agree with what has just been said. But we recognize that *Compañero* Llovio is a good revolutionary. Therefore, before we move on to the next candidate, let us have a round of applause for Llovio!"

Although he couldn't know it, Benigno had just done me a favor. Since any reopening of *La Dolce Vita* threatened my plans, it was better to have the process stopped in the worker assembly than to have it continue into the party investigation and joint meeting, from which every lurid detail of my supposed crimes would soon leak to the grapevine. Even if I survived this assault on my character, I'd lose by winning; I definitely did not want to join the party and be under even more scrutiny.

Now it was my turn.

Iglesias had made two serious errors. One, he had contravened party rules by canceling my selection as an Exemplary Worker; the vote of the assembly was sovereign. Two, he had been too sure of himself, not reckoning with my response.

I had to react or I would be accused of not having "revolutionary combativeness." And so I wrote Iglesias a long letter describing my objections to what had occurred and requesting a private meeting with him and *El Dúo*. Then I recounted the facts of the case to Alfredo Guevara. Finally, I sought out an acquaintance, Humberto Massop, a high-level executive and party member. Once Humberto heard the facts, he took it upon himself, as I'd intended, to denounce Benigno and *El Dúo* to the Central Committee. Meantime, Iglesias called me to his office for the late-afternoon discussion I'd requested.

"Look, Llovio," he said. "The fact is that I didn't have time to read your papers or your biography. Besides, I didn't have a chance to talk to *El Dúo* about your case. Unfortunately, I've been having problems recently. They've taken up all my time. You do agree the time isn't right for you to be designated Exemplary Worker, don't you?"

"I thought I made that evident when I first spoke to you long before the meeting, remember?" I said. "And I did so because it didn't seem very politic to make certain matters public."

Then I indirectly reminded Benigno that an airing of my role in *La Dolce Vita* might force disclosures embarrassing to certain high officials of the party who themselves were only now recovering from the scandal. "Your forgetfulness," I emphasized, "has placed me in a delicate position that doesn't make for peace of mind. Now, of course, I have to respond to the fact that the three of you went against the sovereign vote of the assembly."

"What do you plan to do?" Benigno asked, concern in his voice.

"It is not what I plan to do, but what I've already done," I answered dryly. "And that is my affair. You'll know through the proper channels and at the right time."

As it turned out, Iglesias received his due in short order. Massop's denunciation led to Benigno's removal from the secretary general's job, a demotion rationalized by the image-conscious party in its claim that Iglesias had found it impossible to combine his administrative and his political duties. As for *El Dúo*, they were replaced as well.

Having survived this battle, I was now free of worries about party membership. The membership drive came to an end. Never again at ICAIC would the topic of my candidacy for this great honor be brought up. However, this episode was only my first relatively mild taste of political warfare. In time, I would encounter much more dangerous men than the party Priest.

The trial of will with Benigno Iglesias validated, I thought, the resolve I'd made eighteen months before at the Hotel Riviera. My Communist revolutionary facade was intact and I emerged from the encounter much more confident of my command of the revolutionary power game.

However, my double life exacted an appalling price, far more of a burden than I had ever anticipated. I had to look on with feigned approval as the revolution bled Cuba dry. Futile and foolhardy though it would have been to decry the falsity and corruption, I was more repulsed than ever by it all.

The sense of constant danger bore down on me as well, and there was not even the compensating thrill I'd always known in the face of hazard. Since my moments of turmoil and revulsion on the Malecón in 1965, after MININT conscripted me in its investigation, that old familiar taste of excitement at looming peril had vanished. The only flavor now was of ashes.

After my divorce I discovered a further abyss of desolation. The need to share, that family sense of commonality I was born to, was as basic to my nature as breathing. I had never taken this spirit of belonging for granted. But once it was withdrawn—now that I had no role as a son or brother, nephew, cousin, husband, or, most especially, as Marielle's father—all that was left for me was the shell of existence. As the Stranger and my true self wrangled interminably within me, arguing point after point of conduct and attitude, the acute anguish of a hollow life also kept stabbing afresh.

The pain sometimes threatened to overcome my capacity to manage it. At these times, I'd head out on foot to roam Havana, not really caring where I went as long as the scenery kept changing. One such despondent evening, about the time of my confrontation with Benigno, I was out scuffling along, shoulders hunched, in the streets of the Vedado when I met up with Julio Gómez Plana, the merchant marine captain who had escorted Marie Christine to our sealed apartment after my arrest in March of 1966. Julio knew what had happened to my personal life since then.

"What's going on, Llovio?" he asked amiably. "Nobody's seen you for a while."

I mumbled something about the press of work at ICAIC.

"You look tired," he said after a moment's consideration. "You ought to take it easy. I'm going to Miramar to visit a friend whose family is terrific. Why don't you come with me?"

I was happy for Julio's company and more or less indifferent to any destination. Numbly, I fell into step with him toward Miramar, a pleasant residential neighborhood just up from the Malecón and east of Vedado.

Julio's friend turned out to be the younger of two daughters in the family of a respected mathematician and his wife, a warm, sensitive woman from Oriente. I found both parents and daughters immensely appealing. They were uncommonly affable, full of welcome—a true family. Within a few weeks I was an occasional visitor to their house in my own right, and within a few weeks more, I felt myself being drawn in particular to the family's older daughter, Maggie.

She had recently given up studying biology at the university and was enrolled in the Havana School of Design. Maggie was also very interested in the theater and belonged to a semiprofessional troupe that held rehearsals most evenings, and so we got to know each other only gradually. For the longest time I was simply pleased about the occasions when I found her at home and we could talk along with the others, enjoying a new friendship—heightened, for me, by the subtle chemistry of affection.

There was much in Maggie to admire, from the allure of her remarkable green eyes to her soft grace and wit. But there was much in me, once I identified my genuine attraction to her, that

mocked and derided the possibility of a serious emotional attachment. If I had not anticipated at the Hotel Riviera the loneliness that would engulf me, I also hadn't considered its opposite:
love and its many complications for me. "Why do you go on with
this absurd game?" asked the Stranger. "In no way does she fit
into your plans."

Nor did I fit into Maggie's. She was uncompromisingly independent in her thinking. I knew from the start that Fidel's magnetic personality did not touch her. On the other hand, she did
admire some of my old friends and acquaintances, revolutionaries such as José Antonio Echevarría, Camilo Cienfuegos, and
Ché Guevara.

Much was left unsaid between us as we both cautiously
allowed our relationship to gather its own momentum. We went
for strolls together, visited the beach, and exchanged our thoughts
on paintings, films, plays, and music, slowly discovering how
much we had in common. Maggie knew from our earliest acquaintance of my divorce and my time in UMAP, but we never
discussed it in detail. All areas of possible conflict were skirted
until one night, as we walked through one of Miramar's lovely
old parks of graceful willow trees, Maggie forcefully brought her
own unspoken concerns into the open.

"I'm a fool," she said suddenly, and then let forth with an
uninterrupted discourse. "I've realized for a long time that what
we're doing makes no sense, that it's wrong for me. But you can
see I haven't been able to stop it."

Before I could say anything, she hurried on.

"There's something I haven't told you," she said. "I have
been making arrangements to leave the country. My family may
be part of the revolution as are you, but I am not. And I'm
prepared to go alone.

"I stopped studying biology so I wouldn't have to join the
militia, and I have taken up design not only because I enjoy it
but also because there aren't so many political demands at the
school. I also believe in God and I go to church, but I'm always
afraid when I do. I have to go in secret and I worry that some
extremist I know will find out."

She was angry and adamant.

"I can't approve of a system," she continued, "where everything is obligatory, where freedom of thought and action don't
exist. They try to make everything black-and-white, but human
beings are made of shadings. What do you do? Do you pretend?

Do you say yes when you think no? What are they trying to do, create a country of hypocrites?"

I listened with what I hoped was a thoughtful expression that gave nothing away.

"I know you believe in this revolution," she said. "I respect your ideas and I want you to respect mine. But that doesn't happen here any longer. That's one of the reasons I want to leave. So far, nothing I've tried has worked out, and it's very possible I won't be able to go. In any event, I want you to know what my intentions are."

When she finished speaking, Maggie indicated no expectation of a response from me. There was nothing I could say, or would say, at that moment. But her candor had had a galvanizing effect. Inside me, there was no longer the question of should I love this woman, but how would I manage it? When could I ever tell her who I really was without endangering us both? I could not believe the irony of my posing this momentous question for a second time. And how would I solve the infinitely more complex challenge of getting us both out of Cuba? Yet, in Maggie, I knew I'd found the strength and renewed sense of purpose to persevere and ultimately to prevail. I would not close my heart to that possibility, and for once the Stranger was silent.

"TEN MILLION ON THE WAY"

The new light Maggie brought into the bleakness of my life contrasted sharply with the accelerating decline of the country's mood. By the late 1960s, the revolution's domestic initiatives, from Special Plans to the Revolutionary Offensive, had so ravaged the island's economy that the foreign debt, owed mainly to Socialist creditors, had reached an all-time high. Nowhere was the enfeeblement of Cuba's economic infrastructure more glaringly evident than in the country's main industry, sugar. According to a trade agreement signed in 1966, Cuba was to ship the USSR 5 million tons of raw sugar in 1968 and another 5 million tons in 1969. In fact, only a total of 3.7 million tons for both years would ever be delivered.

Fidel had long since reversed his belief that Cuba was overly dependent on sugar cane as a cash crop and instituted, in 1966, an ambitious capital investment program designed to modernize the industry. He had a long way to go. Most of Cuba's sugar mills were antiquated community facilities, some built as long ago as the early nineteenth century. Cane-cutting technology generally had not progressed much beyond the primitive man-and-machete level. The island's 5,500 miles of sugar-industry railway were deteriorating from lack of maintenance, and most of the industry's locomotives were vintage steam engines, fifty years out of date. There was also a shortage of sugar freight cars. Finally, the industry lacked the proper sugar storage and port facilities to handle any more than the 6 million tons of annual production that it was somehow able to sustain.

No capital program on any scale was going to rescue the sugar sector from its doldrums any time soon. With the tasks ahead of planning, procurement, installation of advanced technology, and the inevitable management headaches of making new mill processing systems efficient, the modernization plan might begin incrementally to improve production above 6 million tons a year only by the early 1970s.

No special acumen was necessary to recognize these facts of economic life; even I, then having some experience in building movie theaters and basically ignorant of the sugar industry, could tell by a glance at the old mills and crumbling railroad system that only a miracle could generate any near-term rise in sugar production.

As a consequence, I was astonished to hear among the revolutionaries the buzz of something truly stupendous in the offing. Fidel had decided to commit Cuba to a 10 million-ton sugar harvest in 1970!

Based on the projection of 10 million tons of production, the Soviets then agreed to purchase half of it at a more than 50 percent premium over current world sugar prices. Another 2.15 million tons would be earmarked for the international market, thereby earning the revolution some much-needed hard currency. The rest was to be shipped to other Socialist countries and to be used for the domestic market.

The Soviets surely harbored no illusions that Fidel could actually produce 10 million tons of sugar in 1970. This was clear from the January 1968 microfraction's "deviationist" analysis of the harvest, based on Soviet thinking, which had landed most of those PSP veterans in jail. "As may be observed," the microfraction had concluded to their own detriment, "to judge the present size of our sugar-cane crop, the years that remain, and the difficulties we have met, it will be almost impossible to reach 10 million tons by 1970."

Still, Fidel had in that same year, 1968, swallowed his pride to endorse the Soviet invasion of Czechoslovakia. He had to be promised something in return for the damage done to his prestige. The Soviet oil allotment, such a point of irritation in early 1968, was increased after his August 1968 speech. Machinery and other aid began to flow, including 1,000 Soviet-built cane-cutting machines that were given a provisional tryout during the 1969 harvest.

Unfortunately, the USSR grew sugar beets, not cane. The machines had therefore been designed to cut the plant close to its roots, thus killing the cane, which otherwise regenerates for at least five years. The *campesinos* baptized the Soviet cutter "Attila's Horse," because everywhere it went, cane plants died.

As subsequent developments would reveal, Moscow was prepared to tolerate another economic disaster in Cuba. The USSR had a coherent long-range strategy for dealing with Fidel, a plan that took into account his vagaries and anticipated their consequences, which the Soviets would use to yoke him finally to their point of view.

Fidel had entirely opposite expectations for the harvest. Not only would it ease Cuba's debt burden, but a successful harvest would exonerate the revolution from its poor international reputation for economic management. To Fidel, image meant everything, and earlier excuses for mistakes—alibis such as the leadership's youth or inexperience, Cuba's underdevelopment, and the U.S. blockade—were no longer being bought in the marketplace of world opinion.

Then there was the tired Cuban population itself to address. Promises of prosperity "in the future" had lost their ability to inspire. They were too elastic, too distant; a more concrete and immediate objective was needed. Ten million tons of sugar in Cuba's storehouses by the end of 1970 translated directly into well-being that a skeptical people could see. At all costs and sparing no effort, the harvest had to succeed.

As its originator and principal fan, Fidel sought to stir Cubans for the toil ahead with can-do exhortations. "When you see someone who says 'I don't know,' look at him with distrust," he had told a crowd in the Plaza de la Revolución in September of 1967. "When you see someone who says 'I can't,' look at him with suspicion. When you see someone who says 'This is too much,' look at him with reservations. What we have to say, all of us, you and us, is 'Yes, we can! And what we don't know, we'll learn!' We have to say that nothing is too much for us!"

Eight months later, in a provincial address that followed by less than four weeks the launching of the Revolutionary Offensive, Fidel had forgotten his deep concerns over the people's many weaknesses. "So," he said, "on the question of whether or not we shall succeed in producing the ten million-ton harvest, we haven't the slightest doubt. Our country's honor is pledged to this. Our country's prestige. This goal will be attained because it is a challenge to the tenacity and iron will of our people."

The spirit of Fidel's public-relations offensive—triumph assured before the battle was joined—was neatly captured in its slogan: *¡Los diez millones van!*—"Ten million on the way!" It was proclaimed on posters and plastered over walls from one end of the island to the other. Radio announcers shouted it: *¡Los diez millones van!* People heard it on television, read it in their newspapers and recited it to each other in their assemblies.

¡Los diez millones van!

In time, it began to seep into their conscience; once more, many seemed ready to put their shoulders to the wheel. Of course they had no real choice. Cubans one and all were going to be mobilized for the harvest, although Fidel coyly ventured the hope that massive mobilizations would not be necessary. I thought that no one in Cuba, including Fidel, could honestly believe that, but he did manage to make his countrymen think, if for the last time, that hard work under his visionary leadership would make the dream come true.

Officially only one voice was raised against Fidel's declaration. Through many sources, I learned about what happened at one of the meetings held in preparation for the harvest. After prodding his ministers, deputy ministers, and directors about the delayed arrival of equipment and parts, Fidel had turned to Lieutenant Orlando Borrego, head of the Ministry of the Sugar Industry (MINAZ) to ask him about the most pressing problems facing his ministry. Borrego, who until then had remained silent, began to enumerate objectively the technical problems that in his opinion could not be solved in such a short time. Fidel wanted to begin the 1970 harvest in July, while it was projected that the 1969 harvest would end in May; that is, in most of the mills there would be a margin of only two months to make new investments and finish the repairs that were needed at the end of each harvest. In Borrego's opinion, the sugar industry could not take on the enormous volume of milling planned for the 1970 harvest in such a short time and with so little preparation. Fidel was silent while Borrego made his detailed statement, and when the analysis was finished, Fidel, without any preamble, attacked his minister, calling him fickle, a skeptic, a defeatist.

"We'll make our ten million," he said, rebuking Borrego, "and it's the people who are going to produce them despite the skeptics, in whose ranks we find the man who until this very moment had been sugar minister."

So much for the voice of reason.

LENIN PARK

The 10 million-ton harvest may have been unique in its epic sweep, but otherwise this colossal undertaking was utterly consistent with the revolution's inclination for the grandiose. As preparations for it proceeded apace, so did the planning for another epic project, the construction of Lenin Park in the extreme southern reaches of Havana.

I was assigned from ICAIC to the executive council for the park, accountable to its sponsor, Celia Sánchez, Fidel's longtime companion. She had assembled the *crème de la crème* of Cuban architects, engineers, and decorators, who were encouraged to give their fertile imaginations free rein in designing Lenin Park. The site, hundreds of acres of hilly desert land, lacking roads and water, was as unpromising a stretch of ground as could have been chosen for a large recreational facility. Yet upon my return from an initial inspection of the terrain, I saw in the project office scale models and sketches of a tropical Xanadu.

At Fidel's order, the engineers were planning to build a dam with a capacity of more than 3 billion cubic feet of water in a spot just outside the park, a place that the *campesinos* called "Dry Pass." The dam would supply water for an artificial lake planned for the center of the park, where there would be a floating stage for productions of popular shows. On the banks of this lake the planners would erect a sculpted stone copy of the interior of a Roman coliseum.

Celia's team also intended to construct the most luxurious restaurant in Cuba, a building with several rooms featuring huge stained-glass windows created by René Portocarrero, the national painter. Complementary decor included antique art nouveau lamps, colonial furniture, and a gigantic Baccarat crystal chandelier.

Another component of the plan was the aquarium in the shape of a seashell to be built on a hilltop. Tanks of heavy green-tinted glass would be embedded in the walls of the shell to display the most typical species found in Cuban oceans and rivers.

Futhermore, the team was considering the construction of a stable, with strict European orientation, for lovers of horseback riding; a rodeo of such proportions that it could "compete with any similar North American installation"; a modern amusement park with equipment imported from Japan; an exhibition gallery surrounded by beautiful gardens, a corner dedicated to artistic and literary discussions called La Peña Literaria (The Literary Circle); several restaurants and cafeterias with exotic backgrounds; a huge outdoor movie theater; and various shops that would sell candies, hot dogs, cold drinks, fine pastry, and so forth. The park would have a picturesque miniature train so that children, accompanied by their parents, could see the enormous site in comfort. And finally, in order to solve the problem of bare terrain, the planners intended to transplant several thousand mature trees, such as ceibas, carobs, mahoganies, and eucalyptus. In short, the park was just the sort of project well within the reach of a poor, underdeveloped country.

My responsibility in this plan centered on the construction of the open-air movie theater, but even this apparently simple work could not escape the designers' enthusiasm for originality. To begin with, we would have to shape a large concave space and seed it with special grass suitable for people sitting on the slopes of the theater. Then we needed to construct a gigantic screen of steel plates almost a hundred feet wide and more than twenty-six feet high, fastened to the ground by a complex iron structure. The projection room would be placed inside a then-nonexistent hill, which we would erect by moving some 3.5 million cubic feet of earth. We would hide the hill behind a curtain of bamboo to preserve the unspoiled atmosphere of the park. And six towers would have to be erected to support the enormous loudspeakers.

To accomplish this task I mobilized the best architects and engineers from the Architecture Department at ICAIC. Although they were amazed by the complexity of the project, they took on the work without a word.

To build the hill I asked Comandante Derminio Escalona, in charge of building the dam at Dry Pass, if we could borrow his dump trucks. "Of course, Llovio!" he answered with great solicitude. "I can't send them all to you right now, but I'll help out. Listen, Chico, your hill is nothing compared to what we're doing here. You'll see, we'll have your hill built for you in no time. This dam is really a great idea of the Commander in Chief's. We'll be able to irrigate thousands of acres. We'll provide water for the lake in your park—for all Havana if you're not careful. Just one good rain and you'll see."

The cloud of dust and the constant traffic of dozens of Berliet trucks dumping rocks and earth for the dam curtain indicated a feverish activity. Derminio showed me his work with pride. "And all this happened even though we've had problems with some *campesinos* who refused to leave their land," he said as we walked over the site. "I don't understand them. It's a great deal for them. In exchange for their land they get an income for life, and on top of that a new apartment with all the conveniences. And besides, Chico, they're so superstitious! They say the water won't stay in the dam, that this earth will swallow it up, that there's a reason they call it Dry Pass, and I don't know what else. As if Fidel didn't know what he was doing!"

Naturally, I did not comment.

Our executive committee met once a week, when developments in each of the projects, their special difficulties, and their progress toward meeting the deadline were reviewed. I listened in a state of stupefaction to the exquisite requirements of the architects and to their complaints about delays in receiving modern Canadian door handles, Italian ceramics for the restrooms in the restaurants, Spanish easy chairs for the projection room in the aquarium, and sculpted stone for building the tiered seats in the coliseum.

The mobilization of resources and the effort that went into construction of the movie theater were incalculable. For example, in order to fix the gigantic metal screen and its sustaining structure, we had to fabricate a compact base of reinforced concrete 115 feet long by 33 feet wide and 20 feet deep. For several days, this almost stopped delivery of concrete from the factory at Rancho Boyeros to other industrial projects in Havana.

The most difficult process was the installation of Soviet projection equipment inside the hill. To bury these huge seventy-millimeter projectors, we needed a frame that could withstand the weight of the earth. After an extended search, the solution was found in the prefabricated arches used to form part of the underground hangars for hiding MiG 21's. It was extremely difficult to obtain these modules. Despite the personal intervention of Celia Sánchez, MINFAR was reluctant to give up its arches. But the greatest imbroglio came when we tried to move them. The double-platform trucks took up two lanes, creating huge traffic jams whenever they made a turn.

In the midst of all this, I was assigned to another special project, the remodeling of San Rafael Street, the main thoroughfare in what had been the most popular commercial center of prerevolutionary Havana.

San Rafael Street had become a shabby relic of its former self. The facades of its once-elegant stores were dirty, the sidewalks broken, and the electric signs dilapidated. In the shop windows the elegant displays had been transformed into strange amalgams in shockingly bad taste, including portraits of martyrs and tawdry propaganda posters plastered with cardboard stars or hung with colored paper and ribbons. Equally unappealing were the timid displays of cosmetics or textiles manufactured in Cuba.

Under my direction, an architect and several well-known decorators devised a plan in which the facades along San Rafael would be repainted, the old electric signs would be replaced, and cafeterias and ice cream parlors would be opened. As for the shop windows, it was agreed they would display the finest works of Latin American folk art the country had to offer. The National Museum and some private collections would lend their most valuable pieces. In this way the street would be turned into a kind of outdoor museum that could be exploited for Socialist propaganda.

I asked myself what kind of mind could conceive such displays of originality in a country with so many other needs. It seemed as if the country's financial resources were going to be drained by a grandiose park—or by an even more grandiose harvest.

THE HARVEST:
ON BATTLE ALERT

¡Los diez millones van!

Any Cuban *campesino* knows that optimum annual sugar-cane yield is obtained at the plants' peak maturity, from December until early spring of each year. When this fact of nature is taken into account, along with attention to the variables of temperature and the proper application of irrigation and fertilizers, sugar grades as high as 11–13 on the quality scale are routine.

But Fidel had commanded that the 1970 harvest begin in July 1969, a sort of headstart toward the goal of 10 million tons. The hope was for sugar at an acceptable grade, 7–9. What was achieved with the first cutting was an inferior grade 3, a sweet glop somewhere between honey and brown sugar. Abruptly, the premature harvest was halted until October.

Fidel had also called for "simultaneous war" throughout the harvest. That is, he had directed national dedication to business as usual in all sectors of the economy even while the sugar harvest was in progress; the harvest was not to interfere with other productive activities. When it recommenced in autumn, however, the effort demanded by the harvest effectively strangled the rest of the already ailing Cuban economy. Factories stopped producing, and serious difficulties arose in the distribution of basic goods. Meat, cooking oil, bean, and rice deliveries were delayed. Detergent, toothpaste, shampoo, and deodorant disappeared from the markets. Many of these items were left to spoil in the heat of Cuba's warehouses.

At ICAIC, film production was disrupted, and we had to close many movie theaters. Restaurants also shut down, or remained open with restricted menus, service, and hours. The government bureaucracy froze. Everyone, revolutionaries especially, was out cutting sugar cane.

This backbreaking labor was the easy part of the harvest. In one of my own "volunteer" turns with a machete in fields near the village of Placetas in Las Villas Province, I saw the piles of cut cane rise higher and higher as the mechanized lifts used to load them onto trucks continuously broke down under the strain of constant use and inexperienced operation. Traveling on ICAIC affairs throughout the major cane-producing provinces of eastern Cuba, I watched the harvest fall out of overloaded trucks at every pothole they hit and at each turn in the road. I also drove past frequent train derailments, cane-laden freight cars upended when their locomotives ran across deteriorated track.

The greatest chaos was at the mills. The operators resented the illogical demand that they process rivers of sugar cane with outmoded and poorly serviced machinery. Sometimes they were harried into using new equipment before it had been properly installed and adjusted. Or, if new machinery such as the giant tandems for crushing the cane actually worked, the mill would often lack the boiler capacity for cooking the cane or the centrifuges for separating the sugar.

More cane had been cut than the mills could possibly handle, even if they operated at full capacity, which few did, owing to constant breakdowns. For optimal sugar yield, the cane should have been crushed within three days of cutting, but it was now delayed to a national average of six days before it was fed into the tandems. Then, because of the transportation and milling snafus, the cane processing was interrupted, with the further effect of forcing the sugar mills to burn expensive oil. Ordinarily, a mill can be fueled by the bagasse—the shredded cane fibers left over from processing. If milling is interrupted, however, the only recourse is to use oil as fuel, the result of which was the thick black smoke that spewed from Cuban sugar-mill stacks all through the harvest.

Gross mismanagement also hobbled the harvest. Fidel, the party, the Sugar Ministry, and practically every other arm of the revolution kept issuing a welter of confused and contradictory directives. Even when the lines of authority were clear, as in Oriente Province, which for many years had been run as the personal fiefdom of Party First Secretary Armando Acosta, incompetence and Acosta's own corruption insured further inefficiency.

Oriente was vital to the harvest; this province alone needed to produce 3 million tons of sugar if the goal of 10 million was to be met. When Acosta's lavish life style and poor leadership began to affect harvest morale in Oriente, he was removed and later banished to La Mulata, that graveyard of revolutionary careers. Acosta was replaced by Comandante Guillermo García, a Politburo member notable for his weak intellect, stubbornness, and Fidel's explicit confidence in him, as García had been one of the first fighters in the Sierra Maestra.

García militarized Oriente, declaring the local harvest on "battle alert" from his "harvest headquarters" set up near Bayamo. The new imagery of warfare did nothing to boost production, but it did follow the evolving tone of the faltering harvest as ordained by Fidel himself. "The struggle being waged by Cubans today," he said in a cane field on January 1, 1970, machete in hand and surrounded by hundreds of North Vietnamese students studying in Cuba who were toiling along with him, "is just as important as that waged by the fighters for independence in 1868 and 1895. It is just as important for the attainment of the country's happiness, well-being, and independence."

By March 1970 it was clear that Fidel's goal was unreachable. But of course, nobody dared say a word. Orlando Borrego's experience was still fresh in the leaders' minds.

At a meeting of the Politburo early in April, Fidel conceded what everybody knew: It was impossible to reach the 10 million. Yet, he said, it was necessary to produce the maximum tonnage in order to get as close as possible to the goal. Furthermore, he declared, it would be counterproductive to inform the people, as that could affect their "combativeness" and thus lower production. The people would be told nothing until the last moment.

Fidel did order a final desperate measure. Ministers, deputy ministers, directors of institutes, and other important bureaucrats were sent to manage the sugar mills and other sugar-processing installations. Fidel was sure that these high-placed leaders could find a way out of the chaos, but again his effort failed. These gentlemen, ignorant of the complexities of the harvest, made decisions that interfered even more with its operation.

How I wondered, is Fidel going to explain the harvest failure to the people? How would he wriggle away from this major reversal, or rationalize it after committing his full faith and reputation to the harvest?

As it turned out, sworn foes of the revolution handed Fidel his opportunity. Early in May 1970, a group of Cuban exiles living in the United States kidnapped eleven Cuban fishermen in Bahamian waters, an ill-timed, pointless provocation for which Fidel must have been rapturously grateful.

The Revolutionary Government seized on the exiles' caper almost as if another Bay of Pigs invasion were under way. The army went to battle stations. Torpedo boats were dispatched to the vicinity of the incident. MiG 21's screamed aloft and out over the Caribbean, flying as close to Miami as they could while still over international waters.

At the same time, the Cuban people were mobilized by their CDRs and workplace organizations to begin demonstrations. Day and night, outside the old U.S. Embassy on the Malecón in Havana and throughout the country, the crowds shouted their indignant demands for the fishermen's return. After months of the maddening harvest mobilizations, Cubans could vent their anger in a national catharsis of protest.

Fidel squeezed every ounce of advantage he could from his lucky break. The Revolutionary Government orchestrated a crescendo of outrage, splashing the story in the print, radio, and television media and issuing news bulletins frequently. The spontaneous anger of the Cuban people was a major theme; government reports noted that the "mediating" action of the police was needed to "contain" the aroused masses. When the fishermen were released by their captors, a massive demonstration was organized to welcome them home. "From the workplace to the American Embassy" was the rallying slogan for the affair, and its main attraction would be, of course, Fidel himself.

On May 19, I joined the huge crowd gathered on the esplanade in front of the Embassy. The expectation was that Fidel would attack the North Americans, and he did. His eternal litany against the CIA and imperialism opened the speech, but this time—because the fishermen had been taken near the Bahamas —he included the English, charging that "British colonialists were the fathers of the Yanqui imperialists, in the spiritual sense and in the political sense."

"Never in our country," he exclaimed, "have we held a rally that was so symbolic; symbolic of solidarity, the solidarity of a nation of eight million people in support of the lives and fate of eleven humble fishermen, workers of the sea!"

Fidel had devised an amazing strategy. First, he equated the return of the fishermen to a victory for the people, because of the mass demonstrations he claimed had led to their release. "And what happened?" he asked. "The enemy surrendered immediately after the first salvos, and there were still plenty of weapons in the people's arsenal." Second, he warned of the danger of imminent attack. "We should all be aware," he said, "of the fact that the imperialists are preparing new plans against us, plans on a large scale."

He was resorting to a favored political ploy—fostering tension within the people. "What do the imperialists have in mind?" he went on. "They figure that if we don't score the supreme victory of the ten million tons, that will be the prime psychological moment for attacking our country and giving the counterrevolutionary a boost."

With this brief mention of the harvest, Fidel had forged his first link. Before a supposedly spontaneous gathering of Cubans inflamed against the kidnap of eleven countrymen, Fidel had cheered their victory and then suggested that the Yanquis were about to pounce on the island if the people's morale weakened, as the imperialists apparently hoped it would should the harvest fail.

As his agitated audience mulled over this threat, Fidel moved quickly to make it seem a more concrete possibility. His voice took on a sincere tone. "I must tell you frankly," he said, ". . . We have had difficulties. Are we going to blame somebody for this? No! Are we going to blame the imperialists? No!"

Then he added for emphasis: "A revolutionary people doesn't have to go around blaming anybody for its difficulties."

This was news. For eleven years, the source of all Cuban problems had been the United States and, sometimes, the Soviets. But at this moment in his oratory, Fidel was focusing on passion, not excuses. He wanted to stoke the people's collective patriotic conscientiousness.

"Naturally," he said, "if a revolution sets itself an objective and does not achieve it, it hurts all of us, deeply wounding us, in our hearts, pride, and dignity. But if you want me to tell you clearly just what the situation is, I can tell you that we won't reach the ten million-ton mark."

Fidel should have been mortified at this admission; after all, he was eating his own words. But he had cunningly couched the news—acting as if he, too, had just learned it—in the totally unrelated context of impending U.S. aggression and wrapped it in an emotive appeal to Cuban national pride, neither of which had anything at all to do with the failure of *his* harvest.

Having banished rationality from his discourse, Fidel then went on to a preposterous proposal. "Victory," he ventured, "might have led to relaxation. Victory might have led us to the notion that all our problems had been solved. In victory, we would have had to guard ourselves from an excess of optimism."

Only the complete disregard for his people's reasoning power could have led Fidel to make such an assertion.

"We have won an important political battle," he said of the kidnap episode. "And we have won it employing a minimum of our resources. Let's use our heads and wait. Let's be satisfied with this great victory of the people. No one should be sad, thinking this is the last battle. Our Revolution still has many battles ahead of it. The people will have many opportunities to demonstrate their valor and staunchness and show the stuff they're made of. In the face of this, we must all work harder than ever!"

No Cuban could fail to grasp the deeper import of what he was saying. A time of great demands and more sacrifice was coming; a time of more work. The vast crowd gathered to be inspired by Fidel's oratory instead came away with the sour understanding that the prosperity and ease promised by the success of the 10 million-ton harvest was only one more vain and bitter illusion.

The next day, May 20, 1970, another speech by Fidel was announced, a television address. He now appeared before the cameras surrounded by papers, maps, and posters that justified the errors committed during the harvest, all the factors that his ex-minister Borrego had dared to warn him about more than two years before. When he stated that "our ignorance of the sugar industry contributed to our not realizing in time, discovering in time, seeing in time the variety of problems," I thought of how much the country might have saved in grief if, as a result of this experience, Fidel really had become aware of his ignorance of economic and production matters—if he had listened and set aside his pride, his desire to know everything and to meddle in everything.

Throughout these tumultuous public events, my private life continued to be a harbor. Maggie's determination to leave Cuba raised the specter of a second abandonment, a dreadful ironic pass I'm not sure I could have withstood. But, despite all her efforts, Maggie could not find a means of exit.

As our relationship deepened, I considered at length whether I should drop my Communist revolutionary facade in front of her and tell her precisely how I felt about Fidel's revolution and my plan for escaping it. The temptation to candor was strong; my closedness had destroyed my marriage with Marie Christine. In addition, making a clean breast of it to Maggie would cement the relationship, adding to friendship, love, and mutual respect a common ideal and shared objective: escape.

The countervailing considerations were compelling too. Comparisons are odious; Maggie was not at all like Marie Christine, and I was a different person from the self-assured youth who six years before had cockily set out to rescue his uncle with little thought to his actions' possible consequences. But there was one constant: the need for caution in everything I did.

Maggie was very close to her family, especially her mother. If she knew the truth, she'd have to share it with her mother. Suddenly, at least three people would be responsible for protecting a dangerous secret. If as was necessary I insisted that Maggie say nothing, it would force her into an unwonted falseness at home and everywhere else. Why should she also have to play the Communist revolutionary? What was to be gained by saddling Maggie with the enormous stress with which I was all too familiar?

The more I pondered the problem, the clearer it became to me that I was the only one who could possibly gain from telling Maggie the truth. If she could love me, as she had come to avow that she did, despite her disapproval of my presumed Communist revolutionary consciousness, then we could be fulfilled together even if my silence persisted for the time being.

Maggie and I were married at her family's home on January 23, 1971. Even choosing the proper date for the wedding entailed some neat figuring. I knew it would be politic to invite a reasonable number of revolutionary leaders to the ceremony, but I kept their possible attendance to a minimum by selecting a day when a plenary assembly was being held. Papito Serguera and Alfredo Guevara came and were welcome; I liked them both and so did Maggie.

The next day we left for the tranquil setting of Varadero Beach, where, free for the time being from thoughts of my work at ICAIC, my plans for escape, and the many problems of Cuba, I was able to relax for a few days with my new wife.

AN OFFER TO RESIGN

The kidnapping of the fishermen in May of 1970 deflected the Cuban people's anger for a while, but the humiliating failure of the 10 million-ton harvest was a blow to the Revolutionary Government's credibility—too serious a blow for a stroke of felicity (or Fidel's suggestion that losing was better than winning) to defuse the crisis of confidence. Something much more dramatic was needed—and quickly.

The Cuban people were drained and disillusioned. Cuba's shops and stores were going to remain as empty as Fidel's promises, and the people's daily lives would be emptier still. The routine of work and sacrifice wasn't just difficult, it was boring, an unbroken grind not relieved by any readily available amusement or diversion or even a companionable glass of beer.

Not that Fidel had a substantive remedy to offer for the economic disasters his policies had wrought or the meanness of his people's lives. What he had was a psychological strategy, a scheme based on the patent illogic of his May 19th speech at the old U.S. Embassy, and dependent for its success upon his extraordinary thespian skills.

Act II of the drama unfolded in Havana at 1970's July 26th celebration in the Plaza. After several intermittent thunder showers had soaked the crowd, and Todor Zhivkov, first secretary of the Bulgarian Communist Party, had bored them with a tiresome address, Fidel took the stage.

First he was presented with a certificate as Cuba's "Millionth Cane Cutter" by Jorge Risquet, the Captains' Club veteran who'd been restored to good order from his minor party post in Santiago de Cuba, where Marie Christine and I had visited him so many years ago. Risquet was now Cuba's labor minister. While such ceremonial presentations were common on celebration days, this one subtly connected Fidel to the collective labor of the recent harvest, emphasizing that he was one of the people.

He humbly accepted the piece of paper and then started his speech with the customary recitation of the Revolutionary Government's efforts in the fields of education, public health, and social security. These were the positive areas he had to cover, the source of much pride. But Fidel was quick to assure his listeners that more than self-congratulation was on the agenda. In fact, it was time for some of Fidel's brand of intense revolutionary self-criticism.

Fidel had with him sheaves of reports and statistics which he said, in a suitably confidential tone, contained "the secrets of the economy, one of those things that are written and discussed in secret so that the enemy won't learn of them." The crowd in the Plaza was being led to believe they were to share information of the highest strategic value.

In a strongly emotional voice Fidel detailed at length Cuba's economic failures. The country's serious problems in providing meat, dependable electrical power, and sufficient, reliable farm equipment led the list of shortcomings, but he did not stint at all in the comprehensiveness of this supposedly self-critical evaluation. Fidel painted a bleak economic portrait in every area of production from rice to toothpaste.

The content of his words was repetitive, depressing, and when read later, stultifyingly boring. But the scene in the Plaza was riveting. Although what Fidel was really describing was the incredible botch he personally had made of the Cuban economy, what the mob heard was the thrilling voice, the soaring oratory.

It was as if Fidel were doing highlights from *Hamlet*. Using every trick of inflection and gesture he knew, he made shortfalls in shoe production sound fierce and heroically tragic, disruptions in the manufacture of glass bottles epic episodes. He penetrated well past his audience's powers of rational thought, seducing them into sharing his ignominy until they and he were one, embattled, angry, and proud. Fidel grew more and more hysterical, grasping at the podium and bouncing up and down in his soul-wrenching *mea culpa* until the frenzy in him had fully ignited the crowd. Then he struck.

"I believe," Fidel cried, "that we, the leaders of this Revolution, have cost the people too much in our process of learning. . . . The people can replace us whenever they wish—right now if you so desire!"

The plaza mob was whipped to the mania point. "FIDEL! FIDEL! FIDEL!" they chanted ecstatically. "NO! NO! NO!"

It was a fascinating performance; and it succeeded brilliantly. Once the crowd had given Fidel its acclamation for the rest of Cuba and the world to see and hear, he turned down the supercharged current and proceeded calmly.

First, Fidel condescendingly flattered the people, saying that in them could be found "the really revolutionary spirit of which Marx and Lenin spoke." Then, in lamblike innocence, he turned to his Prohibition policy. Cuba's bars had been shut down for two years at Fidel's explicit directions. Yet now he cheerfully made Prohibition seem like a peripheral oversight that might easily be corrected; someone else was to blame.

"We have asked," he said, "the *compañero* in charge of this matter to analyze the question of recreation centers (bars, clubs, and cabarets) in order to decide on which days they should be open. And the workers should be consulted in the analysis of this matter."

Suddenly, it had become necessary for him to involve the masses in a higher level of decision-making.

"And if the neighbors make a mistake, they are allowed to make mistakes. It may be hard, but it's their decision. If the workers in a factory err on deciding on a problem of that type, it is hard, but it's the people's decision."

Clearly, Fidel was suggesting that from then on he would change tactics and revise his methods. Before he left the podium he bid his audience farewell. "All that remains to be said in the name of our Party, our leadership, and in the name of my own sentiments," he said, "in view of the attitude, confidence, and reaction of the people, is thank you very much."

Seconds later, Fidel returned to the microphones. He had forgotten to mention another plan whose execution required the consent of the people. Through the mediation of Arguedas, former Bolivian minister of the interior, Fidel found himself in possession of Ché's diary of the Bolivian war, his death mask, and most important, his two hands, perfectly preserved. "What are we going to do with Ché's hands?" he said now.

"Preserve them!" shouted the crowd.

"Then this is the proposal we want you to take into consideration," he said. "Conserve in a sober design that has been made—framed by the olive-green sleeves of his uniform and his major's stars and enclosed in a glass urn—Ché's death mask and his hands, the hands in which he held the weapons of liberation."

Knowing Ché intimately, with his profound revulsion toward this kind of "Communist worship," toward the retrograde Soviet custom of mummifying heroes just as the Egyptians did with their pharaohs, Fidel was nevertheless attempting to create with those hands a native replica on the Plaza de la Revolución of the Lenin Mausoleum on Red Square.

He never spoke of the matter again. It seems that this macabre idea, which clashed with the most authentic Cuban traditions, was definitely rejected after more careful reconsideration by the people.

Fidel's magic in front of a microphone had not deserted him; in the worst of times he was able to work his spell on a crowd. But the domestic chaos of the late 1960s, culminating in the failed sugar harvest, had snapped the bond of trust between Fidel and the Cuban people.

SECRET DEFIANCE

There is no question of open revolt in Cuba; the "system" takes care of that. By means of the ever-vigilant CDRs, through MININT, the party, the unions, and the other mass organizations, the Revolutionary Government easily isolates Cubans from one another. These institutions prevent the disaffected from forming blocs or organizing themselves into an opposition, hidden or otherwise.

But if Cubans cannot express their anger actively, there is a passive alternative, a way of opposing the Revolutionary Government in secret defiance, the true "collective consciousness" of Cuba from the late 1960s onward.

It began as a silent epidemic of indifference whose early symptoms were as common as the state-employed truck driver who did not care if he wasted fuel or the waiter who had somehow misplaced his courtesy or the bus passenger who paid for his fare with an old button or washer. The spirit of self-sacrifice and belief in the future that had sustained the Cuban people through the difficult years of the 1960s gradually gave way to a lethargy measurable in its dramatic impact where it hurt the Revolutionary Government most—in productivity.

Secret studies of the time revealed that in the vital agricultural sector the average workday had shrunk to four hours. The government bureaucracy grew fatter and slower. The quality of Cuban education, a source of great revolutionary pride, slowly deteriorated; teachers taught less and pupils were graded by increasingly lax standards.

Fidel, whose policies had set the tide of this defiance in motion, was powerless to reverse it. In fact, he unwittingly accelerated the process. One of his ideas, the so-called Consciousness Schedule, did away with standard business hours and left it to the workers' "revolutionary consciousness" to determine when each of them came to work or went home. This rule made secret defiance even easier to practice, elevating the decision to take a walk or to stay home into a legitimate, approved exercise of one's revolutionary commitment.

To compound this enticement to sloth, workers were encouraged more than ever to concentrate what efforts they did exert on going to assemblies and rallies and other nonproductive activities where they earned political merits. In this way, and not by hard work and attention to their duties, they progressed toward another goal: "communist labor consciousness." Once they'd arrived at this level, workers or their families were guaranteed 100 percent of their salaries in the event of sickness (easy to feign), retirement, or death. Fidel had institutionalized laziness as one of the revolution's highest virtues.

The continuing discontent and decline in productivity were evident to everyone, even if no one in Cuba dared mention their obvious causes. Abroad, however, the dimensions of and reasons for Cuba's economic morass were being discussed more and more openly and being criticized by erstwhile admirers in ways that were too much on target for Fidel to pass off as imperialist propaganda. His image was in tatters; Cuba was no longer the example, the showcase of revolution and Socialism.

These voices had to be stilled. Inside the country, the people needed to be remotivated. Fidel was going to try something new. Surveying his dwindling options, he hit upon the bold idea, first hinted at in his July 26, 1970, speech in the Plaza, of giving the people a voice, an outlet for their anger and frustration. Cuba was about to try some Socialist democracy.

A month following his July speech, Fidel called and presided over a massive three-day meeting in Havana, attended by the Politburo; the first secretaries of the party in the provinces; national and provincial leaders of the mass organizations such as CDR, the Federation of Cuban Women, unions, ANAP, and the Communist Youth; as well as those in charge of political activities at MINFAR and MININT.

The meeting's exclusive purpose was to examine Cuba's political and economic problems. First, the participants discussed mistakes of the previous years. Then, new efficiency and waste-reduction strategies for the workplace were proposed and analyzed.

To reduce the amount of money in circulation, Fidel decided to boost some cigarette prices from the equivalent of 20 cents a pack to $2.40, and the cost of alcohol, now that it was available again, would be tripled. Residential rents, which Fidel in 1959 had promised to abolish by 1970, were maintained.

Unrelated to specific economic problems but a matter of great concern nonetheless had been the Communist Party's role in and responsibility for the mismanagement of the past. Adopting the Soviet line that the party was above error and must be insulated from any criticism, Fidel said that henceforth the party would restrict itself to political responsibilities such as setting ideology and raising the revolutionary consciousness of the people, rather than the administrative responsibilities of running the government.

Finally, and most important, worker attitudes were examined. The chief difficulty here was absenteeism, a widespread phenomenon that Fidel preferred to see as a minor isolated problem among a very few workers. The Revolutionary Government could not acknowledge that the majority of the Cuban work force had rejected the glories of labor and sacrifice.

Nevertheless, to regenerate spirit—and to create a safety valve for the people's discontent—the meeting's critical outcome was the decision to revitalize Cuba's long-dormant unions and through them develop a channel for the masses to speak. Criticism was going to be encouraged.

Fidel unleashed his new policy to combat absenteeism and increase productivity at the Provincial Plenary Assembly of the Central Organization of Cuban Trade Unions (CTC) of Havana

Province on September 3 and 4, 1970. Before the meeting the party cells at work centers were ordered to encourage the workers to air their complaints and criticisms of state deficiencies and to expose problems that interfered with productivity.

The great CTC theater was jammed. From my assigned place on the balcony I could see the back wall of the stage, covered with an enormous banner on which was printed one of Fidel's phrases: "We must know our weak points, we must know in what sense we should advance and how we should advance." Fidel, surrounded by ministers and party leaders, presided over the assembly.

From the start, the theme of absenteeism dominated the discussion. The damage it caused was described; during July and August of 1970 it had reached levels never before seen in the province. The so-called "certificates of complacency" were condemned. Unscrupulously issued by some doctors as a favor to absentees, they certified that the worker was suffering from a particular disease. Enrique Gutiérrez, first secretary of the CTC of Havana, insisted that the campaign against absenteeism should not follow traditional methods. "We should employ methods that emerge from the masses themselves," he stated. His words served a particular purpose: to encourage the workers themselves to ask for the law against absenteeism.

The minister of labor, Jorge Risquet, who shortly afterward would be fired again for his incompetence, proclaimed the existence of a general consciousness among the people, a national clamor, a pressure on the part of the masses that demanded legislation against absenteeism and shirking. Of course Risquet had found no other way to expose a situation that was acute. It was the first time that a high-level bureaucrat had alluded to low productivity in the country or suggested the existence of a stratum of absentee workers.

The participants' comments from the floor were directed at the negligence and carelessness of the administration and even referred to abuses of power and ostentation among the leaders. Some people denounced the excessive quantity of merchandise thrown out at the port, particularly the thousands of jute sacks left to rot on the docks. Others cited coal that was lost because it was kept on swampy ground.

The litany of complaints was long and varied, and no sector of the economy was omitted. From time to time Fidel would interrupt a statement to find out more about a specific point or to add his opinion, but his attitude was that of a supreme judge who hears the arguments in a trial for the first time and has had nothing to do with the origin of those ruinous problems.

"This revolution has never lacked 'inventors,' or 'experts,' or 'intellectuals' who have invented disastrous things," he observed at one point. "If you respect the people, you should think over your formulas, shouldn't you?"

"What is so funny?" the man sitting to my left in the auditorium asked me with revolutionary zeal. He looked at me in irritation as if at some great impertinence.

Without my even realizing it, a smile had appeared on my face, a reaction to the absurdity of Fidel's statement.

Startled by this and immediately aware of my offense, I quickly and calmly reassured the *compañero* that I was only recalling a funny story Fidel had told earlier. From now on, I thought, the Stranger would have to more completely neutralize my true self and control my impulses. In a different, less anonymous context, such a slip might have had serious consequences.

Fidel's patchwork of new programs dramatically opposed the "idealism" of the radical 1960s. The sudden revival of the unions and the abrupt severing of the party from an administrative role—policies once urged in secret by the microfraction in 1968—were two examples of this reorientation. A third demarcation from past policy was the slower, more subtle de-emphasis on moral incentives in the workplace. The certificates and banners didn't disappear overnight, but this foundation of Ché's New Man ideology also began to crumble.

These changes did not affect Fidel's role at all. He continued, as always, to exert complete control over whatever shifts in policy had been decreed.

His handling of the harvest failure was characteristic. After asserting that the setback was, in fact, a boon, he nevertheless singled out a scapegoat for the failure, the Sugar Ministry. At the September 1970 CTC meeting, Fidel scolded MINAZ. "The technocrats, the 'brains,' the 'geniuses,' and the 'superscientists,' " Fidel said in sarcasm, "all of them knew exactly what should be done in order to produce the ten million tons of sugar. Well, first of all, it was proved that they didn't really know what was what, and, in the second place, they exploited the economy, channeling large amounts of resources to that sector."

To absolutely no one's surprise, Fidel gutted MINAZ leadership, including Francisco Padrón, Orlando Borrego's successor, who was sent to Cienfuegos to manage Latin America's largest fertilizer factory. As was usual in such instances, Fidel acted as if he had just recently discovered the MINAZ officials' malfeasance.

Fidel's renovation and restructuring campaign was not confined to Cuban administrative and workplace practices. He also reached into the daily life on the island. In the summer of 1970 he launched what he evidently hoped would be the revolution's death blow to Christmas.

Addressing the Plenary Assembly of the Ministry of Basic Industry, Fidel stressed that Cuba was a sugar-growing country, and that it was precisely the end of the year when the work force was needed most for the harvest.

"I'm not going to decide on any of these problems," he said in his new tone as the people's obedient servant. "I'm simply stating my opinion. There is a reality. Do we have traditions? Yes! Very Christian traditions? Yes! Very beautiful traditions? Very poetic traditions? Yes, of course! Have we been educated in these traditions? Yes! Isn't it true that by the time December 24 rolled around, visions of Christmas trees danced through our heads? Yes!

"But, gentlemen, we don't live in Sweden or Belgium or Holland. We live in the tropics. Our traditions were brought in from Europe—eminently respectable traditions and all that, but still imported. Then comes the reality about this country. Ours is a sugar-growing country. What are the best months for working, from the standpoint of climate, our country's principal product and constructions? From November through May. Listen, if they had set Christmas Eve for July 24, we'd be more than happy, we wouldn't have any objections at all. Traditions by themselves are historic, they come from way back, but they are also a subjective phenomenon. And we can certainly substitute one tradition for another."

From 1970 onward the annual extra quota of Christmas pork was sold on July 26. And the traditional distribution of children's toys (two per year per child) was moved from January 6— Epiphany—to July. The Magi from the East were transformed into the Three Wise Men from the tropics dressed in olive-drab.

But if Fidel thought he could wipe out Christmas Eve in Cuba he was mistaken. Even his leaders tried to limit the amount of work that day. At home, behind closed doors, the people always had their roast pork, black beans, and yuca with garlic sauce. Surreptitiously, they would continue to celebrate Christmas Eve; the tradition was hidden, but alive.

NO MORE CRITICISM

What was the net effect of all these changes? There is no question that some of the more basic adjustments in revolutionary philosophy produced positive effects that could be seen in a modest rise in the standard of living for 1971, compared to the scarcities of 1970. This small relative improvement was due in part to the measures adopted at the beginning of 1971 that gradually, over a three-year period, would tie salaries to productivity in the various sectors of the economy. In other words, material incentives.

In his speeches Fidel was euphoric about the increased productivity. But I was struck by the fact that the claimed increase in productivity—30 percent, 70 percent, 100 percent—had occurred in so short a time, from 1970 to 1971. Although it is true that there were some improvements, they did not correspond to Fidel's overly enthusiastic statistics.

In the first place, increased productivity in 1971 was based on a comparison with productivity in 1970, a year in which, except for MINAZ, the other sectors of the economy had reached low production records.

In the second place, the approved standards were extremely low. An average worker met them in less than 50 percent of his work time. But why were the norms scaled so low? The answer lay in the method used to establish them.

The revolutionary government was mostly obliging toward such abuses of the democratization process. Where it drew the line, however, was at any open challenge to its authority. In the spring of 1972, I was in Santiago de Cuba on my way to a meeting about building theaters for sugar-mill workers, when the studénts of that city's university held an assembly. Following the national guidelines, there was open criticism—on this occasion of Comandante Guillermo García, the new Politburo delegate to Oriente assigned there during the 1970 harvest. He was accused of abusing power, of flaunting privileges, of not being concerned with the well-being of the people of Santiago or the rest of the province. At the same meeting, five young people expressed their guarded reservations concerning Fidel's tendency to one-man rule and the very limited participation of the people in the decisions taken by the government. Fidel, informed of what had happened by Guillermo García himself, suggested to the party that they hold a second meeting in the same location.

Two days later there was another assembly, this time even more general than the one before, to which I was invited by an acquaintance from the Ministry of Construction, a relative of one of the five young men. The boys repeated their statements accurately, this time in the "surprising" presence of Fidel, who listened to them patiently with hardly any interruptions.

When they were finished, Fidel began to speak. He praised their sense of civic duty. He exhorted them to continue to combat anything that might diminish the prestige of the revolution. He touched again on the theme he had brought up a thousand times: the heroic struggle of the people against the inheritance of Yanqui imperialism.

Once he was certain of having won the approval of the assembly, he very subtly turned his speech around and began to ridicule "salon critics" who from their comfortable position rather than from direct contact with the sweat of the workers dared to cast a shadow on the immaculate good name of capable and honest men like *Compañero* Guillermo García.

The next day, under party pressure, the faculty senate expelled the five students from the university, and a student assembly then ratified their expulsion. They were sent to the countryside to do farm labor. Two years later in 1974, my co-worker's relative was still on a farm near the city of Bayamo, "erasing his political stain," waiting for the "pardon" that would allow him to return to the university. That pardon did not come until 1976. A fine example for those who still tried to risk honest criticism within the revolution.

The episode of the five students typified the Revolutionary Government's self-contradictory essence. Cuba boasted one of the highest literacy rates in all of Latin America, a tribute to the regime's strong emphasis on education. But the ability to read and write in a closed Socialist society is not promoted by its leaders to foster intellectual growth in the people. Free inquiry, the challenge of open debate, the power to examine ideas critically, on their own merits, are anathema in Cuba. The people are given the tools of reasoning, but they are forbidden openly to make use of them.

Moreover, the Revolutionary Government in the early 1970s was beginning to encounter severe difficulties in its pursuit of universal education. As more and more Cubans from all walks of life took advantage of the open-admission policy at every level of education—up to and including advanced university instruction—no provision was made to improve these institutions' teaching faculties. Poorly qualified instructors were pressed into duty, put in charge of teaching subjects they themselves didn't fully understand. In many cases their pupils were also handicapped by insufficient prior training. Increasingly, Cuban education became a matter of the blind leading the blind.

The revolution was able to mask these shortcomings in the same way it statistically adjusted the figures on worker productivity. Each educational institution's output was expressed as just that: output—the number of students passed and promoted each term. Whether or not they'd absorbed any knowledge, pupils marched ever onward in their studies, graduating in all sorts of highly technical specialties such as medicine and engineering.

These problems and many others too apparent to ignore—widespread absenteeism in the schools, repeated reports of sexual relations between students and teachers, the abuse of books and other resources, and instances of vandalism—were discussed at an April 1971 First National Congress on Culture and Education. Eighteen hundred delegates attended the Havana meeting and there proposed exactly the sorts of solutions that the Revolutionary Government might be expected to try when confronted with such a set of difficulties, mostly of its own making. Students and faculty who did not attend class regularly, it was decided, would be made liable to military service. Another of the many reforms adopted at the congress was the establishment of a new course of study in the rules of Socialist morality.

On the culture side, the meeting was preoccupied by State Security's March 20th arrest of the poet Heberto Padilla. He had long been considered too independent, too confrontational in his thinking and his writing. In 1968, his book of poems *Fuera de*

Juego (*"Out of the Game"*) was harshly attacked by those who believed Padilla had characterized the Revolutionary Government as authoritarian. Raúl Castro himself, writing under the pseudonym Leopoldo Avila, had attacked Padilla and another writer in the pages of the official army magazine, *Verde Olivo* (*"Olive Green"*).

With such powerful detractors, Heberto Padilla was living on borrowed time. The Revolutionary Government—while accusing him of nothing specific—kept the poet in jail for a month after his arrest, then brought him out for a humiliating act of contrition, a filmed confession of his traitorous, criminal skepticism.

Padilla's staged self-abasement fooled no one. A few days afterward, sixty-one preeminent international writers and thinkers, including Jean-Paul Sartre, Marguerite Duras, Alberto Moravia, Tamara Deutscher, and Pier Paolo Pasolini, wrote Fidel an open letter. "We believe," it began, "it is our duty to communicate to you our shame and our anger. The pitiful text of the confession signed by Heberto Padilla can only have been obtained by methods that are the negation of revolutionary legality and justice. The content and form of this confession, with its absurd accusations and delirious statements . . . recalls the most sordid moments of the Stalinist period, its prefabricated trials and its witchhunts."

The letter closed: "The contempt for human dignity involved in forcing a man to accuse himself in a bizarre fashion of the worst betrayals and vileness does not alarm us because in this case the man is a writer, but because any Cuban *compañero*—peasant, worker, technician or intellectual—can also be the victim of similar violence and humiliations. We would like the Cuban revolution to become again the revolution that once made us think of it as a model within socialism."

Fidel counterattacked furiously in his closing speech to the Education and Culture Congress, describing capitalist Europe in decline "like a sinking ship," and adding: "With the ship in this tempestuous sea of history, the intellectual rats will also sink."

As for the Latin American intellectuals who had also protested the Padilla affair, Fidel dismissed them as "pseudo-leftists." Then he discharged against them the greatest threat possible. "As far as Cuba is concerned," he declared angrily, "they will never again—Never!—be able to use her, not even pretending to defend her." Fidel was enraged. "Now you know it," he said.

"Bourgeois intellectuals and bourgeois libelants, agents of the CIA and intelligence services of imperialism; that is, of the intelligence and espionage services of imperialism, you will not be allowed to come, just as UPI and AP are not allowed to come to Cuba!"

AN INTIMATE EVENING
WITH FIDEL

Fidel's troubles with the revolution's supporters of the intellectual left were indicative of his image problems everywhere. Except for the victories churned out by his propaganda machine, there was precious little to be proud of on the economic front over the past several years, and much that the government was preoccupied with explaining away.

Then, in November 1970, Salvador Allende Gossens was elected President of Chile. In Fidel's analysis spelled out at the 1967 OLAS conference, the peaceful accession to power of a Marxist like Allende was extremely unlikely. But no guerrilla of any sort had any role in Allende's lawful election: In fact, since the OLAS conference no guerrilla had wrested victory anywhere in Latin America.

Much had transpired, however, since Fidel's confrontational declamations of 1967. First of all, he had dismayed many of Cuba's radical admirers by his endorsement of the Soviets' 1968 Czech invasion. Second, the worsening crisis of the Cuban economy had become a near-constant distraction.

Partially because of these economic problems, Fidel had not been able to sustain the all-out guerrilla offensive he had launched after the OLAS conference. But even with the considerable support he did give several Latin American liberation struggles, after an initial burst of promise each withered and failed.

Most damaging to Fidel's aspirations had been Ché's death in Bolivia. It was a crushing psychological reversal, poisonous to the spirit of revolution everywhere in Latin America. Even Fidel, so personally responsible for Ché's ill-starred expedition, was sobered by its disastrous outcome.

As a consequence, by 1971 the old rhetoric of armed insurrection in Latin America had given way to a new reality. With no official fanfare, Cuba now emphasized diplomacy in her foreign policy and was actively seeking to establish official governmental ties to nations throughout Latin America.

With this revised international outlook, Fidel saw Allende's election as a boon, the chance for a splashy diplomatic event. In the late autumn of 1971, Latin America's first avowed Marxist chief of state would travel to Chile to demonstrate solidarity with its second.

Allende was an old friend of the Cuban revolution and was in basic agreement with most of Fidel's ideas, although his focus of action was different. Before becoming President of Chile he had made several visits to Havana. During one of them, I'd met Allende in the ICAIC projection rooms, where he came frequently to watch the Cuban films he liked.

His style was very different from that of most Marxist leaders. Allende kept his gray hair combed carefully. He wore impeccably fitted *guayaberas* or tailored suits, and his French cologne stamped him as conservative, even "bourgeois." He had a very deliberate temperament, an exceptionally genteel manner, and he was very well spoken.

He firmly believed in the peaceful road to Socialism, in the bloodless revolution—"but don't tell Fidel because he'll get angry," he told a group of us jokingly as we discussed his ideas. The high-level MINFAR and MININT officials at this meeting listened to Allende with apparent respect, but behind his back they called him a doddering old fool. Nobody—including Fidel—imagined at the time that here was the future legitimately elected Marxist President of Chile.

A 600-member advance team from MININT went to Chile ahead of Fidel's entourage to guarantee maximum security for his November 10-to-December 4, 1971 visit—Fidel's first to Latin America since 1960. While he was there, the Cuban media saturated the island with news of his every speech, action, and interview. And before he returned, the party set about feverishly to prepare the grandest possible welcome home.

The entire population would be mobilized. Every noncritical activity, from factory work to teaching, would be suspended. A few days before Fidel's return, I was in Comandante Papito Serguera's office at the Radio and Television Institute, where I listened in on a very peculiar argument over the proper way for TV announcers to refer to Fidel at his moment of arrival and during the drive to Havana from the airport, both of which were to be covered live on Cuban radio and television.

Was Commander in Chief best? *Líder Máximo?* Prime Minister Fidel Castro? First Secretary of the Party? Consultation calls were placed to Celia Sánchez and to Oswaldo Dorticós, President of the Republic. This was handled as a matter of transcendent importance, even though Fidel had often declared that Cuba had no personality cult. Finally, the officials settled on calling him Fidel. As they explained it to each other, Fidel sounded more "familiar," "closer to the people," more "affectionate."

The mobilization of December 4 was one of the largest ever. The entire population of Havana, recorded on radio and television, turned out to welcome their leader. No factory, no workplace functioned as the people, free for one day from the tedium of their labor, gladly greeted Fidel.

At the end of that month, Maggie and I were invited to New Year's Eve supper in Miramar by Comandante Diocles Torralba, the army chief of staff, who was married to one of Maggie's cousins. We arrived early that evening and found no one downstairs in the big house. As Maggie went up to the second floor, I took a short walk around the grounds to the back terrace.

"Isn't anybody here?" asked a familiar voice behind me.

"They're upstairs," I answered automatically, turning to face my interlocutor. It was Fidel.

"The door was wide open," he added. "Where are those people?"

Fidel was accompanied by Pepín Naranjo, Fidel's aide-de-camp and minister of Food Producing Industry. Pepín, Fidel, and I stood together on the terrace chatting for a couple of minutes until Torralba, his family, and Maggie came down. Fidel greeted each one affectionately; he was in a very good mood. Then his brother, Raúl, and Raúl's wife, Vilma Espín, walked up as well.

"We're going to eat some guinea hens at Núñez's house," Fidel explained of his little party. "But first I wanted to stop by and say hello. If you like, you can come along too. I don't think that Núñez counted them out so exactly," he said with a wink.

So the Torralbas canceled their dinner party and we all walked down the block to the manorial home of Antonio Núñez Jiménez, a charter member of the Captains' Club and the former head of the Agriculture Ministry, where he'd been responsible for the coconut-and-snakes episode. He was now president of the Cuban Academy of Sciences. I noticed as we went along that the street was patrolled by at least a dozen guards and that soldiers equipped with long arms and walkie-talkies were stationed at both ends of the block. Three burgundy Alfa Romeos were parked in front of the Núñez Jiménez house.

Antonio Núñez Jiménez, a colorless man, was known by various nicknames: *Ñico Mentira* ("Nico the Liar"), *Ñico Cuevitas* ("Nico the Caveman"), and *Hombre Foto* ("Photo Man"), this last because he invariably managed to appear in any photographs being taken near him. In Cuba they say that, after Fidel, he is the most photographed man in the country. But he preferred to be known by the various titles he gave himself: anthropologist, geographer, speleologist, and writer. Everybody knew that his books on geography, on history, and his other intellectual "merits" were ghost-written by a group of specialists who worked for him. Everybody also knew that Núñez was a servile flatterer, the perfect buffoon for the First Minister and his brother, and for that reason untouchable.

Antonio was smiling, effusive, and solicitous when he received us that night; obviously flattered by Fidel's presence, Núñez Jiménez tried to monopolize his exalted guest from the start. Fidel accommodated him, putting his arm around his shoulder and nodding at his exclamations of welcome. Antonio laughed out loud at his boss's every witticism, and he paid more attention than anyone else to Fidel's words.

The after-dinner conversation was enlivened by a dialogue between Fidel and Raúl, who exchanged their favorite childhood anecdotes, including stories of Fidel's writing poems to his girlfriends and his youthful rebellious escapades. From time to time Fidel would get up, walk around the table covered with plates full of guinea hen bones, and sit down again. During one of his circuits he stopped suddenly, and looking at Maggie, he asked:

"Who is that girl? She can't deny she looks like a bourgeoise."

"You can't deny your bourgeois background either, Comandante," Maggie replied.

Due to the informal and intimate setting, Fidel's reaction to this statement was not explosive, as it would have been had someone said this at an official meeting. But Fidel couldn't let the comment pass. Slowly, with apparent calm, he began a detailed explanation of his, as he put it, "peasant, not bourgeois" family. We all knew that his background was as bourgeois as that of everyone else at the table, but we listened to his proofs respectfully.

When he finished, Fidel sent out to his famous closed van stocked with food and liquor for a case of pisco, a fiery drink made in Peru. Wherever Fidel went in Cuba, the van was always close by.

Now fortified with a glass of the liquor, Fidel somehow managed to get away from Núñez Jiménez and joined the circle of women who'd gathered at the piano. He was in a happy, expansive frame of mind. He entertained the women with jokes and expounded on romance.

The source of Fidel's good humor that night was evident: He still was basking in the afterglow of his recent trip to Chile. But what he cheerily had to say in private at the end of 1971 was astonishing. Fidel was pleased to offer an unperturbed refutation of his heartfelt ideology of just four years before.

"We've never been better off," he said, holding his glass of pisco. "We're breaking the Yanqui diplomatic blockade. Now they can't say we support guerrillas or send arms to other countries on the continent. The South Americans don't need us; they rebel on their own. Who would have thought there'd be a Marxist government in Chile? Who could have imagined ten years ago that there would be an anti-imperialist revolution in Peru? And who knows about Uruguay? Those people are strong, and it's very likely that they'll win with votes, with votes!"

I could see that he'd dropped none of his Bolívarian ambitions for the continent. He spoke of Latin America as his private arena. This sense of his destiny as leader underlay even his analysis of the situation in Chile, a circumstance for which Cuba could take little credit.

"I feel as if my spirit has been renewed by breathing again, in our America, the air of a country in the midst of revolutionary change, by sharing the animation of a people inspired by the kind of ardor we had in the early years," Fidel said to start a little speech. "The Chilean people responded very positively to the revolutionary moves made by Unidad Popular [Allende's coalition of Communists, Socialists, radicals, and others]. I wish you could have seen how animatedly the workers talked, with what liberty of expression! And with what enthusiasm they received us everywhere! Sympathy and admiration for the Cuban revolution is widespread. That gave me the measure of how important we've been to the liberation process in Latin American countries. Now we're gathering the fruits!

"I'm satisfied because the principal political objective of the trip was achieved. We gave the Chilean government the support of the Cuban revolution and contributed to the cohesion among the parties of the Unidad Popular. But you can't imagine the time Allende wastes trying to solve the differences between the parties. Hundred of hours that he could use for other essential matters! Really, there's no political maturity on the left; even MIR [a far-left hard-line revolutionary group once supported by Fidel before Allende came to power], the most radical party in the Unidad Popular coalition, suffers from an immature impulsiveness that's very inconvenient just now. It's not the time for divisions, especially with the unity on the right that could be dangerous because it is supported by the Yanquis.

"The most alarming thing is that even under these circumstances Allende is still reluctant to arm the people. He refuses to discharge senior army officers, and he doesn't even try to break down bourgeois structures like the trade unions and the political parties. The 'old man' is very stubborn. He lives in a world that is too full of illusion and poetry. He is tied to his constitutional ideas. He trusts in the impartiality of the military. And he is certain that it will always defend the legitimate government.

"They'll try to screw him the first chance they get."

Fidel predicted that Allende would ultimately have to arm his supporters, fire the officers and all the rest if he intended to retain his power. "From this point of view," he said, "I feel closer to MIR despite its recklessness. Now they have to be calmed down, but if a confrontation with the army is necessary in the future, then we'll behave differently [i.e., help them]. We should have a contingency plan so that we can be prepared in case there's a critical situation, even if Allende doesn't agree. He'll learn!"

Fidel's explicit threat to back the radical MIR, should Allende's Marxist government begin to totter, was a sure signal that the spirit of *Revolution Within the Revolution* hadn't died. And his private opinion of the Chilean Communist Party was consistent with the philosophy he had openly expounded four years before at OLAS.

"Their conciliatory attitude toward the opposition is disconcerting," he said. "Those people don't learn. They don't draw conclusions from historical events. There is no reconciliation with reaction! Imagine if we had left the political parties, the armed forces, and the congress intact. We wouldn't be here to tell the tale!"

Yet Fidel seemed torn between the competing forces of reality and ambition, accepting for the moment the requirements of keeping his own revolution afloat while still determined to drive the destiny of the continent—*his* continent.

First, Fidel the Pragmatist: "We're not going to interfere [in Chile]. We can't afford to look for more problems. It's their affair."

Then, Fidel the Liberator: "The consolidation of the Chilean revolution means we can count on a springboard for infiltrating our ideas into Argentina and Brazil. Our 'Yanqui friends' know that, and of course they'll do all they can to prevent it. But they'll have a hard time! The revolution in Chile is irreversible, and if the time comes to fight, we'll fight alongside the Chilean people. We'll encourage civil war if necessary. We'll do everything we can. In this sense, our 'unofficial' contact with MIR is vital."

The rest of us, including Raúl, said little that night; in Fidel's presence, one was compelled to listen. Besides, his powerful charisma made him an arresting conversationalist.

As he moved from subject to subject with his ease of expression and formidable command of detail, he was very different from the melodramatic Fidel of the speaker's platform or the willful Fidel I'd seen when he was among his subordinates.

Tonight he was relatively calm, relaxed. Throughout the evening, whenever jokes were exchanged, his rejoinders were always witty. Even as he discoursed on his main topic, politics, about which Fidel is passionate, his voice and demeanor were almost serene.

That is, until the subject of Mexico was brought up.

I was amazed at how he spoke of Mexico, the only Latin American land that had maintained relations with Cuba after her ouster from the OAS in 1962, and a country Fidel always honored in his public utterances. But this night he testily called Mexico a country "going under because of its dependence on the Yanquis, governed by thieves without the least interest in true sovereignty."

He dismissed Mexican diplomats in Havana as "scoundrels who make a fortune out of visas and the jewelry they steal here."

He called the Mexican national leadership "lackeys who allow the CIA to photograph and register Cuban diplomats and officials who are constantly mistreated at the Mexico City airport." Some of his grievances were very old; Fidel said he still didn't forgive the Mexicans for "the obstacles and pressures we suffered when we were preparing to launch the *Granma*."

Fidel seemed to gather strength from talking; he is a compulsive communicator. Returning to the topic of Chile, Fidel reiterated the importance of assisting the Allende government and his determination to influence affairs in Chile. Aldo Santamaría, chief of the Cuban Navy, happened to be among Núñez's guests. "Aldo," Fidel said, "we'll soon be having a visit from the Chilean sailing ship *Esmeralda*. We have to regale her officers. We have to look for receptivity in the crew. It's very important that we penetrate ideologically."

He spoke all night. By dawn I was exhausted, along with the rest of the guests, but I dared not show my tiredness. Fidel was livelier than ever. He had paced and sat, paced and sat, for several hours while talking nonstop. At first light he seemed to make a move to leave, but then returned to the living room and took up a discussion of Peru, where the recently successful military junta was in express defiance of the United States.

"This is a new approach that can be spread among the more progressive members of the military in Latin America," he began, exhaling a huge cloud of cigar smoke. "Of course, it doesn't even approach ours in magnitude, but there's no question that the Peruvian process constitutes a radical change. I was surprised that they began to apply revolutionary means. Within the tradition of Latin American military coups, there's never been anything like a handful of military men proposing to apply agrarian reforms and to nationalize North American companies. Their daring has gone beyond the simple adoption of progressive or reformist measures. That's why I've decided to wait and see what happens. Those anti-oligarchical measures with a nationalist stamp tell me that something new is happening in Peru, that the Peruvian military is really prepared to free the country from Yanqui tentacles.

"We definitely have to help them, encourage them, and of course, monitor them very closely. We have to try with all the means at our disposal to transform that process into a real Socialist revolution."

Fidel went into some detail. "It is necessary," he said, "to neutralize the action of some leftist groups in Peru who, blinded by their habitual sectarianism, can't see beyond their own noses. When I read what they're calling the military, it makes me want to tell them, 'Stop being assholes! Don't you understand that this process is superior to the earlier situation?' The Communist Party is clear about supporting it [the military junta], but they're not a significant political force. Besides, their support can become a factor that's more negative than positive, because it gives international reaction a chance to begin an anti-Communist campaign.

"But there are still two factors that make me distrust the Peruvian process. One is the contradiction between revolutionary goals [giving power to the people] and the military's fear of giving greater participation to the masses. The contradiction confuses me, but we must try, officially and unofficially, to eliminate it.

"The other factor is very dangerous. It's the corruption that exists among the military, their inclination to take advantage of power to get rich. That can be fatal, but we can't do anything; we can't even comment on it. What contradictions there are in politics! The corruption that we hold against the governments in Latin America can now turn against a revolutionary process itself."

The small audience followed his words carefully. Despite our fatigue no one presumed to interrupt him or ask a question, much less express an opinion. The others seemed seduced by the overwhelming personality of the orator. But Fidel did not want simply an intimate chat with friends. He had a very specific agenda.

"The situation in Peru is complex," he continued. "It isn't easy to find the right person, who is intelligent and capable, to represent us there. But I think we have the man right here," he added, turning directly to Núñez Jiménez. "Núñez, you'd be an excellent ambassador. Besides, those famous ruins you like so much are waiting there for you. Isn't that a good idea?" he asked, looking around him.

Fidel continued playing with the other guests, alternating flattery with jokes about some personal trait, showing off his ingenious wit. Again he spoke to Maggie, this time to beg her pardon.

"Don't be offended by what I said a while ago, *compañera*," he said gallantly. "I meant it as a compliment, because there's no denying that bourgeois women are the most beautiful. Your husband isn't jealous, is he?"

Fidel continued talking without a pause until almost nine in the morning. Everyone except for him was bleary-eyed. When at last he stirred to leave, Raúl came up to each of us and very quietly expressed his gratitude for the special night we had given his brother. "He needs times like these," he said, obviously moved. "It's a shame they don't happen more often."

It was clear that Raúl held Fidel in sincere affection and great admiration. Fidel's fondness for and absolute confidence in his younger brother were just as obvious. He left happily, as fresh as when he arrived. "Happy New Year, everybody," he said. "And courage. We have lots of work to do!"

When we arrived home, Maggie went right to sleep. Exhausted as I was, I sat down immediately to write down Fidel's comments while they were still fresh in my mind.

CUBA—USSR:
THE SECRET ACCORDS

Fidel's conflicting observations that night on the desirability of Cuban restraint and the need for Cuban intervention in Latin American affairs were a puzzle to me. Only when I reflected on his statements in the context of all the other peculiar policy and program shifts preceding that night did I begin to realize what was taking place in Cuba. The Soviets were calling in their chips. At last Fidel was being held accountable for the economic chaos of the 1960s and the deepening crisis in production culminating with the ruinous 10 million-ton harvest.

In the late 1960s, given Cuba's irreversible alienation from the United States and indebtedness to the USSR as her sole source of financial support, Fidel had realized that the USSR was Cuba's only salvation. At the same time the Soviets, "grateful" for the Cuban response to events in Czechoslovakia and for the Cuban position vis-à-vis the Chinese, had begun to offer more effective unconditional economic aid in 1969.

I picked up the trail of the key events in the Soviet strategy in December 1970, when Carlos Rafael Rodríguez, the former PSP member who was on excellent terms with the Soviets and who served as president of the Cuban–USSR Intergovernmental Commission, had attended its annual planning meeting in Moscow. Rodríguez spoke several times with Nikolai Baibakov, president of GOSPLAN, who offered generous support for all sectors of the Cuban economy. As a result, the Cuban Soviet Commission for Economic, Scientific and Technical Cooperation was established, through which the USSR began to provide Cuba with massive aid in equipment, factories, and technical specialists. All that Cuba had to do was—for the first time—meet its promised deliveries of sugar and other exports to the USSR.

Later, in April 1971, on a visit to Havana, Baibakov held new talks with Rodríguez and met with Fidel. They agreed that the Intergovernmental Commission would have its first Havana meeting in September 1971, presided over by the president of the Council of Ministers of the USSR, Vladimir Novikov. The Soviets had continued to offer unlimited technical assistance.

Late in October 1971, Alexei Kosygin, then the Soviet premier, arrived in Havana for a widely publicized visit. At every ceremony Cuban-Soviet friendship was exalted, the first Socialist country in the world was honored, and "the immense gratitude of the Cuban people toward the Soviet people, without whose aid it would have been impossible for our Cuban Revolution to exist" was manifest.

Quite a change.

Kosygin returned to the USSR having accomplished the two fundamental goals of his visit: the writing of a Cuban-Soviet communiqué expressing Cuba's support of Soviet foreign policy, and Fidel's acceptance of an official invitation to visit the USSR. That would be the ideal time to speak calmly about mutual interests.

On May 2, 1972, Fidel began a long tour of several African nations and European Socialist countries, culminating in the agreed-upon visit to the USSR. The Cuban press gave little information about the topics discussed by Fidel and the Soviet leaders, but subsequent events revealed that this trip confirmed the beginning of a new phase in relations between the two countries.

Shortly after Fidel's return, a document was circulated at high levels of the Revolutionary Government. In it the Soviets advised Cuba to join the Socialist countries' Council for Mutual

Economic Assistance—COMECON—as the only way "to over-come underdevelopment." The Cuban government then announced that Cuba would request official membership in COMECON in July 1972—a surprising decision, because until then Fidel had privately refused Cuban membership in COMECON. He had said repeatedly that to buy equipment from mainly Socialist countries, with their antiquated technology, would be equivalent to putting the brakes on the country's technological development.

Another telling sign of the turnaround in Cuban-Soviet relations was Fidel's new evaluation of the Soviet Union. In a major meeting held at the Karl Marx Theater, Fidel presented a panoramic view of his recent visit to the USSR to more than 3,000 party members and government administrators. The moving stories about Soviet workers, the marked praise of Soviet economic plans and industrial efficiency, the enthusiastic comments regarding the "high standard of living reached by the USSR"—this speech in praise of the "overwhelming progress of the Soviets in recent years" made it clear that old quarrels were forgotten and that the Soviets had finally succeeded in setting their *enfant terrible* on the right track.

Some months after the New Year's Eve dinner of 1971–72, I gained access to the series of secret documents, negotiated by high-ranking Cuban officials over many months, by which Cuba was now bound to the USSR. These agreements illuminated for me the events of the past four years, beginning with Fidel's attack on the Soviets for limiting Cuba's fuel allotment, through his surprise endorsement of their Czech invasion eight months later, and the subsequent generosity shown by Moscow with renewed and expanded aid programs leading to the 10 million-ton harvest failure, and finally the domestic political administrative changes that Fidel had begun to hint at in 1970.

Ever since the mid-1960s, the Soviets had wanted a Cuban government that offered a semblance of democratic organization like those of other Socialist countries, not one that looked suspiciously like a case of one-man rule. Although the Soviet economy was in crisis, the Soviets wanted a Cuban economy that worked, one with a coherent system of management controls, relying on material incentives and featuring independent but accountable, profitable centers of production. The Soviets also wanted ideological and foreign policy conformity. The New Man was going to have to be buried, and there could be no more deviation from the Socialist international policy.

Fidel's requirements were much more basic and critical. Cuba was broke and he needed the Soviets to bail out her economy. Thus, the deal-making.

Cuba entered COMECON under favored-nation status, meaning she would receive extra credit, lower interest rates, and better import and export prices than other member states enjoyed. The USSR agreed to purchase Cuban sugar at prices much above those quoted at that moment in the international marketplace and to pay for them partially in hard currency. Also, interest payments on Cuba's burgeoning debt to the Soviets would be postponed until 1986.

In return, Moscow received a pledge of loyal cooperation across the board. In party matters, Fidel agreed to restructure the Cuban Communist party on the standard Socialist model. The Cuban Communists assented to a closer working relationship with their Soviet counterparts. These were not onerous conditions, but there was one bitter pill for Fidel to swallow. Under the secret accords, he was to call a meeting of Latin American Communist parties in Havana, where one and all would study their differences and hammer out a common line. After years of attack, Fidel was going to act in solidarity with his brother Marxists of Latin America.

As for government, Cuba agreed to "institutionalization"—the establishment of a Council of State, a National Assembly, and structures called People's Power Governments. In the areas of foreign and defense policy, Cuba was to adopt positions on imperialism that were consistent with those of other Socialist bloc nations and to adopt the same system of military rank as all the Socialist countries. She would be much more circumspect in encouraging revolutions in Central and South America. A mechanism for crisis consultation between Havana and Moscow was to be set up. And Fidel was to seek more Cuban influence in the movement of Non-Aligned Countries, aiming to win the organization's presidency by 1979. Furthermore, Cuba would combat among the non-aligned countries the thesis of "two imperialisms"; that is, the neutral world's belief that both the United States and the USSR were imperialistic.

In economic affairs, Cuba would embrace material incentives and apply the Soviet economic system taught to Cubans in the Soviet Union. Soviet advisers would be introduced at every level of the economy. Five-year plans in coordination with those of other bloc countries would be implemented. And every five years Cuba was to hold a Party Congress to approve these development plans.

Cuba's secret accords with the Soviet Union addressed issues of paramount concern to both governments. As far as the Cuban people were concerned, however, they did not make an iota of difference. For them, the reality of sacrifice and hard times continued unaltered, a general privation in vivid contrast to the luxuriant lives of the revolutionary elite. Whatever the system called itself, and no matter what accommodations and reorganizations Fidel implemented, the revolutionary order would remain unaffected.

MAYIMBE: THE ELITE

The apex of power and privilege in revolutionary Cuba is, of course, the *Líder Máximo*. The next stratum down the pyramid of power is made up of the Politburo and the Secretariat of the Central Committee of the Communist Party, the deputy ministers of the Executive Committee of the Council of Ministers, some ministers, the highest officials at MININT and MINFAR, and the provincial secretaries of the party. These men—nearly all of them white—are the elite of the "revolutionary bourgeoisie," and the Cuban people call them the *mayimbes*, ironically an Afro-Cuban term that means "ruling or powerful class," the bosses.

A *mayimbe* does not socialize with persons from the lower levels, or else he limits his contacts only to those that are absolutely necessary. The *mayimbes* see one another, visit one another, share one another's privileges. They inhabit an exclusive world in which the rest of the people's living conditions are not only not mentioned but are barely even known. In short, a closed caste has been created, separated from the rest of society by an abyss that grows deeper each day.

The *mayimbe* does not know the meaning of a work schedule. The assumption is that he lives fully committed to the cause of the revolution, that he carries out his duties when he thinks it convenient, free of anyone else's control. He works in a comfortable air-conditioned office with several telephones and an adjoining room furnished with a comfortable bed, a refrigerator, a color TV, and a VCR in case he needs to distract his mind with a western film between work sessions. An efficient executive secretary takes care of the smallest details, even his family problems, so that he can be spared any kind of upset.

If he happens to be at work at lunchtime or suppertime, he knows that he always has at his disposal a special chef and a private dining room. Cracklings and corn mush, perennial dishes in the workers' dining room, never appear on his varied menu, which is well supplied with first-quality meat, good cheese, ham, milk, fruit, and Coppelia ice cream.

For the *mayimbe*, transportation problems do not exist— except, perhaps, his having to choose between his Alfa Romeo, his Lada 1600, or his Jeep, vehicles that never lack air conditioning, a telephone, a stereo tape deck, a shortwave radio, and a driver, whom the *mayimbe* may use depending on his destination.

He is very prone to amorous adventures. Regardless of his physical characteristics, he will always find a young lady eager to acquire foreign clothing, expensive perfume, good shoes, and the comfort of luxury hotels in the city or in the national tourist centers in the rest of the country. These moments of pleasure can complicate a *mayimbe*'s life because he often falls in love. Generally, he feels assured that he has found true bliss with his new love—who may be twenty or thirty years younger than he—and jettisons his wife and the mother of his children in favor of a second marriage.

Traditionally, it is the *mayimbe* who leaves his house to his children and ex-wife—which is no great sacrifice, since he automatically receives another house as comfortable and beautiful as the first (it is always Fidel who personally solves this little problem for him), where he builds his new love nest.

The *mayimbe*'s house is in no way inferior to a millionaire's, since they are the very same houses that Cuban millionaires lived in at the time of the triumph of the revolution. They are in the best districts, solid, spacious, and beautiful. Their furniture is the finest, they have the latest audio and video equipment, they are almost all centrally air-conditioned, and they are surrounded by beautiful gardens, some with a pool.

I once visited a house that had a huge greenhouse at one end of the garden. The *mayimbe*, a high-ranking MININT official, was especially fond of exotic plants and showed us with real pleasure the ones he cultivated. I remember that we spent most of the time in the library-sitting room, entirely paneled in rare wood. Sitting on comfortable easy chairs, we saw two North American films—the *mayimbes* don't like Socialist movies—that he had taped himself, since he owned not one but two video machines and a splendid library of tapes.

The Revolutionary Government believes that because of their great responsibilities, *mayimbes* should not be tormented by domestic worries, and so all needs of that kind are instantly taken care of. The infamous ration book is of no importance to them. There are no shortages in their houses. In their refrigerators (they have at least two) and their large freezers they keep meat, fish, and lobster that are often gifts from the heads of cattle plans or officials from the Ministry of Fishing. Their stores of meat include food for their animals, since, as a general rule, the *mayimbe* loves hunting dogs and German shepherds, and if he owns them he cares for them and feeds them magnificently. The *mayimbe* often receives baskets overflowing with fresh fruits and vegetables from some minor head of an experimental plan, and at least twice a year he gets the baskets he loves most: the ones full of delicacies, compliments of Fidel.

When he gets sick he does not go to an ordinary hospital. *Mayimbes* have an exclusive hospital with the latest medical equipment, staffed by the best specialists in the country. If he must be admitted, a comfortable room is prepared for him with an extra bed for a companion.

The *mayimbe* dresses, or thinks he dresses, impeccably. To this end he shops in special stores, but he prefers to buy clothes on his trips overseas. He likes Italian shoes, custom-made suits, elegant safari jackets, embroidered *guayaberas*. His wife and children always wear clothes from "outside" too. At school the *mayimbes*'s children stand out from the rest because of their high-quality shoes, or because they have cassette players and digital watches with complicated dials which their fathers give them as presents. These contrasts have created certain social problems, which in time will disappear because the *mayimbes*'s children tend to congregate in certain schools. Most of their children study for the diplomatic corps when they go to the university, unless they have a strong vocation for another career. Their fathers have passed on to them by osmosis a preference for that which is foreign.

The fifteenth-birthday parties—the *quinceañeras*—of the *mayimbes*'s daughters rival and often surpass those of the old Cuban bourgeoisie. The display and ostentation include the traditional waltz danced by the celebrant and her father along with fourteen other couples. And so the Almeidas, the Mirets, and other *mayimbes* are proud and happy to provide their daughters with the same celebrations they criticized so harshly when the old bourgeoisie held them. These birthdays are usually celebrated in the family mansion, although Las Mercedes Ranch, an exclusive social club near Havana, is frequently selected as an ideal site for such occasions.

The *mayimbes's* annual vacations are typically spent in Varadero, in one of the beautiful mansions in the old Du Pont district, where there is an armed guard on E Street to keep out intruders. An excellent cook, solicitous servants, a yacht for night fishing, and a speedboat for water-skiing are some of the amenities that help round out these well-padded vacations.

What is so surprising is that, to lead this kind of life, the *mayimbe* needs no money at all. His salary, even though it is among the highest in the country, is not relevant to him. His only wealth lies in power, and to preserve that power he is capable not only of turning his freedom of thought over to the system, but even of bartering away his dignity.

But the *mayimbe* also has his anxieties. If he makes a mistake, if he forgets one of the rules he's been taught, he is immediately replaced. The Commander in Chief unhesitatingly excludes him from the inner orbit and puts him in charge of unimportant matters, almost always in production. He suddenly feels powerless, stigmatized, solitary, forgotten.

Not every *mayimbe* can adapt to the new life; most dedicate themselves body and soul to an incessant struggle to climb the pyramid of power again. They try to erase their guilt with humility and to display their abilities until they win the sympathy and confidence of an indulgent *mayimbe* who will intercede on their behalf. As for the others, those who know that no matter what they do they will never wipe out the stain, there are some who choose the escape of suicide.

In general the *mayimbe* has not reached a very high educational level. Before the triumph of the revolution, because he was poor, he could not attend the university. Later, because he held such high posts, he could not devote much time to his education. As the years passed and the Revolutionary Government became aware of this lack, the *mayimbe* was obliged to enroll in special institutions called "party schools," which offer degrees just like the universities. In these schools the subject matter is simple, the exams easy, the teachers understanding, and of course, a *mayimbe's* grades are always high. Even so, it is a great effort to go back to school as an adult, but like a good revolutionary the *mayimbe* obeys the slogan of the First Secretary of the Party, "You can always do more," and he manages to graduate in four years and obtain a diploma in political science. From sixth grade to a university degree in four years: That is indeed one of the revolution's accomplishments.

There are also exceptions. Some of the more quick-witted are granted a doctorate by decree, without passing examinations, by the authority vested in the system.

But in all fairness to the *mayimbe*, he does deserve a doctorate in a very peculiar branch of knowledge; no treatises have been written about it and no schools exist to teach it, except, perhaps, the school of the revolution. In this field you need great facility for transfiguration and intensive training in changing direction instantaneously. Here the *mayimbe* has shown both a profound vocation and vast knowledge. It is what he practices every day, every second of the day, because it is his source of success and power: the art of being a chameleon.

LIBORIO: THE PEOPLE

The Cuban people are chameleons, too, but their circumstances could not be more different from those of the *mayimbes*.

In the early decades of this century, Cuban cartoonists introduced a character called Liborio, with whom the people identified in opposition to the rulers of the republic. Liborio represented the common man, the worker, the *campesino*, the ordinary laborer who continually suffered political disillusionment and the social consequences of corrupt governments.

When the revolution triumphed, Liborio disappeared from the newspapers. The political, social, and economic circumstances that conditioned his existence supposedly had been eradicated forever. The revolution had freed him from exploitation; from now on he was master of his own destiny and would never again be victimized by politicians' lies.

But Liborio continued to exist, even though he could no

longer hope to appear on the pages of the newspapers, much less express his political dissatisfaction, even indirectly. He lives every day in Fidel's Cuba, and his life is as filled with difficulties as his counterpart's was fifty years ago.

Liborio's first daily challenge is transportation. He knows very well that transportation grows worse every day and that he has to get up at dawn to get to work on time. If Liborio is unfortunate enough to arrive late, his supervisor will take him to task, give him a lecture to awaken his consciousness. Points will be taken away from him in the annual competition to be named a front-line worker. Liborio knows that without that award he will never get the refrigerator he needs so desperately, the television set his children clamor for daily, or the washing machine that his overworked wife has been longing for, for years.

At twelve sharp it's lunchtime. A long line in the dining room filled with crowded tables waits for Liborio. On a dirty, greasy metal tray he will be served his ration: broth with hard smoked mackerel, rice, and a piece of cold sweet potato. This menu alternates with cornmeal and a piece of omelette thickened with flour. On special days he will receive a surprise treat: some slices of Russian meat, a few red beans, and an unidentifiable custard.

At 5:00 P.M. his workday ends, but it isn't always easy for him to go home. There may be a production assembly where his work record is examined or his acts of revolutionary consciousness are reviewed. At other times he will be obliged to participate in a meeting that commemorates some historic event. On occasion he will have to go to the Plaza de la Revolución to listen to the words of the *Líder Máximo* or to a designated spot in the city to welcome some dignitary from a friendly country. His trade union, whose functions have turned out to be very different from what he had been promised several years back, exists to organize these activities. In principle, it is supposed to listen to his opinions, but the union has become a mere party tool to indoctrinate him, control him, and overburden him with duties that are not intrinsic to his work. Only if none of his many possible obligations is scheduled is Liborio free to return home, suffering once again the agony of transportation.

If Liborio is old enough, he may still reside in the same house he occupied in 1959. If he is younger, although he may be married and have any number of children, he will have become accustomed by now to living in his parents' house or in the house of his in-laws for an indefinite period of time, because the rate of housing construction is extremely slow.

The revolution made by him gives priority to construction of "the most modern industrial works in Latin America," "the biggest zoo in the world," "the most rapid train in the hemisphere." Some years ago, in 1970, the Commander in Chief promised him that 100,000 housing units would be built each year, but this figure has been reduced to 12,000 for the sake of the country's development. Liborio sees how the cement he so badly needs is exported, and he smiles bitterly when he reads in the paper that cement factories in the country have tripled their production since 1958.

The housing shortage causes Liborio countless conjugal problems that almost always end in divorce, especially if his wife and her mother-in-law or her brother-in-law don't get along. Sometimes, for sheer lack of physical space, Liborio cannot even live with his wife in his parents' house or his in-laws' house. The married couple must meet when they can in hotel rooms or houses of assignation.

It's not that there is no way to get housing. There are certain routes, but the road is as difficult as taking a trip to the moon and Liborio thinks twice before undertaking it. Once a year the ministry he belongs to or its provincial delegation gives away a house or an apartment that he and all his workmates, whose situations are the same or worse than his, argue over at a general assembly. After hours of fights and the public airing of dirty laundry, the cleanest will finally be chosen—that is, the worker with most merits, who is also supposed to have the greatest need, although this is not always the case.

The other route, the microbrigades, is the product of another of the *Líder Máximo*'s inventions. The microbrigade is a group of thirty-three men to whom the state assigns a specific plot of land and provides basic materials for building their own housing. The microbrigadists leave their regular jobs for three or four years to work ten or eleven hours a day building uniform structures under the direction of someone with slightly more training than the others in building techniques. One can easily imagine the quality of buildings constructed by these men, most of whom have never held a shovel or hammer in their hands. But nowadays the microbrigades are practically the only way that Liborio can obtain housing.

The effort would be worthwhile if Liborio could be absolutely certain that he would get one of the apartments. However, that is not always the case. Once the building has been completed, a good number of apartments are reserved for certain officials whose important responsibilities have not allowed them time to join the microbrigade. Other apartments are given to Latin American political exiles. These exiles are protected by the government and live in hotels or communal lodgings. The rest of the apartments are distributed among the microbrigadists according to their need and, of course, their revolutionary merits. It might very well happen that despite working night and day for three or four years, Liborio still will not have an apartment. If he is very persistent, he will begin the process again in the hope of getting one in the next building.

But let us suppose that Liborio already has his house or apartment. When he finally reaches his neighborhood, tired and ill-humored after his odyssey on public transportation, it is very possible that he will find the district in darkness. This does not frighten him: The infamous blackouts are now a part of his daily life. Whole neighborhoods in Havana receive electric current for only five or six hours a day, almost always during daylight hours. At night, families frequently have to gather in the dim light of a candle, and from the tallest buildings in the city you can see large stretches of darkness occasionally lit by the headlights of a car. The same or worse occurs in provincial cities and villages.

An intensive campaign to save electricity has been going on for years. Liborio is very irritated when the president of the Defense Committee on his block comes to remind him to turn out some of his lights. He knows that steel mills, textile factories, and other industries use their electrical systems for the whole day in order to produce in eight hours what could be produced in two or three. He also knows that the lights and air conditioners in the offices are left on day and night due to administrators' carelessness. As always, he has to pay the piper. At the beginning of the revolution the Commander in Chief nationalized the electric company and ordered a lowering of rates, but the good times are over.

Water is also scarce, a problem which is especially difficult for Cubans, whose national habit is at least one shower a day. Liborio has acquired two or three tanks of varying capacity to help correct this situation, to which he is resigned; there are other citizens in much worse circumstances. Those who live in some areas of Old Havana, for example, have already forgotten the pleasure of seeing water come out of a faucet. These unfortunates depend on the tank trucks that periodically park on the street corners to provide them with precious water. It is not unusual to see housewives lowering a long rope from their balconies with a bucket tied to the end so that some willing child will fill it up in exchange for a few coins.

If the electricity comes back on, Liborio will watch television—if he has one. If not, he goes to watch TV in a neighbor's house. When the Revolutionary Government is not broadcasting some patriotic ceremony, he can choose between the two channels whose programs offer the following possibilities: a tedious musical show, a North American movie from the 1940s, a Socialist film with lots of weeping women with kerchiefs tied around their heads and heroes of the Soviet Army facing the Nazis, an educational program, or a Cuban soap opera such as the never-ending *Horizontes* (heavy in revolutionary content) that idealizes the life of the worker or the *campesino*.

Recently, other series with a little more action have been broadcast—*It Had to Be in Silence,* for example, which allows Liborio to enjoy the adventures of a bold and resourceful Cuban security agent as he fights the shadowy CIA, whose stupid agents are always defeated.

Once a week, on Saturday night at eleven, Liborio can look forward to seeing on TV a new North American film. Also once a week, at eight-thirty, he attends an informational meeting or a study circle organized by his neighborhood Defense Committee.

The workweek ends at noon on Saturday. Liborio has a day and a half of rest—unless he has guard duty, or there's a call from his military unit, or his union has planned some productive work in agriculture for that weekend. Every month he is obliged to do two shifts of night guard duty, one at his work center for four hours and another three-hour shift scheduled by his CDR on the block where he lives. If the call comes from work or his union, Liborio will have to get up even earlier than usual to catch his truck. But productive work on weekends is a picnic compared to the mobilizations that his union organizes every year: a month or forty-five days of field labor, almost always scheduled for the time of the sugar harvest.

From time to time Liborio is also called by his CDR for Sunday morning street-cleaning, to fill potholes, prune trees, paint buildings, or cut little paper figures to decorate his block for the next historic occasion. The committee makes many such requests, including an annual blood donation.

Occasionally Liborio can enjoy a full day and a half off. Then he faces the problem of where to go, and not because there are many choices. One of his favorite pastimes is dancing. Fortunately, the worst excesses of the Revolutionary Offensive are over. Nightclubs and cabarets operate normally, although they are not as splendid, not as much fun as they used to be. But Liborio's budget doesn't allow him go to out very often, since drinks are very expensive, and he saves such outings for special occasions.

A second option would be the beach, but the idea of facing his worst enemy—transportation—makes him reject this possibility. The last time he went to the beach he didn't have a very good time. He left his house at six in the morning, intending to catch one of the first buses and enjoy the ocean during the best hours of the day. When he arrived at the bus stop, he saw that many other people had the same idea. The line was endless; he had to wait almost two hours to leave the city. When he got to the beach, it was crowded, and he couldn't find a place to have lunch. Then, on the way home, the bus broke down and he spent four hours on the highway. In short, Liborio spent three hours on the beach and six in transportation.

In light of these circumstances, Liborio usually decides to go to the movies, a healthy and accessible form of entertainment, although the programming is not always to his liking.

During his vacation, Liborio rarely thinks of renting a house on the beach, much less one in Varadero. Getting a house in Varadero is like getting into heaven. If his union local happens to have one of the houses, they probably won't assign it to him, and if by any wild luck they do, he'll have to get into a very long line at the centers set up by the Ministry for Tourism so that a computer can tell him where he will stay. Of course, the exclusive districts in Varadero are not entered into the computer, since they have already been reserved for the *mayimbes*.

It is argued that Liborio has within his reach a way to participate institutionally in the running of the Cuban state. Beginning in 1976 in the people's assemblies where accounts are rendered, Liborio will be able to express himself freely, state the problems that affect him, denounce deficiencies, propose solutions, and demand a concrete response to the questions he has previously raised.

His litany of complaints and suggestions at the accountability assemblies is immediately transcribed by the meeting secretary under the approving eye of an official. This official ends the meeting by stating the outcome of his efforts to resolve the questions raised at the previous meeting. But here is an account of what actually happens during an assembly, from Liborio's point of view:

"At mid-morning it's only natural to eat something to keep us going until lunchtime, or to have a drink when it's hot and we are thirsty," says one of the participants. "It is almost impossible to satisfy this need. You can hardly find a place to get a drink of cold water, much less a soda or a shake. If you order a croquette or a hot dog, what usually happens is that it comes without bread, but when you pay the bill, the cost of the bread is included. There's no way to convince the waiter that the price should be lower because there's no bread."

Another raises his hand and asks to speak. "I've often observed how dishes and flatware are washed in many cafeterias," he says. "They don't even use hot water, much less detergent, and they barely rinse them with cold water. What do we plan to do to protect public health?"

"I agree," adds a third person. "Every day waiters are more careless, more negligent. Their hair is uncombed. They're unshaven. Their uniforms are dirty. And they're lazy. I'm a witness, and I watch many of them wasting water. They let the faucets run until there's no more water and they have an excuse for not working. Sometimes you can spend hours waiting for somebody to clean off a dirty table and tell you to come in."

But Liborio continues to patronize these establishments. This is a new habit he has acquired with the revolution. In the old days he went to restaurants on special occasions—a wedding anniversary, a birthday, a social engagement. Usually he preferred to eat food prepared at home and enjoyed in a family atmosphere.

With the revolution, however, he has been obliged to change his ways. If he doesn't have much money he will patronize a pizzeria, a cafeteria, or a second-rate café. If, however, he has enough money, he will go to a luxury restaurant where the prices are high but where he has his only opportunity to eat his fill of filet mignon or ham steak. And if he's lucky and there is a change in the menu that day, he might be reminded of the taste of those creatures called shellfish, which have almost disappeared from the Cuban diet despite the fact that Cuba exports 100 million dollars' worth of seafood every year.

Back to the assembly.

"Something should be done to ease the burden of food shop-

ping for housewives, especially for those of us who work," demands a middle-aged woman. "I'll use my own case as an example.
To buy produce I use an establishment two blocks from my
house. But to buy oil, condensed milk, sugar, and other groceries,
I have to walk three blocks in the opposite direction. As if that
weren't enough, meats and eggs are distributed in a third store. I
have no choice but to run from one place to the other.

"But the most unbearable part is the meat delivery. It's only
three-quarters of a pound per person, most of the time it's late,
and it's not enough to watch for the moment it arrives. You have
to stand in line the whole time, because if you lose your turn, you
have to wait for the next delivery nine days later, as the meat is
all gone. Isn't there some way to organize a more rational distribution of food?"

An old man stands up and says, "Speaking of quality, gentlemen, what is happening to the bread? At best it has the consis-
tency of gum. Most of the time it's like a rock."

"I want to say something about the ration book for consumer products," interrupts a young woman. "If you want to buy
a mattress, for example, or a fan, what should you do? When you
find out they're in the market, there's a long line of people
outside the store forty-eight hours before they go on sale. These
people apparently don't work. They sleep on the line, and they
distribute numbers among themselves so they can relieve each
other. How do they find out? I think the clerks tell their friends.
Their buddies are the only ones who can get these articles, and
often what they do is resell them at a higher price."

Liborio sincerely admires anyone who can decipher a ration
coupon, let alone use it. There are three-month, six-month, and
annual coupons. Deodorant, for example, is three-month, a shirt
coupon is good for six months, and a pants coupon is annual. But
there are also boxes on the coupons that every three or six
months give you the right to choose between a pair of under-
pants or an undershirt, a pair of stockings or a pair of shorts, a
lipstick or a can of talcum powder, a pair of women's under-
pants or a brassiere. And to complicate matters even more, there
are the famous coupons for rare articles—fans, mattresses, irons,
record players—among which you can choose just one a year for
each family unit.

"I don't understand what's going on with the personnel on
duty at the hospitals," complains another participant at the
assembly. "Two weeks ago I took one of my children who had
broken his arm, and there were all these patients waiting, look-

ing very upset, while the jerk of a doctor came in, went out, came back in, and whispered to the nurses without taking care of anybody. It's an outrage!

"And forget about the clinics. You get up at dawn, you get in line, and when you finally think it's your turn, the nurse calmly refuses to give you an appointment, saying they've all been taken, even if you're there at regularly scheduled hours. And if you get lucky and see the doctor, the only thing he does is send you to the hospital. So why go to the clinic? What's the point? The fact is the doctors don't want to work.

"The same thing happens at the pharmacy. An immense line and only one employee, hard as nails—he barely moves. You get tired of waiting, and often they don't have the medicine that's been prescribed, or they sell you the wrong one."

These assemblies drag on for two, three or four hours. Liborio is hopeful. He unburdens himself of his calamitous tales of woe. From hospitals he moves on to Cuban taxi drivers, *Los incapturables*, "escape artists," reckless and rude and apt to overcharge. After taxis he discusses the dry-cleaning shops from which clothing is often returned stained, torn, or with buttons missing. In principle one has the right to demand a receipt to replace the article of clothing in the shops, but it isn't worth the bother, because new items are of such poor quality.

From dry cleaners he could go on to potholes, or the lack of space in the day-care centers, or the scarcity of replacement parts for stoves, refrigerators, and TV sets, or the problem of garbage collection, a constant theme at all the assemblies because of the foul smell of the overflowing cans in the meeting room corner. He can speak of interrupted telephone service, stopped drains, floods after the rain because of the overflow from sewers, or the alarming plague of mosquitoes, cockroaches, and mice, which are on the increase.

When the assembly is over, Liborio returns calmly to his house. All of the problems have been discussed. No doubt things will now improve.

Months later there is another meeting. The delegate begins with a list of solutions or explanations for the issues that had been raised:

"As for the coupons in the ration books, a complete report will be in the pamphlet *Magacín* [a pamphlet published twice a month by the MINCIN to instruct housewives in the difficult handling of the ration coupons], on sale at newsstands. As for the behavior of commercial workers, we ask for the help of the population, whose demanding attitude can help to make certain that administrative orders intended to guarantee good service are observed. The time will come when commercial workers who do not give good service to the public will not be allowed to work in any establishment.

"Concerning bread, the central task is for all of us to demand better quality and distribution. In the hospitals we are applying a new system for care, and we are gaining valuable experience. In every clinic or hospital there is a box for complaints and suggestions, and when there is a deficiency in service the patient should go to the director, who is obliged to solve the problem. In the pharmacies there is a lack of personnel when they are most crowded. Now there is a 'pilot plan' in effect in some pharmacies, in which technical personnel also work at the counter to raise the quality of service and avoid mix-ups in medicines."

At each assembly Liborio will hear, without major variations, the same kind of response: "We are working on . . ." "We are discussing . . ." "We are applying a new system . . ." "We are gaining experience . . ." "The moment will come when . . ." Invariably it is a palliative, an excuse, an allusion to the future.

The assemblies continue to take place, but out of habit, or, rather, because of an imposed discipline. The energy once mobilized for complaints is conquered by yawns, because Liborio loses his combativeness and resigns himself once more to living with inertia, inefficiency, and apathy.

LIBORIO'S TRICKS

No matter what happens, Liborio must show willingness to perform the tasks that the revolution imposes on him. If he does not, he knows, because it has been demonstrated to him, that his life will become hell. At his workplace, in addition to the members of the union and the party, there is always an *extremista*, someone whose job it is to keep an eye on him, carefully watching his political behavior. The same function is assumed by the never-sleeping eye of the Defense Committee on his block, constantly alert to the slightest changes in his personal life.

With this in mind, Liborio, who is astute and has many

years of experience, has become a master of simulation. He understands that for the moment it is easier to create appearances than to resist, since what matters most is his emotional stability and the security of his family.

And so Liborio will go to any lengths to attend any assembly that he's told to or any productive work that is organized. And he will go even further to be there always in the crowd on the Plaza de la Revolución to listen to Fidel. He will shout *"¡Patria o Muerte! ¡Venceremos!"* without stopping to think what the slogan means; he will scream "Down with the Yanquis!" although at bottom he might have preferred to go and live in the United States a long time ago; he will frantically applaud when he is told that his quota of sugar or coffee will be reduced, although the measure breaks his heart; he will volunteer to fight in the name of proletarian internationalism, although in reality what happens in other countries doesn't matter to him very much; he will let himself be talked to about problems and hear them analyzed minutely through a paternalistic lens as if he were retarded; he will listen without protest to one excuse after another, one promise after another; he will allow them to postpone his prosperity until 1990, until 2000, until the time of his grandchildren or his great-grandchildren, although he has not forgotten the words that the *Líder Máximo* spoke a few years earlier: "We are not making a revolution for future generations; we are making a revolution with this generation and for this generation."

When Liborio returns home after the long speech, exhausted by so much applauding and hoarse with so much shouting, he will ask himself: "But what does he really think? How far does he plan to take us?" In a whisper he will unburden himself to his wife, if he trusts her and doesn't plan to divorce, and he will blame himself for being so docile. But then, as he looks at his sleeping children, he will forgive himself because he understands that for the moment there is nothing else he can do. The next day he will get up again very early to go to work, he will wash his face and shave, and before he leaves the house he will put on a convincing expression.

A great deal of work is demanded of Liborio, and in return he is paid a monthly salary that normally does not average more than 148 pesos, equivalent to 128 U.S. dollars. The minimum wage in Cuba is about 85 pesos, roughly equivalent to 68 U.S. dollars. Ambitious production goals are imposed and are supposed to be achieved in a short period of time. But this doesn't bother him. He knows from experience that if the goal is not met, the world does not come to an end. His superior will invent explanations, and Liborio will go on earning the same salary. It is true that if he surpasses the goal he will earn a little more money, but he prefers to go slow and not to wear himself out, because the whirlpool of responsibilities never ends. The best policy is to conserve energy for political duties and earn his pesos in an easier way, through some clandestine business.

When Liborio arrives at work he will mark his timecard, and if he belongs to the bureaucracy he will go to his office for a moment, shuffle the papers on his desk, make a few changes in his date book, and leave to take care of some personal business. If he works in a factory he will glance at his machine and exchange a few words with his fellow workers until nine, when it's time for a break. The administration sets fifteen minutes for the break, but Liborio has been gradually stretching the time and now he habitually takes a half an hour or even longer. Usually on his break he has a piece of dry pancake and a glass of watery lemonade or strawberry-flavored drink that doesn't taste like lemon or strawberry.

Fifteen minutes before lunch Liborio stops working. He gets up, makes some comment on the news, and gets ready to go to the dining room. After lunch he takes over half an hour to rest, talk, or take a walk. When he gets back he remembers that he has to make a phone call. Liborio is a very social being; he never forgets his girlfriend, his wife, or his friends when he is on the job. He calls them every day and talks animatedly for a long time without caring that he's not working. From time to time he remembers the production goal, sees that he has produced very little during the day, and returns to his machine or his desk. Then some official from his union comes up and tells him that next Sunday there will be productive work in the country. Liborio feels like inventing some excuse, but he remembers that he did that the last time, and he also knows that it's close to the time for distributing household appliances. He needs to accumulate merits to get his refrigerator. And so he puts on his best smile and very emphatically answers: "Of course, *compañero*. Put me down on your list! We don't step back even to get up steam!"

On Sunday, Liborio gets up very early, muttering under his breath, to go to the spot where all his *compañeros* are supposed to meet. At six sharp he's on the designated corner, but the truck doesn't come until eight, which makes him happy because now he'll work less time. Two hours later, after performing miles of acrobatics to hold on to the railing in the truck, he reaches the field where he is supposed to work, but now the man in charge is nowhere to be seen. Someone goes to look for him, and meanwhile Liborio passes the time watching young girls, who chatter happily.

After an hour the man in charge of the land shows up and, after some hesitation, shows them the field where they are going to work. There isn't much to do. The union didn't let the man know far enough in advance that they were coming, and now there are more people than potatoes. How wonderful, thinks Liborio. This way he won't be so exhausted when he gets home, and he'll be able to take his children to see a French film that is supposed to be very funny.

The following Sunday it's Liborio's turn to be on guard duty at his workplace. What a pain! His shift is from two to six in the morning. On Monday he'll feel tired and irritable. Still, Liborio relieves his workmate right on time, signs the guard book, locks the door carefully, and without turning out the light lies down to sleep on the most comfortable sofa. It's idiocy to keep watch this way, but by now he's tired of wasting his time looking for sabotage that never happens. Besides, if there *was* a problem, he couldn't do a thing because they don't even give him a weapon to defend himself.

Occasionally, Liborio has the time and energy to attempt the household repairs his wife insists are urgently needed. The state sells none of the materials he needs for this work, but a friend who works in construction has sold him two cans of pilfered paint and some plaster—at inflated prices, of course, because that's how his friend earns extra money.

He has to be very clever to get the cans of paint into his house past the watchful eye of his Defense Committee, although he knows that even the president does the same thing if she has to.

Liborio has many friends in the black market and in other equally dangerous businesses. He is afraid for Cheo, his neighbor, who is constantly risking his skin playing the *bolita*, or the numbers. The *bolita* is an illegal game that Liborio knows was very popular in Cuba before the revolution. It consisted of guessing the last three digits of the winning number in the national lottery. Even though the revolution has abolished the lottery, in the last ten years it has made a comeback and is more popular than ever. The game is now based on the winning lottery number in Caracas. Liborio knows that in Havana certain places are known as spots where it is easy to place a bet: The Esquina de Tejas, the Rancho Luna restaurant on L Street, and on 23rd Street at the corner of G Street. He dared to play a number once, with such good luck that he won 300 pesos. With the money he got a new pair of elegant jeans for 120 pesos, and he bought a pair of shoes for his wife for 100.

Of course Liborio loves blue jeans, nice clothes, good shoes, tape recorders, electrical appliances. Since he can't get any of these things in the stores, he tries the black market and uses all his inventiveness to make more money, because the black market is very expensive. So, slowly, thanks to Liborio's daring, the *bolita* is coming back.

The theft of state goods is also rampant. Clandestine trading with farmers and foreign technicians has developed, and the labor of many craftspeople has flourished; with materials stolen from the state, they make sandals, bags, and clothing.

It is impossible to describe all of Liborio's tricks. But they will not be Liborio's only strategy for coping with the meanness of his existence. Cuban history shows the rebelliousness of its people. Liborio filled the streets with disturbances during Machado's regime, fought against Batista's dictatorship, rose up whenever he felt his rights were being violated. In the last century his ancestors, the *mambises*, armed only with machetes, successfully freed themselves from Spanish colonialism. For the present, Liborio pretends, endures, waits. But his soul is filled with resentment toward those who, in the name of equality, live so well while he lives so badly. This bitterness is growing, and one day, when he finally loses his patience, the docile Liborio will sharpen his machete once again and take the offensive as the *mambises* did, in an explosion of uncontrollable rage.

CLIMBING THE
PYRAMID OF POWER

A NECESSARY CHANGE

My discovery in early 1972 of Marielle's koala bear effectively cancelled any further emotional life save for my attachment to Maggie. The Stranger, now in full control, no longer had to debate with my true self, for that true self had disappeared.

Nothing outside of Maggie could move me.

I was often surprised at what a dependable computer the Stranger made of me. I was remarkably quick to assess every situation and then to know exactly what I should or should not do, what I should or should not say. The intrigues I encountered grew unbelievably complex, but I always adopted the correct attitude and followed the most prudent course of action. My political facade was immaculate and, now, impenetrable. In this sense I was invisible—even to myself.

As for my determination to escape, my marriage had introduced a new challenge. Cuban officials traveling on state business to foreign countries did not, as a rule, take their spouses along. I was not so naïve as to try to include Maggie in an official trip.

There had been rumors that the party might begin authorizing worker vacations in Socialist countries, but I had no reliable way of knowing when, or if, such a program would ever start. For the time being, the only solution I could see was to arrange somehow that we be sent separately and simultaneously by the government to an Eastern European destination as in my original plan, and that our flight schedules coincide so that we could, at a refueling stop in a Western nation, ask for asylum together. I didn't care to reflect on how many factors could go awry, or how much rare luck would be necessary. I had to treat the plan as a reasonable possibility; otherwise there could be no sustaining hope.

Remote as our escape possibilities seemed at this point, getting us out of Cuba was always uppermost in my mind, my first thought upon waking each day and my last reflection each night. Much would depend upon circumstances, but I could set about laying the groundwork. This meant encouraging Maggie to raise her revolutionary profile, both to enhance my position and to put her in line for a foreign travel assignment.

Even before we were married in 1971, Maggie had joined the Revolutionary Militia and her local CDR. She understood that political integration would be vital for her professional life once she graduated from the School of Design. Maggie loathed the prospect of associating herself with the revolution's true believers, but she understood, as did most other Cubans who had failed in their efforts to leave the country, that the only way to lead an even passably normal life in Cuban society was to play the revolutionary game.

In 1972 she finished her studies in design with high marks, and I immediately set about helping her find a position at the National Council of Culture. I was able to arrange for us to have a short conversation with Lázaro Marcos, then the Council's executive vice-president. Marcos obliged us by finding Maggie work as a graphic designer on the Council magazine, *Revolution and Culture*, where I knew she would face a minimum of bureaucratic rivalry.

Lázaro Marcos was typical of most Cuban cultural officials. He was an army man whose erudition left much to be desired and whose interests were not focused on artists and their concerns. "These people are not easy to manage," he explained to me during our interview. "They think because they can write, paint, or sculpt they deserve everything. They can't understand that the revolution comes before they do."

Above Marcos on the Council pyramid of power was Félix Sautié, a former Communist Youth leader and lapsed Christian like my colleague at ICAIC, Benigno Iglesias. Sautié suffered from the delusion that he was a priest. His boss, Council President Luis Pavón, late of MINFAR's magazine, *Olive Green*, was a heavy drinker whose aesthetic feel was best reflected in the mediocre poems he wrote.

In all, such officials guaranteed that the Council would operate chaotically—precisely the sort of administrative environment that best suited Maggie's advancement as a revolutionary. Her lack of political background went largely unnoticed and we were even able to risk falsifying a few dates on her job application. In one instance, we back-dated her membership in the CDR five years.

It was also very helpful that she had returned to the university to study for a degree in art history. Soon after she began working, she joined a study plan that had been especially established for workers. It offered night classes three or four days a week. This decision not only contributed to her professional development but also brought her respect and admiration in her work center. Educational improvement was considered a high revolutionary merit. All of this, added to her artistic ability and her sense of responsibility, meant that before the year was out Maggie was considered one of the best staff members on the magazine. She was subsequently named its artistic director.

Although Maggie was pleased at being recognized for her achievements and capabilities, she was not especially happy about her substantial new responsibilities, for which she would receive no increase in salary. I, however, was secretly glad Maggie was gaining the trust of her superiors and eventually perhaps travel privileges as well.

For me, too, 1972 proved to be a professional watershed, a chance to take another step up toward the peak of my plan, foreign travel. Word of the New Year's Eve gathering at Núñez Jiménez's house in Miramar had spread almost instantly throughout Fidel's closest circle of revolutionary leaders. To have been included in such an elite circle and then, as it happened, to have spent another long evening with Fidel at Diocles Torralba's house that January gave my revolutionary image a significant boost. I took it as no coincidence when, at the end of January 1972, a call came for me to meet with Miguel Figueras, the MINAZ deputy minister for economy.

Figueras, one of Cuba's outstanding economists, had an intimate working knowledge of the sugar industry. He was not about to allow either of these attainments, however, to complicate his life. When Fidel forswore economic controls in the 1960s, Figueras followed orders at MINAZ, even though he was fully aware of the probable consequences. Years later, when Fidel changed his mind, Figueras revealed himself as the classic Communist revolutionary chameleon by condemning the old policy, or rather those who had implemented it, ignoring the fact that he had acted as one of its staunchest partisans.

I was almost certain Figueras was going to offer me a job, but knowing what I did about him and the sorry condition of the ministry following the failure of the 10 million-ton harvest, I didn't see the coming proposal as an unalloyed joy. To get out of Cuba, I knew that sooner or later I'd have to reach a higher level of power. But MINAZ could easily prove to be a Sargasso for me if I was not extremely cautious—both because of the inevitable power struggle that accompanied any position of power and the fact that at MINAZ, I would no longer be under Alfredo Guevara's protection.

Figueras welcomed me cordially into his office. He had a slow manner of speech and heavy-lidded eyes that gave the impression he was always tired or bored. I guessed both might be true as the deputy minister gave me an ironic smile and moved at once to his reason for seeing me. I was to consider taking the post of head of capital investment plans at MINAZ. Just as quickly, he then went on to catalog the sugar industry's innumerable problems, including specifically the lamentable shape of its capital program, MINAZ's biggest headache by far.

"As you can see, Llovio," Figueras said, "we're bogged down."

"I know economics and administration fairly well," I told him, surprised that I was being offered such an important and sensitive post, "but I don't know the particular characteristics of the sugar industry. I have only a very superficial idea of the production process. Besides, according to what you've told me, there's a lack of authority and discipline, and those are very negative factors. To create a capital investment plan on the basis of the present chaos is bound to be a complex task."

"All right, we'll talk about these things when you're working here," he answered evasively. "You need to finish up your work at ICAIC as soon as possible. We'd like you to begin with us next month."

"I don't think there'll be any problem in finishing up quickly at ICAIC, but before I settle in here, it would be a good idea to spend some time at a sugar mill and begin to learn something about the industry, don't you think?" I suggested.

"You're right," Figueras replied. "We can put off your joining the ministry. I'll make the necessary arrangements so that you can work at a mill near Havana, okay? You'll see how everything will work out. I know that you were in charge of investments at ICAIC. This is a little broader and more complex, but you won't have any problem."

This is a big step forward—no doubt about it, I thought when the meeting was over. Perhaps the job went further than I might have liked, especially as far as responsibilities were concerned, but it was a key post in the country's economy and could open the desired door for me. In 1972, I believed that Maggie's and my escape was close to becoming a reality.

*   *   *

Benigno Iglesias heard the news of my transfer with delight, as he would inherit my responsibilities. For the first time he did what he could to lighten the burden of my duties, and in a short while I handed over the capital investments in process. By this time, my work on the two special projects had ended.

San Rafael Street had been renovated, painted, and lit, an artistic jewel in Havana's center and an amazing contrast to its surroundings. But the people were not so easily deceived by the disguise of precious objects in the windows. At the door of J. Vallés, a store that had been used as the center for our renovation work, we heard a young man comment on opening day: "Instead of showing this shit, what they have to do is sell more clothes and shoes. With these little clay figures I can't put clothes on my body or shoes on my feet."

Nor did the glitter last very long. Some months later the art was returned to its former homes and the windows were empty again, or as cluttered with junk as they had been before.

Against all odds the "greatest park in Latin America" was completed too. The installations were put up almost exactly as they had originally been planned, including the large open-air movie theater, which was a spectacular failure.

For all my skepticism about the project, not even I ever dreamed what a disaster the theater would prove to be. It was impossible for audiences to sit for more than five minutes on the grass, because a swarm of hungry mosquitoes would attack any human being they came across. At first the administration arranged periodic spraying, but it finally became clear that the number of spectators was not large enough to make the difficult task worthwhile. Surely anyone would prefer the comfort of a traditional movie house, even if the screen was smaller and the environment much less exotic. Finally, after a year, the humidity in the booth ruined the equipment, and the movie theater failed.

The mosquitoes loved Lenin Park. According to a popular joke, eating dinner there was like visiting a flamenco show: Patrons clapped continually in their efforts to ward off the bugs.

Cubans really had to want to go to the park to get there. Except for those who had a car—the leaders and a very small percentage of the population—you had to spend hours waiting for the park bus, which ran less frequently than buses on other routes. Even if you succeeded in getting to the park, it was a long trek from one side to the other, since the famous little train sometimes ran and sometimes didn't, depending on luck. The shows were not performed very often, and they were unappealing, so the greatest incentive for going to the park was the mosquito-infested restaurants—where at least the service was better than in the city—or the treats such as fine caramels or chocolate kisses that were sold only at the park. But these frivolities were too expensive for the workers. Among themselves, the people changed the name from Lenin Park to "Das Kapital," because of the amount of money needed to enjoy the park.

The most resounding disappointment was the Dry Pass dam, the only hope for the planned lake and its floating scenery. The dam filled up when it rained, but then the water drained out through the cracks into the subsurface. Engineering efforts by the Ministry of Construction were useless; no matter how many thousands of cubic meters of concrete were poured into the cracks, the water continued to leak out. I remembered the wisdom of the peasants: "The water goes through here; the earth swallows it up. That's why it's called Dry Pass."

Thus, there was no water for the lake. As a kind of consolation, it was filled by a well-pumping system. But then the scenery sank, and with it sank the marvelous dream of watching waterborne spectacles in an atmosphere of historical fantasy. The scenery had to be attached to the bottom of the lake and left motionless in front of the coliseum.

Cubans began to see the park for what it was: an ostentatious display that mocked their real needs. If the project had not been so showy, if so many millions of pesos and so much energy had not been wasted, and if the people's priorities had been treated with more respect, they surely would have appreciated the park more.

Still, the park partly fulfilled its goal. Lenin Park offered another recreational option as well as more grist for the propaganda mill. Any foreigner who came to Havana was taken to see one of the largest recreational facilities in Latin America.

As for me, I felt that the park was important for the people, who had so few places to relax or take their children. If it had been built more realistically—an amphitheater that wasn't a Roman imitation, a cinema screen half the size of this custom-built one, aquaria with standard, not specially-treated, glass instead of Calobar—it might have been affordable for more of the country's citizens. All the cement, iron, imported materials, and labor that had been mobilized toward this luxury park in an underdeveloped country: It was folly. At least in the sugar industry I wouldn't have to contribute to such grandiosity.

IN THE MINISTRY
OF SUGAR

From February until June of 1972, I acted on my request of Figueras and familiarized myself with the basic workings of the sugar industry at the Friendship Among Peoples sugar mill near the town of Güines, about an hour's drive south of Havana. Since my friend Alayón, the barber, who had been my closest companion during the UMAP months, was from Güines, I took this opportunity to find out what had become of him.

I had lost track of Alayón after seeing to it that he was both transferred with me to MINFAR Camagüey headquarters in 1967 and then put on the list of those first to be discharged from UMAP. Later, I was contacted by State Security about an application Alayón had made to leave the country. Hoping I could push the painful process ahead for my friend, I told the man from MININT that I thought Alayón was a peaceable person concerned only about his family. Furthermore, I said, it was my understanding the barber would leave behind an eminently habitable dwelling in Güines. Whatever effect my words had, I was very happy to learn now that Alayón had indeed been allowed to emigrate and lived in Hialeah, Florida, with his family. The news of his successful departure heartened me in my own, more complex scheme to follow suit.

During my stay at the Friendship Among Peoples mill I tried to learn everything about sugar production from the time the cane entered the mills until the sugar came out of the centrifuges. I studied the machines in detail—their parts, their interrelationships, and accompanied the technicians while they worked, talking with them and listening to their experiences. I analyzed the laboratory reports and learned the technical meaning of each of the dials and gauges. Then I traveled the railroad that transported the cane and examined its relationship to other means of transport. In the administrative office I mastered the mechanisms of MINAZ management. At night I read, delving into the inner workings of this industry I knew almost nothing about.

Whatever weekend I could, I traveled to Havana to be with Maggie. She of course was not happy with the separation—neither was I—but she understood the importance of this period of apprenticeship for my future progress at the ministry.

When the harvest was over I concentrated on the annual disassembly of the mill, observing the dismantling of the equipment, piece by piece, and noting the details of maintenance. At the same time, I listened in as the mill's managers decided upon their annual capital investment program. The plan bore no particular relation to the mill's needs or to any coherent scheme of production expansion. In fact, it was little more than a wish list sent up to the MINAZ provincial offices, where, I also learned, such requests for available equipment and materials were filled not by a regional plan but according to how needy the individual mill managers made themselves sound.

The second part of my education in the sugar industry included many tours of MINAZ installations around the island. I saw widespread waste and underutilization of countless resources. Much equipment was badly warehoused, or not even inventoried. When I ordered an inventory of imported equipment that had not yet been installed, the total came to $42 million!

The situation at the ministry headquarters, located in an eleven-story building on the Rampa in Vedado, was the mirror image of what I found in the provinces. The latest MINAZ minister, Marcos Lage, was a young engineer who exercised minimal real authority and who commanded insufficient respect inside MINAZ and among his fellow government ministers. He had no direct access to Fidel. Lage exacerbated the lack of discipline at the ministry with his arbitrary management style and his habit of dispensing MINAZ's equipment personally to provincial offices or even to mill administrators themselves.

The headquarters building itself housed 1,200 MINAZ employees, all constantly scurrying around in a convincing simulation of busyness and hard work. In truth, MINAZ was a dispirited agency, crawling along on inertia.

A prime reason for this malaise was Fidel, who still bore MINAZ an unreasoning grudge for the failure of the 1970 harvest. Childishly, after pouring resources into MINAZ for his 10-million-ton project, Fidel now punished the ministry and crushed its

Fidel with a typical crowd in the Plaza de la Revolución

Maggie resting from volunteer
work in the fields of Havana
Province

House, confiscated from one of
Cuba's millionaires, where I had
a room in spring 1972 while
studying the sugar industry

Painting of Ché
in my office at
Finance, 1977

With First Vice President Kazeruk *(left)*, **our Soviet adviser,
and the First Secretary of the Soviet embassy
in Havana** *(second from right)*, **spring 1977**

The only surviving picture of me *(extreme right)*
with Fidel in Havana

Maggie in the 1970s

While trying to find Marielle, Paris, May 1979

In Panama while conducting the audit with Nilda Rodríguez *(center)* and an embassy official, December 1979

My work identification cards from the Ministries of Sugar, Finance, and Culture

**At Varadero Beach, the day I finally
told Maggie the truth, August 1980**

**Maggie in Mirabel Airport the day
of our escape, December 13, 1981**

Twelve days later, Christmas 1981 in Montreal

In Guadeloupe on the way to see my mother, January 22, 1982

Reunion with my mother, Caracas, January 1982

**With Marielle after sixteen years,
June 1982**

Marielle today

morale by ignoring it, strangling the sugar industry even though sugar provided Cuba with 85 percent of her export earnings.

I walked into this bleak picture knowing my two immediate predecessors had been fired because they could not untangle MINAZ's capital investments, and aware that my responsibility to control the distribution of every mill component, every one of MINAZ's more than five thousand miles of railway track, each auto and air conditioner, made me an easily isolated target when, as was certain, something went wrong.

Miguel Figueras soon proved absolutely indifferent to the mess he had acknowledged I was inheriting. He was very distant in our conversations, more concerned with his own ambition— and safety—than he was in my struggle to organize MINAZ's capital investment program. The rest of my new colleagues tended to shun me, too, although for different reasons. I was treated a bit like a disease-carrier among them, stigmatized by the dangerous and seemingly hopeless job I'd undertaken.

As I had seen at ICAIC (and knew to be true in every Socialist bureaucracy), the all-white board of directors at MINAZ was divided into cliques, *piñas*. Each coalesced around a leader and made common cause based upon shared ambitions against other cliques. Since MINAZ managed the oldest and largest industry in the country, its cliques were deeply rooted. Each deputy minister formed a *piña* with his directors and department heads and eventually formed alliances with other *piñas* against third-party cliques. The bigger the *piña*, the more voracious its appetite until it had devoured everything in sight, or began to devour itself. Fortunately, I was unaffected by it; as yet I had no power, and besides, these officials were too busy attacking one another.

At first I was dogged by my paranoid suspicion that my assignment to the sugar industry was a setup; that I had been sent to MINAZ to fail, perhaps by the same unseen enemies who'd first entangled me in *La Dolce Vita*. But as the summer months of 1972 passed, it appeared that perhaps I'd been assigned to do precisely what I was trying to do: introduce some rationality and organization to the capital investment plan. Unless I detected signs of an attack on my work, I had to assume that my isolation at MINAZ had no sinister meaning.

That autumn I also enrolled in law school, not because I wished a career in the profession but because my being a law student would give me access to the important library volumes of international law. In the library I could study in peace, country by country, the statutes that applied to those seeking asylum and know the surest gamble for us.

With Maggie also working and enrolled in evening classes, our time together was telescoped into a few hours on Sundays. By week's end we were both so exhausted that we rarely stirred from the apartment, and then only to see a film showing nearby. Difficult as this schedule was on us and on our marriage, Maggie never once complained or asked what good was our enormous effort when so many revolutionaries among our acquaintances prospered handsomely on next to no exertion at all. She fully believed that I was a pure Communist revolutionary who would never take advantage of his position. And it was in her nature to work as hard as she could.

Toward the end of 1972, I began to get a clearer picture of why I had been chosen to tackle the capital investments at MINAZ. Diocles Torralba, the army chief of staff through whom we'd had dinner with Fidel, was a veteran of the Sierra Maestra who had seen his career temporarily derailed in the sectarian crisis. But since 1962, Diocles had distinguished himself in several capacities, including his term as a student at a Soviet military academy and as party secretary in Pinar del Río province. Very sobersided, with hermitlike habits, Torralba at the time of the New Year's Eve party had been about to take another giant step up in power. In the fall of the year I accepted the post at MINAZ, he was preparing to join the executive committee of the Council of Ministers, where he would be vice president responsible for overseeing the ministries of Agriculture, Sugar, and Food, a position of great influence within the Revolutionary Government.

Torralba was far too subtle to claim any hand in my appointment to MINAZ. Rather, during our frequent informal discussions of the ministry, he listened carefully to my explanations of the MINAZ morale problems and revealed by his conversation his aim to restore the sugar industry to discipline and to renew its institutional vigor. As MINAZ's chief of capital investments, I naturally figured large in this scheme.

Torralba had to move with extreme caution. Important as the sugar industry was for Cuba's economy, it was still on Fidel's least-favored list. What is more, while Diocles sought to pump life into MINAZ with new resources and to improve its organization, he had to contend with another confounding factor.

Before the revolution, the Cuban sugar industry had been

almost fully integrated, from management of the cane fields to the operation of its mills. Fidel had come to power believing this organizational structure was inherently capitalistic and therefore had to be destroyed. Thus he'd ordered that the industrial side of sugar production be put under MINAZ control while cultivation and cane cutting had been made the responsibility of the National Institute for Agrarian Reform (INRA). With further interference in the 1960s from the party and other organizations, sugar production had become hopelessly fractured, pulled every which way by one hierarchy and then the other.

Torralba's answer to this chaos was the delicate strategy of reintegrating sugar production without allowing Fidel to realize what he was doing. He persuaded Fidel to establish a sugar industry "coordinating" group called the Harvest Sector. Responsible exclusively to Torralba, the Harvest Sector became his tool for remeshing sugar production from top to bottom.

Little of Torralba's overall scheme was apparent to me at first. All I knew was that the capital investment plan was quickly becoming the center of action at MINAZ. It didn't take my colleagues there long to intuit my connection to Diocles as the new emphasis on discipline and organization deepened, and I soon found their old aloofness replaced by a respectful, cooperative attitude. In no time, coherent lines of authority began to be built. Minister Lage, to whom I directly reported, was ordered to hold meetings with MINAZ provincial officials at which an umbrella strategy for capital investment was discussed and each player told to act in accordance with the plan as it developed under my direction.

The first violators of the plan—those initiating capital investments without approval—were treated very severely, but matters soon leveled out. Everybody knew the source of the new policy, and they also knew that Torralba was not a vacillating man.

In spite of Diocles Torralba's efforts to create a more productive sugar industry, he met with obstacles he could not overcome.

The test of the new capital investment plan was not its effectiveness. All that mattered was that it be implemented. Socialist efficiency is, more than anything else, a matter of appearance. And this appearance is measured not by return on investment but by the size of the investment itself; an example of what I call Socialism's "quantitative rule."

To the Socialist mind, the quality of goods or services produced or the soundness of the plan for producing them do not matter as long as impressive statistics can be cited. The first consideration is always propaganda.

In a typical instance, a Socialist state may boast the production of 10 million pair of shoes (which may be true), and yet in the nation's stores there are no shoes, or only shoes of inferior quality. Likewise, in the area of health care, gains are quantified statistically, as in a claim that 100,000 psychiatric exams were conducted in a given time frame. It is unimportant that those consultations were mostly fifteen-minute chats. In another case, Cuba's restaurants and cafés may be drab, poorly staffed, and offer a limited range of unpalatable food. But if Fidel can announce that 1 million or 2 million meals have been served, the state's goals have been met.

In short, the bigger the better. Not a single person asked of the MINAZ investment plan if it was going to be hard currency well spent. And I was frequently ordered to make capital investments that were demonstrably counterproductive. But since I knew these inspirations came down from on high—at least as high as the Politburo—I carried them out with no questions.

Second, Fidel's decisions and their ramifications would always affect the sugar industry, which was still the essence of the Cuban economy, and Torralba could do nothing to stop him. The Soviets—now, under the secret accords, a much more powerful presence in the economy—nevertheless had been unsuccessful in trying to bridle Fidel's many idiosyncrasies and instant enthusiasms. In one way, they demonstrated their shrewdness. Henceforth, their assistance to MINAZ—about 250 million rubles a year at that time—would be separated completely from their aid to the rest of the economy. Their reasoning was very simple: They did not want Fidel misappropriating the resources for his own pet projects.

But they could not control Fidel's independent internal policies, a gap in their direct influence demonstrated by the "remodeling plan"—the project to modernize Cuba's forty-two sugar mills over a three-year period.

The program was very expensive. More to the point, it actually impeded the goal of streamlining the Cuban sugar industry. Fidel at that time did not consider the sugar industry capable of overseeing a successful building plan of new mills, and so he had ordered a remodeling plan that poured immense resources into old wrecks from the turn of the century. I had to control what I

knew was a vast waste of resources, although it was to be hailed
as a major success within the Cuban bureaucracy.

The forty-two mills had indeed been modernized, but they
would always have breakdowns; the changes were window dress-
ing. Cuba desperately required new mills to process her main crop
as efficiently as possible—but she wasn't going to get them soon.

The Soviets had approved the plan, believing it was certainly better than the status quo—no plan at all—but Fidel had
made this decision without a sober economic evaluation. As was
made clear to me from my earliest days at MINAZ, the *Líder
Máximo* had gained scant wisdom from the debacle of the ten-
million-ton harvest.

In addition, Fidel continued to insist on beginning the harvest in November or December and extending it at many of the
mills until June, even though it was common knowledge that the
ideal time for milling cane in Cuba is from January to March,
when the yield is high. The result: The average yield went down
and the cost of production rose.

Another fatal decision was to eliminate the sugar industry
agronomists, who were "unnecessary bureaucrats," according to
Fidel. Without a technician to select the highest-yield cane for
milling, the crop was cut indiscriminately, so that the quota was
met but the yield was low. Not even sugar cane could escape the
"quantitative rule."

The most curious aspect of this string of errors is that
despite past experience, there were still those who dared to make
recommendations or give accurate warnings of consequences.
Andrés Sarasola, director of accounting at MINAZ, wrote an
exhaustive report in which he proposed paying the farmer according to the quality of the cane that he brought to the sugar
mill. Fidel rejected the suggestion, arguing that the difference in
payment would give rise to inequality among the *campesinos*
and would favor the emergence of a capitalist-style farmer.

And then there is the example of a variety of cane called
Barbados 4362. In 1972 a highly qualified technician from INRA
made a detailed study of this strain, which apparently was very
profitable because of its rapid maturation and high sugar content but was also very susceptible to a disease called rust. In his
study he advised sowing this type of cane in small quantities and
in widely separated plantings so that if there was an outbreak of
rust, it could be more easily controlled. But this advice went
against Fidel's thinking: He was enthusiastic about Barbados

4362 and had ordered its massive sowing on 30 percent of cane-growing land. "What could that stupid little technician be thinking of?" he exclaimed in irritation when the study reached his desk. "Send him to the cane plantations. Let him learn something about sugar cane and he'll stop talking so much shit!" ordered Fidel. Cuba would pay the price of his impatience.

A BRIEF CONSUMER'S PARADISE

Fidel's brainstorms and dreams had practically ruined the Cuban sugar industry by the early 1970s, driving annual production down from a steady 6 million tons a year in the 1960s, and the balloon production of 8.2 million tons in 1970, to 5.9 million tons in 1971, 4.3 million in 1972 and 5.3 million in 1973 before Diocles Torralba's administrative acumen started turning the industry around. Still, the dramatic output-collapse from the world's second-largest sugar producer (after the USSR), together with production shortfalls elsewhere, led to a worldwide sugar shortage that soon began to drive prices to historic highs. It was the first such boom time for sugar since Cuba's "Dance of the Millions" in the 1920s.

Before this price run-up was over, a pound of raw sugar would jump from around 6 cents to about 60 cents, an incredible potential bonanza for Cuba. For the first time since the triumph in 1959, she could begin to level out her balance of payments. It was the perfect opportunity for the prudent development of Cuban industry. Finally, the people could actually see a shining future based not on promises and grandiose schemes but upon cold cash. Deliverance might have been at hand, except . . .

"Accept all the credit they'll give you—that's business!" Fidel instructed high-level officials in Foreign Trade.

The Western countries opened their vaults with generous lines of credit, gleeful at Cuba's sudden shopping spree. The North American economic blockade did not prevent the country from being flooded by Western technology from all over the world, including the United States.

Radios, stereos, textile products, and perfumes began to appear in the stores at very high prices. But that didn't matter: The Cuban consumer was avid for goods. Rarely in a small underdeveloped country has there been such a favorable upturn in so short a time. But no other stage was so harmful to the Cuban economy as this one.

Almost every day Fidel met with his officials to authorize the most scatterbrained purchases. It would be impossible to relate in complete detail the misuse of money during this euphoric stage of the sugar boom in 1973–74. But some instances are particularly outstanding.

MINAZ acquired ten torula yeast factories of French and Austrian manufacture. Torula yeast is a special cattle feed made from a sort of honey derived from the sugar milling process. At this time it, too, commanded high prices on the international market.

But the purchase of these factories, at a cost of $200 million, was made without a prior technical-economic evaluation. Because of the construction industry's low capacity, the equipment for these factories was kept in crates for years. Much of it, like that for the factory in the city of Cienfuegos, was warehoused near the ocean. When the factory was finally ready for assembly, over half of its prefabricated components had corroded.

A comparable situation arose with the purchase of mills for producing cornmeal and with the installation of cornflake and oatflake factories. No one ever studied the potential domestic market for these foods, which proved to be nil. Low demand forced the factories to be shut down except for one for each product, more than enough to satisfy the national market.

"Cuba, the country of sugar, will be the first producer, consumer, and exporter of the highest-quality candy! We will emulate the French, the Swiss, the English." I listened to Fidel say so to the workers at the candy factory in Trinidad, one of four imported from the West. And in fact Cuba began to produce high-quality candy. But three important details had been overlooked. First, the factories consumed a great quantity of sugar needed to meet international commitments. Second, open markets for sale of the candy did not exist abroad. And third, special paper was needed for wrapping the candies, extremely expensive paper manufactured only in the West. As a result, just one of the four factories was kept in operation, and its output was committed to the luxury hotels and the shops for foreign technicians.

Factories for producing Fresquitos—cakes manufactured by

mixing flour and fish in predetermined proportions—were imported from Argentina. The factories had not been operating very long when the minister of fishing, Aníbal Velaz, told Fidel that production would have to be interrupted because of a lack of fish. "More flour and less fish" was Fidel's suggestion, and his advice was followed, but the high density of the new mixture destroyed the machinery, and then the only recourse was to close the factories. Years later, in 1980, a contract for repair of the equipment was negotiated with Argentina.

During this time Fidel examined the fishing industry, too, and decided to automate the processing plants around the Havana docks. So, again on credit, Planta Habana, the largest fish cannery in the country, was built. As carefully thought-through as all the rest of the purchases of the time, Planta Habana still was not open in 1981, because the process it uses would have left the entire city chronically short of fresh water.

These few examples give an idea of the incongruities in investment policy—if a policy ever existed—during this period. Fidel assured everyone that sugar prices would stay high for at least a decade, and he continued piling up debts as if the day would never come when they would have to be paid back with interest.

Until that point, Cuba had an excellent repayment history. Now no one in Cuba realized how much the country was borrowing—and if they had, they couldn't have said a word in any case. For Fidel, foreign debt was only a product of the economists' bureaucratic mentality. "In the future it won't be necessary to ask about or wonder what went wrong; what will cause astonishment is how the country didn't go under, considering how ignorant revolutionaries are," Fidel said on one occasion.

He was right. The island of Cuba must be made of cork; that's the only way to explain the fact that it's still afloat.

TWO ENEMIES

The sugar boom turned into another disaster for the Cuban economy, but while it lasted life at MINAZ was relatively easy for me. With the industry once again in favor with Fidel, and Diocles Torralba securely entrenched as my protector, I had only to produce larger and larger annual investment plans that each year were rubber-stamped by the staff at the country's economic planning board (JUCEPLAN). As long as I followed the quantitative rule, my service to the revolution was seen as completely meritorious.

Then inevitably the period of calm ended.

In December 1974 the Cuban Politburo issued its "green book," an outline of the procedures involved in obtaining party approval for every executive appointment or transfer within the government and the party itself. Called *nomenklatura,* a term borrowed from the Soviets, the process had as its main aim absolute party control of executives.

Without this approval, no executive could be appointed, dismissed, or even continue in his current position. In my case I was required to submit a written autobiography to Minister Lage, who would forward it to the Secretariat of the Central Committee. After analyzing the biography, the party would then review my administrative record and make a complete political evaluation of me, which would include a personal interview by the appropriate party official. The interview was the key step in the political evaluation.

Finally, my approval or rejection would be communicated to Lage, who was responsible for informing me in *his* name, not the party's of my suitability to retain my job.

This time I was confronted by two enemies, one old and one new.

"Chino" Mayans, head of Villa Marista during the time of *La Dolce Vita,* and one of former Minister of the Interior Ramiro Valdés's "young tigers," had always felt deep resentment toward me. Ever since my arrest I had continuously denounced the theft of my belongings, which he had authorized. When Ramiro Valdés had been replaced in 1967, Mayans had also been relieved of his post and transferred to Pinar del Río Province. But by 1974 he had regained power as head of economic policy and of counter-espionage in Havana. His rancor was still alive, and one of his subordinates, Raimundo, was the official designated by State Security to be in charge of the Sugar Ministry.

MININT assigns one of several officials to each central agency of the state. Their function is to watch over the workers and leaders, to detect any enemy spy, and to authorize or deny a temporary exit permit to travel on state business for each administrator. MININT also uses these officials to learn and interfere in the inner workings of the administration and the party. The party considers this procedure illegal, but it continues despite the objection.

Under Mayans's direction, Raimundo hatched a plot to eliminate me. It didn't take me long to find out about it, since in the struggle to survive I had created an information network with some of the leadership and officials at MINAZ, who favored me because I was so close to Torralba. I would warn them in similar situations, and they in turn reciprocated. "Watch out for Raimundo. He's saying terrible things about you. I heard him defaming you in front of party leaders," one of them told me, and immediately added, "Please, this is just between you and me. I'm telling you because I know you're a revolutionary and you'd do the same for me."

My information network was correct. In fact, Raimundo was telling the story all over the ministry, especially to the party leaders—of my arrest during *La Dolce Vita*, my time in UMAP, and my marriage to a French heiress.

Months later, Raimundo's intrigues would be duplicated by a high-level official who had recently joined the ministry.

Two years after my arrival at the Sugar Ministry, at Torralba's suggestion, Minister Lage began to evaluate candidates for the position of deputy minister for the economy, which had been vacant since Miguel Figueras's appointment as deputy minister at JUCEPLAN. My choice was Octavio Medina, MINAZ delegate in Camagüey Province, with whom I had an excellent working relationship, and whom I regarded as a friend—in the revolutionary sense of the word.

Sadly, for many years, I was obliged to live without the kind of real friend in whom one places complete confidence and from whom one can always expect the truth. This spiritual solitude, learned through hard personal experience and through my observation of those around me, was a hard pill to swallow.

One of the first of these disillusionments had occurred in 1967 when I returned from my punishment in Camagüey. I had no job, I was at loose ends, and I needed the support of a friend more than ever before. It was then that I thought of going for help to Pepín Naranjo, my old *compañero* in the underground since 1953, who still held the post of First Party Secretary in Havana and was a personal aide to Fidel. For several years he and I had lived in the same boarding house; we had shared plans, dreams, and many dangerous moments. I considered him a good friend and thought that, given his solid position in the government, it would be very easy for him to help me find a new job.

When I went to his office in the Provincial Party building on M Street del Vedado, as I had done so often in the days before my punishment, I was sure I would find the encouragement I needed so desperately. But I was mistaken. All Pepín had for me were a few curt excuses, which were passed on to me by his secretary: He was very busy just then, couldn't possibly see me, and would I leave my phone number.

This indifference lasted for a long time. He was distant when we happened to meet in public places or in the homes of mutual friends, and he treated me with the kind of impersonal courtesy that one shows the most casual acquaintance. Our friendship had been dissolved from the moment my name appeared on the list of those punished because of *La Dolce Vita*. Years later, when I began to hold important posts, Pepín became warm and affectionate with me again.

Several experiences of this kind made me realize that the concept of friendship had lost all meaning in Cuba, that unwritten but powerful laws had undermined and shattered its legitimacy. I met many people who, for political reasons, had been pushed to one side and forgotten by their former friends, and I saw others who were sought after and flattered for the same political reasons. I witnessed hypocrisy, disloyalty, and treachery, and I knew of countless betrayals motivated by cowardice or political opportunism. In Cuba denunciation is considered a revolutionary merit, and is rewarded and noted as an honor in the personal dossier of the informer.

The daily occurrence of events like these has caused a deep-rooted lack of confidence in the minds of Cubans, who trust no one—friend, colleague, or even relative. Political fear inhibits and falsifies all human relationships.

This sad reality did not prevent me from feeling and showing esteem toward many people or keep me from knowing when I was esteemed in return. But I grew accustomed to not expecting too much from anybody, and I limited myself to sharing moments of leisure with those who offered me some human warmth. I never believed in these people politically, and I think I could count the sincere revolutionaries I met on the fingers of one hand.

I quickly learned how mistaken I had been about Octavio Medina. Three or four weeks after his nomination, he already showed his true personality. He was a certified accountant and he had solid experience in the sugar industry, but these qualifications, instead of benefiting him, worked against him, since they tended to lure him into proud, obstinate behavior.

My efficient information network did not take very long to warn me again: "Be careful. Medina wants to screw you. It seems he's Raimundo's ally and wants to stab you in the back." By this time, the advice came as no surprise.

Medina in person and Mayans, with Raimundo as his agent, focused their efforts against me through the *nomenklatura* process.

This was a crucial time for me. I had to move very cautiously, protect myself from my two detractors, and try to make them fall victim to their own limitations. Without intending to, I found myself totally involved in a struggle for power that for me meant much more. If I did not respond to Raimundo's and Medina's attacks, I was accepting the possibility that at any moment I could be dismissed through the *nomenklatura* process, which in turn meant losing all the ground I had gained and giving up my plan to escape.

Before I had time to figure out a way to fight back, my conflict with MININT had an unexpected resolution. Certain of Mayans's backing, Raimundo had been overconfident and carried his campaign to extremes. Not satisfied with his conniving inside the ministry, he'd carried his accusations against me in a report to Alfredo Menéndez, chief of the department of the Central Committee in charge of MINAZ.

But his plan had backfired. The officials at the department had consulted with Torralba, who, aware of the malicious intent of these accusations, spoke personally to the leadership at MININT. Soon afterward Raimundo suddenly disappeared from the ministry. I learned this from my information network, since Torralba never spoke to me about the matter.

I also stopped worrying about the guiding hand behind the plot. Accustomed to sniffing out ill winds, Mayans retreated immediately and did not lift a finger to help the man who had been his tool. My path was now cleared, I thought. Held back by fear and his own opportunism, I was sure Mayans would not dare try to harm me again, at least not for a long time.

The situation with Medina also seemed to be settled in a way that was favorable to me. His troublemaking had not been confined to me alone. He'd imprudently attacked the other deputy ministers, who in turn openly criticized the quality of his work. His own problems led to his failure.

Even so, early in 1975 an incident occurred that showed me that the end of my stay at MINAZ was close at hand. The problem originated with the capital investment plan for 1976–1980. According to Fidel's projections, sugar prices on the world market would stay at around 25 cents a pound for the next five years, and on that basis JUCEPLAN prepared the five-year investment plan for the country. But it was my opinion, and the opinion of other officials, that Fidel's calculations were too optimistic. Foreseeing possible fluctuations in supply and demand, I prepared a rather conservative capital investment plan for that five-year period, although I made sure the plan wasn't *too* conservative, in light of the quantitative rule that I knew would guide those who reviewed it.

At first Medina raised no objections to my plan. But some days later, at a private meeting with Lage, he repudiated it and accused me of not having incorporated all his suggestions. In its place he proposed another plan that was much more ambitious.

This placed me in an embarrassing position not only with the minister but with the entire ministry, since Medina took pleasure in publicizing the matter throughout the building. MINAZ finally sent JUCEPLAN an investment plan completely different from the one I had prepared.

A few months later, in mid-1975, sugar prices dropped to 15 cents a pound, which heightened the already critical situation at JUCEPLAN. The sum of the projected expenditures calculated by each agency was triple the total currency that would supposedly come into the country, even if sugar had stayed at 25 cents.

And so in July 1975, Fidel ordered JUCEPLAN to prepare a high-priority study in order to readjust the national plan to the new economic conditions. The meetings went on for more than a week, many of them with Fidel's participation. He was evidently alarmed, apparently forgetting his own optimistic predictions. In his usual temper tantrums, he discharged his rage at everyone around him. There was an outpouring of recriminations and insults toward those who had "imagined that Cuba was a wealthy country and that resources grew on trees."

His irritation with the officials at JUCEPLAN, whom he accused of being "unrealistic," led him to name a commission headed by Osmany Cienfuegos whose purpose was to revise the 1976–1980 quinquennial plan and prepare a new one.

The commission's judgment would be a double-edged sword for me. If it approved Medina's plan, he would be sure to discredit me further. If it rejected his plan, my future looked even worse, since the wounded pride of a Socialist administrator turns him into a vindictive beast. This line of reasoning led me to conclude that it was healthier for me to take the initiative and change jobs before it was too late.

AN APPEARANCE OF DEMOCRACY

The *nomenklatura* process was only one of the many provisions of the secret Cuba–USSR 1972 accords that were beginning to be implemented in 1974. The Soviets were most concerned with the restructuring of the Cuban government, party, and economy. The USSR was insistent that the Cuban administration be recast according to its rigidly hierarchical model. As evidenced by the specificity of the *nomenklatura*, the Soviets put great stock in precise titles reflective of sharply defined responsibilities, an attitude as unfamiliar as snow to the revolutionary leadership.

Nevertheless, a group of Soviet-trained Cuban economists, men like Humberto Pérez, then president of JUCEPLAN, and José "Cheo" Acosta Santana, all associated with Raúl Castro, were grouped together after the accords to work in secret as the Committee to Establish the System of Planning and Direction in the Economy (SPDE). These "experts" strove gamely for many months to hammer out the new system, which was made public in late 1974.

Based on economic reforms in effect in the Soviet Union since 1965, the committee's guidelines for economic management were hugely complex and would be deeply irritating to the Revolutionary Government, from Fidel down.

Throughout the government, leaders accustomed to discharging their duties in a manner after Fidel's example found themselves confronted with unfathomable new demands for statistical analyses, detailed report-writing, and the application of formulae and models well beyond their comprehension or patience. Material incentives to production—bonuses, rewards, prizes, and the like—were to be gradually introduced. But most offensive to the individual chiefs of national ministries and agencies was the decentralization of authority. All enterprises, from agriculture to heavy industry production, were now going to be independent, at least theoretically.

Although every executive warmly endorsed this reorganization, they all resented it and worked surreptitiously to undermine it. Thus, unimportant or marginal enterprises such as local pizzerias and movie theaters were allowed to operate under provincial control. But the bases of real economic power, such as sugar mills, were kept under effective central control by the simple exercise of the ministries' budgetary powers. The administrators of these installations soon realized that their capital programs, indeed their continued existence, were contingent upon pleasing their superiors at MINAZ. Whatever the Soviets' expectations for their reforms, the revolutionary leadership, starting with Fidel, effectively resisted any true changes in business as usual.

The reformation of the Cuban government also had the propaganda aim of institutionalizing the appearance of democracy. Its essential feature was the establishment of the so-called People's Power Government, with local and provincial assemblies and, above them, the National Assembly. Now Cuba would have Socialist elections and could not be accused of being under one-man rule. Fidel also decided to subdivide Cuba from six provinces into fourteen, which he believed would make the country more manageable.

The result was an increase of bureaucrats. At each level, the number of officials went from six to fourteen, far more than were needed.

Many of the domestic reforms that grew out of the 1972 secret accords were only petty annoyances to Fidel. He continued to control the Cuban economy totally. And although he and his leaders chafed at the cumbersome controls of Soviet-style economic decision-making, the overall effect of the changes was to institutionalize Fidel's hold on power. A self-perpetuating Socialist system was at last in place.

By contrast, in the sphere of international relations, Fidel was now much less independent. My first direct measure of Cuba's new fealty to Moscow had come with Leonid Brezhnev's visit to the island in early 1974. I was ashamed for Cuba at the adulatory tone of the First Secretary's press reception. Typical of the gushing flattery I read and saw everywhere was this ecstatic copy in the pages of the magazine *Bohemia*: "The political significance of the event has no parallel in the history of the nation," *Bohemia* enthused. "Never before in Cuba has there been such a demonstration of solidarity, joy, admiration and affection, in homage to a visitor from other lands."

Fidel himself had been every bit as effusive at a rally in Brezhnev's honor held in the Plaza. "Our people gather in huge and enthusiastic crowds to express to you, *Compañero* Brezhnev, and to the Party and Government officials who accompany you," said Fidel, "our feelings of friendship, affection and brotherhood for the great Soviet people and for the heroic Party that under the leadership of the immortal Lenin carried out the first Socialist revolution in the history of the human race."

Then I observed Fidel close up at a Soviet Embassy reception talking with Brezhnev. His mien was significantly altered. For the first time ever, I saw Fidel behave discreetly and with restraint. His laughter was controlled. He walked slowly. He spoke calmly. In fact, he did nothing to attract attention to himself, behaving humbly, an extraordinary posture for Fidel in his own country.

The joint communiqué of February 2, 1974, had summed up the new USSR-Cuban relationship. Both heads of state expressed their "full unanimity of ideas regarding the current world situation and the foreign policy obligations of Socialist states." In other words, Fidel was publicly keeping his end of the bargain.

Privately, however, Fidel later advanced a different view of the episode. According to what he told the Cuban leadership, it was the Soviet Union that had aligned itself with *his* foreign policy!

For Fidel, the most personally distasteful provision in the secret accords was the agreed-upon Conference of Communist Parties of Latin America and the Caribbean, which was finally held in Havana in June 1975. The universal symbol of violent revolutionary struggle, the conference was a humiliation he had managed to delay for three years. The mere fact that the Cuban Communist Party was even speaking to the members of parties Fidel had historically vituperated and scorned was an insult to him. Even worse was that the conference unanimously approved a document that maintained positions diametrically opposed to the proclamations made under his direction at the Tricontinental Conference and OLAS in 1967.

This final document demonstrated once again Fidel's acqui-escence to Soviet wishes in foreign policy. It stated that armed insurrection—that is, guerrilla warfare—was no longer the prin-cipal objective of the most progressive groups, who now had to support Communist parties working toward development of the proletarian struggle within each country's political system. And not all democratic or dictatorial governments in Latin America would be enemies; from now on it was convenient to go along with the "nationalist" position of some of these regimes. For some time to come, Fidel's relations with Latin America would assume a diplomatic character.

On the other hand, Cuba's military leadership was growing restive. Exhaustively trained and constantly alert to the U.S. invasion that never materialized, the armed forces were also filled with young officers who had had no opportunity to ad-vance their careers and prestige in actual combat. Taken to-gether with Fidel's own revolutionary ambitions, these factors dictated some sort of action, and Africa was now Fidel's target.

I did not know in the summer of 1975 that Cuba was getting involved in Angola. I was so consumed by my job at the Sugar Ministry and by my attempts to avoid my enemies there that I did not pay attention to the fact that some workers were disap-pearing. They had been summoned by the military committees and immediately mobilized without being told of their destination.

Such a summons was a normal occurrence for Cuban men. For one reason or another we were called routinely and asked if we would fight for the liberation of other countries. Of course the answer was always yes. But now the recruits—most of them black and mulatto at the beginning of the war—were instantly sent to secret camps.

When word spread that something serious was afoot, those who tried to make excuses suffered stern government reprisals. They were publicly dishonored at general assemblies at their workplaces, where the mass of workers were forced to show disapproval by insulting them. Then they lost their jobs, and if they belonged to the party they were immediately expelled. It was through cases like these that the people—and I—learned of Cuba's military inter-vention in Angola, and from then on there were no more excuses.

Draftees accepted the call to leave for Angola without pro-test, and they fought beside Angolan troops not so much because of a true internationalist or revolutionary spirit but because they had to survive, on the battlefield and in their own country.

Cuban reservists were not only forced to fight in a foreign country; together with regular army troops they also became the main protagonists in the war. Returning soldiers told stories about the lack of aggressiveness in Agostinho Neto's Angolan soldiers, who were ready to surrender or retreat at the slightest setback.

No casualty statistics were ever published, but thousands of Cuban families went into mourning as a result of the war. And they did not even have the consolation of burying their dead. According to rules established by the Cuban government, the dead were buried "in the country where, with their blood, they had watered the seed of liberty." In fact, the return of the corpses to Cuba was prohibited in order to avoid the negative repercussions that the burials would have had on the morale of the people—and on world opinion.

The same situation was repeated in 1978, when Cuba intervened at the request of the Ethiopian government to stop the invading armies of Somalia. The attack was quickly repelled by the Cuban forces, and later on they were reduced to a minimum.

But that was not the case in Angola. Here, Fidel fell into a strategic trap similar to the one Vietnam became for the United States. The Cuban presence in Angola, which Fidel had claimed in private would last no more than a year, has lasted from 1975 until today and has become absolutely necessary for the survival of the Angolan government. Fidel has stated that Cuban troops will withdraw from Angola only if the Angolan government officially requests them to do so, but if for any reason the request was made and the Angolan revolution failed as a result, how would Fidel justify to the Cuban people the death of so many sons in a lost cause?

This situation affected me emotionally and practically. I was deeply saddened by the Cuban lives sacrificed only because of Fidel's ambitions to be a world figure. And, as a member of the reserve army, I could be mobilized at any moment for two years, which would certainly jeopardize my plan. Fortunately, as long as my work at MINAZ was in such a key economic position, I would not be drafted.

Since I had to do all I could to maintain that protection, I also had to continue my war with the system. My next front would be the most dangerous: my evaluation for the *nomenklatura*.

THE DREAM MERCHANT

A final major provision of the 1972 agreements between Cuba and the USSR was the call for a Cuban Communist Party Congress, a rite, common to all Socialist states, at which progress of the recent past is reviewed and exalted and the goals of the next national five-year plan are presented for ceremonial ratification by delegates to the Congress. As a nonmember of the party, I could not attend the working sessions of the Congress, but via the press, public and secret documents, and detailed discussions I held with those who were privileged to join the meetings, I was able to piece together a detailed portrait of what transpired behind closed doors.

This information was vital to me. Even though I expected to leave MINAZ, I needed to know what its real programmed goals were for the coming years in case I remained at the ministry. Also, it was after this Congress that I would face my first *nomenklatura* evaluation. I needed to be alert to any changes or alterations approved at the Congress that might affect my own situation.

Another consideration was the possibility of any change in the mechanisms and procedures for joining the party. If the rules were to be different from those I'd encountered in my quarrel with Benigno Iglesias at ICAIC, I had to be aware of them.

It was not enough simply to be bloodless and calculating, as I had been since the incident with Marielle's koala bear. I had always to be prepared, aware of any abrupt changes in the rules of the game—*nomenklatura*, party membership, and other procedures that could threaten my always precarious foothold. The Congress in its secret deliberations might generate some surprises.

At work I accepted and implemented without reflection every directive handed to me, knowing that most of what I was told to do was counterproductive or plainly wrong. No matter. If it was noon and Fidel said it was midnight, for me it was midnight.

I had no wry inner reaction, for example, to the tub-thumping and blare of the pre-Congress propaganda drive. A single theme dominated. On huge fences along Havana's avenues and all the provincial highways, on thousands of posters distributed throughout the island, in pamphlets, newspapers, and magazines, the same emblem invariably appeared. It was a gigantic number one. In its center were a Cuban flag and a red banner held high over a stylized crowd of people carrying raised machetes and rifles. In the upper part of the numeral was the single word *Congreso* and in the lower part, the initials *PCC*. It was the graphic representation of the December 1975 First Congress's historic import, "the most transcendental event of the revolution," as the faithful referred to it.

The center of this seismic occasion was to be the old Rosita de Hornedo Theater, a few blocks from Maggie's family's house in Miramar. The largest such facility in the country, it had been totally renovated and renamed the Karl Marx Theater for the Congress; later it became an officially designated national monument. The 3,116 delegates and invitees to the meetings, including members of 85 foreign delegations, nearly filled the theater to capacity.

Among the foreign leaders of Socialism attending were Mikhail A. Suslov, the Soviet Union's leading ideologue; Todor Zhivkov from Bulgaria; János Kádár from Hungary; and leading Communists from the important parties in Latin America and other countries.

Maggie and I had front-row seats from her parents' house as we watched the many dilapidated mansions of the Miramar area undergo refurbishment for the foreigners who would occupy them during the Congress. The dirty and discolored Malecón was cleaned up as well. Everywhere the invited guests might wander was replastered and repainted. In fact, there had never been so much quality paint available in my recollection. Those in charge of distributing it at the Ministry of Construction had plenty left over to thin with water and then sell to their black market connections at 20 pesos a gallon.

Suddenly, I saw Havana's shops stocked with imported clothing, electrical equipment, and cosmetics. Food markets sold a whole range of Socialist canned goods. Maggie and I noticed that the restaurant menus were diversified and the lighting was improved on the busiest streets. New trash cans were distributed in our building. Trees were planted along the avenues. Buildings that had stood half-finished for years were completed. Empty lots were turned into parks. The activity was unceasing. On several Sundays, I joined mobilizations by my Defense Committee to fill in the potholes or to do maintenance work in the parks. An effort was made to build an elegant facade in a hurry, to acquire a varnish of beauty and prosperity to impress the foreign guests. "If only they held a Party Congress every year," I heard people say.

My first priority was to read a copy of the 1,200-page report that had been distributed to each delegate for study. I doubt that even the most fervent party members had the sustained interest to consider fully this mountain of statistics and tiresomely repetitive discourse. But I avidly pored over every page of the copy given to me by one of the delegates.

Then there was Fidel's 243-page Central Report, which he read for interminable hours at the fully televised opening session of the Congress. I watched the entire speech. First came Fidel's historical analysis of the revolution. The rest of his report was divided into several chapters explaining the economic and social development of Cuba since 1959. I heard Fidel point out the considerable increases in electrical power output, construction, steel production, production of herbicides, textiles, footwear, pasta, beer, and baby food. He read pages devoted to progress in education, public health, and social security.

For all the revolution's alleged advances, only in this last area did its achievements have concrete reality for the man on the street. Human beings can't wear steel or eat fertilizer. Scarcity remained the central fact of Cuban life. The paper was a compendium of hollow victories and rewarmed promises of future development.

At the time, my single interest in the report was to memorize its many assertions and disclosures in order to understand Cuba's situation as Fidel saw it. That most of the document's boasts were based on cooked numbers and its projections purely a matter of fancy did not matter to me. Later, however, I compared what Fidel said in this report with his past pronouncements on production.

In a 1969 speech Fidel had said, "In six years time we may

possibly find ourselves first in the quality of food. Quality also means quantity. That is, there will no longer be limitations on quantity, and the quality will be better."

Rice is one of the most important components of the Cuban diet. In 1968, Fidel had promised "a third of a pound daily" for each person. Now he was blaming the droughts for his inability to keep his word. Meanwhile, the Cuban people continued with their four-pound-a-month ration.

Despite his previous promises about meat, the weekly beef ration of three quarters of a pound in Havana and one quarter of a pound in the provinces was exactly the same in 1975 as it had been in 1968.

Cuba, the country of sugar and tobacco, would continue to enjoy a monthly ration of four pounds of sugar and three packs of cigarettes. But the worst was that in 1968, Fidel had pledged that 225,000 housing units would be built between 1973 and 1975. Now he declared that "between 1959 and 1975 just over 200,000 houses were built."

Undaunted, Fidel in his 1975 Central Report went on to make new promises. The grandest pledge was for an annual average rise of 6 percent in economic development. "This is not an exaggerated figure," Fidel insisted. "This means that in 1980 we will have a gross social product thirty-four percent higher than in 1975. In only eleven years, the country's economy will have doubled." It was clear that the "dream merchant" had not learned from, and in fact had ignored, one of the most repeated phrases of his speechmaking: "This revolution has been characterized by facts, not by promises."

Fidel did insert several *mea culpas* into his report, a survey of mistakes entitled "Errors We Have Made," which was a final repudiation of Ché Guevara's economic principles. Among these mistaken methods, according to Fidel, were "the elimination of all commodity forms and the abolition of charges and payments between units of the state sector." He also mentioned other erroneous directions, such as ignoring fundamental economic relationships and the failure "to take account of remuneration according to work." Although he never explicitly acknowledged it, Fidel was accepting blame for not being Marxist-Leninist in his thinking.

He also confessed that "we were not always capable of discovering the problems in time, of avoiding mistakes, of overcoming omissions and of acting absolutely in keeping with the working methods that should guide the direction and the functioning of the Party."

On this point, the pristine sanctity of the party, Fidel waxed fervent.

"The Party is a synthesis of everything," he emphasized. "Within it, the dreams of all the revolutionaries in our history are synthesized. Within it, the ideas, principles and strength of the Revolution assume concrete form. Within it, our individual-isms disappear and we learn to think in terms of the collective. It is our educator, our leader and our vigilant conscience when we ourselves are unable to detect our errors, our defects and our limitations. Within it, we are closely knit together, each one of us is a spartan soldier of the fairest of causes, all of us together forming an invincible giant. Within it are guaranteed our ideas, our experiences, the behests of our martyrs, the continuity of our work, the interests of the people, the future of our homeland, and our indestructible ties with the proletarian builders of a new world all over the world."

Fidel's final theme in his Central Report was integrity. "As a revolutionary principle, *compañeros*," he said, "self-criticism will always be one thousand times better than complacency. And self-humiliation will always be preferable to self-praise!"

To complete his idea he added, "What does history show? That men have had and abused power. Even in revolutionary processes, certain men acquire extraordinary power, especially in this phase, especially in the early years. . . . In this phase that all of us lived through in the revolutionary process, the dangers were great: the danger of vanity, the danger of conceit, the danger of deification, the habit of having authority, the habit of having power, the exercise of power. How many risks are in-volved? And how many errors have been committed throughout the history of humanity because of them!"

Hours later, Fidel and the full membership of the Central Committee presided over a public rally in the Plaza de la Revolución where I saw the second act of the play performed, this time with the public as audience.

"If in the Karl Marx Theater the Congress of the Party met, here in the Plaza de la Revolución the Congress of the People meets to express its support of the decisions reached by the Congress," said Fidel to thunderous applause. "But if we vote there we should vote here, too. If we discuss there and approve all the proposals, here, before all the people, we should also vote and ask our people if it supports or does not support the decisions of the Congress."

The Plaza crowd—which was only vaguely and incompletely aware of the decisions—automatically erupted into applause and shouts of "Yes!"

"Here we can also ask if anyone is opposed."

Shouts of "No!"

"Then we unanimously approve the decisions of the Congress."

The wild finale of universal approval is the standard conclusion to Fidel's speeches. I recall one such day in the early 1970s when Fidel roused a crowd in the Plaza with a particularly grand speech on Cuban solidarity with Chile. He told the audience that he knew Cubans would give their blood for Chile. What he asked was that each citizen provisionally donate a pound of their sugar ration to the Chileans.

The crowd responded on cue with its boisterous approval, but as Maggie and I were walking home with the rest of Fidel's audience, we heard someone bitterly commenting on the new sacrifice he'd been cheering only minutes before.

"What was that sonuvabitch thinking of?" he asked those around him. "Bye-bye, my pound of sugar. I'll never see you again." And he didn't.

More frequently, the people's disaffection manifests itself in humor. Two of the more sardonic jokes that emerged anonymously after the First Party Congress and spread very quickly by word of mouth reflect the people's true feelings about the decisions of the Congress that had been "unanimously" approved at the mass rally.

In the first tale, the members of the Politburo are traveling with Fidel by plane to the eastern provinces of the country. One of the officials goes to a window and throws out a twenty-peso bill.

"Why did you do that?" asks Fidel, very surprised.

"Because with that money at least one Cuban will eat."

"Then I'll throw out two ten-peso notes so that two Cubans can eat," says another traveler.

"And I'll throw out four five-peso bills so that four Cubans can eat," says a third.

Fidel, with his higher economic consciousness, speaks up and says: "The most rational thing would be to throw out twenty one-peso bills so that twenty Cubans can eat."

Just then the pilot, who has been listening to the conversation, shakes his head and shouts to the passengers: "Why don't you all throw yourselves out the window so that all the Cubans can eat?"

The other joke, which was also very popular, went as follows:
Fidel is giving a speech to the people in the Plaza de la Revolución after the First Congress has ended. When he finishes speaking, he presents to the public his special guest, Superman, who also gives a moving address on the marvels of Socialism. When he finishes, Superman says good-bye to Fidel and to the people to return to the United States. He raises his arms toward the sky, gives a little jump, but doesn't move.

"You see, *compañeros*, even Superman has his doubts about returning to the belly of the imperialist beast!" shouts Fidel enthusiastically, trying to derive some political advantage from the situation.

"You're wrong, Fidel," answers Superman. "I can't fly with this crowd hanging on to my cape."

AN ENCOUNTER WITH THE PARTY

It was at about the time of the First Party Congress—ten long years since I'd returned to Cuba—that my plan of patience and alert discipline seemed about to pay off. Around the middle of 1975, I learned that I was to lead a MINAZ delegation to Eastern Europe, to visit sugar-production facilities and, ostensibly, to absorb from my counterparts in the Eastern bloc a better command of the new economics then being grudgingly applied for the first time in Cuba.

Immediately, I set about exploring the possibilities of Maggie's taking a similar trip at the same time. It was a hopelessly premature opportunity; Maggie was still too junior an official at the Culture Council to qualify for foreign travel on such short notice. Nevertheless, I kept postponing my departure through the second half of 1975, trying to buy time for a miracle. Finally, in September, I had to fly off in bitter frustration for a working tour of Czechoslovakia, East Germany, and Poland.

The weeks-long trip was entirely uneventful, mostly wasted

in idle conversation and toasts during long banquets, except for a disconsolate moment at the East Berlin side of the Wall. Standing alone, I allowed myself one fleeting recollection of a carefree vacation trip to West Berlin in the early 1960s and of the youthful mournfulness I'd felt at my first sight of the Berlin Wall. Many years later, viewing the same gray barrier from the inside out, I just barely checked a spasm of shuddering despair.

Still, upon my return to Cuba just before the Congress, I took heart that there would be more such travel opportunities. Meanwhile, I had to keep attending to the cultivation of my Communist revolutionary image, work that now brought me to my first encounter with the *nomenklatura* process.

I was well prepared by the secret documents of the Congress to handle the initial phase of the procedure, my political evaluation. Knowing generally what to expect, I then made a discreet study of my appointed interviewer, Godwald Reina. My sources indicated Reina was a typically mediocre party functionary with the usual consuming lust for power. Furthermore, I had to expect him to be influenced by Raimundo's mischief of the preceding year; Godwald Reina was probably going to be ill-disposed toward me.

My interview appointment was set for 1:00 P.M. at the old Comodoro Hotel in Miramar, on a sultry winter day in early 1976. Around the hotel, then the provisional offices of the Central Committee bureaucracy, were several asbestos- and cement-roofed sheds that were used as offices because of lack of space inside. Godwald was waiting for me in one of these airless, stifling enclosures, sitting sweating behind an old desk on which a sheaf of papers, my political file, was clipped together.

He began the interview with the customary questions about my education, my work experience, details of my relations with the union and the party at MINAZ, my participation in the activities of the Defense Committees, in voluntary labor, and in the clandestine struggle.

"*Compañero* Llovio, we must pause now to clarify certain issues," he said suddenly, interrupting the long questionnaire. His voice had taken on an authoritarian tone. "We, the party, believe that there are certain aspects of your life that stand out because they are difficult to understand in a revolutionary. We cannot understand what induced you to leave Cuba in 1958, abandoning the insurrectionary struggle. And we cannot understand your residence in France for so many years, even after the triumph of our revolution. And we certainly cannot understand your marriage to an heiress, when the most natural action in a revolutionary would have been to fall in love with a girl of humble background. It is unacceptable that while our people engaged in a fight to the death to survive only ninety miles from imperialism and suffered the blows of an unjust economic blockade imposed by the United States, you enjoyed the comfort and abundance of a consumer society. And what is more, on your return to Cuba you did not hesitate to become part of the deplorable conduct of a few misguided men who obliged our Revolutionary Government to take drastic measures."

He droned on and on with this nonsense, the unmistakable product of Raimundo's intrigues. I listened to him calmly. By now I was used to that string of dogmatic sentences that revolutionaries use with so much pleasure, especially those who carry the "card," the members of the party most interested in showing their proletarian facade. Apparently, Godwald confused my silence with fear. Sure of the crushing effect of his words, he observed, "Undoubtedly your bourgeois origin has weighed heavily on your political trajectory. While you were born on linen sheets, thousands of Cuban children, children of poverty-stricken *campesinos* or the unfortunate marginalized classes, died of hunger or terrible diseases. While you swam at the best private beaches, the poor, the blacks had to sneak into the ocean near the reefs. While you enjoyed the pleasures of the most exclusive clubs, or the toys you received on Epiphany, while you studied in the best schools in the country, many children roamed the streets naked and barefoot for lack of anything better to do, without receiving even the most elementary education. You must recognize that such a background is a burden for any revolutionary."

"Look, much of what you've said is true," I interjected to short-circuit Godwald's speech. Then I launched into my obligatory round of revolutionary self-criticism. I told Godwald of my guilty feelings for having left the unfinished revolution in 1958; my later shame for living in Paris in the early 1960s while the Cuban people were fighting the Yanqui economic blockade; that I was foolishly self-indulgent to marry a French noblewoman; and, finally, that my involvement with *La Dolce Vita* was regrettable hedonism at a time I should have joined with the other revolutionaries in the struggle against imperialism. But my personal list of shortcomings stopped in 1967; for the past nine years, I had been a perfect revolutionary. Exemplary.

After conceding my past errors, I backtracked to one of Godwald's huffy observations in order to skewer him. "There is one point," I said, "on which I sincerely disagree with you. Your judgments concerning the determining influence that a privileged background can have on a revolutionary seem somewhat exaggerated to me. Those judgments would also pertain to the Commander in Chief, and according to your hypothesis it would be necessary to allow that—"

"What are you saying?" he interrupted brusquely, shooting up from his swivel chair as if he had bounced on a spring. "That shows disrespect!"

"Calm down and I'll explain what I've just said. If you get so excited it would be better for me to call Alfredo Menéndez and discuss the matter with him," I told him without changing expression, knowing that I had pushed the right button for stopping any party official. Menéndez was then head of the Central Committee's sugar department, and my investigation had indicated Reina wanted Menéndez's job.

"It is not necessary to call Alfredo. Go on," he murmured in a lower tone while he wiped away the large beads of perspiration running down his face.

"It's very simple, Godwald," I said. "You accuse me, among other things, of being born between linen sheets. According to your line of reasoning, I would think that the Commander in Chief must have been born between linen sheets edged in gold. His life must have been more comfortable than mine, since his family was much richer than mine. The schools he attended were as bourgeois as mine, or more so. According to your theory, the Commander in Chief must also be damaged by his background, isn't that so?"

"Well," he stammered in reply, "you haven't understood me correctly. Or perhaps I haven't expressed myself clearly. I've had so many interviews every day recently. It . . . it isn't easy. Of course . . . I mean . . . everybody comes from a bourgeois background. Even I."

Godwald smelled the possibility that he'd made a mistake, and he wasn't going to risk further confrontation with me. By the end of the interview I was convinced that I would pass my political evaluation with no difficulty.

For the balance of 1976, I was absorbed in my struggle at MINAZ. My successful interview with Godwald did not deter my enemies. Once the Politburo Commission of Osmany Cienfuegos rejected the Medina-Lage five-year capital investment plan in favor of one very similar to mine, Octavio Medina intensified his attacks on me. I remained as prudently aloof as I could, but the deputy minister for the economy was an implacable foe. I decided to talk to Diocles Torralba. He listened very carefully while I told him how my situation in MINAZ had been worsening to a point that the only solution was to get a transfer out of the ministry. I knew he would help me.

Here, the *nomenklatura* presented one potential difficulty. The Central Committee Party Secretariat would have to approve my transfer to a new position, which meant a second scrutiny of my record. I had no interest in opening the past again, and I was concerned that Medina might try to interfere with my political evaluation in the party cell, another possible complication to my transfering out of MINAZ.

Luckily, Diocles Torralba's special interest in my circumstance made Minister Lage quite tractable. He even offered me an alternative position at MINAZ, understanding my reasons for not wishing to work around Deputy Minister Medina any longer.

This conversation, according to the rules of the hierarchy, was preceded by a meeting with Medina himself. I informed him officially of my every complaint against him, an important part of correct revolutionary behavior and a necessary prelude to repeating these objections again to Medina, in the presence of Minister Lage.

As it turned out, Medina emerged from our confrontation with a wider reputation as a refractory troublemaker and chronic malcontent. On January 31, 1977, I formally withdrew from the ministry and set forth on what would prove to be the final and by far the most perilous stage of my secret struggle to escape revolutionary Cuba.

ON THE PYRAMID OF POWER

Among my new job opportunities I considered a return to ICAIC, where Alfredo Guevara would have welcomed me and political strife was minimal, but the chances for foreign travel at ICAIC were rare. The State Committee on Economic Collaboration (CECE) also had a position open, and I knew that frequent foreign trips were a standard perquisite there. CECE, however, was then run by Héctor Rodríguez Llompart, a member of the Central Committee and an exemplar of scheming opportunism. He'd surrounded himself with executives who struggled constantly among themselves for travel privileges and permanent foreign assignments. CECE was just the sort of place I had to avoid.

A third, more interesting opportunity was suggested to me by Raulito Roa Kourí, then an adviser to Carlos Rafael Rodríguez and a close friend as well of Francisco García Valls, minister-president of the newly established State Finance Committee (CEF).

The Finance Committee, created in November 1976 as the last of the new governmental agencies under Cuba's reorganization, was to be one of the most important economic agencies of the country. Under the new economic system, CEF would prepare Cuba's annual budget according to the current economic plan and then control all expenditures in the budget through the National Bank. It was empowered to establish the new taxes to be levied against the various state enterprises. CEF was in charge of Cuba's so-called invisible currency, both the "soft" money of the Socialist nations and the spendable hard Western currencies necessary to cover the expenses of Cuba's foreign representatives, including diplomats, government officials, and executives.

Most important, in a high-ranking job in such an important committee I would be guaranteed trips abroad. As a result, I listened eagerly as Raulito explained that García Valls needed a top assistant to get the new committee up and running.

But working at CEF also entailed significant risks. In 1966, Fidel had summarily abolished its predecessor organization, the old Hacienda Ministry (or Finance Agency), calling it in his "idealistic" phase an "inoperative, bureaucratic, and unnecessary" agency. For the eleven years since, Cuba had had no budget, no organized economy, no system of financial relationships at all. This was the way Fidel preferred to run the country, and I could not assume that the Soviet-mandated committee, even though it was to report directly to Fidel via Osmany Cienfuegos, was going to be any more popular with him than the Hacienda Ministry had been.

What is more, CEF's authority to plan and implement Cuba's financial affairs was a blow to the power and influence of other agencies, such as JUCEPLAN, which formerly had independent authority to map and direct the economy, and the National Bank, which had been solely responsible for dispersing funds throughout the bureaucracy. These and other agencies now regarded CEF as a usurper and treated it with jealousy and rancor. Together with my worries over Fidel's attitude, I wondered if the official animosity might quickly reduce the Finance Committee to the abused stepchild of the Cuban bureaucracy.

My chief consideration, then, would be the strength of the man in charge at CEF. And here again I had reason for concern. García Valls, whose work was so important for the state, had no powerful protector as I had in Diocles Torralba; in fact he had been named to his job for want of any other qualified executive, at Carlos Rafael Rodríguez's suggestion to Fidel. More important to me, García Valls was an old-line PSP Youth member, which implied a mind-set deformed by rigid party discipline and a personality accustomed to fear and denunciation. I remembered very well how the PSP members had fallen upon one another in furious denunciations in the aftermath of the sectarian crisis, and I knew that I could expect García Valls to support me only so long as his loyalty to a subordinate created no threat to his own position.

Another complicating factor at CEF would be the quality of the staff García Valls was putting together. His principal source of middle-level executive talent and technicians was the Personnel Exchange, a commission recently established by the Politburo to funnel the pool of available bureaucrats to the newly created agencies such as CEF. The idea made some sense, but the person in charge at the Exchange was the remarkably dense Commander Guillermo García, previously noteworthy for his militarization of the 10-million-ton harvest in Oriente. García ineptly allowed the Personnel Exchange to become a repository for the flotsam and jetsam of the revolutionary bureaucracy, a convenient place for agencies to assign their least competent cadres, from which unfortunate executives such as García Valls were forced to select many of their executives and technicians.

And yet, this was no time for faintheartedness on my part. It was now twelve years since I'd trapped myself in Cuba, and six since Maggie and I had been married. I recognized that the Finance Committee post was a gamble, but I was as ready as I was going to be. I had disciplined myself to machinelike emotional neutrality. My mind was an information processor, my thoughts directed entirely to waging the war for survival and escape. I felt certain that I had mastered every intricacy of the real internal politics of the Revolutionary Government, so different in my experience from the revolution's public face.

But I still had much to learn about how devious and petty one had to be to survive in a Communist bureaucracy.

My interview with Francisco García Valls was mostly perfunctory. He was tall, rather heavyset, with a long face and blue eyes that peered unblinkingly from behind the metal-rimmed glasses. His prematurely gray hair and gravely aloof manner made García Valls appear older than he was.

"What I want, Llovio," he said, "is a person I can trust. Someone competent to work directly with me. I need someone who can function as my adviser, my right arm. At first, you would be executive director of my office. After the new organization is complete, you would become chief adviser."

Since we both already seemed to have made up our minds, I had little to say. Nor did García Valls waste words. After going over a few details with me, he ended the conversation with a businesslike summation. "Aside from the recommendations of our mutual friends, including Raulito Roa," he said, "I've received other recommendations. I spoke with José Abrantes, with Alfredo Guevara, and with Diocles Torralba. There'll be no problem. We'll still have to take care of approval from the *nomenklatura*, but I don't think we'll have any difficulties with that. In any event, I'll speak with Alfredo Menéndez at the Central Committee."

My new workplace was located on Obispo Street at the corner of Cuba Street, in the very heart of Old Havana. This area, historically and architecturally the most interesting in the capital, showed signs of neglect everywhere. The old palaces and mansions were in desperate need of repair. The walls of the buildings were dirty and peeling. Many of the balconies and roofs had to be shored up against collapse. The sidewalks were broken, the sewers stopped up, the streets foul-smelling and full of potholes, and the corners blocked by overflowing cans of garbage.

The building for the Finance Committee, chosen by Fidel, had not escaped the general state of disrepair. Its facade was a vague mixture of three different styles, the result of various additions to the original 1930s construction. The interior looked as if it had been through a war. The colors of the wall mosaics were hidden by a mixture of dust and grime. The marble floors were filthy and cracked and the windowpanes were broken. The stairs had partially collapsed; the ceiling was warped into a convex shape. All seven floors of the building were scheduled for complete refurbishing, at an estimated cost of more than a million pesos. But first, fire hoses had to be used to loosen the layers of filth on the floors, and a thorough fumigation was needed. The project produced several fifty-five gallon tanks full of mice and cockroaches.

The seven-story building's deplorable state was a metaphorical echo of what I encountered in CEF's executive corps. Even those who hadn't come from the Exchange—senior administrators such as First Vice-President José Acosta Santana, better known as "Cheo," and Humberto Knight, vice president for administration—were notorious for their corruption and incompetence. Acosta had been a member of SPDE Commission and its specialist in finance, which he'd studied in the USSR. He seemed to know a great deal of financial theory, but his work was disorganized, indecisive, inefficient; Acosta was incapable of holding a firm opinion about anything. His protector was his close friend Humberto Pérez, then President of JUCEPLAN.

Humberto Knight had an even more powerful sponsor. Although Knight had been denounced several times, even by MININT, he always managed to keep his head above water thanks to the help of Carlos Rafael Rodríguez. Knight took very good care of himself in this post. There was never a shortage of fine foods and the best imported liquor at his house, a place that was much sought-after because of his "generosity."

Neither Acosta nor Knight—or hardly any other of CEF's executives except for García Valls—showed much dedication to their new work, so vital to the restructuring of the country's finance system. Perhaps this was just as well; none of them was particularly competent. However, their lack of productivity did create a staggering workload for the rest of us.

At first I was given a narrow office, separated from the minister-president's office by a varnished door eaten away by termites. Our offices lacked almost everything; there were no files, the plywood desks were rickety, and the wooden chairs were uncomfortable. I took these conditions as a first clue to Fidel's overall enthusiasm for his new Finance Committee.

This irritating lack of basic conveniences further complicated my work, which proved to be a good deal more demanding than García Valls had indicated during our first interview. I was his right-hand man. He delegated to me almost complete control of the committee. I had to give orders to the vice-presidents and the director and make sure that everything went smoothly.

The secret documents from the party and the state flooded
my desk every day. I had to digest them in order to know what I
could and couldn't do. In almost all cases I had to advise the
minister-president which path to follow and how to act on the
accords of the Executive Committee of the Council of Ministers,
of which I was the CEF representative.

The information I received daily revealed to me how the
country was doing and where it was going. For my own purposes
I needed to assimilate every detail in order to survive.

But that was not all. I also had to supervise the Soviet
advisers, which was not an easy task. To make them respect me,
I had to employ a delicate mixture of aggressiveness and diplomacy. I had to be forceful but could not go beyond certain limits;
neither could they.

My position at CEF carried with it certain privileges appropriate to rank. I was assigned a late-model Soviet-built Lada to
drive, and I dined everyday with the rest of the senior staff on
fare the average Cuban could obtain only on rare occasions from
the black market. But I scrupulously avoided taking advantage
of the many other privileges my colleagues enjoyed. Quite apart
from not coveting these advantages, I recognized that accepting
them could one day destroy all hopes of escape.

The seventeen-hour workdays García Valls and I routinely
put in at CEF would have precluded much dissolution, anyway.
Finance was a much sterner test of my physical and intellectual
stamina than even the early years at MINAZ, when I was struggling to master the complexities of the sugar industry while
studying for my law degree. However, a major difference between my job at MINAZ and the finance post was the technical
assistance we received from our Soviet advisers. The Soviets'
deep involvement in my daily work was an added complication
to an already difficult life.

One of the most demanding aspects of my work in the Finance Committee was my responsibility for overseeing the Soviet advisers to CEF, with whom I had to have very close
relations. Through its very sophisticated use of such advisers,
Moscow exercised its control of every sector of the Cuban
bureaucracy.

The large scale introduction of nonmilitary Soviet technical
advisers to Cuba began in 1971, and by 1974 they were firmly
entrenched in every sector of the country. Less than three months

after the committee was established, a dozen advisers hand-picked by Soviet Finance Minister Garbuzov and headed by Vassilly Petrovitch Kazeruk, the first deputy minister of finance for the Ukraine, were on hand at CEF.

Kazeruk, who acted as principal adviser to García Valls, proved to be very well informed. When I asked him a question, he answered immediately and with great accuracy. I could see the absolute control he exercised over the others.

Selected CEF administrators were each assigned a Soviet specialist in his field. The adviser's job was to clear away doubts the executive might have, to devise methodology, and to analyze financial information as it was submitted to him. If a disagreement between the Cuban bureaucrat and his Soviet adviser could not be resolved, Kazeruk took up the matter in private, first with me and then with the minister-president. He made every effort not to undermine the Cuban administrator's authority. As a general rule, Kazeruk's advice was accepted, and a few days later García Valls, or one of the vice-presidents, would declare a dispute's resolution as if it were his own decision rather than the result of Kazeruk's intervention.

The Soviets maintained strict discipline. It was inconceivable for them to take liberties beyond those permitted by their superiors, much less dare to criticize individually any measure adopted by a Cuban administrator. Once a week they went to the Soviet Embassy for the regular party meetings, and they frequently exchanged opinions with Soviet advisers at other institutions. At CEF meetings or in councils held jointly with other agencies, the Soviets were always in full agreement regarding every question.

Outside the office, our Soviet advisers socialized only with high-level Cuban officials. We frequently invited them to luxury restaurants or to the Tropicana nightclub, which fascinated them. The Soviets usually invited us to parties at their homes to reciprocate the committee's celebrations of Soviet national holidays.

As a pretext for continual drinking, they liked to make toasts for any reason at all. At first the toasts would be related to political or patriotic themes, but when these were used up they kept going. "To the beauty of the Cuban woman!" "To the pleasures of the tropics!" We Cubans had to eat constantly to remain standing, since each toast required us to drink a whole glass of vodka in one swallow. Throughout these parties, I stuffed myself with butter, the best prescription for counteracting the effects of the vodka.

It was evident to me that these Soviet advisers lived in perpetual fear of conflict, of committing an error. They were meticulously efficient in their work and desperate to obtain the highest evaluation. They knew that although the minister-president signed their evaluations, these documents had to be proposed and prepared by me—and their future depended on their evaluations. As a result, their relations with me were very different from those with the rest of the CEF executives.

The Soviet advisers were well aware that a poor evaluation would mean a return ticket home—and the loss of their very privileged existence, a standard of living they could never maintain in Mother Russia. Technicians from Socialist countries, including the USSR, lived very well in Cuba, in comfortable houses in quiet neighborhoods or large apartments in luxury buildings; in their own countries these same technicians had much smaller and more modest apartments. Special stores were established for them, facilities that gave rise to a fairly widespread business in Cuba. It was very common for them to resell products to Cubans at black market prices and obtain extra income in Cuban currency—the only instance where the advisers strayed from their usual careful behavior. The Revolutionary Government decided to ignore this illegal traffic.

I was in the same position as they were, in relation to my own country, and I watched their behavior carefully. They were the beneficiaries of fifty years of wisdom about how to stay out of trouble within the system. And so I never took liberties beyond those permitted by my superiors and never criticized any measures adopted by them. The Soviets and I had come from different countries, but the same rules applied—and I was more determined than ever to master them.

MININT STRIKES AGAIN

My several episodes with rivals as I struggled to survive on the power pyramid—from my confrontation with Benigno Iglesias at ICAIC through the troubles I encountered from Raimundo and the truculent Octavio Medina at MINAZ—had taught me the necessity of an active strategy in dealing with potential enemies. Like everyone else, I had to assume that the people around me were all pursuing some ulterior scheme to use or to destroy me. This sense that each day was a life-and-death chess game for me informed my handling of the wily Captain Erasmo, whose advent at the Finance Committee was a prelude to the most fantastically complex bureaucratic warfare imaginable.

Erasmo at CEF, like Raimundo at MINAZ, was our man from MININT; that is, he was the Finance Committee's officially designated monitor. His real name was Miguel Camineiro; MININT officers work under aliases, new ones for each agency they are assigned to. In each state agency these operatives ferret out the disloyal, remain alert to any plotting—especially possible CIA activity—and are very watchful of those Cubans with foreign connections, whether family or friends. They are zealous in all facets of their work for good reason; if some spy or traitor emerges to embarrass or harm the revolution, it is MININT that is held responsible.

However, an official as cunning as Captain Erasmo also tries to build a power base in the agency to which he is assigned. It was Erasmo's intention, as I would see, to augment his influence at CEF through an intimate personal knowledge of the staff and his skill at manipulating certain of García Valls's senior executives.

For me Erasmo represented not only MININT, which was my enemy from the days of UMAP and Raimundo's continuation of those false accusations in the Sugar Ministry, but also Mayans, Erasmo's boss, who would do everything he could to get rid of me since I had denounced him.

The saga began almost a month after my arrival at Finance, at one of García Valls's regular 7:00 P.M. organizational meetings. A half hour after the minister-president, other executives, and I had begun our discussions, Humberto Knight staggered in with alcohol on his breath. Humberto was often drunk by this hour. García Valls at the moment was absorbed in a document and didn't notice Knight's condition. But when he finished examining the paper and turned to Knight for his opinion of its content, García Valls discovered the deputy minister in charge of administration and protocol, the General Customs Office, and the Agency for International Insurance sloppy drunk and asleep in his chair.

The minister-president prodded Knight, who came to in a fluster, mumbling through his thick tongue: "Well, uh, I don't know. I mean, uh ... Well, whatever. What do you say?" The meeting was quickly adjourned and all of us, excepting Humberto Knight, were excused.

The next morning I noticed Captain Erasmo as I was inspecting the renovation work on the first floor of the CEF building. "What did you think about Knight being drunk at the meeting last night?" he asked, after affably introducing himself.

"Let's go up to my office, all right?" I answered instantly, registering all over me the sticky touch of Erasmo's spider web.

We rose to the fourth floor in the ancient freight elevator, Erasmo all the while smiling broadly to reveal his full set of even white teeth. His look of affected ease was intended to reassure me of MININT's goodwill. Amused by the patent falseness of this expression, I smiled back down at him.

By Erasmo's first remark I could assume that Humberto Knight was a special interest of his, meaning that MININT had secretly targeted the deputy minister for some reason. In a quick review of those who had attended the meeting, I settled on Leónides Méndez, CEF's party secretary, as Erasmo's likely source of information. The motive, I learned as soon as I could tap my information network, was MININT's disapproval of Knight's wastrel ways—and revenge. Two MININT officials, I was told, had denounced Knight's corruption while he was still head of CAT, the state enterprise that dealt with foreign technical aid. But it was they who had been ultimately punished in the fray, thanks to the intercession of Knight's protector, the powerful Carlos Rafael Rodríguez. Knowing the long memories at MININT and its accustomed ways of squaring old debts, it was easy to imagine these two officials casually questioning their colleague Erasmo about Knight's behavior at CEF, signal enough to the ambitious captain that his personal prospects for advancement might improve in direct ratio to Humberto Knight's problems at Finance.

In my office over coffee, Erasmo communicated a second, equally clear indication of his interest. "You're probably surprised," he said, eyes gleaming, "at my approaching you so abruptly about a matter as serious as last night's incident."

No, I wasn't. But I said nothing.

"In fact," Erasmo continued, "the question was really a pretext for my speaking to you, since I haven't had the chance before this. MININT has to establish good relations with you, *Compañero* Llovio. It's a high priority for my superiors. We would like certain unpleasant situations from the past to be forgotten."

Like hell they would.

Erasmo had correctly identified me as a key player at CEF, the only way to gain access to Francisco García Valls. With such a contact, Erasmo would have a pipeline to the richest source of information at CEF—the minister-president himself. And information was the base of Erasmo's work.

But above him in the MININT hierarchy was Chino Mayans, my old nemesis from *La Dolce Vita*. It had to be from Mayans that Erasmo had been informed of the "certain unpleasant situations"; I was being told that Mayans wished to heal our animosities. Of course, Mayans wished me the worst possible fortune in the world. This truce or treaty, as Erasmo proposed it, was nothing more than Chino Mayans trying to buy time before he started plotting against me again.

Erasmo and I spoke for some time that morning, and nearly every day thereafter. Soon, and despite my efforts to curtail such conversations, he made me familiar with Humberto Knight's exact liquor consumption in his office and the precise quantities of committee provisions that the deputy minister surreptitiously transferred to his house. He even told me the details of Knight's love life to prove how widely cast his net of information was.

Cheo Acosta's activities came up in these discussions too. Cheo was tainted in MININT's eyes, in part because of his drinking and indecisiveness; lack of spine is a serious personality flaw in the macho revolutionary world view. But Cheo was being watched also, as Erasmo told me, because of his wife, Migdalia Agüero. She had once been held at the Villa Marista on suspicion that she was a CIA agent.

Erasmo showed me with malicious glee one bit of the evidence he was collecting against Cheo Acosta and his wife. It was her special shopping list of CEF provisions she wanted for their vacation house at Varadero Beach. The list was lavish and long, a detailed request for luxury provisions, from lobster and shrimp to ham, beer, cheese, and rum.

Neither of Erasmo's targets, Knight and Acosta, appeared to feel at all threatened by him. If anything, the two of them grew more overtly abusive of their positions as the weeks wore on.

I attributed this fearlessness to their experience; with protectors as powerful as Humberto Pérez at JUCEPLAN for Acosta and Carlos Rafael Rodríguez for Knight, both men might have assumed they were beyond MININT's reach.

Furthermore, each of them controlled a large and powerful *piña* at CEF, allies they kept in line through favors and gifts. In return for the privileges they received from their bosses, Acosta's and Knight's underlings were always first to sign up for voluntary work and maintained the best attendance records in the Finance Committee.

But Erasmo was an experienced *piña*-builder too. When the chief of executive personnel at CEF had to be removed because of her poor work, Erasmo supported as her replacement Leónides Méndez, a servile and easily manipulable bureaucrat from the Culture Ministry. García Valls accepted Méndez into CEF, first because Leónides as a party member would cause no problems with the *nomenklatura* and, second, because Erasmo had become an important source of information for García Valls about his own ministry—and García Valls wanted to appease him.

The captain completely dominated Méndez. Soon, Erasmo was personally approving each new executive and technician brought into the committee, thus securing their allegiance and aid before they got inside the door. And because Leónides was also General Secretary of the CEF Party Committee, Erasmo knew everything that occurred at each supposedly secret meeting of the CEF party cell and also could influence its deliberations.

CEF was a snake pit. I watched Erasmo's machinations, knowing that my turn to come under MININT attention could come at any moment. Every day, I reviewed and analyzed his actions and words, trying to anticipate the captain's next move and planning how I might foil any attack on my security.

It was obvious, for example, that he was detailing Knight's defects and peccadilloes to me in order to force me to discuss them with García Valls. If I hesitated, I knew I would be vulnerable to charges of administrative laxness and indecision for not acting on what I knew.

Yet once I took Humberto Knight's case up with García Valls, Erasmo as my chief informant could use the matter as a wedge to open his own channel of communication with the minister-president, thus undercutting my power as the gate through which all matters passed before reaching García Valls. I had to act.

One afternoon I had a private chat with García Valls in which I communicated the gist of Erasmo's investigation. At the same time, I offered García Valls the friendly advice that although the captain had proved very conscientious and useful in discharging his duties, his closeness to Leónides Méndez and the elaborate *piña* he appeared to be constructing might be seen by some as interference with both the administration at CEF, which was solely García Valls's responsibility, and with Finance's party functions, in which case Erasmo's activities might be construed as verging into the sacrosanct internal life of the party.

Both possible interpretations of Erasmo's role at CEF positively froze an old PSP man like García Valls with consternation. From that moment forward, I was sure, the minister-president would be acutely mindful of Erasmo and the potential danger to his safety that the captain might represent.

Then I suggested a course of action in Humberto Knight's case. I advised García Valls that he should consider visiting Knight's protector, Carlos Rafael Rodríguez, with Erasmo's troubling dossier. In that way, the minister-president would have acted properly in bringing the matter to a senior party member's attention. Also, Erasmo would for the interim be obliged to stay his hand until Rodríguez had considered the problem.

Following my advice to the letter, García Valls discussed each of Knight's problems with Carlos Rafael, who decided that Knight should be given a chance to mend his ways. As a warning to do so, García Valls replaced three directors who belonged to Knight's *piña*.

In my judgment, this slight a reprimand was insufficient to curb Knight's excesses; eventually he would have to be removed. I began to plan ahead by considering the best candidate to propose to García Valls as his replacement, someone who would pose no threat to me. It didn't take many weeks for the inevitable to come to pass.

Not only did Knight persist in his drinking and corruption, but he also joined forces with Cheo Acosta in a campaign to bring down the minister-president; Cheo, who originally had been considered for García Valls's job, still coveted it. This conspiracy was fueled by more than Acosta's ambition, however. Cheo's protector, Humberto Pérez at JUCEPLAN, continued to be deeply resentful of his loss of power to CEF and was pleased to do what he could to damage the committee and García Valls.

Acosta kept Pérez informed of everything that happened at Finance, and Pérez used this intelligence to attack García Valls, publicly and privately, whenever he could. As the minister-president told me (and the documents I saw attested) Pérez savaged García Valls in the New Economic System meetings while Cheo sat silently by at the table.

In the meantime, Captain Erasmo patiently continued to build his case against Knight and Cheo Acosta. By the middle of 1978, Erasmo had detected Knight's complicity in Cheo's plotting against García Valls. Taken together with Humberto Knight's unreformed personal conduct, his behavior was too much even for Carlos Rafael Rodríguez to abide. He had no recourse when shown Erasmo's latest evidence but to withdraw his protection of Vice-President Knight. On November 21, 1978, the *nomenklatura* told García Valls to remove Humberto, who was punished by the party and later demoted to an office job with a Ministry of Construction brigade in the coastal city of Mariel.

Cheo Acosta's *piña*, like Knight's, was dismantled by the replacement of some of his directors and his wife, who was transferred to the Academy of Science. In all, fourteen CEF directors and department heads were eventually swept away.

But the ousters of the Acosta and Knight *piñas* in no way settled the difficulties that continued to beset the Finance Commitee, and me.

In particular, there was Manuel Castro, head of the Finance Section of the Central Committee, known sarcastically as *El Topo,* "The Dummy," because he was manifestly slow-witted. I had earned his enmity by openly refuting some of his stupider proposals during our business meetings with the Central Committee. Castro had widely known ambitions to become a vice-president at CEF.

As a result, I was not a bit surprised when Leónides Méndez sidled up to me one day with his firsthand report of the previous day's meeting of those in the party cell who were responsible for my ongoing political evaluation. "Llovio," Méndez said with a simper, "yesterday there was a meeting about your political evaluation. The results were satisfactory, although there were some objections. Manuel Castro tried to influence your evaluation negatively on the basis of an unfavorable report from the Ministry of the Interior."

Castro was trying to injure me with Raimundo's old slanders, his MININT report prepared during my time at MINAZ.

When, some months earlier, he had brought the report to García Valls's attention, the minister-president had calleld José Abrantes, the head of State Security, who'd informed him that Raimundo's accusations were "inoperative." García Valls had told me about it at the time.

At the meeting Leónides Méndez had attended, *El Topo* tried to introduce the MININT report again. As I learned from Leónides, García Valls had been late to the evaluation meeting. Seizing this opening, Castro brought up the MININT file, only to have García Valls enter the room at precisely the moment Manuel was discussing Raimundo's report.

García Valls, said Leónides, coolly asked Castro if he didn't recall his converation with José Abrantes.

Castro tried to act surprised and then quickly found his memory, apologizing for the oversight. "Castro pulled back," Leónides told me, "and repeated several times that it was all a misunderstanding. So you know, really, you have no problem. Your evaluation is perfect! Congratulations!"

Méndez's bonhomie grated on my nerves almost as much as Erasmo's unctuous eagerness. He knew as well as I that Castro would retreat only so long as he felt it politic to do so. Then Castro would come skittering out in another sally against me. I further expected Captain Erasmo, more powerful now than ever, to begin subverting my authority after he'd erased Humberto Knight and Cheo Acosta. How long and with what determination Francisco García Valls (himself under daily threat from Humberto Pérez) would support me against Erasmo and Mayans was anyone's guess.

Yet even as the multiplayer chess game grew more complex—I had to devote long hours every day to thinking and strategizing—my work itself at CEF was becoming much more demanding.

Humberto Pérez, when he wasn't busy harassing García Valls and the committee, managed to complicate our lives simply by being Humberto Pérez. He had emerged in a very brief period from his position as an obscure economics professor to become president of JUCEPLAN and a leading party official; he was vice-president of the executive committee of the Council of Ministers and an alternate member of the Politburo. His association with Raúl Castro was one ingredient in Pérez's success formula. The other was the Soviet-directed reorganization of the Cuban economy. What Pérez knew about economics and administration was negligible, but in the land of the blind the one-eyed man is king.

*   *   *

The operations of JUCEPLAN under Pérez were a paradigm for the inept functioning of the bureaucracy as a whole. Each year, in June, JUCEPLAN initiated the next year's budget process by sending to every ministry and institute a proposed invididual economic plan for the coming fiscal year. By August, each of these agencies returned the JUCEPLAN proposal with comments. Invariably, several sectors of the government insisted they would need additional funds and supplies to meet the proposed plan, requests that Humberto Pérez's staff at JUCEPLAN were incapable of analyzing and assessing. Every October, JUCEPLAN cobbled together a national economic plan so removed from the reality of what Cuba should, or could, accomplish in the coming year that it annually underwent radical surgery performed by Fidel himself, assisted by Osmany Cienfuegos, secretary of the Executive Committee of the Council of Ministers. The shredded, slashed, stretched, and sutured document then came down to the Finance Committee, where it had to be deciphered and somehow shaped into a budget.

The exercise was useless and time-consuming. I hated to pay with a sixteen-hour workday for others' inefficiency. But at CEF we knew that a budget had to be presented in December to the National Assembly, no matter what. And so I did what I had to do.

FOR A FEW
DOLLARS MORE

Month after month I studied the reports of the National Bank, and month after month I saw the country's foreign debt mounting. The money Cuba owed to capitalist countries such as France, Japan, Spain, and Canada was increasing, but the hard-currency income wasn't. Something was badly wrong.

Fidel's investment plans, particularly his grand projects and massive borrowing during the sugar boom of the early 1970s, had pushed Cuba to the brink of default. As explained in a secret National Bank report dated June 30, 1978: Without an influx of hard currency the country would be unable to continue meeting its international obligations after 1979.

Fidel would not hear of such a thing. "Cuba," he said in meeting after meeting, García Valls reported to me, "will pay every last cent! This country will never renegotiate her foreign debt!" His confidence was based on past experience. The Soviets always had compensated for the Revolutionary Government's economic deficits.

But times had started to change. Now First Party Secretary Brezhnev was meeting stiff resistance in the Politburo toward handing over more dollars to an anarchic leadership still stumbling in spite of the new economic system it had adopted.

An internal commission, led by Carlos Rafael Rodríguez, was established to develop new export products and create mixed enterprises in Panama, Mexico, and Canada in order to gain a foothold in the international market. Among the export items considered were cotton clothing, crafts, works of art, cement, some derivatives of steel, and naphtha, a by-product of Soviet oil refined in Cuba for reexport.

It was not going to be easy to compete in free markets saturated with high-quality, low-cost goods, but revolutionary aggressiveness faced the challenge with optimism. According to the Ministry for Light Industry: "The production of Rodeo Brand blue jeans, with their exquisite cut and magnificent fabric, will easily displace the market for blue jeans made in the USA." The government not only believed this statement but included in its economic planning the dollars the country would supposedly receive from these exports.

Finally, it took Fidel's fertile mind to devise an expeditious plan to bring in abundant U.S. currency. This plan, which would be characterized as a "spontaneous and humane" gesture when announced to the rest of the world, was in fact calculated down to the last detail.

In 1977, Fidel called a closed meeting of more than 3,000 party members in the Karl Marx Theater. His five-hour-long speech, which I later read, had as its principal theme the country's difficulties in obtaining hard currency. Fidel explained that sacrifices were required to earn more hard currency, including the possibility that the luxury hotels in the cities and at the beaches would have to be available to foreign tourists year-round, thus possibly denying Cubans their vacations. He told the party gathering that such measures were urgently necessary to obtain hard currency in order not to default on international obligations. Videocassettes of the speech, which I saw, were shown to all party members in the country. From them, the news quickly spread to the rest of the population. The terrain was being prepared.

With my access to official information, I could reconstruct Fidel's strategy. At first he moved quietly. Early in 1978, a secret economic report, which I saw at CEF, forecast that the country could soon expect an infusion of between $50 million and $60 million in hard currency. The secret report did not say where the money was going to be found, but in fact, after nearly two decades of rabid vilification, character assassination, and general calumny, Fidel was going to supply money from the pockets of thousands of Cuban exiles who would be welcomed back to visit the Fatherland!

No hint of the secret preparations could be allowed. In May 1977, for example, U.S. television personality Barbara Walters interviewed Fidel and asked, "Will you allow Cubans to visit this country, to visit their families?"

While at the moment that was exactly what Fidel planned to do, he replied to Ms. Walters: "I believe, at this time, the required conditions do not exist, because until relations between the United States and Cuba are normalized, we cannot permit this type of visit."

The first step in Fidel's plan was to identify groups of young Cubans who had immigrated to the United States in the early years of the revolution and who were not actively antagonistic to the Cuban revolution. Thus the Antonio Maceo Brigade was born, named for a Cuban patriot of the last century and composed of young Cubans, or North American-born children of Cubans, who either wanted to touch native soil again or see it for the first time.

Fifty-five of them came to Cuba early in 1978 and were given an extensive tour of the island. They were permitted to visit their relatives and were warmly welcomed by some of the highest officials. Of course, the press recorded their every step while ICAIC filmed a documentary entitled *Fifty-five Brothers*, which I saw before it was released. Armando Hart, member of the Politburo, wept with emotion before the ICAIC and television cameras when he met the group, whom he called "*Maceítos*, the children from the Antonio Maceo Brigade."

The brigade's purpose was obvious: It was necessary to improve the Cubans' image of the exiles, who had so frequently been denigrated to them.

Following the brigade's visit, Fidel held meetings with representatives of Miami's Cuban exiles, as well as conversations both with North American reporters and with journalists from the "Cuban community abroad." In his initial press conference, held on September 6, 1978, I watched Fidel, smiling, affectionate, exploiting to the fullest his charismatic qualities. Like a good fisherman, between smiles and jokes he threw out his line to the Cuban exiles in a fraternal atmosphere.

His first gesture was to agree to the eventual release of political prisoners and to allow 14,000 former political prisoners and their close relatives to leave Cuba. Both concessions created a positive image for the revolution in terms of human rights policy, then an important international issue thanks largely to Jimmy Carter's emphasis upon it. But they masked a second objective that mattered much more to Fidel.

Those 14,000 former political prisoners were a hindrance, a dangerous thorn, since neither they nor their families had been reintegrated into the revolution. Then, too, it was difficult to find work for so many people. The same was true for the 3,000 current political prisoners who, in just three or four years, would swell the ranks of Cuba's rebellious and embittered unemployed. Their departure would be a boon to the revolution.

Talking to the U.S. press in Havana in December 1978, Fidel shrewdly emphasized that the problems of Cuban political prisoners would be solved exclusively "among Cubans"—from Cuba *and* from the United States. "The United States government has absolutely nothing to do with this, absolutely nothing!" he stressed several times to the reporters. Knowing what considerable pressure Cubans in the United States would bring on President Carter to accept the 14,000, Fidel would at the same time promote goodwill among the exiles and seem to have taken the human rights initiative away from Carter. Carter had already made friendly gestures to Cuba, which had led in September 1977 to the opening of an "interest section" in Havana and in Washington, D.C., which officially opened the lines of communication between the two countries for the first time since the early 1960s.

I was very surprised when I saw Fidel sharing with the press his newly revised sociohistoric understanding of the exiles' experience. I knew that he had to be cooking up a scheme. For the first time ever he spoke in positive terms about these people, a community that "tries to maintain its national identity. . . . They try to hold on to their language, want their children to speak the language." Suddenly, the despised "worms" had turned into butterflies. As for past aspersions, "I think," he said, "these expressions resulted from the heat and the passion of the struggle. I have been the first to use the term *Community*, and I plan to continue doing so."

Now a symphony of soothing tones was played to the Community back in the United States, while Fidel's own people were prepared for a round of official hospitality to those whom they had been taught to hate. That same year, toward the end of December, Cuba opened her doors to the Cuban Community abroad. Finally, after so many years of absence, more than 100,000 exiles would visit their country again. As Fidel had hoped, each group came with billfolds bulging; not 50 million, not 60 million, but more than 80 million in exile dollars would come to rest in Cuban coffers in 1979.

Each visitor was permitted to come for one week. The trip cost approximately $800 and included round-trip passage, a luxury hotel room, and three meals a day. But the great majority of the returning exiles hardly made use of these privileges, as Fidel had predicted. Their only interest was to reunite with their families, and logically enough, they preferred to sleep less comfortably and eat less sumptuously in their relatives' homes in order to take full advantage of the short time at their disposal. The net gain, therefore, was rather high for the Revolutionary Government.

And Fidel found a way to bleed an additional $75 from each visitor. Their U.S. passports were not accepted. In order to travel to Cuba the exiles had to reactivate their Cuban passports in the United States and receive them in Havana as their only valid identification. It did not matter that the brand new Socialist constitution, approved in 1976, did not recognize double citizenship. The charge was $75, and dollars mattered.

We at the Finance Committee, which controlled Cuban customs, also did our share to separate the exiles from their money. Initially there were no baggage restrictions; each visitor brought in as much luggage as he or she wished. But the customs officials complained about having to open ten and even fifteen suitcases for each person. Later in 1979 the visitors were made to pay for each excess kilo until, toward the end of April, through a "noncommercial tariff" law I had to work on, baggage weight was limited to forty-four pounds. Moreover, the bags' contents, according to an established tariff, could not exceed 1,000 Cuban pesos, or approximately 1,200 American dollars in value.

This CEF regulation also restricted the free entry of special articles. To bring in tape recorders, radios, or cameras, for example, the exiles had to pay a "guarantee" that would be returned upon presentation of the article when they left the country. The Revolutionary Government had a specific reason for taking this step: to accumulate money, since most of the visitors left their equipment with their relatives and therefore could not reclaim their deposits.

Much to Fidel's chagrin, he was going to have to pay a price for that money. For nearly two decades daily propaganda had created the image among Cubans of the exiles in the United States and in other countries as discriminated against and mistreated, going hungry and barely surviving in a fiercely competitive society. The older people had listened with skepticism and kept quiet. But for the younger people the only truth that existed was the official one. In school, from the time they were very small, they had been indoctrinated with the deepest hatred and contempt for those Cuban "traitors," who were enemies of the Fatherland as much as the Yanquis themselves. The media prepared the news for them; the "bestialities" of imperialism were the cause of all the evils in the world.

Then the "Community," as Fidel called it, suddenly burst onto the scene. Fidel was tranquilly confident that his people now had sufficient "political maturity," in his words, to face any eventuality. Revolutionary consciousness had developed to such a level that it was impermeable to any other ideology, he believed. There was no risk of any kind in allowing the presence of the exiles with their deep pockets.

By the middle of 1979 more than 50,000 exiles had come for their short stay on the island, and they proved to be rather a different lot from what had been expected by the Cuban people, especially by the younger people. The sisters and brothers, the aunts and uncles, the cousins from the Community had healthy and happy faces. Their way of life as they described it was not at all unpleasant, despite what Cuban newspapers had claimed. They showed photographs of their houses, their cars, and, what was most important, they brought suitcases full of gifts. The coveted goods of the consumer society flooded Cuban homes. The child of the most modest family could listen to prohibited music on a modern stereo tape recorder, or wear clothes and shoes comparable to those of the child of the highest official.

These goods continued to pour into the country despite our customs restrictions, which soon led to protests by party members and leaders, who were strictly forbidden to take visitors into their houses or to accept gifts from them.

"Comandante," Fidel read from a letter he'd received, "I'm a revolutionary and I have to allow my neighbor and his children to receive from the Community what I, by working honestly, cannot have." The letter, which I heard on videotape, was read to a closed party meeting at the Karl Marx Theater, a gathering Fidel was forced to call because of such complaints. His speech centered on the terrible domestic conditions in the country, caused by the international economic crisis, and on low sugar prices. He suggested that, for the time being, the return of the exiles was a necessary evil.

But I knew, as did the revolutionary leadership, that Fidel had too much confidence in that "conscious and austere" people who gave him wild ovations in the Plaza de la Revolución and frenetically shouted revolutionary slogans. "I'll trade two uncles who are party members for one poor uncle from the Community," was the biting joke about a Cuban child who envied his schoolmates' new shoes and tape recorders; it clearly reflected what was occurring throughout the island.

At Fidel's order, Minister-President García Valls then tightened the customs restrictions further, but because money was money, the former Sears store in Havana was also opened for the exclusive use of the Community. Everything they could not bring in could be bought at Sears. The most varied imported goods, in addition to coffee, meat, and sausage, were sold to the Cuban visitors for U.S. dollars. For example, prices for Lee and Levi's jeans, on average, were several times higher than the exiles would pay for the same jeans in North America. A pair of these jeans cost $80 to $120, but the exiles were willing to pay it in order to provide for their needy relatives on the island.

In this way, by exploiting family love and by trading on human feeling, the Revolutionary Government was generously enriched by $84 million.

But there was more to come. The Cuban Community would be the unintentional catalyst for a dissatisfaction that had been gestating for many years and would, within less than a year, shake the country and make headlines all over the world.

REVOLUTIONARIES ABROAD

At the time that Fidel was putting together his plan to bleed the exiles, Humberto Pérez's analysts at JUCEPLAN were whipping up another of their annual economic fictions. Like that of the year before, it would have to be completely revised by Fidel and then sent to CEF, where I foresaw another long siege of work to produce a final budget for 1979.

About the time the process started, as my resentment at Humberto Pérez for causing this totally avoidable labor began to build, Maggie was suddenly told that she was going on official Culture Ministry business to Moscow! At last, we had both arrived at the point where my escape plan could work, and in any other circumstances I very likely could have engineered a foreign trip to coincide with Maggie's.

But this was no ordinary circumstance. I could not possibly propose a trip for myself just as the Cuban national economic plan landed on our desks for processing. Distraught, infuriated, and ready at that moment to wring Humberto Pérez's neck, I remained at work in Havana unraveling the mess I'd been handed while my wife and our first concrete opportunity for escape flew away.

The chances of leaving Cuba with Maggie on a joint business trip now seemed even more remote. It could be years before Maggie was sent on another such trip—and there would always be complications. I had to find a surer and more feasible way of escaping. At this time, in 1978, there was renewed talk of a program that would allow tourist trips to Socialist countries. This now seemed to be our only hope. It was the safest and most reliable way to proceed. The higher I rose in the hierarchy, I told myself, and the more secure Maggie became in the Culture Ministry, the more certain it was we'd qualify for a variety of possible trips as soon as the program began.

Meanwhile, my work at Finance kept me busy in Maggie's absence. Besides its mandate to promote orderliness and rationality in annual expenditures, the Finance Committee through its information-gathering function was also the vehicle for introducing the alien concept of economic controls throughout the Cuban state. Every transaction of any consequence ultimately was reported in some fashion to CEF, or could be inferred from the mountains of statistics we processed.

We were able to establish, for example, through an investigation by our auditors, that somewhere between 300 million and 350 million pesos' worth of state property was stolen by workers and often by officials each year in warehouses, workplaces, and throughout the service sector. The party called the CEF report "exaggerated and incorrect"; such massive, systematic pilfering simply could not occur in Cuba's "revolutionary, hardworking, and disinterested" laboring class, the party insisted. It was necessary, as usual, for the party to deny or hide the truth. And it was of paramount importance not to anger Fidel with such information.

García Valls should have taken heed at this official repudiation of the evident. CEF's power to quantify and to pinpoint corruption was obviously a double-edged sword, especially should that power seem to threaten the sacred prerogatives of the revolutionary elite. Nevertheless, and to my deep consternation, when another such situation confronted the minister-president, he proceeded to act on it.

Even a glance at Cuba's hard-currency account ledgers confirmed that significant sums were being wasted or disappeared altogether each year, principally in the country's embassies and among the legions of traveling revolutionaries. While it was impossible to know for certain the exact amounts being misappropriated or wasted, several millions of dollars a year is probably a conservative guess. Aware of this problem, the Executive Committee of the Council of Ministers decided that an intergovernmental economic commission should be formed to look into it. CEF was designated the lead agency in the study.

In the spring of 1979, García Valls ordered me to inspect the financial affairs of Cuban embassies in Czechoslovakia, East Germany, France, and Spain.

I had no choice but to do as I was told.

My trip was coordinated with the minister of foreign relations and with MININT, who would send coded messages to the ambassadors and chiefs of the intelligence centers in each embassy, informing them of my inspection and ordering them to give me all the information I requested.

But now I did not harbor any illusion as to the trip's potential consequences for me. If the sword swung, it was going to be my neck it would catch.

Nevertheless, I could not ignore the excitement that stirred in me when I learned my itinerary, for one of the cities was Paris, where at last I could look for my daughter. Marielle would now be eighteen years old; I hadn't seen her in twelve years.

I flew to Prague on May 19, 1979, where I met with Leopold Lér, the Czech minister of finance, to discuss salaries for the 4,000 Cubans then working in Czech industry. Since 1977, Cuba had been exporting workers to several Socialist countries on the pretext of providing them with technical training. The real reason these men and women were shipped away was part of a secret government plan to arrest domestic unemployment; joblessness is unacceptable under Socialist doctrine.

My orders from García Valls were to negotiate a 40 percent rebate of the Cuban workers' salaries to the Cuban state. This cut in their pay was supposed to erase disparities between the standards of living of these workers and those in Cuba. It was necessary to preserve "revolutionary consciousness" and the sense of austerity, and to this end these workers' power to consume had to be curtailed. Moreover, the state had other uses for this money.

Certainly the daily life of Cuban workers in Czechoslovakia was far from comfortable. After Fidel's support of the Soviet invasion, the Czechs had lost sympathy for the Cuban revolution and the Cuban people. In the factories as well as on the street, there were unpleasant altercations between Cuban workers and the Czechs, whose irritation and disappointment had turned into a kind of political racism.

Before I left Havana, I had been warned by Cuban specialists in foreign protocol never to toast the Soviet Union. Now I saw why. The Czechs did not hide their distaste for anything having to do with the Soviets. They scarcely mentioned them, and when for unavoidable reasons the subject came up, expressions of scorn registered on their faces.

To my relief, the three long sessions I spent at the Cuban

Embassy in Prague turned up only minor irregularities in its financial management, too small to worry about, which meant one less problem to handle on my return.

In Berlin, I stayed at the residence of Ambassador Julio García Oliveras, my old *compañero* from the clandestine days and one of the few Revolutionary Directorate fighters left in a position of power after *La Dolce Vita* in 1965. By chance, Fidel Vascós, minister-president of the State Committee on Statistics, was at Oliveras's house too. He told me that on the day before he had left Cuba, Cheo Acosta, first vice-president at Finance, reportedly was replaced and transferred as financial analyst to Raúl Castro's staff.

Since this news came as no surprise I said nothing.

There were 5,000 Cuban workers in East Germany, as disliked as their countrymen in Czechoslovakia. After working out with Finance Minister Blüm a salary protocol covering them, as I had in Czechoslovakia, I began my inspection of embassy finances.

The accounts in Berlin appeared to be more or less in order. But according to "Camilo," the chief of Cuban Intelligence in East Germany, the Berlin Embassy personnel commonly supplemented their incomes by currency trading. Before Ambassador García Oliveras had prohibited travel to and from West Berlin without his express permission, they would trade their East German marks for dollars brought in by visiting Cubans at the artificially high official exchange rate. Then they would spend their dollars in West Berlin or trade them back into East German marks at the discounted open-market exchange rate. These dealings, said Camilo, were hardly affected by García Oliveras's travel ban. The Embassy officials were now plying their business in marks and dollars on the East German black market and prospered nearly as well as before.

So far, my investigations had failed to implicate any Cuban official powerful enough to threaten me with retaliation. As I looked ahead to Paris, however, I needed no imagination to guess what I would find in that playground of the revolution. Since the early 1960s, when I'd lived in Paris, revolutionaries' behavior could only have gotten worse. Still, as I boarded the airliner for France, my thoughts were not of my mission. Every feeling was swallowed by a much more profound disquiet, the tense apprehension of a father determined after nearly twelve years to see his daughter again.

AN ENCOUNTER WITH THE PAST

The Stranger, so long accustomed to controlling my computerized daily existence, argued his cold, logical objections to my intent, but now Marielle was outside his domain. He might, as he did after the incident with her koala bear in 1972, drive Marielle's memory from my active consciousness. But my need to see my daughter again, given the opportunity, was primal, instinctive. I didn't know if she remembered me, or what I would say if we met. I was not even sure if she still lived in France. No matter; once my inspection at the embassy was complete, I knew I could not leave Paris without searching for her.

As I was en route from East Germany, her image suddenly came to me with such force that I crumpled in my seat. I can't say how long I stayed in this reverie, but I was shaken from it by a stewardess whose voice at first seemed far, far away.

"Sir?" she said, holding a tray of food. "Sir! Don't you want lunch?"

I looked up at her surprised expression.

"I'm fine." I smiled to reassure her, wondering how long she'd been trying to rouse me.

When she moved on to the other passengers, I breathed deeply, exhaled, and listened to a nervous lecture from the Stranger.

"This is really serious," he said. "If you allow your feelings to show so much that even a person you don't know is shocked, then you're lost."

My first concern was to gather my wits in order to face Nelson Nuevas, the head of Cuban Intelligence in France, who was expecting me at the Embassy in Paris as soon as I arrived. By training and experience Nuevas was keenly alert to any signs of forced or unnatural behavior, and would be suspicious if he detected anything unusual in my actions. With every ounce of energy I could muster, I willed Marielle's image out of my mind and concentrated on my assignment. By the time we landed at Orly, I was back in control.

I went straight to my hotel and then to the Embassy to meet with Nuevas. He got down to business quickly. Nuevas explained that Ambassador Gregorio Ortega, then on vacation in Havana, set the work example for Embassy employees. He worked only two hours in the morning, and so did the rest of the personnel. Some of them, with his consent, charged their personal expenses to the Embassy's account. It seemed this practice was quite common in most Cuban embassies. In addition to saving all the money they could from their low salaries, Embassy personnel used a variety of tricks to obtain more dollars, bring goods back to Cuba, or buy a Soviet automobile with hard currency.

The ambassador's residence served as a hotel for Ortega's friends and high-level leaders in the Cuban government, who stayed there, ate at the Embassy's expense, pocketed the money for travel expenses they saved, and later reported the money as spent when they settled accounts in Havana.

In the Embassy books I found various "private subaccounts" in French francs, totaling nearly $200,000, mixed in with the Embassy's accounts. The list of names was headed by Osmany Cienfuegos and included members of the Council of Ministers as well as high-level party members. These funds were clearly for the unofficial, private use of the revolutionary leadership, substantive proof of the system's real attitude toward individual sacrifice and its double standard of rectitude. Needless to say, their discovery also placed their discoverer—me—in serious personal jeopardy.

Nelson Nuevas was also eager to explain and document for me the activities of the permanent representatives of the Ministry of Fishing in Paris, which operated independently of the Embassy. Their standard of living was much higher than that of the diplomats. Entertainment expenses for the ministry's leaders had no ceiling; they never went anywhere more modest than the Lido, Maxim's, or the Moulin Rouge. According to Nuevas, they had been living like this for more than seven years, and although he'd denounced them, his reports had no effect.

Nuevas's complaints amplified my already well-founded fears that this investigation could only do me harm; the officials involved in the corrupt practices were immune to denunciation, the most powerful men in Cuba. In essence, my case against them would become their case against me.

In the midst of my stressful and dispiriting work at the Embassy, my only relaxation came in conversations with the internationally renowned Cuban writer Alejo Carpentier, who served there as cultural adviser. Carpentier was always fascinating to listen to, a man of fine intellect who cared only for his work. His company was a refreshing and stimulating contrast to the revolutionary cant of the rest of the embassy staff.

Finally, I could turn my full attention to finding Marielle. The first person I went to see was Maître Jean Budin. By then in his seventies, Uncle Jean welcomed me as warmly as ever, although his own life had been permanently saddened by the death many years before of his wife, the vivacious Aunt Alla. We talked a great deal about the past, the happy days we all had spent together at his château at Vaumain, where Marie Christine and I had been married. But Uncle Jean, who was Marielle's godfather and, as he explained a little reluctantly, had represented Marie Christine in our divorce, said he knew nothing of my daughter or her whereabouts.

"It is as if the earth had swallowed up both of them, José," he said. "I haven't heard anything about her or her mother for many years."

It surprised me greatly that Marie Christine had allowed what I knew had been her great and sincere affection for Uncle Jean and Aunt Alla to lapse. Perhaps, I thought, seeing them prompted too-painful memories of our serene lives in Paris before the return to Cuba.

I can attest that I myself felt a bittersweet tug of nostalgia just being in Maître Jean Budin's presence, an ache reinforced almost everywhere I went in the capital. It seemed as if every street corner, café, and park sparked a recollection, not so much of Marie Christine as of a lost time. I resisted these feelings with all my strength, aware that opening myself at this moment to my past could foreclose my future. Back in Havana there loomed the greatest test yet of my wit and nerve. In Cuba, the Stranger's terrain, there was no room for happiness, anger, or any intense emotion of any kind, only for calculation.

The search for Marielle brought me back into the company of my French friends from twenty years before: Jocelyn and Marie France (who had divorced), Christian, Bernard, Prisca, and the rest. With them, too, I avoided rekindling any intimate connection and conducted myself with amiable distance. I could tell they sensed I was changed in a fundamental way, but none of them asked about the reasons for my reserved behavior. Also, not one of our old circle of companions knew where my daughter was.

I had only a few days in which to look for Marielle, and without my friends' help it appeared as if I'd have no luck. I kept asking them, especially Bernard, to think of anyone they might know to trace Marie Christine's whereabouts. They all seemed unsure of the wisdom of my search and of their own proper role in furthering it. While this reticence was understandable, I was frustrated by it until one night at dinner at Bernard's house when he took me aside.

"I'll help you, José," he said. "I'll try to find out Marie Christine's telephone number. But first I want to ask you a favor. I know you very well, and I know what you're capable of when you set your mind on something. If I can reach her, I beg you to abide by her decision. Please understand how delicate this is for me. And besides, this has to do with your daughter; you have to behave very prudently."

I accepted Bernard's conditions. After several phone calls that evening, he managed to obtain Marie Christine's number in a small Dordogne town where, he told me, she had been living for several years. In 1975, Marie Christine had remarried and had borne another child.

Bernard communicated these details after speaking with Marie Christine for several minutes. "She didn't know who I was at first, José. She didn't remember my name," he said when he hung up the phone. "She was cold, but I seemed to detect great turmoil in her voice when I told her you were here and wanted to see Marielle. She asked for a few minutes. I'll call her back in a little while."

Fifteen minutes later Bernard spoke to her again. He explained my intentions as persuasively as he could, but Marie Christine was immovable. She and her husband, she told Bernard, agreed that I should not be allowed to see Marielle.

I didn't even try to mask my anger. "Calm down, José," Bernard insisted when he saw my eyes. "Please, don't do anything on your own. You'd put me in a very difficult position. Be patient. Time takes care of everything."

I was shaking with violent emotion, but I agreed and promised Bernard I would follow his advice. By the end of the night my fury had turned into a confused welter of emotions in which impotence predominated.

In the morning, I decided to go to Dordogne to visit Marie Christine's aunt and uncle, the Meynards, hoping they would intercede with her on my behalf or would help me to find a solution. To cast no suspicion on me, I took "Gonzalo," vice-consul for Cuba in France, a Cuban Intelligence agent, along with me. That way this leg of my trip would be accounted for.

The Meynards received me with their usual loving warmth; despite all that had transpired between me and their niece they showed me a compassion for which I am eternally beholden. After exchanging news about our lives, we started to speak about my daughter. The Meynards told me they understood Marielle was at boarding school in Perigueux, but that they knew very little about Marie Christine. She had stopped coming to see them, too, a long time ago. Then I revealed my reason for coming to Dordogne and Marie Christine's objection to it.

"It would be better to abandon that idea for now," Pierrette Meynard said after some reflection. "At least this time. Her mother, and especially her grandmother, have filled her with negative ideas about you.

"If you dare to go and see her you will only complicate things even more, José," she said. Both of them insisted that I should wait, that in time Marielle would come to me.

Certain as I was of their good faith and judgment, I reluctantly had to accept Pierrette Meynard's reasoning.

For the eight days since I'd left East Germany—indeed, from the moment in Cuba I'd known I was coming to Paris and resolved then to search for Marielle—the tension within me had mounted steadily. Then to discover where my daughter was but to know I should not see her was an unbearable anticlimax. The thread of hope for the future seemed thinner than ever as I turned myself over once again to the Stranger.

Before leaving Paris for my last stop, Madrid, I went for a second time to see Maître Budin. I wanted to give him for safekeeping the transcriptions of my conversations with Ché and my meetings with Fidel, along with several volumes of notes I had carried with me from Cuba under protection of my diplomatic passport. I also wanted to tell him what had happened since 1965, a version of the truth to help him understand what I was entrusting him with but not enough to upset him.

When I handed him the papers, he seemed pleased to be given what I obviously regarded as an important responsibility.

"You've done the right thing, José," he said. "Could a father deny a request from one of his children? You can rest easy. I will take care of these papers as Jean Budin, your friend and your father, and a professional too. Don't forget, I'm still a lawyer."

Then I told Maître Budin my real reason for leaving for Cuba in 1965, what had happened in *La Dolce Vita* and some of the saga of the fourteen years since we'd last met. Through it all, I carefully avoided details of the situation with Marie Christine; there was no reason to embarrass him for having acted as her divorce attorney.

Maître Budin took in these revelations, and then spoke. "José," he said slowly, "I discover you again as you were when you lived in Paris. The only thing that shocked me—and I can tell you now after hearing the whole story—was the expression in your eyes. Your look was so glassy and a little terrifying."

I apologized to Uncle Jean for my coldness and explained as best I could the necessity of it. It was beyond Maître Budin's experience as a Western European to understand what a system like Socialism in Cuba does to the individual, but he could accept the truth of what I told him. "Alla and I never believed you were a Communist," he said toward the close of our conversation. "For all these years we've thought about you a great deal and asked ourselves what could have happened to you. But we never imagined the hell you were living through."

With that, we said our farewells at his door. It was to be the last time I ever saw him, and in a way I cannot account for, I knew it then.

The next day I flew to Spain. At the Embassy, "Eliecer," the head of Cuban Intelligence in Spain, took me to the conference room adjoining the ambassador's office to speak to me privately. The walls of this room had been specially treated to impede any outside interference. Following the same orders received in Berlin by Camilo and in Paris by Nelson Nuevas, Eliecer offered me his help in carrying out my inspection.

The picture in Madrid was like the one in Paris, except that the volume of abuse was greater. Thousands of Cubans passed through Spain each year with the sole purpose of buying goods and enjoying themselves. The bureaucrats at Foreign Trade went to Madrid on the pretext of making official purchases—a function that was supposed to be carried out by the commercial adviser at the Embassy—and then prolonged their stay for months.

"They all save their money in other countries so they can

shop in Madrid," Ambassador Alfaros told me angrily during a meeting that lasted for more than five hours. "But it is the state that pays their expenses for room and board. And what can I say about our people passing through? I have to put them up at the residence. I tell you I'm not an ambassador; I spend my time traveling back and forth to the airport, transporting the big shots, eating with them in restaurants, acting as their guide to the city. When do I have time to take care of my own work?"

The old gentleman did not stop talking for a moment. "Another thing," Alfaros continued. "A little while ago one of those men was here who's protected by a big name. He bought articles for his personal use with no sense of limits. Do you know what he did? He filled my house with packages. I had to intervene with Cubana de Aviacion so they'd let him fly home with two thousand kilos [about 900 pounds] of excess baggage."

"Ambassador," I replied, "there must be a mistake. Two thousand?"

"Kilos! Yes, sir! Iván Espín [Raúl Castro's brother-in-law] carried on two thousand kilos. But that's not all. I had to take ten thousand dollars out of the 'revolving account' to pay for everything he bought, and then, to make room for his suitcases, I had to take goods off the plane that one of the ministries had urgently requested."

In theory, the revolving account was a sensible means of covering the costs of entertaining visiting Cuban officials. But as I had now seen in four Cuban embassies, the revolutionary elite's duty to the public trust meant little to these men. And it certainly would not help my predicament.

On the way back to Havana, exactly one month from the day I'd left, I began considering how to package my report so as to cause me the least damage. None of the alternatives appeared at all promising.

I was relieved on one score, however. On my return, when Maggie—who knew only that I had gone to Europe on official business and that I had intended to look for Marielle while I was there—asked me if I'd seen my daughter, I answered "No" without a trace of the turmoil and disappointment I'd been through. My answer felt to me, and sounded to her, no more strained than as if I were relating incidentally that a business lunch had been postponed. She did sense my deep sadness, a trait Maggie had recognized in me from our first acquaintance. But by our tacit understanding, she never questioned me about it, nor did she say anything now. At least my poise was intact for the looming battle ahead.

García Valls stared at me without saying a word. The results of my investigation obviously disturbed him, not so much because of the facts themselves but because it was now his job to send the report on to higher levels. García Valls had to make sure the report I would prepare got as high as Fidel, whose knowledge of its contents would be our only possible protection against the vengeance of those revolutionary officials implicated in the corruption.

"The best way to reach Fidel is through State Security—and that means Abrantes, Minister," I said, after reviewing every avenue open to us. "He can meet directly with Fidel. This information will affect many interests; Abrantes is the only one who can intervene."

García Valls decided that I should prepare a detailed report, naming names, for Fidel's eyes only. A second very general paper, which would not include names, would go to Fidel's Invisible Currency Commission. The fewer people who knew exactly what I had found the better.

On a Friday afternoon García Valls talked to Abrantes. The next day he called me at home to come to the committee offices immediately. "Fidel is waiting," García Valls said. I heard the tension in his voice. "He wants to know the details and the names, especially those connected to the Madrid Embassy."

Fidel was suspicious and disbelieving; he asked insistently if there were documents to prove my allegations.

"They're all in a sealed archive in the accounting section at the Embassy," I said.

That was the end of the meeting. On that same night, García Valls later told me, a high-level official of State Security left for Madrid, and a short while later the incriminating documents were back in Cuba.

I knew that once Fidel saw this proof, my fate would be decided swiftly, within a day. When, after twenty-four hours, we heard nothing from him, it seemed I was safe, at least for now.

My problems, however, were not over. I had to survive, I figured, for at least one more year, until the summer of 1980, when I believed Maggie and I could take our tourist trip together. Although Fidel had spared me, the messenger, for bringing him the news that his leadership was systematically looting the national treasury, if and when he decided to punish the offenders my role in their undoing would become known. It was not a recommended way to win friends.

Thus the central question for me became: Would I get out before my time ran out? Thanks to Leónides Méndez, this soon became a more immediate question.

One morning Méndez approached me very discreetly. "What I'm going to tell you is a party secret," he said coyly. "I know you'll keep it confidential. Last night, at a meeting of the Party Cell of the Presidency, I proposed and got them to agree to the elevation of your case to the Municipal Party for membership processing. I believe you deserve it. Your political trajectory and your daily work vouch for you. What do you think?" he asked, looking at me like someone who expects great demonstrations of gratitude.

"It's a great honor for me, Leónides," I answered. "I thank you very much."

I wanted to step on him! As if I didn't have enough on my mind, Leónides had practically guaranteed that one of my greatest worries, party membership, was going to become an issue again. Unlike my previous brush with this much-to-be-avoided honor in 1968, the new party rules adopted at the 1975 Congress called for candidates proposed by the party to be preinvestigated by the party before their nomination at worker assemblies.

This meant that I had already been reviewed in the workplace cell and that the party at that level had found me qualified enough to open the membership process. Next would come the worker assembly. There, ordinary workers still could spontaneously nominate their candidates for Exemplary Worker, as they always had. I, however, would be proposed at the assembly by some party member, a sign to everyone that my final acceptance was all but assured. Although the process from nomination to approval might stretch out over a year, neither luck nor wit was likely to save me from the straitjacket of party discipline.

I consulted my calendar—it was now the summer of 1979; the summer of 1980 looked impossibly distant.

BACK TO SQUARE ONE

JUCEPLAN's balloon of fantasies burst on schedule in 1979, despite the millions and millions of dollars Fidel was bilking from the Community. Fidel lashed out, in meetings, against Humberto Pérez's analysts' "unrealistic" economic calculations. "We will have to limit imports and save every penny of hard currency"—Perez quoted to me the Commander in Chief's words from one of these sessions. "The population's subsistence level will have to be reduced."

Years before, I might have smiled at Fidel's words, knowing as I did what evidence of official waste and profligacy Fidel had in his hands. But now I showed no reaction at all to Pérez; I listened with an expression of attentiveness and respect.

By November 1979, when the annual battle of the budget began anew, I hoped against logic that my report to Fidel the previous June had been buried and would stay that way. With any luck at all, I believed, this was going to be my third and last year at CEF, in dubious warfare with JUCEPLAN's fantasy projections as Fidel had revised them with Osmany Cienfuegos.

I was right about one thing: This was to be my final budget grind. As for my summer escape plans, a new assignment would take care of them. García Valls, with a very worried expression on his face, called me into his office that November to announce that once again I was to explore the world of the embassies, this time in Panama.

He told me that I was ordered to investigate every account in Panama City and to report fully on what I found. For traveling Cubans, Panama was the New World Madrid, an obligatory stop and an ideal place to shop. Its proximity to Cuba and the low prices of consumer goods there made Panama City so attractive that I could easily imagine the situation there to be worse than what I'd found in Spain.

I did what advance investigating I could in the various ministries that had regular dealings in Panama. I also wanted to take along a witness whose credentials were impeccable, something I had regretted not doing in Madrid. Nilda Rodríguez, a department head in the Office of Currency and leader of the party committee at Finance, was the perfect choice. I also packaged the balance of my notes in the expectation of shipping them to Maître Jean Budin from Panama. Hoping that I wouldn't have to explain the extra luggage to Nilda, I arrived for our December 1, 1979, departure at the Havana airport nearly an hour early.

To my dismay, there she was waiting for me. "Oh," she said, "you have a lot of luggage!"

"It's not full of clothing," I answered, trying to make the extremely heavy bag of notes look as if it held little. "I brought along an extra suitcase to have room for the papers we must get in Panama."

When we landed, I went through the same pantomime, hefting my many pounds of notes through the airport as if the bag were feather-light. As soon as I could, I posted the documents to Paris.

For the next two weeks I moved through the most sophisticated spheres of corruption among Cuban officials. The Embassy personnel in Panama City had once again been advised of our visit by MININT and the Ministry of Foreign Relations and ordered to cooperate. But they did not know our purpose, and so our presence intrigued them. The ambassador, Miguel Brugueras, was a close associate of Comandante Manuel Piñeiro and an outstanding member of Cuban Intelligence since the beginning of the revolution. He kept reminding me that he had only recently been named to the post. His laments recalled those of the ambassador in Madrid.

"We're simply intermediaries," he told me at our first interview. "I don't know and I don't care where they get the money from, but somehow this carnival should be stopped. Until now all we've done is entertain officials passing though the city. Every day they want more and more. You have to give them high-level treatment and facilitate their shopping. The quantity of VCRs, color TVs, tape recorders, record players, and air conditioners that leave here for Cuba is incredible."

I told Nilda to go over the accounts and make photocopies of every document that might reflect some irregularity, while I met with the heads of the ministries represented in Panama. Almost all of the ministries, in violation of established regulations, had large amounts of dollars deposited in checking and savings accounts in Panamanian banks.

The representatives of the Ministry of Fishing, as always, were the most audacious. This ministry, first headed by Emilio

Aragonés, had historically been characterized by its lack of rigor in the control of currency. Its leaders had the advantage of fishing boats, the perfect cover for avoiding customs inspection, and they brought everything into the country, from a package "on commission" to an automobile.

Most of the private accounts were in the Embassy's commercial office, where one official's full-time job was to transport leaders to the Free Zone in Colon City; there, duty-free goods were sold at very low prices. The same official was in charge of taking care of orders placed in Havana.

The greater the power the less the concern with covering traces of wrongdoing. In a Panamanian bank we found an account for $750,000 in the name of Omar Vázquez, who said he was an adviser to Guillermo García, a Politburo member recently promoted from the Personnel Exchange to become minister of transportation, and who came to Panama every month to do his chief's personal shopping.

I discovered Fidel's personal account, certainly well nourished, was in the name of Rodolfo Fernández, office manager for Celia Sánchez. His receipts showed purchases of great quantities of luxury items, many of them exclusively for female use. Raúl Castro's receipts were mixed in with MINFAR's. His personal aides traveled frequently to Panama to buy special orders. I didn't want to pry into these two accounts, but I wasn't certain if it was a good idea to make exceptions. Perhaps Fidel himself did not know the means by which he acquired the goods he kept or gave away; I did not dare hide something, in case I was accused of being deceitful later.

Nilda and I returned to Havana after two weeks, loaded down with hundreds of photocopies, any one of which would demonstrate that revolutionary austerity and honesty were no more than a myth. "Just wait till Fidel finds out," commented Nilda ingenuously. "Poor man! He works so hard and then they do this to him."

"Yes, just wait till he finds out," I said, asking myself if the woman was really so innocent or if, on the contrary, she was so astute that her mask of naïveté was completely in place.

While in Panama, as I uncovered evidence of the deep corruption within the leadership, I felt there were bound to be tremendous repercussions when I returned. Now, with all the facts in my suitcase, I knew for sure that I was going to face the wrath of the gods and would have to focus all my energies on trying to come out of this unharmed.

Back in García Valls's office at CEF, I watched the minister-president sink into his chair as if he wanted to escape to another dimension while he listened to my report. He stared at the white wall, his chin wrinkled, his lips pursed, his eyebrows raised. This time the problem was not simply our having to inform Fidel. It was a matter of bad timing. In recent days Fidel had been highly irritable because of Cuba's unremitting economic troubles and because Celia Sánchez was gravely ill; his inseparable companion and confidante of so many years was dying from lung cancer.

Just as before, we decided to prepare two reports: an exhaustive one for Fidel that would reach him through Abrantes, and another more general one, referring only to the ministries, that would be submitted via official channels. These were sent on December 28, the equivalent of April Fool's Day in Cuba. When García Valls and I realized the date, we looked at each other and agreed it was a poor choice of days to send this particular report.

Celia Sánchez died on January 9, 1980 and her death may have been the hardest personal blow Fidel had suffered since the triumph of the revolution. Her body was put on view in the Plaza de la Revolución at the foot of the monument to José Martí. For one whole day it was under constant guard; the trade union in each workplace organized a parade of workers past her coffin. An army detachment headed the procession, and at the cemetery she received the highest military honors. And rightly so. Celia Sánchez had been part of the Moncada assault, a fighter in the Sierra Maestra, and from that time on, the woman closest to Fidel. To the Cuban people she represented one of the greatest examples of the revolutionary woman.

I had no way of knowing how much of what followed was due to my report, but a few days after I sent it to him, there was much scurrying around in high levels of the party and the government. The ministers and other leaders mentioned in my reports did all they could to erase every trace of guilt, from the luxuries in their homes to the tape decks in their cars. The most notable was Rafael Francia Mestre, then minister of agriculture and a member of the party's Central Committee. Mestre pulled out the wall air conditioners in his house one night. By early the next morning, not only had the units been removed to the ministry, but every sign that they'd been installed at Mestre's residence had been erased. All the mounts and apertures were plastered over, and even the house's walls were repainted. That's what's called Communist efficiency!

On January 11 the front page of *Granma* announced the largest ministerial massacre of the revolution. The Central Administration staff was reduced from forty-three people to thirty-five. Nine ministers were "unemployed" and eleven were replaced by a decision of the Council of State on January 10, 1980. Of course, this was reform, revolutionary-style; those who were dismissed became new ambassadors or simply moved down to a slightly lower level on the pyramid of power. Mestre, for example, shortly after being dismissed was appointed ambassador to Angola. That's how the revolution "punished" its naughtiest children.

But in mid-January 1980, in García Valls's office, the new minister of fishing, Fernández Cuervo, held a long discussion with the minister-president, the outcome of which left me petrified. The Ministry of Fishing, as my report confirmed, was the most corrupt of all the state agencies. At Fernández Cuervo's request, the CEF auditing office would carry out a general audit at Fishing and its enterprises—and I would be the one delegated by García Valls to do it. After discovering gross irregularities in this agency outside Cuba, I could imagine what I'd find inside Cuba.

The Ministry of Fishing had always enjoyed special status, which allowed its leaders to handle hard currency with almost absolute independence. They protected one another and had formed a *piña* that was very difficult to combat. Realizing this, Fernández Cuervo, who was not part of the corruption, had asked for the investigation so that he could take action based on concrete facts.

The kingpin of this "mafia" was Antonio Carrillo, one-time ambassador to France, back from his long-ago disgrace for having hidden his fugitive nephew, who was AWOL from UMAP. Carrillo had climbed long and hard to become deputy minister of fishing since 1975. There, protected by Pepín Naranjo and Osmany Cienfuegos, he was able to resume the same opulent and licentious life as one of the "untouchables." He also belonged to the glorious ranks of the revolutionary vanguard—that is to say, the party, an honor bestowed on Carrillo personally by Raúl Castro.

From the first day we uncovered illegal activities. Expenses for Fishing "representatives" in capitalist countries reached $200,000 annually, but there were no receipts to document them. Fishing boats were removed from production, ostensibly for maintenance but in fact for private fishing parties whose members indulged in every pleasure imaginable.

As for Carrillo, we found that he had a new motor for his private Mercedes-Benz, personal bank accounts in Spain, France, and Japan, 100,000 pesos invested in the expansion of his private home with the excuse that he had to entertain wealthy Spanish businessmen, and hundreds of luxury articles that he gave to his friends and girlfriends.

But this thievery was minuscule compared to administrative operations. In December 1979 the Ministry of Fishing had proclaimed that it had fulfilled its export plan of $100 million, and then-Minister Aníbal Velaz had even sent a letter to Fidel to inform him of this "success." Now our audit revealed that the "success" was nothing more than a gigantic hoax, that $52 million corresponding to these exports were not in the National Bank.

As part of this sham accounting, the Ministry's enterprise for the export of fish and shellfish, CARIBEX, had recorded as a completed sale a large quantity of lobster and shrimp, valued at $25 million, that had not yet been sold; it was stored in freezers in Canada. The remaining $35 million were still owed to Cuba by businessmen in Spain, France, and Japan. Because the officials at the National Bank of Cuba were afraid of Carrillo's power, they had said nothing about this abuse.

Worried by the seriousness of the audit's revelations, García Valls asked for an urgent meeting with the vice-president of the Executive Committee of the Council of Ministers in charge of Fishing, Flavio Bravo. Flavio Bravo seemed alarmed at the meeting, although he almost certainly knew the facts, since he was part of the group that received "gifts" from Fishing's leaders. But Bravo said only, "I'll have to discuss this problem at a higher level. I ask you to be patient and have confidence in the party." His higher level was Pedro Miret, another of Carrillo's intimate friends.

Days later Flavio Bravo called another meeting to tell us that the case "was in the hands of party leadership." The heads of MININT who were at the meeting, as well as García Valls and myself, understood perfectly what that meant—that nothing at all would be done—but no one said a word.

Meanwhile, the very influential Carrillo had begun to wage an intensive campaign against the audit among the high-level leaders. I learned of his attacks against the State Finance Committee from several sources. I also learned that I was the principal target of his campaign. One rumor he launched was that the investigation was dominated by personal problems between him and me.

At the beginning of March, Osmany Cienfuegos sent to every ministry involved a copy of my Panama report and a handwritten note demanding, on behalf of Fidel, a discussion of the report between the CEF and each of the ministers involved. A shudder ran through my body when at the end of the last page of the copy of my report I saw: "Prepared by José Luis Llovio." It was not common practice for the person who had prepared this kind of document to be openly associated with it. Suspecting Carrillo's hand in this, I found myself exposed to the wrath of almost all the high officials in the party and the government.

Two days later we received a letter from Carlos Rafael Rodríguez, now member of the Politburo and chief of the External Sector, written in an ironic, almost threatening tone. One of the paragraphs read: "As always, the organisms in my sector are involved. . . . I suggest a meeting of Vice Ministers of Economy from these organisms, presided over by a Deputy Minister of the CEF and with the participation of *Compañero* Llovio, who, of course, must prove his accusations."

I said to myself, *José Luis, this is your death sentence.*

Three days later, Maggie was waiting with a message for me as I walked into the apartment. "García Valls called you twice," she said. "He's at the Committee and says it's urgent you get in touch with him."

Urgent calls from García Valls had become habitual in recent months. After a brief telephone conversation with him, I left for the Finance Committee.

The old building was even more depressing at night. The ground floor was dark and almost deserted. Two young women in militia uniforms were on guard duty, impatiently waiting for the arrival of their relief. The sound of the elevator broke the silence with a long trail of echoes.

No one else was on the seventh floor. García Valls had retired to his office, where he was leaning on his desk, absorbed in reading a document. A light very close to him projected his curved shadow onto the wall. When he heard my steps he raised his head and turned to me.

"Llovio," he said without emotion, "I have to tell you my decision. From this moment on you are no longer my chief adviser. Because of your involvement in *La Dolce Vita* and your prolonged stay in France, you've been replaced." His voice broke when he pronounced the last syllables.

I was silent for a few moments. Since I'd received the report with my name on the last page, I'd had presentiments of this moment. But now I didn't want to believe it. His words resounded in my ears.

"I don't understand, Minister," I said without expression. "I've been working with you for three years. In all that time you haven't pointed out a single error. I've received the highest administrative evaluations, and I presume that my party evaluations have also been favorable. I've worked as hard as you have. Together, we've built CEF out of nothing. I've shown my competence for the post, and I'm a revolutionary. Then what's the reason for replacing me?"

"Llovio," he answered—or, rather, didn't answer—me, "I repeat: Because of your involvement in *La Dolce Vita* and your stay in France you are replaced. That's all. There's nothing more to say. If you ask me again I'll repeat the same thing. Do you understand?"

In spite of the firmness of his voice, I knew he was lying; García Valls, too, had been reduced to a tool. This categorical decision against me came from much higher up, probably from Lionel Soto, the member of the Central Committee responsible for economic affairs. The only way I could be dismissed was through the *nomenklatura* for Finance, of which Soto was the head.

"And when should I leave?" I asked García Valls coldly. "And unfinished business—who should I turn it over to? What will you tell the other directors and workers on the committee?"

"You should leave right now," he said. "As soon as you've collected your personal belongings. I'll take care of unfinished business, and on Monday there will be an assembly to inform the workers."

"And what reasons will you give them?"

"They'll be told that you don't meet the requirements for the post," he answered, avoiding eye contact. "The same thing will be told to the party cell."

"Why don't you tell them what you just told me?" I challenged him with revolutionary aggressiveness. "Why don't you tell them that after five years in a *nomenklatura* position at the Sugar Ministry, and more than three years as your chief adviser, I'm being replaced because of what happened more than fifteen years ago?

"Why don't you tell *me* the truth?" I went on, raising my voice. " 'You don't meet the requirements.' That doesn't say anything. I could be an imbecile, a drunk, a thief. You preach honesty and now you want to hide the truth. Why don't you say that what *they're* trying to do is destroy me politically!"

I collected myself for a moment, and then spoke slowly, without equivocation. "García Valls, you can tell Lionel Soto and the whole Economic Department of the Central Committee that I will not sit still for this. I'll respond as violently as I've been treated. And I'll do it in the open; not like a hypocrite, not like them."

García Valls was mute in his humiliation as Lionel Soto's errand boy. When he reached meekly for the open document on his desk, I strode from his office and went to collect my belongings.

But before leaving the building I wanted to emphasize my determination to fight. By nature, by the code of revolutionary conduct, and as a matter of survival, I could not accept this punishment.

"I have nothing against you," I said to García Valls from his door. "You're simply following party orders, although you know very well this is an injustice. I'll win this fight, García Valls. I don't care where the blow came from. I assure you I'll win this fight."

Back on the street my rage strangely altered my perceptions. The familiar surroundings suddenly lacked precise forms. I was sensible only to García Valls's distorted, disembodied voice resounding in my ears. "You are replaced. You are replaced. *You are replaced!*"

FIGHTING BACK

Back in the apartment I asked Maggie to come to the park with me. She did not know what I had found in the embassies and in the Fishing Ministry, or what terrible jeopardy I now faced. But what she did comprehend at once from my news was my desperate anxiety, which she addressed in a combative spirit.

"It's so unfair!" she said angrily, focusing my own confused thought on the essential dilemma before me. "You have a very powerful enemy."

We talked for a long time that night and throughout the next day. Maggie's fundamental faith in me calmed and steadied me. Through her, I found my bearings again and began rationally to assess our predicament.

Beyond adopting a determined, truculent pose, I had no clear idea how I was going to combat this crushing reversal. I had put García Valls on warning that the matter would not rest, but I didn't have the opportunity to demonstrate my commitment until, a few days later, Olivier Stirn, the French secretary of state, came to Cuba on an official visit. I knew Olivier from my student years in Paris, and before my last trip to Europe, Cuban Intelligence had told me of their interest in approaching him. They had asked me to get in touch with Stirn on my way through Paris, but when I returned I made the excuse that I hadn't been able to reach him. Then they had prepared several gifts—tobacco, rum, and a book about Cuban painting—to send to him in my name as a New Year's present. Ever attentive to nuance and detail, Cuban Intelligence had sent similar packages in my name to our mutual friends Bernard and Christian, so that Olivier's suspicions would not be aroused.

Olivier arrived in Havana two or three days after my termination at CEF and asked Raúl Taladrid, director of capitalist countries at the State Committee for Economic Collaboration, about me. As a result I was invited to a reception in Stirn's honor, a summons to be of use to the state that I categorically refused. The act underscored my stance as a revolutionary man of honor, unjustly afflicted, who would not bow to expedience to curry official favor. This was not a time to appear weak, even though I truly felt helpless.

I expected my unexplained dismissal to raise trepidation among my supposed friends in the revolutionary elite; knowing only that I must have made a powerful enemy was enough to scare everyone away, with the exceptions of Alfredo Guevara, Papito Serguera, and Diocles Torralba. Otherwise, absolutely no one was interested in me. I had fallen into political ostracism, which means total ostracism in a Socialist country.

My thoughts began to slide around senselessly in the growing void of my mind. I felt as if my nerves, my sinews, even my bones were atrophying. The deepest paranoia gripped me. It seemed that many eyes were following my movements, that other ears were listening to every step I took. Remembering MININT's investigation of the microfraction, I believed these cares to be well founded.

They were. I went through my clothing, checked my papers, scrutinized every object in the house. The discovery of two shining tiny pieces of metal confirmed my instinct. Microphones had been installed to spy on me in my own house, one inside the plate that held the living room lamp to the ceiling, the other at the top of one of the bookcases.

My situation was every bit as serious as I had imagined, and so far all I had done was to wait. But wait for what? Wait until Lionel Soto or whoever had ordered my downfall reversed himself? Wait for him kindly to bring my retirement to an end and place me in some unimportant post from which I could never hope to escape? If I did that, I thought, I would never regain the approval of the "system." Even if the party placed me in a new post, I would not be trusted again. As I knew from bitter experience, the "system" had a very long memory. I would have to accept the idea of not leaving Cuba for another ten years, and of never leaving it with Maggie. And acceptance meant my moral death, my defeat.

I knew I could not afford to wait; I had to act, rapidly and precisely. The person behind my dismissal undoubtedly was a high-ranking official powerful enough to make Lionel Soto do his bidding. Somehow, I had to take my case around and over this anonymous foe to the only possible court of appeal: Fidel or Raúl.

Antonio Carrillo was so closely associated with Pepín Naranjo, Fidel's personal aide, that I rejected the idea of trying to reach Fidel. Given the choice between Carrillo and me, Pepín would surely choose his protégé, and his influence would be decisive. That left Raúl, the colorless, humorless little man notorious for his heavy hand and ideological inflexibility; the comandante whom his own officials treated with panicky respect, the frugal soldier inaccessible to most civilians, the leader whose prefabricated image made even the most daring leaders tremble. Raúl Castro, it was widely believed, had and would do anything to protect the revolution's image. I had to gamble that he wouldn't turn his wrath on me. If I was right, there was still some hope for me.

My strategy, which I worked out over several days and through long conversations with Maggie, was to state the facts plainly, but discreetly, and to invite Raúl to thoroughly investigate the situation on its merits; that is, to examine my life in detail to see if anything I'd done justified my dismissal and dishonor.

Everything hinged on the spotlessness of my record over the past fifteen years. I could not be reproached for living opulently. Maggie and I occupied the same apartment I'd had since

1965—and it hadn't even been painted since then. My administrative evaluations had been positive all through ICAIC, MINAZ, and CEF. I knew from Leónides Méndez that my party evaluation was clean. And no senior Communist revolutionary had ever been more scrupulous on the road than I. My expense reports were meticulous: every last dime was accounted for. Anyone in Fidel's government who asked Raúl Castro to review his record, to search back over a decade and a half for any evidence that he was anything but what he claimed, a model Communist revolutionary, had to be sure his record reflected that assertion. I was.

The letter itself required four full days of writing and revision; I hardly slept until it was completed. The language had to be in the correct ideological style, while the wording spelled out my incomprehension at events. Nothing else could seem to lie behind the extraordinary request to be investigated. Only the purest ideological motivations, the desire for revolutionary justice, could appear to have stirred me to write.

When at last I was satisfied with the letter and had signed it, "Revolutionarily, José Luis Llovio," I needed trustworthy advice as to whether I'd pleaded my case correctly and the best means of getting it directly to Raúl.

After much consideration, I decided to consult Comandante Lino Carreras, a member of the Party Central Committee and then a member of the Party Commission of Control and Revision, the unit of the Central Committee that enforced discipline and arbitrated issues of correct party behavior. The commission was the party equivalent of the U.S. Supreme Court, a very useful place to have my arguments known, if and when Raúl acted.

After I gave Comandante Carreras the letter and explained its contents, he looked at me with plain respect. "If you dare to write to Raúl Castro," Lino said, "you must be innocent—or crazy." In accordance with his advice, I then took it directly to Raúl's office at the Central Committee.

MARIEL

Given the extraordinary daring of my request, I knew that I would hear from Raúl very soon. About a week later, on Saturday, April 5, I was with Maggie at the home of Servando Cabrera Moreno, the eminent painter who was one of the few friends we visited during the months of my forced retirement. That day we were listening to stories about his friends, the film maker Carlos Saura and Geraldine Chaplin, whom he had visited during his last trip to Spain, when a confusion of voices and the sound of people hurrying down the street interrupted us. We went out to the small garden in front of the house and saw a large, disorganized crowd of people heading toward the Miramar district.

"Where are all these people coming from?" I asked Servando, intrigued by that sudden uproar in a normally quiet neighborhood.

"It looks like they're coming from the Salón Mambí in Cabaret Tropicana," he answered.

"The party's over, *aseres*! We're leaving!" I heard a man shouting from the street.

"What's going on?" I asked him.

"They took away the guard at the Peruvian Embassy, *asere*. So you know, if you want to get away from the *ñangaras* [the popular nickname for the Communists] get a move on and follow us. But hurry up! There must be a riot down there already. There's nobody left at the Tropicana, nobody!" he shouted gaily as he hurried on his way.

The beginning of what was to be an extraordinary and embarrassing episode for Fidel had come two days earlier when a city bus crashed into the Peruvian Embassy, killing a Cuban guard outside. The attackers—approximately twelve of them—had forced their way in and demanded political asylum. The Cuban government insisted on the return of the attackers, who, in its opinion, did not deserve political asylum, since they were only "common criminals instigated by the CIA." The Peruvian government thought differently and refused to hand over the twelve. With that, the spark was lit.

Fidel reacted arrogantly to the Peruvians by removing all Cuban guards at their mission. It was his belief that only a few hundred of what he called "delinquents" would take advantage of this invitation to seek asylum, and that the Peruvians would be forced to accept the human trash Cuba was happy to see leave.

On April 7, *Granma* published a front-page editorial entitled "Cuba's Position"—anonymous but obviously written by Fidel. "As was to be expected," the editorial began, "a few hours after Cuban guards were withdrawn, hundreds, in their great majority criminals, *lumpen*, and antisocial elements, loafers and parasites, gathered in the grounds of the Peruvian Embassy. After forty-eight hours, there were more than three thousand, chiefly from the city of Havana and the western provinces of the country. . . . None of them were subject to political persecution nor were they in need of the sacred right of diplomatic asylum."

But that was only the start of the refugee flood. Over the next few days an incredible scene unfolded in the courtyard of the Peruvian Embassy. Men, women, and children crowded into less and less available space as an uninterrupted flow of newcomers arrived. Whole families came, carrying only small bundles, not looking back, not caring about the consequences of a decision they had made so quickly.

On the morning of Sunday, April 6, for example, I happened to pass the Embassy. At that moment, I saw the driver and passengers tumble out of a city bus and run into the Embassy, leaving the vehicle in the middle of the street. Similarly, a traffic policeman parked his motorcycle at the corner, jumped the Embassy fence, and minutes later threw his olive-green uniform onto the street.

By April 8, more than 10,000 people had squeezed themselves into the Embassy; Fidel had seriously misjudged the size of Cuba's "delinquent" population. As I later discovered in MININT files, about 1,300 of those who finally made their way to the Embassy did have criminal records or cases pending trial. The rest were ordinary workers seeking freedom.

Of course they all continued to be condemned as "criminals, *lumpen*, and antisocial elements."

"As always," read Fidel's April 7th editorial, "Cuba gladly opened the doors for them, as it had before with all the rabble that opposed Socialism and the Revolution. . . . The historic undertaking of making a revolution and building Socialism is absolutely voluntary and free."

Fidel sought to assume the mask of magnanimity by means of two measures. First, a house near the Embassy was outfitted as a clinic for the refugees, and a Red Cross station was set up, too. The Revolutionary Government also made drinking water and food available.

The second measure, announced in the editorial, provided that "those who entered the Peruvian Embassy after the guards were removed were not considered guilty of forced entry and are, therefore, absolutely free to return to their homes and go in and out of the Embassy as often as they want. The Cuban authorities will not take measures against them. They can go to Peru or any country which gives them a visa."

The truth was a bit different. The area around the Embassy was patrolled, traffic was rerouted, and control points were used to supervise the goings and comings of the refugees who chose to visit their homes. When the returning refugees reached the control points, they were savagely attacked, supposedly by indignant patriots. The real instigators of these putatively spontaneous acts of civic outrage, I learned, were young men sent out from the secret MININT schools under orders to provoke the attacks. Rightfully fearful for their physical well-being, the refugees stopped trying to get back to the Peruvian Embassy and waited at home for the official documents that would allow them to leave the country. This development was then exploited by government propagandists as evidence of the refugees' deep confidence in Fidel's guarantees.

Fidel devoted himself body and soul to this crisis from its outset. He set up what was called his "war headquarters" in a house near the Embassy and from there he directed a three-part strategy aimed at containing the embarrassment of events and, if possible, taking advantage of them.

One thrust was to divert attention away from the Embassy by highlighting social problems elsewhere. The press, radio, television, and films enthusiastically provided more and more news about unemployment and hunger in Peru, Venezuela, Chile, Costa Rica, and the United States. The devastation caused by growing inflation in Brazil and Canada received extensive coverage, as did the troubles in Venezuela, where 100,000 construction workers were unemployed in the midst of housing shortages. Everything that would reflect social discontent overseas was exploited more insistently than ever in the mass media.

Then there was the tried-and-true tactic of mobilization.

"Now the People Will Act" was the title of Fidel's April 14th editorial on the front page of *Granma*. "A million Cubans will march by the Peruvian Embassy on April 19," it announced, "all integrated and united in the indestructible ranks of the Revolution. Fifth Avenue will come alive to the marching of our fighting people and the hymns of the Revolution and the homeland."

It did, and to insure that it did, CDRs all over the city summoned "volunteers" whose participation in the march was meticulously recorded. Later every marcher was presented with a certificate bearing Fidel's signature.

Maggie earned her certificate by marching ten hours that day. The CDR excused me from participating because I had to stay home to guard our empty apartment building.

Granma pronounced the parade a huge success. What *Granma* later neglected to mention was that thousands of those same Cubans who militantly marched before the Peruvian Embassy, shouting slogans against the Yanquis and the "antisocial elements," soon joined in the exodus themselves.

Their opportunity came when Fidel impetuously moved to escalate the crisis. "The announcement has been made," said *Granma* on April 21, of "the arrival of boats from Florida to pick up the antisocial elements who have received permission to leave. ... Of course we will not greet them with cannon fire because they are not coming to wage war and we have no problem accepting the fact that they will take these people away." In fact, on Fidel's orders, Cuban agents and exiles with whom the Cuban government maintained quiet contacts were told to spread the story in Miami that any boat that reached Cuba would be allowed to take relatives out.

On April 24, ninety-four boats from Florida cast anchor in the port of Mariel; on the 25th there were 349; on the 26th there were 958. On the same day, in a new regular section in *Granma* entitled "Note from Mariel," all Cuba was informed as follows: "A passport and definitive safe conduct will be granted not only to the *lumpen* who took refuge in the Peruvian Embassy but also to any other *lumpen* who requests it. They are all 'dissidents' and they all have the same rights. Any discrimination would be unjust and unconstitutional." All a prospective emigrant needed in order to leave from Mariel was a sponsor—a relative who lived in the United States or elsewhere.

It was then that the people really "took action." The country was thrown into chaos. Thousands and thousands of Cubans flooded the designated offices to present their requests for permission to leave. At the workplace the most surprising people left their posts to exit by way of Mariel. Some, lacking a sponsor, pretended to be convicts, shirkers, homosexuals, prostitutes, or any other variety of "antisocial element" in order to obtain permission to emigrate. There were so many that even the police stations had to be used to process them.

The sudden great rush to get out of Cuba, to take advantage of this moment, was more than the explosion of pent-up anger and disaffection from the Revolutionary Government. The flashpoint had occurred a year earlier when so many relatives from the Community had visited the island with their stories of material success in North America and elsewhere. They were prosperous people who worked hard and earned a good living, a vivid contrast to life in Cuba, where there was no point to working at all.

Granma's announcement notwithstanding, it required desperate courage to present oneself for processing. Prospective emigrants, like the refugees at the Peruvian Embassy, were subjected to violent and degrading harassment, incidents approvingly described by the Revolutionary Government as "repudiations." These repulsive scenes were repeated daily all over Cuba. I saw dozens of instances where the "traitors" were forced to parade through the streets in shame, heads lowered, wearing large signs scrawled with the nastiest insults: whore, faggot, pimp, *lumpen*, cuckold, delinquent.

"Let the scum leave! Let the scum leave!" shouted the mobs that followed behind and pelted these people with eggs, fruits, or anything else they could find.

The emigrants had no rest even at home. There the neighborhood Defense Committee—the CDR—could be relied upon to prosecute "repudiation" fully. One notorious case involved Carlos Pimentel, an official from the Ministry of Fishing who lived on 26th Street in the Nuevo Vedado District across from the Acapulco Theater. After requesting an exit permit for himself and his wife, he was besieged in his own apartment for three weeks. His CDR set up a platform in front of his building and from it, using microphones and amplifiers, they insulted and threatened him twenty-four hours a day. Pimentel's electricity, gas, and water were also shut off.

Nor were children spared the brutal fury. Acts of "repudiation" were organized in the schools against students as well as their parents. Children were paraded by their schoolmates through the streets all over the country.

The collective virulence lasted several weeks, a living hell for prospective emigrants. This was the price the revolution made them pay for leaving Cuba "freely." But despite it all, requests for emigration continued pouring in.

In all, 120,000 Cubans left the Fatherland via the Mariel–Florida route.

Fidel had been interested in getting rid of a few thousand, perhaps 20,000 to 30,000 of the disaffected, but he had never suspected the volume of "delinquents" would be so great.

A controlled amount of emigration did favor the economy. Fewer Cubans on the island meant fewer Cubans to feed and dress and fewer that needed housing. It also relieved unemployment, which had become a serious threat to stability. The exportation of Cuban labor to Czechoslovakia and Germany, the thousands of construction workers sent to Grenada, Libya, Iraq, Jamaica, and Angola, the doctors and nurses who offered their services in various countries of Asia and Africa, the Cuban troops in Angola and Ethiopia—even these solutions did not go far enough. What is more, the Revolutionary Government did not know what to do with the thousands of young people who completed their military obligation or graduated from the universities.

But Fidel had a hidden motive, too, for provoking the mass exodus. His scheme was conceived at the very beginning of the crisis in response to the United States' contradictions and vacillations regarding the refugees in the Peruvian Embassy. On the one hand, President Carter had proclaimed that the United States would receive them "with open arms"; on the other hand, the authorities in Miami had threatened to confiscate the boats that returned from Cuba with refugees on board so that the boats could not go back to Mariel to pick up more Cubans.

Fidel's reaction to Carter's welcoming words—"I'll fill his arms with shit!"—was reliably reported among the revolutionary elite soon after he said it. Fidel's plan was to empty Cuba's prisons into the stream of refugees.

Two years before, during his first interview with reporters from the Cuban Community, he had said, "They [the United States] do not want common criminals to go [there], people sentenced for common crimes. We are not going to do anything so ridiculous as to include someone sentenced for robbery. It takes two minutes to find that out. Moreover, it would imply a lack of responsibility, a loss of prestige for the Revolution."

By 1980, Fidel's notion of prestige had grown rather elastic. "Either you leave or you'll rot here!" MININT officials told prisoners in their cells. Even those who had completed their sentences were now warned to head for Mariel or be arrested again. And the owners of the boats were forced to accept groups of these criminals, or they could take no one at all.

Similar actions were taken against homosexuals and the mentally ill. CDRs informed the emigration police, who suddenly appeared at their homes and forced them to leave on one of the boats. According to internal MININT statistics, about 5,300 people with criminal records emigrated at Mariel, although many of them had been imprisoned for "economic crimes" in the formal economy—black marketeering, theft of state-owned materials, or unlicensed self-employment.

The Mariel boatlift also created numerous opportunities for corruption to bloom. Some emigration officials and members of the revolutionary police sold false documents or permits for the equivalent of about $2,400. Months later, more than a dozen of these officials were arrested. Others at MININT and among the leaders of the provincial parties hurried to appropriate for themselves the best houses and apartments left by the emigrants, ignoring the need for housing among the rest of the population. This became so glaringly evident in the cities of Havana, Camagüey, and Holguín that the residents protested and the Politburo was forced to intervene and freeze distribution.

MININT and CDR members also sacked the unoccupied dwellings and took what they wanted. A widely known case involved the chief of police of Havana, "Gallego" Franco, who looted the personal belongings of an aunt who had left through Mariel. The scandal forced Fidel to relieve him of his duties.

Franco's egregious example was not isolated but typical. In Mariel's aftermath, such individuals would be severely punished for their actions. Their behavior had serious internal repercussions for the Revolutionary Government, embarrassing it in front of the people, just as the vast size of the emigration itself embarrassed Fidel in front of the world.

What the Mariel boatlift demonstrated even more dramatically, however, was what tens of thousands of Cubans thought of their revolutionary society. As I watched them go, leaving everything they had, including in some cases family and loved ones, I knew that these were the same people who had shouted "FI-DEL!" in the Plaza, cut sugar cane on weekends, and stood docilely in line each month with their ration cards. All it took was a glimmer of hope, one perilous chance to escape with nothing to a country they'd been taught to despise, for these Cubans to show their true revolutionary spirit.

Fidel was left with several disturbing truths to ponder once the episode was over. For one thing, he had clearly overestimated the public's revolutionary consciousness and the ideological strength he so often extolled in his speeches. All it took was brief contact with their prosperous relatives from the Community for Cubans to begin dreaming of joining them in exile, gladly leaving behind them the scarcity and corruption they saw every day among their leaders.

In this way, without necessarily meaning to, the Community handed Fidel a stunning internal and international defeat. The Mariel experience also caused a fundamental change in the attitudes and assumptions of the Revolutionary Government. Too many trusted low-ranking revolutionaries chose to join the exodus. Henceforth, a fog of suspicion descended over everyone. What had been unthinkable before Mariel became a topic of daily speculation. Who would be next to leave? What revolutionary would suddenly and publicly renounce the revolution? Who, after all, were the real revolutionaries, and who was pretending?

REPRIEVE AND CONFESSION

The outcome of my own plans to escape Cuba was not going to be played out on a dock in Mariel but at the Palace of the Revolution. On a Tuesday morning in late April 1980, about a month after I'd sent my letter to Raúl, a call came for me to see his aide in charge of "conflictive matters," Fabio Raimundo.

That afternoon, an elegant secretary led me to a small room on the third floor of the Palace. Seconds later, Raimundo, obese, with a broad face and a good-natured expression, came in.

"*Compañero* Second Secretary of the Party asks you to excuse him," he said in a colorless voice. "Due to the current situation at Mariel it has been impossible for him to attend to your case earlier. The purpose of this interview is for you to expand on the contents of your letter."

I nodded.

"I may be obliged to interrupt you if it is necessary to ask a specific question," Raimundo went on in his monotone. "Later, I will send a summary to the Second Secretary. If you agree, we will set up a tape recorder. In this way your statements will reach him more directly."

Raimundo paused briefly. "Do you object to our recording the interview?" he asked.

"On the contrary, I prefer it that way," I answered.

Our exchange on the issue of the tape recorder was *pro forma*. One did not refuse such a request. It also would have been pointless to object, since I knew that the interview would be taped whether I agreed or not. The room was equipped with secret audio and video taping devices. Carrying out his part in our charade, Fabio Raimundo left and returned holding a small recorder. He then took a seat next to me.

I began the discussion by repeating the content of my letter, emphasizing its key paragraph. "It would be subjective on my part to affirm that the decision made about me was influenced by my last reports," I had written and now reiterated. "All the reports were made with the greatest honesty and revolutionary discipline. It would also be subjective to assume that the decision was based on a superficial and schematic analysis of my person, but it would be dishonest not to tell you so if I think it is true."

In this paragraph I had tried to formulate for Raúl an indirect but precise message: At the highest levels of the party, reprisals were being taken against me for specific motives that he, as second secretary of the party and therefore second representative of so-called revolutionary justice, was obliged to investigate.

I was taking a gamble. I was almost certain that Carrillo's supporters had kept CEF's Fishing report to Minister Fernández Cuervo out of Raúl's hands in order to protect their friend from Raúl's wrath. In my meeting with Raimundo, I described the three reports I had made, including Fishing. This way Raúl would be made aware of the existence of a third report and would be clued into the reason I was fired. Then I again attacked the reason for my dismissal given to the staff at the State Committee for Finances—my past in France and my life in *La Dolce Vita*. I stated my total disagreement with the methods used, and I demanded my public vindication once the investigation was completed.

I did not attack García Valls directly. I only suggested his lack of combativeness, a notably unrevolutionary characteristic. I thought that his attitude had been weak and even cowardly, but I still did not know the real reasons for his conduct and so I did not want to express a personal opinion.

Raimundo said very little, taking in my speech without expression and tending to his tape recorder. When I finished, he had no questions, and no comments either. If my letter had generated any hostility in Raúl's office, Fabio Raimundo didn't show it.

Two weeks later I was summoned to meet personally with Raúl. Now I knew my letter had hit its mark; Raúl would have delegated any order to muzzle or punish me for bringing my problems to him. In fact, we did not discuss the letter at all. For the brief ten minutes we spoke at the Palace, Raúl confined his questions to the third report on Fishing which, I had guessed correctly, he had not seen.

Then he relaxed his stiff, official mien and offered me a cup of coffee. "What is your opinion of the acts of 'repudiation'?" asked Raúl, referring to the official treatment of those leaving Cuba from Mariel.

I was somewhat disconcerted by the question, since the appalling acts were then at their height. But I adopted the most convenient revolutionary lexicon (I was now an expert) and answered: "It is an error. The revolution is characterized by generosity and respect for human dignity. Those scenes damage its image. Only extremism, or rather opportunism, is realized in them."

Raúl looked at me intently. "You must have confidence in the party and in revolutionary justice," he said, and then indicated that our discussion was over.

I left the meeting knowing that I had won this battle. Raúl would have to correct the great and obvious injustice his party had paid me.

On May 30 another appointment was made for me, this time at the Economic Department of the Party Central Committee.

Manuel Castro, "El Topo," head of its section on finances, together with Germinal Rodríguez, head of the section on cadres,
had been assigned to give me the final verdict. "The party," said
Germinal, "has determined that you can occupy any leadership
post in the government."

"Does this mean that I can resume my functions at the State
Finance Committee?" I asked, moving to the offensive, although
I already knew the answer and had no interest in returning to
CEF. It was not wise for me to work in any agency connected
with Lionel Soto.

"You must understand," Rodríguez replied, wearing the same
uncomfortable look Manuel Castro had, "this decision is not
retroactive. Resuming your post at Finance would damage the
authority of a high revolutionary officer. Minister-President García
Valls was the one who dismissed you."

Germinal knew that I knew he was lying; I believed that
the decision to fire me from CEF had come from the secretary
of the Central Committee in charge of economic matters, Lionel
Soto, and perhaps from someone above him. My letter to Raúl
had forced Soto to reverse himself to the point of absolving
me, but the party was never wrong. I told Rodríguez that I
agreed with him and did not want to work in the economic
sphere again.

Unconcerned for the time being with whatever else Soto had
in mind for me, I told everyone I could the story of my request to
Raúl to be investigated. Since they all knew I'd been restored
from my punishment, knowledge that the second secretary of the
party had intervened on my behalf suddenly strengthened me in
all my dealings—job interviews and my relationships with former co-workers.

CEF and party officials informed me that in the weeks following my dismissal there had been all sorts of rumors as to its
cause, including one story that García Valls and I had had a
fistfight and another, much more serious one, that I had been
axed for ideological deficiencies.

Two of my more active detractors during my period of ostracism, I learned, had been my dear friend Leónides Méndez and
the ever-smiling Captain Erasmo from MININT. Méndez no longer
attacked me in the aftermath of Raúl's intervention.

Erasmo had persuaded García Valls to replace me with one
of Erasmo's puppets, a party member named Morgan, giving the
captain the open avenue to the minister-president he'd lacked

during my tenure as chief adviser. Erasmo had also moved his office to a private perch above the seventh floor in order to pursue more conveniently his romantic interest in a committee employee—and this became public knowledge. Eventually Erasmo's scheming caught up with him—he went too far. He was transferred to a job as a low-level official at the airport.

Another of the active participants, Antonio Carrillo, remained unaffected by the corruption report, although he was dismissed from the party one year later for his part in a scandalous orgy that took place in Panama. Carrillo, who for many years had been denounced repeatedly for serious offenses and failures, known throughout the party and the revolutionary leadership for his corruption, was punished for a casual moral lapse. His removal from the party had nothing at all to do with his systematic abuses of power but for an incident that was impossible to cover up. In time, Antonio Carrillo would rise again toward the top of the power pyramid.

As for García Valls, he called me at home one day in June to invite me, very solicitously, to lunch at his office.

"Have you had any problems?" he asked as we ate. "Are they paying you?"

García Valls himself had ordered my salary suspended from the day of my dismissal and he'd issued orders barring me from entering the CEF building and then countermanded both his own directives.

"No, no problems, Minister," I answered. "They're paying me now." And I smiled.

When we finished, I asked him in affable malice how Erasmo was doing. Since García Valls had not resisted the captain's slander attack on me, Erasmo's abrupt disappearance following my political rehabilitation was worrisome to the cowardly PSP man in García Valls. He told me in a perturbed voice that Erasmo had been reassigned to a minor post at the Havana Airport.

"Don't worry, García Valls," I said as I rose to leave. "Your friend Erasmo will know what to do, just like he did here, to become powerful again."

A few weeks later (and thanks to a contact of mine at the Central Committee), I was able to confirm the full extent of the plotting against me. My ultrasecret personal file had been doctored first to last.

My insurrectionist fighting was reduced to a minimum; my

stay in France was judged as frivolous; my participation in *La Dolce Vita* was emphasized and exaggerated with no mention of my MININT assignment; my work at ICAIC and MINAZ was underrated, my political evaluations at Finance had been modified to my detriment and bore no resemblance to the administrative assessments I'd already seen and signed.

In short, as my *nomenklatura* review for confirmation as CEF chief adviser was about to be taken up by the party Secretariat, my record had been altered to insure my rejection. Lionel Soto and his clique had given in to pressure from Carlos Rafael Rodríguez and the others implicated in my reports.

My dismissal had also been approved by friend Osmany Cienfuegos. And attached to my file was a letter from my other friend, Abrantes, in which he showed himself ready to accede to any decision taken in my case. I deduced that the influence of Carrillo, who was an intimate friend of both men, had been decisive. Osmany's connections with his former *compañeros,* the members of the PSP, had also had an effect.

As for the reports that had started the sequence of events, none of these senior members of the revolutionary elite would ever be touched by them.

By the summer of 1980 the tourist trip program was underway, and with Raúl's protection and support, I was certain it was just a matter of weeks before I'd once again be placed in a high-level job. I had fully recovered from the tremendous blow I'd received—both emotionally and politically.

Finally I was sure enough Maggie and I would get out of Cuba that I was ready to tell her what I had been withholding for almost ten years of marriage. The troubles at CEF in the spring of 1980 had delayed me, but now I felt certain we'd be able to leave—and soon. It was time to tell her the truth.

I chose as the most propitious time for my confession an August day at Varadero, where we had gone to stay with friends. The others left that morning on an excursion to the former Du Pont property nearby, so Maggie and I were alone.

I was relaxed and relieved that the moment of truth had come. We strolled in the early-day sunlight to the beach and waded into the blue-green Caribbean until we were about fifty yards from shore, standing waist-deep in the warm water. The solitude and soothing ripples around us encouraged the feeling of intimate confidence.

At first we both were silent; Maggie knew I had something of importance to tell her and was waiting expectantly to hear it. After we'd taken a few leisurely swimming strokes through the clear sea, I felt distant enough from the shore to begin my announcement.

"I'm glad we're alone today," I said to her. Then it all came out in a rush.

"I want to talk with you about something very important, now that there's nobody around," I said. "I've been wanting to talk to you about it for a long time, but circumstances kept forcing me to put it off. I hope you understand."

As I talked we continued moving farther away from shore. "I am not a Communist," I told her. "I am a revolutionary and I always will be, but not a Communist revolutionary. I have never been one. I returned from France only to rescue my uncle and then was caught in the system myself. When Marie Christine left me in 1967, she also took my only hope of escape. Then my plan was to use a trip overseas to ask for political asylum. I would have done it on one of my past assignments. Last year I planned everything, and I would have told you then if I'd been sure of the plan. We would go as tourists to a Socialist country this June and use the stopover in a Western country to ask for asylum. The plan was ruined when I was dismissed. But recently, since my interview with Raúl, things haven't been going too badly. I'm sure I will be placed again in a position of trust, in a work atmosphere that's not tense. I estimate that by next summer, or perhaps even sooner, we'll have the chance again."

We were, literally, in deep water now, well over our heads. Maggie churned the waves nervously with her arms. She was having a difficult time staying afloat. With her eyes fixed on mine, she finally spoke.

"I suspected it," she said. "Recently you've been sending out signals. Sometimes I thought I was imagining it, but other times I was certain that you were getting ready to tell me something like this. I always wanted you to think this way. I wanted it so much that there were times when I imagined it was true that you were pretending, like so many people pretend. I feel suffocated here; you've always known that. I've tried to swallow my bitterness and adjust for your sake. Now your plan makes me very happy. I don't care about the risk; I'm only worried about one thing—"

"Yes," I interrupted, "I know. I've thought a lot about your parents too. We have a year, more or less, before we go. We can talk about it again, but we should do it only occasionally, and only when we're certain that nobody's around. Do you understand? It's very dangerous. Any hint could be fatal."

Maggie already knew what close interest State Security took in our private lives. One day the preceding spring, just after I'd discovered the microphones in our apartment, she'd come home from work furious about the disorganization at the magazine. Maggie started to vent her frustration explicitly, castigating the sham of revolutionary consciousness, when I immediately jumped up and put a warning finger to my lips.

I grabbed a pad and pen. "Don't speak," I wrote. "We have two microphones in the apartment. Let's go to the park."

The incident disturbed Maggie, of course. And it took a long talk in the park to settle her anger. But once I explained to her how we would have to handle the matter—the need not to let on that we knew of the two microphones—Maggie had adjusted to their presence.

Yet keeping our escape plans a secret for a year or more was going to be a much tougher challenge than living with MININT's listeners. "What do you think about telling my mother?" Maggie asked me a couple of evenings after our conversation. "She's always wanted me to leave the country. I know that she would understand and be able to accept it even if our separation causes her pain. I can't bear the idea of leaving and perhaps never seeing my family again without at least telling my mother. I know I shouldn't look at it this way, but somehow I would feel that I was betraying them. My father is not very strong emotionally. But I know that my mother could stand it; as a matter of fact, I think it would make her very happy."

My concern about secrecy went beyond the danger to Maggie and me. I was sure that after our escape State Security would interview Maggie's family and would investigate how much they had known about our plans. If we didn't say anything to anybody, their surprise would be genuine. But if we told our plans to Maggie's mother, she would have to pretend for the MININT officials, and I didn't know how prepared she was to do that. Investigators from State Security are very well trained. They have a great deal of experience in the psychological detection of lies. A moment's weakness could betray Maggie's mother, and the reprisals in such cases are severe. All these fears inclined me to reject Maggie's proposal, but at the same time I understood her need. It seemed to me that if I opposed her in this I would be asking too much of her.

"I would have preferred that this remain between the two of us," I said to her. "But if you think you have to do it, if talking to your mother will give you some emotional relief, then go ahead. But you must keep in mind that the least slip-up on her part could be fatal, not only for us but for everybody. You have to make that clear to her."

"I'm going to think about it," Maggie said, taking me by the hand. It was our last night together at Varadero. "I'm very glad you understand. If I decide to talk to her I'll tell you, but I won't do anything right away. The later she finds out, the less time she'll have to worry about us. No matter how well she takes it, it's inevitable that she'll worry, whether everything turns out all right or not."

From that time forward, I continued to stress to Maggie all the reasons for absolute secrecy; I appreciated much more than did she how the most innocuous-seeming slip could ruin us.

Then other worries cropped up as 1980 moved toward its close. My first indication that Lionel Soto still had me in his sights came as I looked for new employment. Recently recertified Communist revolutionary that I was, my discussions with various ministries and institutes nonetheless yielded no firm offers. After a few weeks I began to sense Soto's hand behind this. If, through indirect pressure, he could prevent me from moving outside the economic sector he controlled, then in time Soto could avenge himself and his allies on me. I had no intention of giving them that opportunity; the time was fast approaching for a second letter to Raúl. Also, after Ronald Reagan's election in November 1980, Cuba declared a state approaching war against the United States on the grounds that Reagan was a warmongering fascist. The army mobilized reserve officers more frequently than ever. I was involved in numerous military call-ups and had to do special guard duty practically every weekend. An officer at army headquarters had told me that I would be assigned a reserve job in the army sometime in 1981—which would mean more time in the army and more risk to our plans.

Another "voluntary" force, the territorial militia troops, had been created for those not in the regular army reserve or civil defense. Since I was an officer in the army reserve I did not have to join this new militia, but for Maggie it was a "voluntary" obligation, and she could be mobilized at any time during the year.

Then, too, the party had created a commission to verify the authenticity of former Sierra Maestra and underground fighters so that they could be awarded medals. The ceremony was scheduled by the party for late 1981, and attendance was strictly obligatory. Any of these eventualities could coincide with the date of our trip and ruin our plan.

I had no control over the possible problems with the military and the medals, but I did see to freeing myself of Lionel Soto's machinations. In mid-November 1980, I wrote my second letter to Raúl, detailing my fruitless efforts to find work. I also repeated my desire to join an agency of government unrelated to the economy.

The difficulty was resolved within a few days, as a direct result of my letter. On November 20, I began work as an advisor at the four-year-old Ministry of Culture.

Culture Minister Armando Hart, for whom I now worked, was a member of the Politburo and a man who had Fidel's complete trust. He was known for defending all his executives. What had happened to me with García Valls at CEF would not happen with Hart, and this was a great relief.

I worked with Deputy Minister Marcia Leiseca in the areas of theater, dance, plastic arts, museums, and propaganda. After the whirlwind of my problems at Finance, my new duties seemed simple. In this peaceful setting I hoped to accomplish my ultimate goal—to escape.

THE COMMANDER IN CHIEF LOOKS NORTH

The nearly constant military mobilizations Fidel called weren't merely another instance of his familiar use of the Yanqui threat to stir tension in the people. Ronald Reagan, the eighth U.S.

President to serve as Fidel's bête noire, presented a conservative, militant anti-Communism. From the moment he took office, Reagan reintroduced on the U.S. side a confrontational tone in Cuban–U.S. affairs.

It was in this atmosphere that Reagan wounded Fidel's pride by refusing to participate in the so-called North-South Dialogue if Fidel was invited to join. This was a conference of hemispheric heads of state held at Cancún, Mexico, in the summer of 1981. The rejection so upset Fidel that before the conference he went to the Mexican island of Cozumel with the sole purpose of declaring to Mexican President José López Portillo his intention of not attending the North-South Dialogue. Fidel said he did not want to be an "obstacle" to the development of the meeting.

In September, at the 68th Conference of the Inter-Parliamentary Union in Havana, Fidel lashed out at the United States, whose delegates were attending the conference. "I am deeply convinced," he said in his opening speech, "that the group which constitutes the main core of the current U.S. administration is fascist. Its thinking is fascist. Its arrogant rejection of every human rights policy is fascist. Its contempt for world peace is fascist. Its intransigent refusal to seek and find formulas for honorable coexistence among states is fascist."

The United States government, according to Fidel, had openly declared itself "the world's policeman," and was developing a maniacal and unrestrained arms race. The United States was responsible for the grave world economic crisis, for genocidal acts in El Salvador, for the Israeli bombing of the nuclear facility in Iraq, for the brutal Zionist bombings in Lebanon, for provocations in the Gulf of Sidra against Libya, for the "criminal" South African invasion of Angola, for destabilization in Central America, and even for the situation in Afghanistan.

Fidel's extensive list of charges against the United States culminated in matters relevant to Cuba. "The Yanqui imperialists have stepped up their criminal economic blockade against our country," he declaimed, again flourishing his favorite weapon, long since an anachronism.

But Fidel wasn't finished yet. He also accused the United States of waging biological warfare on Cuba.

"Recently," he said in all seriousness, "we expressed our conviction that imperialism was using biological weapons against our homeland. It is not a groundless accusation. In less than three years five serious epidemics have plagued our animals, our plants, and—what is even worse—our population. . . . And in each case they have appeared without any logical or natural explanation."

Fidel was referring to the epidemics and plagues that had ravaged Cuba's people, cattle, and crops in the previous three years: blue mold in tobacco, rust in sugar cane, and hemorrhagic dengue among humans. Of course, it was Fidel's policies that had destroyed the harvest of two of the most productive sectors of Cuba's agricultural resources.

The first of these calamities was the sugar-cane rust blight of 1979 and 1980, a disease infestation of the superstrain Barbados 4362 sugar cane that ruined fully a quarter of the harvest. Instead of heeding as he should have the agronomist who had warned Fidel that Barbados 4362 was susceptible to rust and therefore should be planted in widely spaced fields, Fidel had dismissed his expert as a "little technician" and ordered a massive planting of Barbados 4362 cane. When the rust hit as the agronomist had predicted, Fidel blamed the CIA for causing the plague.

The United States was similarly held responsible for the attack of blue mold that wiped out the entire 1979 tobacco harvest and closed Cuba's tobacco-processing factories for two years. Here again, as I learned in conversations with Arnaldo Milián, the minister of agriculture and a member of the Politburo, there was no sinister or subversive reason for the failed tobacco crop. Milián told me Fidel had tried to save hard currency by reducing to a minimum the amounts of fungicides imported to control blue mold. Fidel, said Milián, argued that previous applications of fungicides were sufficient to protect the tobacco crops and that blue mold was no threat.

Similar reasoning led to the epidemic of hemorrhagic dengue that battered the country in 1981, causing 156 deaths. Year after year the Ministry of Public Health had warned JUCEPLAN of the need to import products to combat the astonishing proliferation of mosquitoes, which had led to the rapid spread of exotic diseases that thousands of Cubans had brought back with them from different African and Asian countries. But Fidel ignored these public health warnings and each year eliminated most insecticides from the importing plans. A singular exception to this policy was insecticide for crop dusters to drop over Varadero beach in June and July, the months when the leaders of the revolution vacationed there. In the rest of the country there was no campaign against the mosquitoes.

As always, action was delayed until the moment of crisis. The hemorrhagic dengue virus appeared and spread through the island with unusual rapidity, affecting more than 100,000 people. It was then that Fidel, not without first accusing the CIA of having introduced the virus into the country by spreading infected mosquitoes from airplanes, declared a state of emergency and authorized the purchase of 40 million dollars' worth of insecticides.

Suddenly the anti-mosquito campaign was the first priority throughout the country. Public-health workers visited private homes, stores, factories, and service centers at least once a week to conduct intensive fumigations. The Defense Committees and the Federation of Cuban Women were also mobilized to inspect standing water and to use insecticides to keep the mosquitoes from breeding. Towns and cities were overrun by large military trucks, donated by the USSR, that sprayed a dense blue smoke in the streets.

The exaggerated remedy yielded rapid results. Not only were the mosquitoes eliminated and the epidemic contained, but also vast numbers of the population broke out in allergies at the overspraying. Hundreds of nontarget animal species were nearly destroyed too.

Fidel's rage at Reagan at the Inter-Parliamentary Union conference was mild compared to the fury he would unleash three months later.

After being elected president of the Non-Aligned Nations in September 1979, to his satisfaction, Fidel had anxiously awaited December, when Cuba seemed sure to score the further political coup of becoming the Latin American representative on the United Nations Security Council. Isidoro Malmierca, minister of foreign relations, and Raulito Roa, Cuban delegate to the U.N., believed that Cuba had the votes of the non-aligned countries in her pocket. And according to Antonio Núñez Jiménez, deputy minister of culture, with these two positions Fidel planned to use his presidency of the Non-Aligned Nations and the Security Council seat to "crack the foundations of imperialism." Unexpected events, however, caused his own image to crack before the non-aligned nations.

The Revolutionary Government had closely monitored events following the successful 1978 leftist takeover in Afghanistan, never imagining that the Soviets would soon intervene militarily to rescue the new government from annihilation by Islamic tribes-people. One day before the December 1979 invasion, Moscow informed Fidel of its intentions through the Soviet ambassador in Cuba and thereby sealed Cuba's fate among the non-aligned countries. Not a single public word of condemnation, not a single allusion to the event, was heard from Cuba, with consequent embarrassment to Cuban diplomats overseas, especially those at the U.N. Fidel, president of the Non-Aligned Nations, found that he could not condemn an action in flagrant violation of the sovereignty of one of those nations! Despite all the painstaking corridor diplomacy at the U.N. by Malmierca and Roa, most of the non-aligned nations withdrew their vote for Cuba for the seat on the Security Council and backed Colombia for the post. Not coincidentally, Colombia soon experienced a sharp increase in leftist guerrilla action by its fighters all over the country.

WAR ON THE *CAMPESINO*

Cuba approached the Second Congress of the Party, which was to be held at the end of December 1980, in a very different mood than it had the First. The main reason for the change was Fidel's secret closing speech before a restricted session of the National Assembly in December 1979. The discreet revolutionary leaders who had attended the assembly had broadcast the principal points to the four winds, seriously demoralizing the Cuban people.

What they learned was that the country needed $250 million to cover the 1979 deficit and $500 million for 1980. As a consequence, the population's standard of living would be even more limited, and there would be more shortages in the people's diet.

But the most pathetic of Fidel's statements came at the end. The goal of prosperity was going to be pushed even further into the future. "We are navigating on a sea of difficulties," he said. "I believe that our people must get ready for a long struggle. . . . We are speaking of perspectives for the year 2000; we must think specially in relation to the year 2000."

After these disclosures, the Second Congress was an exercise in deceit. Once again there was some improvement in Havana's urban transportation system and in the restaurant service. Building facades in downtown districts were cleaned and repaired as well as those in the areas near the Palace of Congresses.

But the Second Congress was irrelevant: excuses for failures, artificial economic progress without any relation to reality, and promises of future well-being. I got very bored reading the materials given to the delegates. Only two aspects of the nonpublic agreements would really affect me. The *nomenklatura* process was going to be more comprehensive in its background investigation, deeper, and the modifications in the process of joining the party meant that, at the end of 1981, I would be asked to become a member. Those two matters worried me a great deal; my escape plan had to be executed as soon as possible.

As for Fidel's Central Report, only three points attracted my attention. The first referred to how much the country had spent in its development. "Capital investment expenditures in the 1976–1980 five-year period amounted to 13.2 billion pesos [approximately $15 billion]. The number sounded impressive, but as usual there was no relation between those investments and Cuban prosperity, evidence not only of mismanagement but of the Cuban people's indifference to national goals. Their languor and secret defiance guaranteed that the country's capital programs had failed and would fail. Fidel and his leaders could pledge all they wanted; the Cuban people were immune.

The second point touched on foreign policy: Fidel's endorsement of the Soviet invasion of Afghanistan. I learned by listening to his speech that circumstances in Afghanistan, like those in Poland with the Solidarity Movement, were the consequence of "ferocious provocations, the subversive actions and the indifference of imperialists and the international reactionaries." According to Fidel, imperialism had brought the situation to such a point that "the aid of the USSR became necessary to save the process and preserve the conquests of the revolution of April 1978." And in the case of possible future invasions by the Soviets, Fidel said; "It is not the least bit questionable that the Socialist camp has the right to safeguard its integrity, survive and resist, to survive and resist at whatever price the onslaughts of imperialism." In other words, what had been good for Czechoslovakia and Afghanistan would be good for Poland too.

On the third and final matter, Fidel was uncommonly terse. "The free peasant market has begun to function this year," he said of his latest strategem to eliminate the remnants of independent, land-holding *campesinos*.

Outwardly, the establishment of a market where the *campesinos* could sell their farm goods directly to consumers without taxes or price controls appeared to be a retreat for Fidel, who had consistently rejected this solution to shortages, employed commonly in other Socialist countries, as too capitalistic. The only overt advantage to him for okaying the free markets in 1980 was to insure a decent supply of food, and the look of abundance at the time of the Second Congress, when foreign politicians and journalists would be in Havana. But the measure was in truth the capstone to a tactic begun three years earlier, another of Fidel's patient and elaborate schemes.

In 1977, Fidel also had reversed himself on the issue of cooperative farming in Cuba, a form of agriculture in which small landowners banded together to pool their acreage and supplies and jointly plan what crops they would produce. Fidel had consistently opposed cooperatives, believing that they fostered independence and individualism. Most of Cuba's private farmers disliked the idea for opposite reasons, preferring to operate on their own.

By this time, only about a fifth of the island's arable land remained under private *campesino* ownership; these were the small farmers who had resisted integration into the microplans of the 1960s. They were also Cuba's most productive farmers, accounting for more than four fifths of the agricultural products officially distributed by the state, as well as the great bulk of the food available on the black market.

Fidel was determined to stamp out this vestigial form of capitalism, no matter how productive the private farmers were, and his means of doing so would be the cooperative. Well before the May 17, 1977, Fifth Congress of ANAP (the Association of Small Farmers), propaganda and direct pressure directed by the party had persuaded a minority of the *campesino* farmers that cooperatives were indeed a good idea. At the Second Congress, this fabricated support for Fidel's revised view of cooperative farming was raised in a carefully orchestrated fashion. The few farmers who favored cooperatives spoke up.

"I believe that you have spoken with great eloquence about what the integration of land means," Fidel then told a closed session of the congress. "And you have done it, moreover, with extraordinary revolutionary spirit." With that, the formation of cooperatives became national policy. All independent farmers were invited to join cooperatives and were offered several inducements to do so. Once they joined, however, they could not withdraw their participation, nor could they sell their land to anyone but the state, which put aside special funds to acquire this land as soon as it might become available.

While exploiting the idea of cooperatives as a step toward outright state control of all farmland was not going to finish off the private farmer overnight, it was an effective new weapon for separating the *campesinos* from their land holdings ultimately. One way or the other, Fidel was determined to make Cuba one vast landholding with a single manager in charge: himself.

The second step of the strategy was the 1980 opening of the free peasant markets, a move widely misinterpreted outside Cuba as a sign of liberalization. Suddenly fruits, vegetables, dairy products, and pork, which had not been seen for so many years, reappeared. The prices were rather high, but not much higher than the black market. The shops authorized to sell these products were crowded with people eager to buy goods they had been deprived of for so long. Cubans who had been limited to a meager monthly quota for years could hardly believe that suddenly they could buy as many pounds of rice or beans as they wanted, and pork, chicken, or any other agricultural product produced in the country—except for tobacco, cocoa, coffee, and beef—without the risks and difficulties of the black market.

In a parallel move, the way was cleared for the purchase of handcrafted goods, which the state now authorized artisans to produce and sell freely. Throughout the island markets were set up where the people could buy clothing, shoes, ceramics, and other handcrafted items.

The absence of any regulation of prices or taxes, as Fidel logically anticipated, promoted undue greediness among the peasants and artisans. Prices rose excessively. At the same time, another factor forced prices even higher. This was the middlemen, those who bought the peasants' harvest, or part of it, transported it to the city privately or in state vehicles, and resold it directly to householders or to the shops set up for this market at a higher price. The party and the Ministry of the Interior were aware of this situation, but they did nothing to stop it. Abundance continued, but for the average Cuban worker to pay 80 cents for plantain, or 3.5 pesos for a pound of pork, or 10 pesos for a chicken was almost impossible.

It was then the protests began to surface, the people's criticism of the private farmer as their exploiter, not their ally.

Fidel's strategy relied on this first, inevitable public backlash. And he skillfully wedded it to the ongoing campaign in favor of cooperatives, which intensified considerably in 1981 when the so-called "Agro Fairs" were opened. These were the state counterparts of the peasant market, where the state sold agricultural products in season at low prices.

The end of the chapter, as I knew from party documents, was programmed for the first six months of 1982, during the Sixth Congress of ANAP. The subject of the peasant market would be presented as a "problem" that had to be solved. The farmers would be exonerated. The middleman would be sharply criticized and eliminated with all the force of the law. But in order to avoid excessive earnings for the *campesino,* the congress would establish the need to regulate the peasant market with high taxes, price ceilings, and other measures that in the long run would discourage the private farmer, who would be obliged at last to choose between only two alternatives: joining a cooperative or returning to the risky path of the black market.

FIDEL

If my adult life and the modern course of Cuban history have a single reference point, it is Fidel Castro Ruz. I have spent many years trying to explain to myself the Fidel I saw in action, the man whose revolution I lived, the politician, and, as I came to understand him, the enemy.

In the mid-1940s, well before the first shots of the Cuban revolution were heard, Fidel Castro Ruz was an impetuous but unknown law student at the University of Havana. He is remembered from those days for a startling revelation he delivered during an informal student meeting. As the session wore on, the young men in the room turned from topical concerns to a discussion of the future and what each of them hoped to accomplish in his life. One student said that he wanted to become a great physician; another, that some day he would be a famous attorney. Fidel listened quietly until all the rest had spoken. Then he shared his dream. "My greatest ambition," Fidel stated firmly, "is to have a line written about me in Cuban history."

But Fidel did not specify what his line in history might be. In the intervening forty years, the efforts to assess his career, to reduce Fidel to his essence, have produced millions of lines of text, a deluge of analysis and interpretation that unfortunately leave him as little understood today as he was little known then. From the time of Herbert Matthews's famous 1957 *New York Times* dispatches from the Sierra Maestra, Fidel has remained the object of fascination, idolatry, censure, mystery, fear, and misapprehension everywhere, including among the Cuban people.

Fidel has actively abetted this confusion. He is instinctively guarded about himself around foreigners, the international press, and any Cuban outside the trusted circle of the revolutionary elite. He is also an artful dissembler, intent upon promoting an image of himself that is often completely at odds with reality. And even when he does speak about himself and key episodes in his past, his habit of explaining events according to his political purpose of the moment has resulted in wildly conflicting statements.

When, for instance, did Fidel become a Marxist-Leninist— and why? He did not openly declare himself a Communist until 1961 and had publicly denied any Communist agenda several times while he was in the Sierra Maestra and afterward. Years later, however, he traced his growth as a Marxist-Leninist as far back as the early 1950s. He has encouraged commentators to reach every conclusion about the reason for his conversion, from the influence of the Marxist literature he read in prison to the necessity of Cuba's embracing Soviet support in the face of U.S. hostility toward his "green as a palm" revolution.

And what is the truth of the 1962 missile crisis? Did Fidel request the nuclear arms from the USSR, and did he have a say in their deployment? From his many official versions of the incident, the answers are *yes, no,* and *maybe* to both questions. As a result of these inconsistencies and Fidel's continued willingness to rewrite history as it suits him, the man has long since become one of the least reliable sources about his own motives, ambitions, and beliefs.

Fidel came to power by dint of determination, daring, luck, and the shrewd use of his consummate political talents. In leading the 1953 attack on the Moncada Barracks, he demonstrated his bravery and his willingness to risk everything to realize his dreams, to escape his political anonymity.

From Moncada onward he placed himself directly within the
Cuban people's tradition of struggle against tyranny. He claimed
that his battle was inspired and waged in the purest ideals of
that tradition, part of a historical continuum. "I carry in my
heart the doctrines of the Master," said Fidel, referring to José
Martí, during his defense at the Moncada trial.

When he came down from the Sierra Maestra, Fidel was not
only the head of the victorious rebel army; he was also, in almost
everyone's eyes, the authentic successor to the generations of
Cuban leaders who had sacrificed themselves for justice, liberty,
and national independence. His message had struck a receptive
chord. This decisive popular support was fully independent of
the people's profound rejection of Batista.

But Fidel immediately showed himself to be an exceptional
leader as well. He had overwhelming charisma, a magnetic personality, extraordinary political skill, and an incomparable ability to communicate with the masses—gifts he exploited to the
utmost. In those days he even misled such disparate and independent figures as Ché Guevara and Camilo Cienfuegos. To them,
and to the rest of the nation, Fidel was both man and symbol, the
living incarnation of the revolution. This belief was the essence
of *Fidelismo.*

Fidel, however, was intelligent enough to realize that charisma and political arts would not be sufficient to sustain him as
a permanent ruler of a nation just ninety miles away from his
mortal enemies, the Yanquis. Fidel was sworn to defy them and
needed a system that would pit Cuba, in absolute antagonism,
against all U.S. interests. He recognized that Cuba required a
powerful ally and that he, as Cuba's unquestioned leader, would
benefit greatly from a political system that lent itself to the
perpetuation and ratification of such power.

Until the proper moment, when the revolution was strong
enough, it was expedient for Fidel not to alienate potential supporters or prematurely to alarm world opinion, especially in the
United States, with professions of Marxist affinities. He chose
instead to lie about his agenda, repeating his "green as a palm
tree" characterization of the revolution until years later, when
he avowed that even in the early 1950s—while the Cuban PSP
was shunning or denouncing him—"I already had deep Socialist
and Communist convictions."

Fidel portrays the evolution of his political thinking in a
more flattering light. Thus, in a fuller discourse with Barbara

Walters on May 19, 1977, he explained: "Before the revolution, our program was not yet a Socialist program. But those who read the Moncada program drawn up in 1953, long before the victory of the revolution, those who read it carefully and analyze it in detail will see that first and foremost it was a program of national liberation, a very advanced program that was close to Socialism. I'd say it was the most advanced program that our people could have understood at that time and in that situation."

Nevertheless, the CIA conveniently provided Fidel with precisely the proper moment to declare the Socialist character of the revolution. After the failed Bay of Pigs invasion there was absolutely no question of Cuba's reaching an understanding with the United States. And most Cubans, still firmly in support of Fidel and his nationalistic ideas, were enraged by an invasion branded as pro-Batista and pro-U.S. It was finally the right time to give a name to what had already been happening in fact. The Cuban revolution was not forced to adopt Communism, as many, myself included, had thought. The Cuban revolution had been moving resolutely in that direction all the time.

This is where Fidel's shrewdness is most evident. Even with the undeniable populist content of his first revolutionary laws, and auspicious timing, Fidel had to be at the peak of his incredible popularity, assessing every detail and variable of the situation, to declare for Cuba a system alien to most Cubans, and to do so in a way that made most of the people willingly accept it. It was simply an astonishing political coup.

But was Fidel really as Marxist as he publicly has claimed since 1961? His behavior from 1961 to the early 1970s does not accord with Marxist precepts. The imposition of moral incentives, the idealistic effort to create the "new man," the abolition of mercantile relations and economic controls, the marked tendency to undervalue money as a means of distribution, the ignorance of the theory of value, the effort to build Socialism parallel with Communism—these were not the principles of someone who understood and practiced Marxism.

Yet, because of the system, Fidel no longer needs the old magic. "It has always been said that power corrupts, that power makes men arrogant and haughty," he told Barbara Walters. "But it should be remembered that we have a doctrine. I am not a *caudillo* whose influence and power are based on personality or personal appeal. My power and strength are based on ideas, on a doctrine, on convictions.... And what is a dictator? I don't identify myself as such."

But can he contemplate any role other than *Líder Máximo*? "It seems to me that it would be an act of selfishness on my part if I were to resign in order to rest, write, and live a less tense life. So I couldn't do that. However, if I felt incapable or incompetent it would be my duty to resign. And if I didn't realize this, most likely my *compañeros* would replace me."

He clearly thinks that possibility is remote. "Perhaps," Fidel went on, "if I am capable until I die, I will be on the job until then. I'm going to have a long life. Then, most likely, I would be President until I die."

That is one definition of a dictator, although Fidel denies he is one. Another hallmark of his strong-man rule is the cult of personality, a blatant phenomenon in Cuba which Fidel also rejects as a fiction.

It is true, as he has declared, that no streets bear his name and no statues are erected in his honor. But many places connected to his revolutionary career are museums or national monuments today. Siboney Farm, outside of Santiago de Cuba, the spot from which Fidel launched his attack on the Moncada Barracks, is a venerated site open to the people and to tourists. Fidel himself shows it off to foreign statesmen and other distinguished guests who visit the country.

The old Modelo Prison on the Isle of Pines is a museum featuring, among other things, the cell where Fidel was imprisoned after the attack on Moncada. The old Presidential Palace, today the Museum of the Revolution, also preserves many artifacts of his past. On one side of the building, in an enormous crystal urn, hermetically sealed and air-conditioned, rests the yacht *Granma*—like a fetish. The old boat is always watched over by an honor guard, and tour guides describe the *Granma* reverentially, as if it were a shrine.

¡Comandante en Jefe, ordene! "Commander in Chief, at your command!" The phrase means exactly what it says. Fidel is the banner raised to motivate any activity, political, economic, or social. For mobilization to the countryside or to the trenches, to surpass goals, to attend demonstrations or receptions, to study, to march off to distant lands to work or to fight, the spur is always the same: Fidel. When children are taught to write, the first thing they learn is that *F* is for Fidel.

Fidel's speeches immediately become study materials in the party cells, the trade unions, and the Defense Committees, where each gives birth to at least one new slogan. It is a widely held belief in Cuba that when the *Líder Máximo* speaks, the entire world listens. In the days following any speech, *Granma* reprints all favorable or admiring comments that have appeared in the world press. And the revolutionary bourgeoisie boast that the voice of the Commander in Chief causes the United States and other enemy countries to tremble.

The first casualty of war is the truth. Certainly Fidel has always been at war in one way or the other, and he has always regarded his political truth as a relative commodity. "Subjective conditions change" is how he often puts it.

One moment the Soviets are cowards and have moved away from Marxist ideology; the next moment they are not. Armed conflict is the solution for Latin American nations, and sometimes it is not. The Communist parties of Latin America are bourgeois and corrupt, and sometimes they are not. Moral incentives move the revolution forward, and sometimes they do not. Money has no value, and sometimes it does. The sovereignty of nations must be respected, and sometimes not. Cubans in exile are condemned, and sometimes they are welcomed with open arms.

Similarly, Fidel's loyalty to any cause or friend is always subordinate to expediency or his political interest. Osmany Cienfuegos, for example, has proven himself corrupt and incompetent at every post he's ever held in the Revolutionary Government. He has been punished, but is always restored to important and highly visible positions.

In contrast, there was the case of Haydée Santamaría, one of the founders of the July 26th Movement. Haydée had been part of the assault group at Moncada and she fought in the Sierra Maestra as well as in the underground. With Celia Sánchez, Haydée was the very symbol of the revolutionary woman. No one was more loyal to Fidel from the beginning.

But Haydée paid a heavy psychic price for her bravery. She suffered in prison and endured the trauma of being shown her brother Abel's dissected eyes after he was horribly tortured and killed by Batista's army. She never recovered fully and finally snapped under the strain of her divorce from Armando Hart. Totally unbalanced, she became hysterical at the thought that

Hart would take his new wife, the actress Norma Martínez, to the annual July 26th celebration in 1980. A few days after the holiday, Haydée Santamaría put a bullet in her head.

Unlike that of her *compañera* Celia Sánchez, Haydée's body did not lie in state at the foot of the José Martí monument in the Plaza de la Revolución. Rather, she was perfunctorily buried, with few official expressions of respect befitting her revolutionary prestige, and no funeral oration from Fidel.

Why? Because the state religion of Communism proscribes honor to suicides, no matter how exemplary their lives or heroic their careers. Haydée's absolute loyalty counted for nothing; the anguish of her later life elicited no official sympathy. As far as Fidel was concerned, Haydée Santamaría had betrayed the revolution.

However, Fidel soon discovered how genuine a heroine Santamaría was to the Cuban people. Once he detected the unpopularity of his action, he directed Cuba's media and the whole propaganda machine to begin acknowledging Haydée's special place in revolutionary history.

Fidel observes the same standard of conduct in his international relations. There is the case of his Algerian friend Ahmed Ben Bella, the man who defended the Cuban revolution to the Arab countries and who dared to visit Cuba in the early years of the revolution in defiance of U.S. pressure. What was Fidel's attitude toward Ben Bella when he was overthrown by Houari Boumedienne's coup? Ben Bella was forgotten and a pact was made with his enemy. Similarly, Fidel gave the people of Eritrea, fighting for the independence of this Ethiopian province, his political support and weapons against Haile Selassie, but only as long as it suited him. Then, when his friend Mengistu Haile Mariam came to power, Fidel transferred that help to Mengistu's forces to exterminate the Eritrean fighters, who by then were considered "counterrevolutionaries." He also used Comandante Douglas Bravo and his guerrillas in Venezuela, supplying them with money and materiel as long as it was in his interest to foment Venezuelan guerrilla warfare. Then he pushed them aside; Comandante Bravo no longer suited Fidel's plans to improve relations between Cuba and Venezuela.

Fidel's political versatility is also evident in his relations with Latin American countries such as Mexico, relations that are apparently very warm. In reality, the seeming harmony between the two countries is contingent upon the Mexican government's support for the Cuban revolution. The Mexicans understand that if this support were to change, their country would experience a rapid increase in student uprisings and a more intensive effort by the radical left to increase subversive activities.

Cuba's domestic economic situation is masked from foreigners. True, visitors from other countries are shown around Fidel's extensive fiefdom, but they see only what Fidel wishes them to see. A foreigner has no access to working-class Cubans, who are too afraid to be candid. If a visitor talks to one of Fidel's leaders, all the answers and apparently spontaneous remarks are exhaustively prepared.

Should the visitor be a writer or a journalist, he or she is often given the opportunity to interview Fidel himself. But writers such as René Dumont, K. S. Karol, Mario Vargas Llosa, and Pierre Goldendorf, among many others, have learned that the warmth of their reception in Cuba is a direct function of what they have to say in print. Because they wrote what they believed instead of uncritically praising Cuba, these writers are now considered "agents of the CIA paid by imperialism."

Despite his constantly decrying the intervention of other nations or opinion-makers in the life of his country, Cuba repeatedly intervenes, directly or indirectly, in the internal affairs of other countries. But Fidel is rarely censured; in fact, he issues his own indignant protests whenever the United States or some capitalist nation flexes its muscles. When he invokes the chimera of the imminent United States invasion of Cuba, he can still rely upon an outpouring of communiqués and documents from radical leftist groups in support of the Cuban revolution and expressions of "concern" by many governments. At the same time, Fidel's open support for guerrilla warfare and the presence of Cuban troops in other nations provoke no comment from these groups and governments. Rather, they respond with the silence of complicity.

Fidel's international schemes are rooted in his obsession with his place in history. "We have made a revolution larger than ourselves," he has said on many occasions, and he strongly believes it. While the Commander in Chief's real glory would be to bring prosperity to his people, his first dream is to be seen as the liberator of the oppressed of the earth.

Consistent with the dream is his coveting of international honors. Some, like his presidency of the Non-Aligned Nations, have been realized. Others, such as a Cuban seat on the United

Nations Security Council, have been scuttled by his inopportune deal with the Soviets. Still others, like the Nobel Peace Prize, continue to preoccupy him.

Fidel also has more modest dreams. He has always wanted to make state visits to Spain and to France. The official trip to Spain has been planned twice and then postponed. The invitation for him to visit France has yet to be extended. Of course, there is an inherent contradiction in Fidel's wishing to visit a country he has often criticized.

Fidel's personal behavior is also not free of contradictions. I recall one typical performance he put on for Barbara Walters, the ABC News interviewer noted for the apparent candor she elicits from her famous subjects. "You are a man of mystery to us," she told Fidel on television on May 9, 1977. "First of all, why the mystery? You come from nowhere; you seem to disappear. We hear you have no one home. You are a man of secrets and mystery."

As I watched the interview in Havana, I felt that it rankled Fidel. In private, he calls such prying questions "a decadent characteristic of bourgeois journalism." Fidel gave Ms. Walters a smile, however, and then an amiable nonanswer.

"I suppose we could say that we're up against the mystery theory, no?" he responded. "I ask myself—I am the first to ask myself—where is the mystery? And who invented it?"

Then, because the question provided an opening for attack on his favorite foreign target, the CIA, Fidel did acknowledge that he kept his plans a secret. "There are things we had to do from the start of the revolution," he said. "If we were about to make a trip, for example, why give the CIA and its terrorists advance notice? Why would we have given them advance notice at that time, over ten years ago, when the CIA used all its means and resources to try to assassinate me? What obligation did we have to make the CIA's work easier? Obviously, we were forced to take precautions."

Fidel then buried the question. "Nothing is more alien to me then mystery," he told Ms. Walters. "I like things to be free of protocol and solemnity. I like them to be as simple and as natural as possible. That's the way I am and how I live."

That is how Fidel *once* lived: the informal, casual guerrilla leader I'd encountered in 1959 in his room at the Havana Libre, his hair sopping-wet from the shower, unselfconsciously pulling on his socks and boots. But by the time Barbara Walters interviewed Fidel in 1977, the simplicity he spoke of was already a fading memory.

One transformation manifests itself in how he dresses. Although Fidel still wears uniforms everywhere, he has a regular and a dress version. They are both cut from the finest imported English gabardine and fitted by the most skilled tailors in Cuba. Likewise, his combat boots are brought in from France or Spain. At social occasions, he favors a high-fashion boot with semi-squared toe and a zipper on the side.

The revolutionary leaders are also required to take care of their personal appearance. If they are civilian leaders, they must wear a *guayabera,* a business suit, or at least a safari jacket to all meetings at the Palace of the Revolution and at important ceremonies. Cuba's military chiefs must be turned out in dress uniforms, displaying their insignia of rank and loaded down with medals. The old scorn Fidel once expressed toward military rank (according to him, ribbons, sashes, and brass were unwholesome reminders of Batista's army) has disappeared completely. Fidel himself affects two special laurel-leaf insignia on his uniforms, no doubt a reflection of his admiration for Julius Caesar.

His passion for medals also provides opportunities for solemn, formal ceremonies; Fidel has over the years developed a weakness for pomp and pageantry. The medals ceremonies are particularly grand. Raúl pins medals on Fidel, Fidel pins medals on Raúl, and they both pin medals on everyone else. At these moments, Fidel assumes an appropriately circumspect posture, accentuated for the TV cameras in close-ups.

This Fidel, mannered and punctilious, bears little resemblance to the bold young man with the full, untrimmed beard who came down in victory from the rugged Sierra Maestra clad in a dirty, ill-fitting combat uniform; the restless guerrilla loved and admired by the Cuban people who, for a time, was an authentic hero to all the underdeveloped world. Some of the change in him is the inevitable work of time; Fidel's beard is gray now and he often tries to contain a spreading belly with a corset. To the young people of Cuba, Fidel is commonly known as *El Viejo,* "the old man."

Still, he cultivates the revolutionary image. His insistence on always appearing in uniform is one conceit; never shaving his beard is another. Beards had been a symbol of the revolution. The guerrillas of the Rebel Army were affectionately known as *los barbudos,* "the bearded ones." After the victory, beards and long hair remained the fighters' distinction and subsequently became a fad. Only then did Fidel, through Raúl, order that beards be forbidden in the army. The right to grow one became Fidel's alone.

Fidel's personal barber meticulously grooms the famous whiskers each week, before every meeting with foreign visitors, and for Fidel's television appearances. The Commander in Chief is also tended to by a manicurist; Fidel makes sure his hands and nails are impeccably maintained.

His life style is as elaborate as his grooming. Fidel has always had several residences. In Havana he used to spend his nights at Celia Sánchez's apartment, and now his principal home is a mansion on 160th Street in Marianao, close to the Palace of Congresses. The house is spacious and offers every comfort imaginable, although it is in no way ostentatious. Its excellent small theater has thirty-five reclining armchairs imported from Spain, and modern video equipment, including a giant screen.

In this private den Fidel enjoys the latest Hollywood movies, his favorites. He prefers westerns, gangster movies, and Mexican *charro*, or cowboy films. Productions of greater intellectual content bore him, and he almost never watches them all the way through. Unlike his closest leaders, Fidel hates pornographic films.

Other important rooms in the Havana house are his library and an audio studio with sophisticated equipment. But Fidel does not like music very much. I've seen his bored expression at musical performances often enough to attest that he attends these public events only to fulfill his official obligations.

In general, Fidel prefers sports to culture in any form. His favored pastimes are basketball, volleyball, handball, and deep-sea fishing. He almost always spends his summer vacations deep-sea fishing on his yacht, the *Tuspán;* he especially likes needle-fishing, a sport about which he is very enthusiastic. Otherwise he can be found at his magnificent house in the Du Pont section of Varadero. In the winter, Fidel usually travels with his entourage through the interior of the country, spending time at one of the "rest" or "visitor" houses of the provincial parties.

Wherever he is, security is extremely tight. Guards are with him everywhere—no surprise, considering the number of times the CIA has tried to kill Fidel. The guards protect him as he sleeps and accompany him on his walks, when he plays sports, and on his vacations. "Shoot first; ask questions later" is their motto.

The life of the *Líder Máximo* is more important than any mistake—and several have been made. The last I know of took place in 1979 in the middle of the Vía Blanca. A car carrying several Socialist technicians returning to Havana from the beach of Santa María did not reduce speed or pull over to the right when it encountered the flashing lights of an Alfa Romeo leading Fidel's motorcade. Out came the machine guns. One technician was killed and several were wounded.

A security force capable of foiling for nearly three decades both the CIA's and many others' determination to exterminate a single target must be first-rate, and Fidel's is. Aside from his scheduled public speeches—such as his July 26th addresses, for which the safety procedures are elaborate and exacting—there are simply very few opportunities to assassinate Fidel. Most of his public appearances are surprises, and even then he is shielded from the public by his watchful bodyguards, alert to every suspicious movement. An old practice, his arriving at the University of Havana for impromptu discussions with the students, has been limited.

One price Fidel pays for maintaining his protective cocoon is isolation and loneliness, especially since Celia Sánchez's death. He was a dedicated womanizer, but every female he met and was enamored of had to be carefully investigated, lest she turn out to be a CIA agent. If the object of Fidel's affection passed this test, a discreet third party invited the woman to the beach, or perhaps on a fishing expedition. Only then did Fidel step in and the romancing begin.

In all, Fidel has enjoyed very little in the way of stable intimacy with women, and almost no family life. He is the father of at least three illegitimate offspring, but he officially recognizes only one child as his: Fidelito, born to Fidel and his first wife, Mirta Díaz Balart, whose family was very closely connected with the Batista regime. Fidelito, now in his thirties, has been put in charge of Cuba's Soviet-built nuclear power-generating plant, soon to begin operation in Cienfuegos.

Fidel must always be the first, the best; never, ever can he be shown up. I recall one vivid example of this pride, an incident well known to Fidel's inner circle. One day in 1972, Fidel was visiting a secondary school recently opened in Matanzas Province. When he came to the volleyball field, accompanied by his entourage and some teachers, he stopped to watch a game among the students. Then Fidel began to joke, to give the players advice. Finally he decided to join them, but a sudden downpour forced him to leave the game and take shelter inside a building.

There he encountered a boy about ten years old who was hitting a ball at a Ping-Pong table. "Okay, let's go. Let's have a game," Fidel challenged the youngster, who was clearly intimidated and bashful in Fidel's presence. "Don't you want to?" Fidel went on. "I really shouldn't do it, but I'll bet my cap against yours, okay?"

With no way out, the ten-year-old agreed to the match, and the game began. Immediately he showed his skill, winning point after point. Soon Fidel was panting and sweating, jumping from side to side, trying in vain to return the ball that his opponent sent to the most unexpected places. Fidel lost the game, and without masking his displeasure he threw down his cap on the table.

"Here it is. Hold on to it, because it won't be long before I win it back," he told the boy. And with that, Fidel stalked away in a foul humor.

Some months later Fidel returned as promised and asked for his opponent. The boy did not have the cap with him, so Fidel sent the boy with one of his drivers to retrieve it. Then came the rematch. But something had changed. This time Fidel did not miss a single shot. It was clear that he had been practicing Ping-Pong intensively in the past few months. He quickly won the game, and to the astonishment of the spectators, he took his cap and left.

Fidel's ego is often manifested in bullying incidents. In a conversation, for example, he must always dominate, either by talking nonstop or by peppering his interlocutors with a withering barrage of questions. No matter how specialized the topic— whether it is politics, the economy, nuclear energy, cybernetics, cooking, or Einsteinian relativity—he must be the expert. If he is unsure of his facts, it never shows. Fidel is capable of improvising with so much certainty, such power of conviction, that those listening are made to feel like intellectual pygmies in his presence, no matter who they are. The greatest danger comes when Fidel himself falls under the spell of his own *ad hoc* reasoning.

Naturally, Fidel allows no intellect to shine but his. His personal aides and the men closest to him have always been easygoing, obliging, optimistic, and energetic enough to follow him around for hours. But they have never been outstandingly intelligent. There are very few men of intellectual breadth or acumen among the top officials in the country. Those few who can think for themselves possess another characteristic that neutralizes this acuity—absolute submissiveness. If an idea occurs to one of them, he or she must use cunning to present it in such a way that it seems to have come from Fidel. It is also a good idea for an official to propose just the opposite of what he thinks. Then, guided by his contradictory spirit, Fidel will order what the official secretly regards as correct.

Fidel does not need to unleash his temper to control his entourage, but he does so frequently, especially when he learns that one of his plans has failed, when one of his leaders commits an error that makes the revolution look ridiculous, or when he discovers that there is not enough hard currency in the country to finance his latest inspiration. Then he is like a wild animal. Those in the room tremble as Fidel angrily strides from one side of the room to the other, shouting insults and curses, stamping his foot, throwing his cap into the air, or furiously tearing up reports. At those times the best thing to do is be quiet and agree with whatever he says, no matter how far-fetched it is.

Fidel's private behavior can be explained by the chief constant in his personality: his obsessive will to power. In this regard, his personal motives exactly mirror those of Fidel the public man; it is impossible to separate the two.

If Fidel the politician and Fidel the man are inseparable beings, Fidel the enemy must be understood in light of another critical trait, his pathological hatred for the United States and everything having to do with the *norteamericanos*.

The seeds of this fanaticism were sown in his boyhood, a period Fidel has ingenuously explained otherwise. "Evidently," he said in *Diary of the Cuban Revolution* by Carlos Franqui, "I was born with a politician's vocation, a revolutionary vocation. It seems hard to believe that in the environment in which I grew up I could have become a revolutionary. What made it possible is simply the political and revolutionary instinct that I had."

The economic circumstances of Fidel's boyhood in the small Oriente village of Birán were decidedly bourgeois. His father was a well-to-do planter, and Fidel never suffered from the poverty and oppression that have molded so many Latin American revolutionaries.

He did grow up in a part of Oriente Province dominated by the United Fruit Company, whose exploitation of the impoverished local *campesinos* was impossible to ignore. Furthermore, his father, who was Spanish-born, inculcated in Fidel his own distilled hatred of the Yanqui government for its intervention and preemption of the Cuban War of Independence. This *norteamericano* act, together with the later disarming of the *Mambises* army and the imposition of the Platt Amendment, has deeply alienated Cubans throughout the twentieth century. Fidel's father was particularly vehement in his feelings, but he was by no means unique.

There was hatred of another sort in Fidel's early years. He was born illegitimate—his mother was the family maid at the time she bore Fidel—and the Catholic Church refused to baptize him. Other children in Birán teased the boy without mercy, calling Fidel *judío*—Jew—not out of specific anti-Semitism but because *judío* was the only term they knew for one not baptized a Christian. Fidel was constantly getting into fights over his humiliating stigma. Finally he had to be sent away from Birán to complete his education in Santiago de Cuba.

It is easy to oversimplify. And yet, these factors do go far toward explaining Fidel's later combativeness, his determination to destroy a social order that victimized him, his desire for recognition, his need to control everything around him, and his selection of Socialism as an effective tool to fight the United States, the prime target of his bitterness and rage.

His agenda was foreshadowed in an often-quoted June 1958 letter he sent to Celia Sánchez from the Sierra Maestra. "When this war is over," Fidel wrote, "a much longer and larger war will begin for me; the war I'm going to wage against them [the North Americans]. I realize that it will be my destiny."

After his official 1961 statement that he was a Socialist, and when he felt more secure in his power, Fidel set up his war headquarters in Cuba. It was then that he began his impetuous aid in the 1960s to every revolutionary movement. Later came the Tricontinental and OLAS conferences, whose only objectives were to feed the currents of armed struggle in other countries, to swell the flood of insurrection, to unleash war on a large scale against "all the phenomena that are the contemporary expressions of what we must call imperialism and whose center, whose axis, whose principal support is Yanqui imperialism." In all other ideological positions Fidel has deviated over the years, but in this theme of defiance and conflict with the United States he has been constant.

After Che's death in Bolivia, the subsequent collapse of Fidel's guerrilla offensive in Latin America, and the pragmatic necessity of following the Soviet line of peaceful coexistence, Fidel moved his war to the African continent. There he found grounds for diverting Cuban military involvement—something he could not risk in his own hemisphere—and was emboldened by the fainthearted U.S. response to both the Angolan and Ethiopian interventions.

Meanwhile, his objectives in Latin America were revised and refined. Beginning in the early 1970s, Fidel courted such countries as Argentina, Venezuela, and Peru, seeking to establish Cuba as a diplomatic force on the South American continent. At the same time, he stepped up his covert support for revolutionaries in nations with more reactionary regimes tied to the United States. His action in Nicaragua was crowned with success. El Salvador continues to be another of his targets. After that it could be Guatemala or Honduras, depending on how the Salvadorian guerrilla war develops.

These are low-risk ventures for Fidel. Cuba trains the guerrilla fighters and conducts their political indoctrination. Arming them is easy; all that's necessary is to provide the rebels with hard currency with which to buy their weapons on the international black market or, as is often the case, in the United States.

When revolutionaries come to power in other countries, it does not matter to Fidel whether or not they declare themselves Marxist-Leninists. What does matter is that those governments declare themselves anti-imperialists, arm themselves, propagate the seed of instability in nearby countries, and show themselves as furious enemies of the United States.

Fidel gleefully recognizes that the United States has no coherent policy toward Latin American nations, and he watches patiently as in case after case Washington tries to solve problems by drowning friendly governments in money. Because that aid rarely generates many jobs and does not go hand in hand with needed social reforms, it creates prosperity for a few and corruption for many. Not only does the United States' attitude foster governments inimical to its interests, but it radicalizes the Latin American left.

Fidel is a shrewd student of United States society, institutions, and government. He is perfectly familiar with how the Congress functions and how long it takes its members to reach a decision. He knows how the United States government acts—or, according to him, doesn't act—during presidential elections. And he understands the limitations on a president's power to act in many critical circumstances.

This knowledge informs his every strategic maneuver and makes Fidel a more dangerous adversary than most North Americans realize. His only weak point is that the hatred he feels toward the United States leads him to oversimplify how power is wielded and who holds it there. According to him—and Fidel never tires of repeating this—all the power in the United States is concentrated in her corporations and among the Jews.

He therefore hates Israel, a political rather than social or cultural form of anti-Semitism. He believes Israel must be destroyed, which is one of the reasons for his close connection to the Palestine Liberation Organization and the Arab countries. "What is Israel? A state instrument of Yanqui imperialism, the real instigator, the protector of that state," he said in his closing speech at OLAS, August 10, 1967.

Fidel's hatred for U.S. capitalists and the world view they represent is no less fervent. But to these enemies he puts on a conciliatory, almost cooperative, face.

He knows that concerns ranging from soft-drink makers to engineering firms in the United States covet the potential Cuban market for their goods and services. And he takes every opportunity to tell them that Cuba and U.S. business share a common interest in lifting the economic embargo that officially bans all trade between the two countries.

Fidel relies on the profit motive to send these capitalists to Washington, where they argue before the Congress and each administration that the embargo should be lifted. In this way, too, he applies indirect pressure on the U.S. government to reverse a long-held policy; to admit that economic isolation has failed to defeat or even contain the Cuban Marxist-Leninist government on its doorstep.

His aim is to score a major propaganda victory. Fidel would call the end of the economic embargo a defeat for imperialism, and it certainly would be a first step toward the normalization of relations between Cuba and the United States, which he earnestly desires for the political victory it would represent. In recognizing Fidel's government, the United States would finally be ratifying Fidel's international status, acknowledging his legitimate role in world affairs.

Nevertheless, in my view Washington should seriously consider ending the embargo and granting Cuba diplomatic recognition. The embargo has long been a myth; through intermediary nations Cuba has access to nearly all the U.S. technology it can afford. Furthermore, a lifting of the blockade would rob Fidel of his favorite alibi for Cuba's economic failures. It is true that U.S.-Cuban trade would open to him a source of hard currency, but it would also open Cuba to ideological penetration. As Fidel's experience in welcoming the exile Cuban Community has shown, his people's revolutionary consciousness remains quite vulnerable to the subversive influence of consumerism.

Fidel is not blind to these potential problems, but he nevertheless remains intent upon breaking the embargo, taking his campaign to U.S. politicians, mostly liberals who are congenial to any measure that might reduce tensions between Cuba and the United States. In the course of this strategy, Fidel privately has made extremely presumptuous statements, especially about visiting U.S. congressmen. In the first place, as he often says, he considers them "ignorant of the details of their own country's foreign policy." Therefore, he thinks they are easy to manipulate, pawns in promoting negotiations toward lifting the economic embargo and eventual normalization. "I turn them into advocates of our cause without their realizing it," he said that New Year's Eve at Núñez Jiménez's house. "They are so naïve that they don't even understand that we are irreconcilable enemies."

Like other Socialist leaders, Fidel sees liberal professions of international amity as weakness to be exploited. That is not to say he holds hard-line conservatives in high regard; Fidel thinks they are all fascists and warmongers. But if he were forced to vote in the United States, it would be for a liberal Democrat.

"If the Democratic party were in power for twenty years, Communism would make considerable progress in the world," he often says.

Fidel, the enemy, speaks of the U.S. media in the same way. In his mind the North American press functions like *Granma*, the propaganda organ of the party—as a mouthpiece for the most powerful interests, the government and the corporations. He

derides the Yanqui press—which he believes is controlled by big
corporations and Jewish interests—whenever it produces a story
about him or Cuba that he perceives as favorable. Of course he
agrees with all flattering comments, but he privately scorns the
free press for making them. For all his careful study of the
United States, Fidel's ideological blinders prevent his grasping
that a free press is an essential strength of an open society. He
specifically denigrates *The New York Times, The Washington Post*,
the U.S. television networks, and the North American newsweeklies
in this regard, but any example of positive notice in the U.S.
press stirs his contempt.

"The best propaganda help we receive in the world comes
from the belly of our enemy, from the Yanqui press," he boasted
at Núñez Jiménez's house. "How many times have we used
insidious text from UPI and AP to our advantage in our speeches?
It would cost us tens of millions of dollars each year to launch a
propaganda campaign like the one the so-called free North American press wages for us free of charge, attacking their government's policy toward us or making statements that we can easily
refute in public. In that country not even the press identifies us
for what we really are: enemies to the death."

Of course, Fidel does not conceive of this conflict in direct
military terms. It is ideological warfare that he generates: to
injure U.S. interests, undermine North American authority in
Latin America and Africa, and circumscribe Washington's latitude of action. On these battlefronts, he has scored several suc-
cesses. First, by surviving in power since 1959, he has demonstrated
that a small nation ninety miles away can successfully defy and
even challenge the most powerful country in the world. From
this base, he has projected Cuban influence onto every continent
and has changed the military and political balance of power in
Latin America and Africa, where Cuba is largely responsible for
the continued existence of two radical Marxist governments. He
has served, as well, as an instrument of Soviet strategic interests,
both as a surrogate in fomenting anti-American sentiment and
as an advocate among the non-aligned nations. Because of the
Cuban revolution, Latin America is no longer a U.S. province as
spelled out in the Monroe Doctrine but has become another
testing ground in the East-West confrontation.

Before the Cuban revolution, Washington dispatched its ma-
rines and gunboats to Latin American trouble spots as a matter
of course. Today, the United States must think very carefully

before projecting its military power into most regions of the hemisphere.

The Cuban revolution established leftism as a real and credible force in Latin America. Until the 1960s, there was practically no forum for the left in the region. Now, many of Latin America's more prominent and influential leaders, including members of the Catholic clergy, espouse left-reform agendas that, while falling well short of Fidel's radical ideology, simply were not heard thirty years ago.

Another more subtle and actually heartening consequence of the Cuban revolution has been the gradual decline of oppressive, right-wing dictatorships in Latin America. The correlation of power has changed; Latin nations see from the Cuban example that they need not always acquiesce to U.S. political interference. But they have also found in the Cuban Socialist example an unpalatable alternative to the old U.S.-backed *caudillos*. And so such countries as Venezuela, Peru, and Colombia have turned to democracy, strengthening themselves through self-government, increasingly unwilling to do as they are told by the United States.

Unwittingly, then, Fidel the enemy has significantly undermined U.S. power in Latin America without achieving a commensurate expansion of his own influence. Instead of displacing the United States, he has discredited himself, because the most effective warfare Fidel has waged has been against his own people.

Fidel had the opportunity, in 1959, to create the fact and not the myth of a truly revolutionary Cuban society. An industrious, hardworking people were united behind him. And most of the world looked with favor on his revolution. A wise leader, intent upon breaking Yanqui domination, would have seized the moment to consolidate his power through elections and then addressed his every effort to making Cuba an independent, prosperous, happy showcase of social reform.

A more self-assured Fidel—a man less obsessed with hatred and by power—would have concealed his unfamiliarity with economics, industry, and agriculture and allowed a self-correcting government of democratic dialogue to guide Cuba's development. He would have given the independent and productive *campesino* farmers their land and not tried to defraud them. He would have improved education, health care, and social security without going on to undo these achievements by his own ignorance.

Instead, Fidel chose to poison the well. He repaid his people's sacrifices with Socialist corruption. He twisted the ideals of the revolution into a system of privilege and poverty. He committed the island's resources to bizarre and harmful fantasy goals. And he willfully squandered his people's lives trying to promote his violent ideology.

Finally, this man who is so full of contradictions, this able politician who has managed to keep himself in power for almost three decades at the very door of the country he says is his authentic enemy, proves once again that power corrupts, and that every revolution in power becomes corrupted.

He has realized his youthful dream to the fullest: History will surely devote more than one line to him, but it will also judge him and, in time, will not absolve him.

THE LAST BATTLE

MY PLAN PROGRESSES

Among those affected by the epidemic of dengue in 1981 was Maggie's mother. According to the doctor's diagnosis, it was because she contracted this virus that she later developed a strange secondary condition that required her hospitalization on July 15, 1981.

Maggie, who was just about to tell her mother the secret news of our impending plans for escape, made distraught daily visits to the Neurological Hospital's intensive care unit, where she sat noon and nighttime with her absolutely motionless mother, sustained by the doctors' assurances that there was hope for recovery. After two weeks, her mother did show signs of improvement. Maggie came home one night with the glad news; the crisis in her mother's illness appeared to have passed. The next day, however, came Maggie's heartbreaking shock. In an anguished voice, she telephoned me at my office with the news that her mother had just suffered a fatal cardiac arrest.

Maggie bore the loss of her mother with stoic dignity. She devoted herself especially to consoling her bereft father and giving him strength. Only when we were alone would she allow the tears for herself and for her father. Knowing she would soon leave him behind in Cuba forever made these days of mourning all the more difficult, a wrenching emotional experience. I supported her as best I could.

But her determination to go ahead with our plan never wavered. As summer 1981 turned to autumn, we both were caught in the tense anticipation of our approaching chance to escape.

Maggie and I each had reasonable expectations that we'd receive the option of foreign tourist trips, the critical first step in implementing our plan. But there was little room for delay. I knew that I could not leave Cuba on any date when I was supposed to be awarded my medal as a fighter during the revolution. I also faced the real possibility of being called to active duty as a MINFAR reserve officer soon after the turn of the year. Last, the specter of party membership had begun to stalk me again. As a reaffirmed revolutionary with impeccable credentials, after Raúl Castro's intervention, I had to assume that soon I'd be made the offer to begin the process for party membership, which would mean additional binding responsibilities and the extra scrutiny of the party.

We faced our first hurdle in October 1981, when Maggie's workplace assembly met to apportion by vote the foreign trip it had been allotted. That day I spent an irritating morning with an official at Reserve Headquarters. He informed me I'd been appointed the reserve army's head of supplies for Havana and also been assigned to a regular army unit. According to him, I was going to have to attend military school and could expect to be mobilized anytime after December 1, at least a month sooner than I'd anticipated.

I came home in a grim humor to wait impatiently for Maggie. By 6:00 P.M. she still had not arrived. I picked up a book, put it down, stood up, and opened the door to the terrace. A soft breeze did nothing to calm me as I intently scanned the street below, searching for her.

I went back into the living room and tried to get interested in the book again. Immediately I set it down, lit a cigarette, and paced back out onto the terrace, where at last I saw Maggie standing on the corner below, waiting for the light to change. She looked up at me and broke into a conspiratorial smile. Success!

"Let's walk for a while," she suggested casually as soon as she came in the door; MININT may still have been listening.

"The assembly didn't last more than fifteen minutes," she said with excitement once we were in our special park. "What luck not to have any opponents! It was all so easy! It's hard to believe, isn't it?"

"What are the options?" I asked.

"We can choose between East Germany and Czechoslovakia. The trip to East Germany is for two weeks and it leaves in the middle of November. The one to Czechoslovakia is for ten days and leaves December first. There's another one to the USSR, but that's at the end of December and lasts twenty days."

"Let's take the one to East Germany," I said, and then recounted the gist of my morning meeting at Reserve Headquarters. "The sooner the better. Every minute counts."

Fortunately I was not going to have to contend with the famous awarding of medals. The commission in charge of the process had found lies in thousands of biographies. So many self-proclaimed heroes of the revolution had materialized that if their swollen numbers had corresponded to reality, Batista would not have lasted in office for more than a day. Our small force of university fighters, for example, never more than 400 people, had mushroomed into 3,000 dedicated revolutionaries. More than 10,000 others claimed to have fought with the Rebel Army. At least 15 alleged combatants whose faces and names I recollected not at all approached me personally for validation of their participation in underground actions that I had been involved in.

The most shameless attitude was that of the old members of the PSP, who had done nothing but boycott armed struggle in those days. Now they all tried to appear as heroes of the insurrection, bent on presenting false documents and citing each other as mutual witnesses to nonexistent deeds. But the commission resisted accepting these falsifications. For the real veterans, the time had come for revenge on these crafty old men.

The renewed conflict between the real fighters and the fakers became so heated that Carlos Rafael Rodríguez was obliged to intervene. He presented Fidel with the long list of those who had been rejected. The Commander in Chief's decision was not long in coming; the old-line Communists would also receive their veteran medals.

"Well, Fidel knows what he's doing. He must have his reasons for agreeing," one of the commission heads, obviously in low spirits, told me. The Commander in Chief had given his consent, and his word was dogma.

Because of all the uproar, my medal ceremony had to be delayed, meaning my group of honorees wouldn't be called until April 1982. By then, I hoped, they could send mine to my forwarding address.

Then came another piece of luck when I succeeded in getting my military obligation postponed for a time. Under the pretext of the many activities that the Ministry of Culture had scheduled for the end of the year, I managed to have the head of Direction One—the paramilitary organization integrated into every central government agency—send a letter to my military superiors asking for a postponement of my training until the beginning of the year.

These delays proved doubly felicitous when we learned that

our papers couldn't be processed in time to take the mid-November trip to East Germany. We had to settle for the December 1st departure for Czechoslovakia.

This was not a problem, because on the way, the Czech flight was also scheduled to make a refueling stop in Montreal; Canada was my first choice of nations from which to request protection, as the laws for granting it were more lenient than in other countries. Although the most crucial time would be when we asked for asylum, I had also thought long and hard about what might happen to us afterward. I knew that the Canadian government gave economic help to political refugees, providing modest financial support until they had found work and established themselves.

Then our luck ran out. "Did you read this!" Maggie nearly shouted to me one morning in early November, pushing a copy of *Granma* across the table at me. The short item she'd found froze my blood. Czechoslovakian Airlines, it said, had announced that due to favorable wind patterns, their flights to Prague would go nonstop starting November 15. There would be no stopover in Montreal on the flight to Czechoslovakia!

Within a day, I was able to confirm, very indirectly, that the Czech airliners would have to refuel in Montreal on their return leg from Europe, and told Maggie this on our customary walk through the park.

"We will have to spend ten days in Prague," I said.

"Ten more days of tension!" she exclaimed.

For the rest of November we quietly and discreetly removed from the apartment and burned our personal papers: diplomas, letters, photographs—all our memories. Difficult as it was to erase every memento back to our earliest childhoods, neither of us could abide the thought of MININT's operatives sorting through our most personal and cherished belongings.

The work filled me with many old memories, but in my computerized, mechanical state of emotion, the recollections played at a distance, as if I were watching a film. They didn't affect me; neither did the knowledge that I'd soon be out of Cuba.

On November 27, just four days before we were to leave for Czechoslovakia, I received a telephone call at home from a close friend of the family, a person who kept me more or less informed about my parents in Venezuela, telling me he had to see me at once.

I dressed quickly and sped across town to his house, where he greeted me at the door. One day earlier, he said, my father had passed away in Caracas. After twenty-three years of separation and only two weeks short of the time that I might be together with him again, death had canceled that chance.

I had no appropriate response to the news; I had no response at all. The grief and sorrow that should have filled my heart were instantaneously frozen and sealed away by the Stranger. Without a flicker of emotion, I thanked my friend for the courtesy and returned to my car.

That night, at a birthday party for Maggie's father, not a person, not even Maggie, suspected what had just happened. Not a word, not a single gesture belied my savagely repressed grief. This was the most brutal proof yet of the degree to which I had succeeded in splitting my personality.

Nor were the fates yet finished with us. On Saturday, November 29, at noon, while Maggie was fixing lunch, I lay down on the living room sofa to enjoy a few quiet moments when suddenly the sharp jangle of the telephone startled me. I picked it up to hear an unfamiliar woman's voice.

"*Compañero*," she said, "we need you to come on Monday morning at nine to our offices at CUBATUR with the payment voucher for your trip."

I asked no questions, but sensed instinctively that this was a serious matter.

Maggie looked at me expectantly. "It seems there's some problem with the trip," I wrote for her on a piece of paper, and then burned it.

I looked at the time; it was twelve-thirty. I couldn't do anything until Monday. It was going to be a hellishly tense weekend of worry and speculation in a void. When Monday came, I would barely have a day to solve whatever the problem was. Once again we were gripped by uncertainty.

Early Monday morning I arrived at the Habana Libre office. A tall, heavy woman, robust and almost mannish, walked toward me.

"Are you José Luis Llovio?" she inquired brusquely. "Come with me, please."

I followed her to a small office.

"Sit down," she said. "I'll be with you in a moment."

The woman left me alone for a few minutes and then returned.

"Look, *Compañero*," she explained, "it seems that the procedures for you and your wife have not been completed. Your papers are still in Immigration at MININT; they've just told me on the telephone. At this point it is impossible for you to be on the flight that leaves tomorrow for Prague. Do you have your payment voucher? If you like we can refund your money immediately."

In the firm voice of one accustomed to authority, I replied, "Don't cancel our passage, *Compañera*. I'm certain there's been some mistake. I'm going to find out right now what's going on. Everything will be straightened out this afternoon."

I left without the slightest idea of what I was going to do. My mind was spinning. Undoubtedly somebody in Immigration had interfered and denied us our exit permit, but who? Time was at a premium. I kept asking myself what I should do, where I should go. I was overwhelmed with anxiety.

Finally I decided to go to the Culture Ministry. There I left a message about my uncomfortable situation for Deputy Minister Marcia Leiseca, and added that I would go to the Office of Immigration to rectify the error myself. I was betting that she would mention my problem to Culture Minister Hart, and that a phone call from him to the Office of Immigration would remove the obstacle.

When I reached Immigration the offices were closed and would not open again until one-thirty. Another wait. The endless worrying was eating away at my spirit. I telephoned Maggie. "Everything's fine," I said to calm her. She thought the phone might still be tapped and asked no more questions.

At one-thirty sharp I went into Immigration, identified myself, and asked for the supervisor.

"I'm sorry, *Compañero* is at a meeting," a young woman dressed in an olive-green uniform said pleasantly. "Can I help you?"

Her expression changed as I explained what had happened. Her voice became dry, she took my documents, and with a dismissive gesture told me to sit down. Her suspicions about my negative political condition were obvious.

Half an hour later the young woman came back, accompanied by her supervisor. He came toward me with a forced smile.

"*Compañero* Llovio," he said, "please excuse us. It's all been a mistake. Here are your documents and your passports. We've already sent the exit permits to CUBATUR. You can stop at the Habana Libre offices this afternoon. I hope you and your companion have a pleasant trip."

In the CUBATUR offices they gave me the official explanation: The coding on our identity cards had "coincided" erroneously with those of other persons who were not permitted to leave the country. The excuse was too ingenuous. The image of Chino Mayans came to mind. Or perhaps Justo Hernández, Antonio Carrillo's close friend, and director of immigration. The Ministry of Culture must have intervened on my behalf. Then I stopped speculating. After all, what did it matter now?

At ten the next morning, Tuesday, December 1, we went to the Habana Libre for a preliminary meeting with the other tourists in our group. For the most part they were Exemplary Workers, traveling overseas for the first time. The state was paying for almost all of their trips as a reward for surpassing a goal or for some extraordinary work merit.

An energetic, nervous little man gave us instructions for the trip. His information seemed to come from some basic etiquette manual, as well as a guide to political rules. No one of us should separate from the rest without telling the group leader first, he said. In order to avoid provocations, it was necessary not to mix with foreigners, especially those from capitalist countries. We shouldn't talk in loud voices. It was preferable to eat using all the utensils of our place setting. And he asked the women not to leave their rooms or go out on the street with their hair in rollers. This Cuban custom, he explained, was considered in bad taste in Europe.

He then informed us that we would have no guide until we reached Prague and announced at the end of the meeting that I was designated group leader.

If I was responsible for resolving the many petty problems that would no doubt come up twenty-four hours a day, I would not be able to be with Maggie—and she needed all my support to get through this ten-day ordeal. I had spent sixteen years perfecting my masquerade; Maggie had never lived under the kind of excruciating tension that awaited us, and I could not let her face it alone.

"I'll be the chief of the group until we arrive in Prague," I said.

"No problem," he said. "Tell it to the guide when you get there." He handed me the group's passports and spending money in Czech koronas. From that moment on I would have to solve any matter related to airport procedures from the time we left Cuba until we arrived in Prague.

*   *   *

At three that afternoon we left our apartment for good. I looked around quickly. What would happen to all our possessions? Who would enjoy our paintings, our furniture, the books we loved so much? Probably whoever got to the apartment first, I thought. But this was no time for bitter sentimentality. I was leaving behind a few people I loved, a handful of acquaintances, and an ocean of pain. Ahead of us lay the hope of being masters of our own destiny, at last.

After registering at the hotel we went up to our room, and while Maggie rested I went out onto the terrace. I wanted to see Havana for the last time. Before me lay the white city, the city of columns, the same city that had so dazzled me more than twenty years before. At the entrance to the bay rose the silhouette of Morro Castle, symbol of colonial power, and to its right the eternally gloomy Cabaña Fortress. Many political prisoners had been sent there in Batista's time. Fidel's political prisoners were there now.

Maggie called me back into the room. Her family had come to say good-bye and we had to go downstairs.

In the lobby one of the members of our tourist group approached me.

"There's been a delay," he said. "We won't leave for the airport until two this morning."

"Do you know why?"

"The plane was held up in Montreal for over six hours," he answered. "Somebody asked for political asylum and they didn't let it take off until his suitcases were found."

What a coincidence, I thought.

After leaving Maggie with her family, I decided to indulge myself in one last stroll through Havana. I stopped for a few minutes on the corner of L and 25th, not knowing which direction to take. I felt the need to say good-bye to the city I loved so much, which paradoxically was so alien to me now. I needed to wander her streets, feel her, breathe her, listen to her.

I took L Street left, going south, and came to San Lázaro, where I found myself once again in front of the great stairway of the university. There was Alma Mater, massive and impassive, her arms always open. In a reverie I once again saw hundreds of young men running like hares to escape the police and their terrible fire hoses. My memory replayed a scene of tumult and shouting as the students threw themselves to the ground and hid behind walls. I heard the sharp report of pistol fire, the sound of running footsteps, cries and shouts of defiance.

Abruptly, the dream dissolved as I was recalled to reality by the sharp sound of someone giving orders to a small formation of territorial militia. They were practicing for an upcoming massive celebration.

I strolled down San Lázaro Street to Infanta, the street once lively with groups of enthusiastic students crowding into dozens of cafeterias. Vividly I remembered the stands that sold hamburgers, fritters, oysters, and also the constant traffic on Infanta. Now the street was badly lit and shabby-looking, with few pedestrians and a solitary, deserted public park.

The church on Infanta was lit inside. Who dared to pray in public? I crossed the street and went in. Hardly a soul was there. A sad old woman knelt and said her rosary in one of the back pews. The feeble flame of a single candle burned in front of one of the images. The church had been forgotten.

Returning to the street I saw the singed and grimy scaffolding of the old Infanta Cinema. People were told the cinema had been sabotaged by the CIA. The truth was that a short circuit in its worn-out electric cables had startled the fire that gutted the movie house.

Then I walked along the narrow sidewalks of San Rafael in the direction of Galiano. My arm brushed against the old facades that begin almost at the street. A twisting thread of black pestilential water ran along the gutter. Around the famous Trillo Park the sordid old tenements still stood, full of little rooms and winding hallways where you could buy anything and not even the police dared go in. They were the nest of the alienated, home to criminals, just as they always had been.

Below Belascoaín Street, on the right, I passed a conspicuous two-story shop. Heavy curtains blocked the view to the inside. This was the clothing and tailoring shop reserved exclusively for the revolutionary leadership. Access by the common man was prohibited.

Then I came to the corner of Galiano and San Rafael, the famous "sin corner." I remembered it as it used to be, an endless anthill of happy, relaxed people, dozens of beautiful women walking haughtily, elegantly, well decorated windows, friendly faces, happy voices.

I walked along San Rafael Street and into Central Park. In the middle stood the figure of the Apostle, José Martí.

It was time to go back. In a taxi I drove down the Prado and went along the Malecón, still beautiful despite years of neglect, its wide gateways lined with columns, now painted green, pink, yellow—harsh colors. I passed by Maceo Park and the equestrian statue of General Antonio Maceo. Behind it rose the structure of the future Hospital Centro Habana; "the monument to inefficiency" as the people called it, completing another year of construction, the fifteenth—or was it the sixteenth?

My taxi stopped for a light on 23rd Street. Nearby was the great marble column, former monument to the *Maine*, its top still crowned by a framework of rusty steel bars that had once supported the imperial eagle. A long time ago, in the first years of the revolution, Pablo Picasso in his enthusiasm had offered a dove to crown the statue, the dove of peace. Time passed, Picasso changed his mind, and the dove never arrived. The taxi turned left onto 23rd Street. On the corner an enormous stockade shouted its useless slogan: MORE EFFICIENCY AND MORE AUSTERITY.

When we reached the hotel, Maggie was waiting for me to go up to the dining room on the top floor with her family. Six hours later we left in a Pegasso bus for Rancho Boyeros Airport.

A strange lethargy afflicted me all that evening at the Havana airport, as if my nervous system had shut down in a protective response to the intense emotional strain I was under. Hoping to shake the lassitude, I went to a men's room to splash some cold water on my face.

Just then, a woman's voice penetrated my torpor. "Czechoslovakian Airlines announces the departure of its next flight to Prague," she said over the loudspeaker.

I raised my head slowly and leaned on both hands on the edge of the sink. When I opened my eyes to look at myself in the mirror, a shiver ran through my body. The face I saw looked just like mine, but it was absolutely lifeless, without expression, so blank that not even I could detect the slightest sign of the tension that was consuming me. It was the Stranger's face, the only one I had shown the world for more than fifteen years, the mask that had allowed me to neutralize the blows of human betrayal and low passions, to survive prison and the struggle for power, and to overcome the succession of obstacles that had appeared right up to the last moment.

I walked out of the lavatory and looked for Maggie. When she saw me she stood up impatiently, signaling that I should help her collect our bags and coats. We walked toward the departure gate and joined the small crowd there, exchanging smiles and jokes with members of our group.

After twenty minutes we were taken by bus to the Soviet Ilyushin airliner.

Getting off the bus I felt an oppressive sadness as I looked at the few paces that separated me from the plane's steps; for an undefined time they would be my final contact with the land where I was born. The feeling lasted only a moment and then my reason, always on the alert and skilled in controlling my emotions, took over. We still faced ten uncertain days in Czechoslovakia, and no mere feeling could be allowed to distract my mind from the dangerous situation that awaited me.

The jets roared, and seconds later the plane began to roll gently down the main runway. Maggie was staring at the ceiling, trying to repress the anguish she felt at leaving her family behind. Her equanimity, her fortitude filled me with the deepest admiration.

Then we were airborne. Each moment was awash with the past. I closed my eyes and everything that had shaped my life began to flow through my mind, a contradictory mixture of necessary and unnecessary risks, small prison cells and large ones, passions and reflections, masquerades and desires.

THE GLASS DOOR

The overnight flight to Prague progressed uneventfully eastward across the Atlantic until near dawn, when the Ilyushin began to shudder violently. For several terrifying minutes, I could feel us making a steep descent. My head was stabbed with pain.

"I can't stand it! My ears!" Maggie shouted above the roar of the vibrating engines. "They feel as if they're going to burst!"

All around us our fellow passengers wore looks of utter panic, craning around to stare at one another. Both stewardesses had made their way to the front of the cabin, where they were administering oxygen to an elderly Polish man who had fainted.

The airliner leveled out, and then a male voice came on over the cabin intercom. "Ladies and gentlemen," he said, "we're experiencing difficulty with our pressurizing equipment and we must fly at a very low altitude. The unexpected consumption of fuel forces us to make a landing before continuing on to Prague. In a few minutes, we will touch down at the Brussels airport."

With the emergency apparently under control, I breathed deeply, closed my eyes, and exhaled. What cruel irony, I thought, would it have been to escape Socialist society only to be killed by faulty Socialist technology.

I also felt Maggie's eyes on me, and I knew her thoughts.

"No," I said to her, "nothing's changed." I wasn't sure enough of Belgian asylum statutes to risk trying them on this unexpected opportunity.

She leaned back with a sigh.

We were on the ground in Brussels for only twenty minutes, then flew for almost two more hours to Prague, where we were greeted after clearing customs by a middle-aged Czech woman who identified herself as Anna, our guide.

She accompanied our group on the drive in from the airport, a dull journey through the winter fog past endless rows of identical postwar buildings.

Our hotel, the International, built by the Soviets after the war, was very similar in style to the Palace of Culture in Warsaw and the buildings in Moscow from the Stalinist period. The first difficulty presented itself in the lobby.

"You have the passports, don't you?" Anna asked me in her precise, albeit heavily accented Spanish. "You should wait until all the *compañeros* have registered."

I glanced at the group, moving restlessly from one side of the lobby to the other, uncomfortable in the strange, cold city. They looked more like refugees than they did tourists, shuffling ceaselessly among their packages and suitcases.

"Excuse me, but my responsibility ends now," I answered, looking back from the crowd to Anna. "In Havana they told me that I would be group leader only until we arrived in Prague."

"Isn't there anyone else in charge?"

"I don't know," I said. "We assumed that a representative from CUBATUR would meet us here."

"Don't worry," Anna replied pleasantly. "Give me the passports. I'll take care of them until tomorrow."

After registering, we all went up to our assigned rooms. Ours was narrow, modestly furnished with two small single beds, a bureau, and a big old radio on a night table. It was connected to the next room by a bathroom with ancient plumbing. There was a very high bathtub and a toilet with a tank just under the ceiling, which we shared with two other guests.

Back downstairs, before we were to leave for our first tour of the city, we met Berta Torres, the CUBATUR representative in Prague. I gave her the group's money and told her exactly the arrangement I'd made with the CUBATUR official in Havana. She didn't say anything then, but I could tell by the expression on her face that she was annoyed. At lunchtime we were taken to a popular old tavern. There Berta Torres said a few words of welcome to the group and then she added: "Since *Compañero* Llovio refuses to cooperate with the organization of the trip, we should elect another more conscientious *compañero* as group leader."

Somewhat surprised by her attitude, I stood up abruptly and declared: *"Compañera,* the group is witness to the fact that I accepted this responsibility in Havana on the condition that it would end when we reached Prague. I've come to rest, not to carry out duties that belong to a CUBATUR official. You don't know me, and it seems to me that you've spoken out of turn."

Berta Torres sullenly begged my pardon and chose a girl as group leader. I had made a new enemy.

After lunch, the money was distributed. Each person was given the korona equivalent of about $6 a day to spend on souvenirs.

Most of the group quickly bolted for Prague's shopping districts, where they spent hours looking for the cheapest goods. The money allotted them was hardly enough to buy a few trinkets, but some knew how to take care of that. The cleverest had supplied themselves with boxes of cigars and bottles of Cuban rum which they furtively sold to Czech citizens. A small group of three or four young girls spent their time flirting lasciviously with Czechs or with tourists from other Socialist countries. The rest stirred even the shopkeepers' pity in their effort to squeeze their pennies to buy shoes for their children or lengths of cloth for their wives.

The group was equally ravenous at mealtimes. Accustomed to scarcity at home, they greedily attacked the abundant meals of Czech cuisine. They ate huge amounts. Some watched the food that their neighbor didn't eat so they could ask for it. On several occasions I caught the waiters' disapproving expressions as they served us.

Mealtime conversations, between mouthfuls, were dominated

by excited chatter over the small purchases each one had made so far. From time to time, the case of the Cuban who had asked for political asylum on the previous trip was also discussed. "Do you think that one of us will ask for asylum in Canada?" one of the people at our table asked.

"Based on the composition of the group, I don't think so," answered a heavyset woman. Maggie and I added our comments as naturally as possible.

During one of the many excursions outside Ostrava we visited a city close to the Polish border. Helicopters were constantly hovering overhead and we saw a large amount of military traffic on the road. This naturally attracted my interest and I asked the guide if there was a military camp nearby. "I don't know," he said. "It's the first time I've seen so much activity."

Maggie and I did our utmost not to count the hours and minutes of each day. But by the time the trip was half over it seemed like an eternity until we'd be once again en route to our real destination: Canada and escape. The problem was not in our remaining patient and appearing engaged in the vacation when our minds were somewhere else entirely. What we couldn't put aside, however, was the certain knowledge that at any moment something could go wrong, something ridiculous like provoking the spite of Berta.

The day before we returned to Prague the new group leader took me aside. "Llovio," she said, "Berta, from CUBATUR, asked me to keep an eye on you and your wife. According to her, your attitude is not revolutionary. I'm telling you so you'll be on your guard. I'll tell her that your conduct has been perfect, but just in case there's any problem back in Cuba here's my address. I'll testify on your behalf. That woman is malicious and she's capable of making up something in a report to harm you."

I thanked her, realizing better than she how right she was. If Berta Torres decided to send Havana a negative report on any Cuban tourist, that person, without knowing why, would never be able to leave the country again. If I wasn't very careful around her, Berta might even complain about me to a Cuban intelligence official there in Czechoslovakia. I couldn't afford to arouse any suspicions.

We spent the last three days in Prague, where we had a good deal of free time away from the group. Maggie and I visited Old Prague, the Malá Strana, or Lesser Town, dominated by its famous majestic castle and full of a special charm. The narrow cobbled streets, the little houses with their sloping roofs and tiny windows created a fairy-tale atmosphere. We stopped at the church of the Infant Jesus of Prague. The delicate image made me remember my mother, who was ardently devoted to Him, and the processions in His honor at the Marist Academy when I was a child.

The day before we left I wanted to buy Maggie an overcoat and boots with the money I had secretly taken with me. Very cold days were waiting for us in Montreal. Before we went back to the hotel we also bought a roll of wide yellow tape to mark our suitcases.

Berta Torres's animosity and the possibility that she would cause trouble continued to concern me until our last night in Prague, when there was a farewell party for the group in a very picturesque restaurant outside the city. During the party, I happened to run into Raúl Caballero, one of the heads of the Cuban Economic Office in Czechoslovakia, whom I had known for many years. As I expected, Berta then inferred I was a person of rank and joined Raúl, Maggie, and me very jovially. When she became aware of my friendship with this official, she didn't leave our little party for the rest of the night. Now, I could tell, Berta was afraid of me. It was her turn to sweat.

There was a long and unpleasant wait the next day at the Prague airport. A crowd of people filled the waiting room in the midst of unbearable excitement and noise.

"*Compañero*, do you have room in your luggage to carry this package for me?" a young girl with black eyes asked me anxiously.

She was a Cuban guest worker in Czechoslovakia, one of perhaps seventy who were taking our flight home. Now, at their moment of departure, Czech customs officials were confiscating consumer goods from their baggage, ostensibly because they were overweight.

"These Czechs are sons of bitches!" shouted a long-haired young man in faded blue jeans. "Nobody gave me this—I sweated for it. They already steal enough money from our salary."

His wife, seeing that the scene was attracting attention, tried to calm him, talking to him very quietly.

"They're bastards, *Chica*!" he went on. "They give us the worst jobs, we earn less money than they do, they treat us like dogs, and now they want to steal what is ours. Who do they think they are!"

In the middle of the disturbance, our departure was announced. About thirty young Nicaraguans joined our group. They were coming from Bulgaria, where they had received military training, and were returning to their country by way of Cuba for a few weeks' vacation. The vitality and aggressiveness of some of them were astonishing. They spoke in loud voices, laughed uproariously, and asked us questions about Fidel and the revolution.

"Fidel's really a wild man," said one of them. "He's cut off the Yanquis' balls. They don't call him 'Stud' for nothing." The others, including the Cubans, responded to the comment with a chorus of laughter.

We all got into a long line that didn't move. Something was going on.

"Move back! We're not leaving for another hour," somebody said.

The hour went by. Then we lined up again and the same thing happened again. By now it was two in the morning. We hadn't eaten since six. We were hungry and exhausted.

On the second floor they gave us tickets good for a sandwich and a drink. While we ate our snack, Maggie and I noticed a frantic commotion in the group of Cubans. A young woman had collapsed on the floor after an attack of hysteria, and several men were picking her up to take her to the airport infirmary.

At 3:00 A.M. we lined up for the last time. Behind us, one of the men of our group repeated the usual comment: "I hope nobody decides to ask for political asylum in Montreal!"

Fortunately, our seats were in an uncrowded section of the aircraft, and those few around us were almost all Czechs. "What luck—I couldn't stand the noise those Nicaraguans were making anymore," I whispered in Maggie's ear. She took a tranquilizer. She was very worn out, but she did her best to appear serene.

Following takeoff I closed my eyes and pretended to sleep for a few minutes. The decisive moment was approaching. I didn't know the layout of the new Mirabel Airport, and I didn't know how we would get to the building once the plane had landed, whether by bus or covered ramp. I played over in my mind all the different scenes that might develop when we asked for protection, and I tried to imagine the best way out of each of them. I had warned Maggie that under no circumstances was she to separate from me, and at no time was she to look me in the eye. I was going to have to plan the actual escape on the spot;

she would have to react instantly once it began. Finally, the intense fatigue produced by the tumult of the last few hours made me fall asleep.

I awakened at about 2:00 A.M. local time to the stewardess's voice announcing our landing in Montreal, where we would have a forty-five-minute stopover. Once the plane was parked at the gate, Maggie and I exchanged a quick, silent look, gathered our carry-on luggage, and slowly filed up the aisle of the aircraft behind the others to the telescoped portable ramp. We came out into the spacious international area, very well lit and full of small boutiques, all of them closed. Our group was the only planeload of passengers in transit at that hour, and those of us who debarked during the stopover were widely scattered. This worked against me, since I'd hoped we'd be mingling in the safety of other travelers when the moment to ask for asylum came.

A quick glance told me that we had a single escape route, a door in a glass wall about fifty feet from the gate. Within our area, in front of the door, was a Canadian immigration officer seated at a desk. To his left, about thirty feet from us, was a row of chairs.

"Let's leave our things there," I said to Maggie. Then we began to wander through the cavernous room with apparent unconcern. We window-shopped, looking over the merchandise and commenting on articles of interest. We also affected curiosity in the building's construction, chatting back and forth about the high-tech ceiling and ultramodern architecture of the airport. All the while, I was taking in every detail, gauging distances, and formulating our escape plan.

We had been walking around in this way for perhaps two minutes when I noticed that a sandy-haired man, tall and muscular, was following us quietly but persistently. *It was a mistake to bring our coats and bags off the plane,* I thought to myself. Long experience with such people told me that the sandy-haired man was a MININT official.

Now, my evolving escape plan had to take him into account. If I could not reach the immigration official, I decided, I would throw one of the chairs through the glass partition wall and yell for Maggie to jump after it. Then I would have to fight, not only with the security man but with the rest of the passengers as well. At that point there was no way I could win, but Maggie would be safe and free, and if I was taken by force inside the plane, the Canadian government would not allow the plane to take off. Still, it would be far better if things did not escalate to that point.

We continued walking, seeming to pay no attention to our escort. Others from the group approached us from time to time and we followed them to see objects they'd discovered, or simply stood talking to them.

Ten minutes into our layover, the MININT man gave up his foot surveillance and took a seat strategically located between our belongings and the single working exit door. From there he followed our movements with his eyes.

Beside me, Maggie's tension was now palpable. Her thoughts came to me in silence. *What are you waiting for?* I felt her plea. *When are we going to do it!* Her nerves were screaming.

Suddenly, the loudspeaker crackled. Our flight was ready to resume after only twenty-five minutes!

Moving wearily from their seats near the door, our fellow passengers began to file toward the ramp. The sandy-haired man rose, too, very slowly, and stood between us and our belongings on the seats, staring at Maggie and me.

At that moment, Maggie panicked. "I'm going to the bathroom!" she said in a voice she could hardly control. Then, for the first time since deplaning, I looked her directly in the eyes and said in a cold voice, "Give me the camera."

Maggie was completely startled by my expression and the request. The camera, after all, had no film in it. But my demeanor shook her from her momentary panic and she dug for the camera in her purse.

Ever since I'd seen the MININT officer, I had been racking my brain for the right moment and gesture to break the psychological hold he had as our watcher. In the instant of Maggie's fright, the camera came to me as the solution.

I took it and began snapping flash shots of the ceiling, letting the other passengers pass by on their way to the gate. Then I felt the MININT man coming, almost at my back. I turned casually and snapped the shutter.

The flash made him blink and disoriented him. "Tell me where I can send you your picture when we're back in Havana, *Compañero*," I said cheerily as Maggie and I made as if to collect our belongings to reboard the plane. He continued walking on with the rest of the passengers while we, once we had our belongings, continued in the opposite direction.

"We're Cubans," I told the Canadian official quickly, in French. "We don't want to return to our country and we ask the protection of the Canadian government."

"*Oui! Oui!*" he answered and ordered with his walkie-talkie that the glass door be opened. It clicked and that was it. We left the international section and were on Canadian territory.

I looked back through the glass to see two or three members of our group still standing at the departure gate, staring at us in stupefaction.

"We want our suitcases, please," I said to the official. "They're marked on both sides with yellow tape. It won't be hard to find them."

Maggie was ashen, her pallor accentuating the dark circles under her eyes. Her lips were as white as wax. Her chin trembled uncontrollably. When she was offered a glass of water, she took it with shaking hands.

While we waited for our luggage, the officials told us the radio was broadcasting unconfirmed news of a Soviet invasion of Poland. Now I understood why there were so many helicopters and so much war equipment in that part of Czechoslovakia. It was an odd sensation suddenly not to care what Fidel would have to say about this supposed Soviet incursion.

I looked at Maggie. Though still in emotional shock, she was in control again. She took a cigarette, lit it, and smoked in silence for a few minutes.

I walked to a window. My legs hurt; I felt stabbing pains and an enormous heaviness throughout my body. I collapsed into an armchair, sank into it, stretched my legs and extended my arms on both sides, letting them fall limp as I leaned my head on the back of the chair. I closed my eyes, inhaled and exhaled deeply. The Stranger had just expired. At that moment, my true self again occupied the place that was rightfully his. He felt like a stranger to me. We were going to have to be reacquainted.

I looked through the window. Outside, in the shadowy dawn, the snow was falling heavily. It was December 13, 1981.

EPILOGUE: REUNIONS

We waited until after dinner of the following night to make our first telephone calls. It did not occur to us to place them from the comfort of our hotel room; Socialist paranoia is a strong habit to break in a day. Instead, Maggie and I trudged outdoors into a snowy, windy Montreal winter's night to contact our relatives from a pay booth.

It was 10 degrees below zero Celsius. We could hardly make our fingers work to dial the international operator, but Maggie finally got through to her uncle's family in New Jersey and Florida. Naturally, her news flabbergasted them, a scene I was about to repeat with my mother in Venezuela.

I remember that the connection to Caracas was quite clear so that I distinctly heard my mother's confusion when a North American anglo accent tried to render my surname. She had no idea who was calling her until I broke in.

"*Mamaíta*," I said in Spanish, "*es Nené*"—my boyhood nickname. It had been twenty-two years since she'd heard my voice.

"Yes! Yes! Yes!" she exclaimed. "Nené, where are you? In Havana?"

"No, *Mamaíta*," I replied. "I'm in Montreal. Maggie and I have left Cuba."

A dead silence ensued. As I later learned, my mother, in shock, gave the telephone to my brother and walked by her guests without saying a word. The visitors were there that evening to express their respect and condolences at the recent death of my father. She went straight to a bottle of whiskey—which she seldom touched—and proceeded to pour herself a neat swallow. Only then, and with no explanation to anyone, did she return to the telephone to continue talking.

I don't know how long we spoke, but it wasn't until both Maggie and I had convinced my mother that we were safe and sound and that she wasn't dreaming that we began to feel the bitter cold around us. Only when we hung up did it strike either of us how ridiculous it was to be standing outside.

"Fuck Socialist paranoia!" I yelled, shivering and laughing and hugging Maggie. At that moment we felt wonderful.

From the outset, the Canadian government officials treated Maggie and me with great courtesy and respect. On that first night, instead of making us wait in the terminal until morning when the immigration office opened, we had been driven in a sealed police car to a nearby Holiday Inn and shown to a room where we could rest for a few hours. We had quickly fallen into a welcome sleep as an armed guard kept watch at the open doorway.

At about eight the next morning we returned to the terminal for a brief interview with an immigration officer and were then sent by taxi into central Montreal and installed at the Hotel de la Salle. That afternoon we met for a more thorough discussion of our situation, rights, and options with Gaston Therriens, a senior immigration official. Throughout this meeting and all our subsequent encounters, Therriens was especially gracious and helpful, both in his official capacity and personally. Maggie and I were particularly grateful that Therriens and the rest of his colleagues in the Canadian immigration service strictly honored our request for anonymity. Neither the press nor anyone else was told our identities.

We stayed at the La Salle for ten days and then rented a small studio, supporting ourselves with the help of our relatives and a weekly allowance from the Canadian government. For Maggie, there were several novel aspects of a consumer society to absorb, including the utterly foreign experience of shopping for our food in fully stocked stores and purchasing needed articles of clothing from a wide variety of choices and prices. She could hardly recall a time in Cuba when rationing and scarcity hadn't been the rule.

We both had to become accustomed to talking freely, even to each other. Over the coming weeks, I explained to her for the first time my misadventures in the revolutionary hierarchy, the details of my special assignments to Cuba's embassies, and all the rest that I had been forced to keep hidden over ten years of marriage. She listened to my stories in astonishment.

Despite Maggie's concern for her father and her worries about how the Revolutionary Government would treat him and the rest of the family still in Cuba, there was no looking back, and no lingering anger on my part at the waste of sixteen years in

Fidel's Cuba. With the death of the Stranger and a world of opportunity before us, I felt whole and fully confident.

On the other hand, my sense of loss was profound. It still is. What was taken from me personally—my freedom, my daughter, and my family—amounts to an irretrievable gap of emptiness in my life. And although I have no hate for Fidel, I do condemn what he has done to my country and my people. My contempt for him is mixed with my sorrow for the Cuban people's ongoing ordeal, as well as my admiration for them and the victory of their secret defiance.

For my long-dead *compañeros* in the struggle, I have found myself in ironic agreement with Fidel's observation on the 1957 attack on the Presidential Palace. He was absolutely right, as experience has shown. The assault did turn out to be "useless bloodshed." If José Antonio Echevarría and the rest of the attackers could have seen the future, they never would have sacrificed themselves. This is true, too, for Frank País and the other martyrs of the revolution whose deaths have had no meaning.

It had occurred to me long before our escape that someday I would openly tell the truth about the reality of Cuba. This determination dates from the 1971 New Year's Eve dinner at Antonio Núñez Jiménez's house when Fidel, feeling at ease, began revealing so much of himself that no one outside the revolutionary elite could possibly know or understand. I felt that I had a responsibility to recount, as accurately and objectively as possible, what I saw and heard.

At the same time, Maggie and I began to make plans to rejoin our families in the United States and in Venezuela. At first we hoped to travel to see Maggie's aunts, uncles and cousins in the Northeast and in Florida before flying on to Caracas to see my mother and brother. But this seemingly straightforward expectation was quickly quashed by one John C. Spiegel at the U.S. consulate in Montreal.

After explaining our situation to a lower-level official at the consulate, we were taken to see Spiegel, who listened to me with his feet propped up on his desk. When I finished the story, he did not respond to what I had said at all but simply repeated by rote all the rules and regulations against the issuance of U.S. visas to anyone without a foreign residence card.

It was useless telling him that Maggie and I had special circumstances. I identified myself as I had to the Canadians, but Spiegel was totally uninterested. At the end of this fruitless discussion, he suggested I compose a telegram to Secretary of

State Alexander Haig and indicated that he would send it to Washington. I wrote the telegram and gave it to Spiegel for transmission, but received no reply.

Spiegel's curious indifference seriously complicated our travel plans. We found that neither the Mexican government, the Jamaicans, nor the British would allow us to change planes in their countries or possessions. Traveling with a Cuban passport, we did not have any way to get to Venezuela. Only after a long search did we discover a connection through Guadalupe in the Caribbean and then received transit approval from France, the single country that displayed any understanding of or sympathy for our visa problems.

On January 22, 1982, we flew south, arriving at midnight at Caracas' Maiquetía International Airport. After meeting briefly with Venezuelan Intelligence officers, we walked out of the international arrival area to see my mother and brother for the first time since 1959. The scene is an emotional jumble in my mind. I remember thinking how stricken my mother looked; my father had died less than two months before. But with a sort of nervous, clumsy joy, we embraced and all spoke at once.

My mother had been living for almost twenty-three years with a long list of unanswered questions about me, mysteries that we spent all night unraveling. She wanted to know why I did not write to her, for instance, a question that could only be answered by explaining a Cuba she did not recognize or understand. As unalterably opposed to Communism as my mother was, she had no clue as to the reality of life in Fidel's Cuba or the necessity for my bewildering behavior.

In time she would come to grasp what had happened in a process of reconciliation through understanding. Sadly, it was too late for me to explain myself to my father. A few days after we arrived in Caracas, I visited his grave in a cemetery outside the city. Standing alone at his resting place, on a windy day with huge cottony clouds overhead, I felt for the first time the full impact of his death. I had found my mother and I could look for my daughter and I could tell them both who I was and why I'd acted as I had. But with my father there was no chance—just a son's cold and empty realization in sorrow that forgiveness and amends were now impossible.

My father was a stern and self-contained man. He and I were never close in the usual sense of the word. When he did take a pointed interest in my behavior, it was generally because I had exceeded my mother's ability to control me.

However, his aloofness was never out of coldness or indifference. Throughout my time in Cuba, whenever I would think of him, I'd remember one day in 1957, when I had returned to Ciego de Avila and was working for the July 26th Movement. I was hurrying out of our front door with a machine gun wrapped in a clothing bag in my hands. Just as I stepped over the sill, I literally bumped into my father, and the weapon clattered to the tile floor.

My father looked at it, then at me, and asked me what I was doing. I said nothing for a few seconds, and then stammered that I was needed somewhere but could not tell him why, or for what. He looked again at the machine gun and at me, and said only, "Be as careful as you can, and don't ever let your mother know."

Whatever action it was I took part in that day, I returned home safely and went to bed that night. The next morning, after my father had left for work, my mother told me that he had behaved strangely all night. She said he'd paced all over the house, obviously in deep reflection and troubled. But he would not tell her why. Nor did he ever tell her, as he did once confide in me, that she need not have clipped my name and photographs from the newspapers during the student demonstrations in Havana. He saw every story and knew everything. Yet he never said one word to stop me.

I know, too, that he was sure I could never become a Communist; that is, until 1965, when I sent for Marielle to come live with Marie Christine and me in Havana. My mother told me that from 1965 until his death, my father was furious in his conviction that I had been won over to an ideology he detested. He forbade any mention of me in his presence.

Over the years, she went on, my mother received occasional letters from her friend in Havana, the one who had informed me of my father's death. These letters had been the single tenuous link between me and my parents. She could never tell my father the little news of me she could glean from these letters. But she could casually leave them in plain sight when she went out on errands. Almost always, my mother told me, she would return to find that the letters had been moved and that my father was sitting alone and silent, tears in his eyes.

In time, my mother and I were able with ease to bridge the long hiatus in our lives. She kept Maggie and me laughing with her dramatic and colorful stories of trying to handle me, her *bellaco* son, describing all the times I came home bloodied from some street fight, how my antics drove her to distraction and, on occasion, to her bottle of tranquilizers.

Soon I was deviling her with jokes and tricks.

"*Nené,*" she said. "You haven't changed at all. You're exactly the same."

I took her remark as a benediction. Although I felt that the travails of all these years had never touched my true self, the hidden me, it was reassuring to hear from my mother that I really was the same son she knew from twenty-two years before.

For other reunions with people I loved it was too late; death claimed them first. In Florida, I would learn from my aunts and my cousin Silvio that my uncle and his wife, then living in California, would not hear my name. They both believed I was an ingrate and worse, that I had violated the blood trust of our family. My only hope was for Uncle Sergio to read my book and then decide about his nephew. But he was taken ill in 1985 and died, as my father did, in the belief that I had betrayed the family.

I found a happier reception from Alayón the barber, my old friend from the UMAP, who was still practicing his trade in a shop in Hialeah.

When I stood in the doorway, Alayón turned to tell his new customer he would be right with him. Then he looked at me as if he couldn't believe his eyes. He ran over and broke into tears. After our very emotional *abrazo,* he told me. "I never thought I should tell you then, but I always did think you were too good a person to be a Communist!"

I called Uncle Jean Budin in Paris several times in 1982. He was grandly pleased at Maggie's and my escape and equally excited about my book. In August 1982, he sent me the notebooks and papers he had been keeping since 1979, and I began working on the text. Several times we talked about my return to Paris and the happiness of a prospective reunion, but before I could go, Maître Budin had passed away.

It was months after our escape in Canada that Maggie and I heard the first trickle of news from Cuba. One source, a neighbor in Havana who later visited us, recounted an amazing anecdote. During our last months in Havana, when Maggie and I so often took walks in our favorite nearby park, she just as often would break into tears. According to our neighbor, a member of our CDR monitored these strolls and reported that the Llovios appeared to be on the edge of divorce.

Many of our paintings, I subsequently learned, now hang in the National Museum in Havana. MININT officials, I am sure, also found the complete set of my official identification cards that I left in our apartment. These were all copies. The originals accompanied the notebooks I had shipped to Jean Budin from Panama in 1979.

Officially, the Revolutionary Government made no comment about our escape and no doubt was grateful that Maggie and I avoided all publicity. There was, I am told, a buzz that went through the international intelligence community that some unknown, unnamed, high-ranking Cuban official had made his way to the West. But for the longest time my identity was a complete mystery to nearly everyone, including the CIA.

This was the way Maggie and I wanted it. When we decided to seek political asylum in the United States, our aim was to live quietly and anonymously in a large city such as New York, where it is easy not to be noticed or bothered. Our social circle would remain restricted to the few Cubans we already knew, our families, and any new friends we made in the United States during the extended period necessary for us to complete my research and writing.

That is how it has worked out. Once U.S. government officials investigated and interviewed us, our application for political asylum was processed with little trouble and was finally approved in October 1984. Aware that it was going to be impossible to keep this public action quiet, I decided to accommodate the inevitable press interest by doing a single question-and-answer session with reporters from four major U.S. daily newspapers. The correspondents asked mostly general questions and published their stories. Since then, Maggie and I have been able to continue living in privacy.

Of course, my central preoccupation since 1967 had been my daughter, Marielle. It was because of Marielle that I could never abandon hope of leaving Cuba, and it was to see my daughter again that I had forsworn any quick and risky escape.

In 1979, when I was in France, I had learned from the Meynards that my mother had written to Marielle through them. For almost sixteen years, although she had never received a reply, my mother had sent Marielle a card at Christmas and on each birthday. Once I was in Venezuela, I found out that Marielle had come from France to Manhasset, Long Island, where she was studying and living with a French family. She had obtained my mother's telephone number from the Meynards, and, from Long Island, she would call Caracas regularly.

On an idle day in the spring of 1982, I was alone in the Caracas apartment when the telephone rang. When I answered, I heard Marielle ask for her grandmother in Spanish. Without thinking, I told my daughter she should call back in a couple of hours. For the duration of this brief conversation, a ghost of the Stranger in me had reasserted himself. I could not reveal to her that she was talking to her father, and I firmly forbade my mother and brother to tell Marielle I was in Caracas too.

Why was I so insistent? At that time I was in the midst of a protracted effort to obtain a U.S. visa, and I did not know when, or how, I would be able to come to see Marielle. After sixteen years I could not bear the idea of our being reunited by a long-distance telephone call.

Within a couple of months, however, my visa was approved. I had my brother, Marielle's uncle, call her to say she should expect a visitor who was bringing something for her from Venezuela. On June 19, 1982, I flew from Caracas to Kennedy Airport and then took a train to Manhasset.

I cannot re-create my walk to the house where Marielle was living. I was in a sort of supercharged state of expectancy and joy that blotted out every physical detail. Images of Marielle as a happy infant in Paris and as a little girl playing on the beach in Cuba crowded one another in my mind. At hand was the moment I had prepared for since 1967, and nothing external to it could register with me. I assume that June 19, 1982, was a pleasant summer day in Manhasset, but I could not swear to it.

At the front door I pushed the bell and waited in a glow of anticipation. Inside, I saw a tall, blond young woman walking toward me. She was very attractive; Marielle had inherited her mother's beauty. She looked at me through the door with curiosity—and recognition.

Then she opened the door and gazed directly into my eyes.

"Ah! C'est toi?" Marielle asked. Is it you?

I smiled and held her in my arms. "Oui, c'est moi!"